American
Political
Institutions
in the 1970s

American
Political
Institutions
in the 1970s

A *Political Science Quarterly* Reader

Edited by

Demetrios Caraley

Columbia University Press/New York/1976

Demetrios Caraley is the editor of *Political Science Quarterly* and a Professor of political science at Barnard College and at the Graduate School of Arts and Sciences, Columbia University.

Library of Congress Cataloging in Publication Data
Main entry under title:

American political institutions in the 1970s.

   1. United States—Politics and government—1945–
—Addresses, essays, lectures.   I. Caraley, Demetrios.
II. Political science quarterly.
JK271.A576   320.9′73′092   76-8494
ISBN 0-231-04106-3
ISBN 0-231-04107-1 pbk.

Columbia University Press

New York   Guildford, Surrey

Editor's Introduction

The 1970s have been nothing if not a time of unprecedented turbulence and change for American political institutions. Who could have predicted in 1970 that before the decade was half over:

—A president would resign his office to escape almost certain impeachment and conviction by Congress for having "prevented, obstructed, and impeded the administration of justice" and engaged in assorted other "high crimes and misdemeanors";

—A vice president would resign his office and plead "no contest" to a charge of tax evasion as part of a plea-bargain to avoid prosecution and possible imprisonment for the tax evasion charge and additional charges of bribery and extortion;

—The provisions of the new Twenty-fifth Amendment would be used twice, with the consequence that a president and vice president would be serving in offices to which neither of them had been elected by the people;

—Subpoenas would be issued and enforced against a sitting president despite his claims of "executive privilege," compelling him to produce evidence of confidential conversations that had been held with his most immediate aides;

—The seniority rule in Congress would be cracked, when in organizing the 94th Congress, the Democratic caucus in the House of Representatives bypassed the most senior member and previous chairman in three committees and chose persons with less seniority as the new chairmen;

—Congress would enact legislation purporting to restrict the president's "war powers" and his ability to "impound," i.e., not spend, appropriated funds;

—Congress would investigate, ferret out, and make public, information about the most highly covert operations of the FBI and the CIA, including the FBI's surveillance of American citizens and disruption of domestic political groups and the CIA's involvement in *coups* and assassination attempts against foreign political figures;

—Trust and support among the general public for our national political institutions would drop to the lowest point since professional poll-taking began in the 1930s;

—The Democratic party would hold a presidential nominating convention which appeared to be controlled more by young, black, and female political amateurs than by professional politicians;

—Feelings of allegiance and attachment to the nation's two major parties would drop, especially among the young, to such an extent that some analysts could predict the end of parties and particularly of two-party politics as it has been traditionally practiced in the U.S.;

—An attempt would be made to sharply alter past campaign financing practices as new legislation, whose constitutionality was immediately challenged, imposed strict limits on donations and spending and imposed new enforcement machinery to implement those limits, while at the same time providing for partial public funding of presidential nominating and general election campaigns;

—The government of the nation's largest city would hover on the brink of literal bankruptcy for almost a year, as it lost its ability to borrow money in the municipal bond market and ultimately had to be "bailed out" with special loans from the federal government.

This collection of articles published in the *Political Science Quarterly* since 1973 does not purport to be a comprehensive overview of all the changes taking place in American political institutions. The articles were written, after all, not in accordance with some overall plan but as particular contributors, on their own initiative or in response to solicitations by the editor, were moved to write or talk about specific topics. As the editor of the journal from which the articles are drawn, I do find it gratifying that the collection as a whole turns out to have things to say about nearly all of the key changes alluded to. It thus reflects the *Quarterly's* deliberate attempt to publish articles that are not only grounded in solid scholarship but also relevant to important issues of lively public concern.

I

The two articles in Part I analyze different aspects of the changing

American political culture, its complex of politically relevant attitudes, beliefs, and values. Samuel P. Huntington is concerned with the most useful "paradigm" to employ when trying to account for the dynamics of change in American politics. He rejects the "consensus" theorists' view that because of agreement among Americans on political ideals, conflict has not played a significant role. He also rejects the progressive and pluralist theses that the most significant forms of conflict have been between upper and lower classes or among economic interest groups. Instead, Huntington argues that focusing on two other kinds of recurrent conflict —conflict between the political ideals to which Americans are committed and their perception of the actual operation of American political institutions, and conflict between the different political ideals and priorities of successive generations of Americans—may yield more useful insights into the dynamics of political change in the United States.

F. Christopher Arterton's article reports the results of an empirical investigation of the political attitudes of children, conducted at the height of the Watergate crisis. Arterton found that contrary to studies conducted in the early 1960s, which found that children had highly warm and supportive feelings about the president, in December of 1973 children viewed the then president, Richard Nixon, as "malevolent, undependable, untrustworthy, yet powerful and dangerous." These findings are highly significant because many political scientists believe that adult feelings about the legitimacy of governmental authority in general are derived largely from early childhood idealization of the president. To the extent, therefore, that such idealization has been eroded and is not rebuilt, the question is raised of whether our political system may be susceptible to a long-run legitimacy crisis for an entire future generation of adults as a product of Watergate.

II

The articles in Part II are about various aspects of changes taking place in the operation of our system of parties and elections. James L. Sundquist gives an overview of the erosion and shift of party allegiances since the New Deal-generated cleavages of the 1930s. Though conceding that a decline has taken place over the past four decades in the proportion of people who identify themselves as Democratic and Republican and a growth in those who call themselves independents, Sundquist questions whether this decline indicates a long-term trend toward the gradual disappearance of the political parties in the United States. Instead, Sundquist suggests that the increase in independent attitudes in the 1960s and early 1970s may have been caused by the rise of three powerfully felt issues—race, Vietnam, and the "social issue" of crime, drugs, student protests, etc.—that happened to cut across traditional party cleavages, thus jarring voters loose from past attachments. If that'has been the case, with the receding of these cross-cutting issues from the center of public attention, Sundquist believes, the central issues of the 1970s may be over the role of the government in dealing with economic problems, and such issues may reinvigorate or recreate attachments to parties that follow the basic cleavages of the New Deal era.

Judith A. Center analyzes the origins and content of the Democratic party's delegate selection "reforms" for its 1972 national nominating convention. She argues that the mandate of the Commission on Party Structure and Delegate Selection that state parties encourage representation on the National Convention delegations of minority groups, young people, and women "in reasonable relationship to their presence in the population of the State" turned into a de facto requirement that minimum "quotas" of the designated social groups be selected. According to Center, this and other delegate selection reforms produced in 1972 the predominantly anti-Vietnam War convention that the antiwar activists felt they had been unjustly denied in 1968. She concludes that by representing a majority of only the party's antiwar activists, the 1972 Democratic convention ignored the broad nonactivist segments of traditional Democratic party followings and produced a candidate—George McGovern—whose narrow appeal guaranteed defeat in the November general election.

Jeffrey L. Pressman and Denis G. Sullivan also examine the impact of the delegate selection rules changes on the 1972 Democratic convention. They contend that it was less the rules changes, and more the weaknesses of the so-called center candidates—Hubert Humphrey, Edmund Muskie, and Henry Jackson—that permitted the McGovern victories in primary campaigns for delegates and later at the convention. Furthermore, according to Pressman and Sullivan, the McGovern delegates were not inflexible purists who wrote their ideological views into the party platform, but showed willingness to compromise on the platform in order to enhance their candidate's chances of electoral victory. Pressman and Sullivan also report on the changes in delegate-selection rules since 1972, including the prohibition of "quotas" and the banning of winner-take-all primaries, and conclude that prospects for conventions producing first-ballot victories have been weakened and those for multiballot, bargaining conventions have been enhanced.

Walter Dean Burnham analyzes the 1974 congressional elections in the perspective of historical and contemporary trends in American electoral politics. He contends that the outcome of those elections are consistent with a two-decade trend of increasing invulnerability to defeat for incumbent members of Congress from both political parties, regardless of the success of their party's candidates for other offices in the same election. Burnham sees this trend as part of a still longer-term one in which party loyalties among the general public are progressively weakening and political parties are becoming eroded as basic components of our political system. Burnham concludes that as party attachments reduce their hold on individual voting decisions, different electoral coalitions will predominate for presidential and for congressional elections, thus adding a stronger political dimension to the institutional separation of powers between the president and Congress.

David Adamany and George Agree analyze the political context and legislative tactics that led to enactment of campaign finance reform legislation in 1974. This legislation placed ceilings on campaign expenditures by presidential, Senate, and House candidates; set low limits on contributions and aggregate donations by individuals; initiated public financing of presidential general elections, nominating campaigns, and nominating conventions; strengthened requirements for full disclosure of campaign financing; and established an independent agency to enforce the various regulations. After critically reviewing its provisions, Adamany and Agree argue that some specifics of the legislation will introduce distortions and inequities in election campaigns and that, more importantly, the legislation's spending and contribution limitations may be unconstitutionally curtailing the First Amendment freedoms of speech and association.

III

The articles in Part III deal with the operation of the presidency, Congress, and the bureaucracy. *PSQ* editorial board members Charles V. Hamilton, Alpheus T. Mason, Robert A. McCaughey, Nelson W. Polsby, Jeffrey L. Pressman, Arthur M. Schlesinger, Jr., George L. Sherry, Tom Wicker, and I give, in a transcript of a discussion we held soon after Richard Nixon's resignation as president, our first impressions about the long-term impact of Watergate on American political institutions. The one proposition supported by everyone was that Watergate and the forced presidential resignation to escape impeachment had revitalized the concept that a president can and should be held accountable if his conduct oversteps certain limits. Many also expressed the view that Congress, the press, and the people had over time contributed to the undue expansion of presidential power by not checking and balancing presidential over-reaching. The press was especially singled out and blamed for its tendency to glorify, if not deify, presidents. Perhaps unexpectedly, the thread running through the entire discussion was that despite the excesses of past presidents, a strong presidency was still desirable and that the problem thus remained of how to sustain such a strong presidency while keeping its occupant accountable within constitutional limits.

The "Watergate Briefs" are the briefs filed in opposition and in support of a request for a court order requiring then President Richard Nixon to comply with a subpoena. The subpoena "commanded" him to turn over for grand jury use tape recordings of conversations held in his office about the Watergate break-in, its investigation, and attempts to cover up the involvement of close presidential aides and the president himself. Such an order to force compliance with a subpoena by a president had never before been issued. The brief filed on behalf of President Nixon essentially advances two premises: (1) that if disclosure of the tapes could be compelled, "the damage to the institution of the Presidency will be severe and irreparable" because "no longer could a President speak in confidence with his close advisors on any subject"; and (2) that since the president had "the power," he "thus [had] the privilege to withhold information if he concludes that disclosure would be contrary to the public interest" and in the exercise of that privilege, "the President is answerable to the Nation but not to the courts." The Special Watergate Prosecutor's brief argues, to the contrary: (1) that the "President is not above the law" and "there is no exception for the President from the guiding principle that the public, in the pursuit of justice, has a right to every man's evidence"; (2) that a claim of executive privilege must be resolved not by the President but by "the Court . . . weighing the need for the evidence against any government interest in secrecy," and (3) that "the rights and obligations of the President and other high executive officers are defined and judicial orders are entered on the premise that these officials, rather than impose their naked power, will obey the law's explicit and particularized commands."

Arthur M. Schlesinger, Jr., examines the method of filling vacancies in the offices of president and vice president under the Twenty-fifth Amendment. This amendment, ratified in 1967, permits vacancies in the vice presidency (caused either by resignation, removal, or death, or by the vice president's succeeding to the presidency) to be filled through presidential nomination followed by approval of the nominee by the two houses of Congress. Abhoring most of all the Twenty-fifth Amendment's making possible the succession to the presidency of a person not elected by the people to be either president or vice president, Schlesinger calls for the filling of vacancies in the presidency by the formula of a temporary acting president and a special election. This, he contends, is what the founding fathers intended. The temporary acting president would be a member of the president's cabinet, as Schlesinger's scheme would completely abolish what he considers to be the "useless," "mischievous," and even "dangerous" office of vice president.

In the article on "Congressional Politics and Urban Aid," I analyze the patterns of support and opposition that have evidenced themselves in congressional voting between 1945 and 1975 on federal financial assistance to large cities. These patterns indicate that legislation authorizing major new kinds of federal aid to cities has been almost impossible to enact unless a Congress with heavy Democratic majorities and a Democratic president were serving in office simultaneously. In the article's conclusions I speculate on the prospects for expanded federal aid to large cities and specifically on whether Democrats in Congress and in the White House can continue to be as prourban as they have in the past, in the face of the continual decrease in the proportion of the nation's population that lives in large cities.

Leon V. Sigal examines the process by which certain information given to Congress by executive-branch officials through informal communication is treated as "officially secret." Although much of what is officially secret in Washington is not secret at all, Sigal argues that official secrecy and the consequent absence of formal, regularized provision of information to Congress about the programs involved seriously impair the ability of congressional opponents of such programs to voice effective opposition. One serious consequence is that the bureaucratic officials in immediate charge of "officially secret" programs enjoy great autonomy; Congress finds it difficult to perform its "oversight" function over such a program, and senior officials in the executive branch cannot easily monitor the program for compliance with their own objectives.

IV

The two articles in Part IV are concerned with the changing role of the Supreme Court. Alpheus Thomas Mason gives a broad overview of the Court's commitment in different stages of its history to "judicial activism," "judicial self-restraint," and "preferred freedoms." Arguing that the Warren Court's identification of constitutional jurisprudence with the Bill of Rights was its hallmark, Mason shows that even with the addition of four new Nixon-appointed justices, the "Burger Court" on the whole continued to protect the Bill of Rights-derived freedoms. According to Mason it is these freedoms that are essential to a "free government."

Harrell R. Rodgers assesses the level of progress achieved in school desegregation in the twenty years since the Supreme Court's historic 1954 decision in *Brown* v. *Board of Education*. That decision held that dual segregated school systems were inherently unequal and therefore unconstitutional. Rodgers, finding that considerable desegregation has been achieved in the South as a result of court action and administrative enforcement of Title VI of the 1964 Civil Rights Act, argues that it has been in the North that progress has been the least. Rodgers explains that "segregation" in the north has not been de jure, or mandated by law, but de facto, a reflection of segregated housing patterns. As a result the Court in the 1970s has not been prepared to order changes in de facto segregated school attendance patterns to bring about racially mixed student bodies unless it found that such patterns were the result of intentionally discriminatory actions. White exodus from central cities to the suburbs has been another factor making it almost impossible to achieve racially balanced school populations. This is because the proportion of white students remaining in inner-city schools, however distributed, is too small to produce balanced school bodies. Interdistrict remedies—such as consolidation of inner city and suburban schools or cross-district busing to bring more white children into the school system—have consequently been required for desegregation. But the Court has held such remedies unwarranted without a finding of actual discriminatory practices in all the school districts the remedies would affect.

ACKNOWLEDGMENTS

My most immediate debt is to the authors of this collection of articles, for having originally published them in the *Political Science Quarterly* and for later giving permission to reprint them in this volume.[1] Mary Ann Epstein, *PSQ*'s assistant managing editor, receives my special thanks for taking on most of the burden of transforming a set of selected articles into copy for a published book. Bernard Gronert has my gratitude for facilitating the publication process at Columbia University Press.

I do, however, also want to use this opportunity to record certain more continuing obligations that I feel as the editor of the *Political Science Quarterly*: to members of the journal's editorial advisory board and other anonymous referees for evaluating article manuscripts and to the board members for providing additional advice; to *PSQ*'s editorial staff—Mary Ann Epstein and Joyce Fine Schultz—for making it possible for me to edit a major journal while also performing my duties as a professor; to William V. Farr, the business manager of the Academy of Political Science —*PSQ*'s publisher—for always being available with helpful counsel not only on business matters but on all aspects of the journal's operations; and to Robert H. Connery, the Academy's president, for being a constant source of support and encouragement.

DEMETRIOS CARALEY

---

[1] The articles have been reprinted exactly as they first appeared in the *Political Science Quarterly*. A few biographical summaries have, however, been updated to reflect the authors' current status.

Contents

Part I.

American Political Culture

1   Paradigms of American Politics: Beyond the One, the Two, and the Many

SAMUEL P. HUNTINGTON

"In American social studies," Louis Hartz observed eighteen years ago, "we still live in the shadow of the Progressive era."[1] The book in which he wrote these words played a major and, in some respects, decisive role in dissipating that shadow and moving the study of American society into the bright, warm, soothing sunlight of the consensus era. For a decade thereafter, the dominant image of American society among scholars and intellectuals was that formulated and expressed in the works of Boorstin, Hofstadter, Parsons, Potter, Bell, Lipset, Hartz himself, and many others. The consensus theory was the product of a new scholarly concern with what was "different" about American society and, indeed, "American civilization." The consensus theory marked not only a rejection of the earlier progressive paradigm of American politics. It also differed from, although it was not entirely incompatible with, the pluralistic model which, from the early decades of the century, had been the most popular paradigmatic child of the American political science profession. The progressive theory stressed class conflict; the pluralist model stressed the competition among a multi-

[1] Louis Hartz, *The Liberal Tradition in America* (New York: Harcourt, Brace, 1955), p. 27.

SAMUEL P. HUNTINGTON is Frank G. Thomson Professor of Government, Harvard University, and editor of the quarterly magazine, *Foreign Policy*. His books include *The Soldier and the State*, *The Common Defense*, *Political Power: USA/USSR* (with Z. Brzezinski), and *Political Order in Changing Societies*.

plicity of groups; and the consensus view, the absence of serious ideological or class conflict and the presence of a fundamental agreement on values. Could American politics best be understood in terms of one consensus, two classes, or many groups? Such was the issue dividing the paradigms.

Even in the 1950s the consensus theory had its critics,[2] but the critics were themselves only additional evidence of its intellectual dominance. For they were in fact *critics*, and in scholarly debate to criticize a theory is to testify to its importance and perhaps to its persuasiveness. A paradigm is threatened not when it is criticized, but when it is ignored, when people find a different paradigm a more compelling and useful way of organizing their thoughts. In the rather turbulent latter half of the 1960s, the criticism of the consensus model intensified, and there were frequent expressions of the need to move "beyond consensus" in interpreting American society and politics. But just what it was one was to move to remained rather vague. Did going beyond consensus mean going back to the progressive or pluralist models? If American politics were not thought of in terms of either the one, or the two, or the many, how could they be thought of? Did not these just about exhaust the possibilities? The purpose of this paper is to review the way in which these three paradigms developed, to analyze sketchily the advantages and disadvantages of each, to take a quick look at American politics in the perspective of comparative politics, and to suggest that the conflicts between ideals and institutions and among generations may provide alternative approaches to the tyranny of the one, the two, and the many in the study of American politics.

Class Conflict and Pluralism

The progressive theory to which Hartz referred was, of course, that reflected in the works of Beard, Parrington, J. Allen Smith, Turner, and other social scientists, primarily historians, at the turn of the century. The two key elements distinguishing the progressive approach were, first, a stress on the significance of economic interests, as distinguished from idealistic purposes, as the motive moving men in history, and second, the emphasis on the extent to which American history could be interpreted in terms of the clash

[2] For the first major attack, see John Higham, "The Cult of the 'American Consensus': Homogenizing Our History," *Commentary*, 27 (February 1959), 93ff.

between two contenders for power: the popular party and the elite party. Over time the particular groups in this conflict might change, but the struggle itself continued. The essence of the progressive paradigm was well summed up by Parrington in some notes which he wrote for but did not use in *Main Currents in American Thought:*

> From the first we have been divided into two main parties. Names and battle cries and strategies have often changed repeatedly, but the broad party division has remained. On one side has been the party of the current aristocracy—of church, of gentry, of merchant, of slave holder, of manufacturer—and on the other the party of the commonalty—of farmer, villager, small tradesman, mechanic, proletariat. The one has persistently sought to check and limit the popular power, to keep the control of the government in the hands of the few in order to serve special interest, whereas the other has sought to augment the popular power, to make government more responsive to the will of the majority, to further the democratic rather than the republican ideal— let one discover this and new light is shed on our cultural tendencies.[3]

In stressing the continuing cleavage in American society between elite and mass, the progressive historians were, as Hartz noted, reacting in large part against the earlier "Patriotic" historians who had celebrated the unity of the country and the beneficence of its founders. They were also echoing a viewpoint which was not, however, unknown among the founders. What the progressives saw as parochial dialectic of American history, the federalists had earlier seen as a common characteristic of all societies. "All communities divide themselves into the few and the many," said Alexander Hamilton. "The first are the rich and well born, the other the mass of the people." John Adams similarly argued that "The people, in all nations, are naturally divided into two sorts, the gentlemen and the simplemen. . . . The great and perpetual distinction in civilized societies has been between the rich, who are few, and the poor, who are many."[4] The difference between progressives and federalists, of course, lay in their evaluations of this conflict. For Hamilton the rich were good; for Adams both were bad (or, at least, could not be trusted); while for the progressives, of course, the poor were good. The federalists accepted the elite-mass division as an inevitable feature of any society, including American society, which was

---

[3] Quoted in Richard Hofstadter, *The Progressive Historians: Turner, Beard, Parrington* (New York: Vintage Books, 1970), p. 438.

[4] Alexander Hamilton, in Max Farrand, ed., *The Records of the Federal Convention* (New Haven: Yale University Press, 1911), I, p. 299; John Adams, *Works* (Boston: Little, Brown, ed. by Charles Francis Adams, 1850-56), VI, p. 185; IX, p. 570.

not in any way unique: "There is no special providence for Americans," as Adams said, "and their nature is the same with that of others." Governmental institutions, consequently, had to reflect this division. For the progressives, on the other hand, the division was bad because one of the parties was bad, and hence governmental institutions should promote the victory of the popular party over the elitist party. Until that victory was achieved, however, American history would be a continuing conflict between the good guys and the bad guys, and, as Hartz pointed out, one of the comforting aspects of the progressives' theory was that it "always had an American hero available to match any American villain they found, a Jefferson for every Hamilton."[5]

At almost the same time that the new historians were setting forth the progressive paradigm, other scholars, primarily political scientists, were delineating a related but also different image of American politics. This pluralist paradigm stemmed from the coming of age of the new discipline of political science. The American science of politics, to use Bernard Crick's challenging but accurate label, was fundamentally a product of the Progressive period in American history.[6] Before the 1890s, the first steps had, of course, been taken toward a more systematic study of politics and government. American students had attended the German universities, absorbed the standards of scholarship and concepts of *Staatswissenschaft*, and returned home to attempt in some measure to duplicate and to apply them. John W. Burgess founded the Columbia School of Political Science in 1880; Johns Hopkins also developed a significant graduate program before the end of the century; Woolsey, Burgess, and Willoughby produced *Political Science* (1877), *Political Science and Comparative Constitutional Law* (1890), and *The Nature of the State* (1896). These and other studies were general, comparative, formalistic, and, in part, historical. This was, as it were, the period in which the preconditions for the scholarly takeoff of the science of politics were being laid.

That takeoff occurred during the first decade of the twentieth century. Political science as it developed during these years became realistic rather than formalistic, reformist rather than conservative,

---

[5] Hartz, *Liberal Tradition*, p. 31.

[6] When capitalized, Progressive refers to the intellectual and political currents generally dominant in the first decade of this century; when in lower case, it refers to the particular ideas and approaches of the "progressive" historians, especially Smith, Turner, Beard, and Parrington.

and parochial rather than comparative. The development of the discipline was one element in the Progressive movement. This take-off involved, in the first place, a shift from a sympathy for conservatism to a commitment to reform. This change was reflected, in part, in the breaking away from the stress on moralism and natural law to a greater emphasis on a pragmatic approach to political life. "To call the roll of the distinguished social scientists of the Progressive era," Hofstadter has argued, "is to read a list of men prominent in their criticism of vested interests or in their support for reform causes. . . ."[7] The means of promoting reform was the exposure of the inequities, vested interests, corruption, and attendant evils which were interwoven into the dominant pattern of political and social life. Hence the emphasis on realism—how people in politics actually behave—rather than upon the description and analysis of formal institutions. The student of politics, as Woodrow Wilson put it, "must frequent the street, the counting-houses, the halls—yes and the lobbies—of legislatures." He must study "the life, not the texts, of constitutions."[8] He must investigate his subject in much the way the superior journalist does. He must, in short, become a muckraker, and that, indeed, was precisely what the American political scientist at the turn of the century did become. No clear line separated the journalistic muckraker from the scholarly one. In both, the emphasis was on the exposure of facts—facts which simply by virtue of their exposure would serve to generate demands for reform. "The documentation of the muckraking journalism and its alleged objectivity makes it only in style and published location different from the empirical studies in the city government that the sociologists and the new political scientists were beginning to interest themselves in. . . . Facts, once put before the people, would do their own work."[9]

In addition to being reformist and realistic, the political science of the first decade was also increasingly parochial. These were the years of the " 'Americanization' of Political Science," in which American scholars less frequently studied in Europe and less frequently read or used European sources: In 1896, for example, forty

[7] Richard Hofstadter, *The Age of Reform* (New York: Alfred A. Knopf, 1956), p. 154.

[8] Quoted in Albert Somit and Joseph Tanenhaus, *The Development of American Political Science* (Boston: Allyn & Bacon, 1967), p. 32.

[9] Bernard Crick, *The American Science of Politics* (Berkeley and Los Angeles: University of California Press, 1959), p. 84.

percent of the books reviewed in the *Political Science Quarterly* were published in languages other than English; in 1915 and 1920, these figures had dropped to fourteen and four percent respectively. The proportion of references to foreign language sources in articles published in American political science journals similarly declined and American government supplanted comparative government as the most widely offered undergraduate course.[10] The progressive historians, epitomized in Beard and Turner, were, of course, almost totally preoccupied with the American historical experience to the exclusion of any significant comparisons of it with Europe. American political scientists similarly became almost totally preoccupied with American politics; the reality which they studied was an American reality. As the "emerging political science," in Crick's words, ". . . tried to become more scientific, it in fact became more parochial."[11] The study of comparative politics in both Europe and America declined; in the United States the decline was more marked, but it was also associated with what can only be termed a more healthy emphasis on the realistic analysis of political behavior, which soon came to the fore in the Chicago work of Merriam, Gosnell, and Lasswell. "The narrow notion of science in politics concerned with the extension of 'hard data' techniques to trends in behavior was the American answer to European theory, but it remained almost exclusively concerned with American problems. There remains a paucity of materials using behavioral methods and dealing with governments and institutions of countries other than our own."[12]

The reformism, realism, and parochialism of American political science led eventually and naturally to a stress on the pluralistic character of American politics and the critical role of groups, particularly organized groups, in shaping the course of public life. The group approach received its most explicit formulation, of course, in Bentley's *Process of Government* published in 1908. In Bentley the emphasis was analytical; it stressed the utility of the group concept as a category for political analysis. In others, the approach became more descriptive; the stress was on the multiplicity of groups as the distinguishing characteristic of American politics. The Ameri-

---

[10] Somit and Tanenhaus, *American Political Science*, pp. 61-62.

[11] Crick, *American Science of Politics*, pp. 111-112.

[12] David E. Apter, "Comparative Politics and Political Thought: Past Influences and Future Development," in Harry Eckstein and David E. Apter, eds., *Comparative Politics: A Reader* (New York: The Free Press, 1963), p. 730.

can pluralists were not, however, generally favorably disposed toward groups as were the English normative pluralists such as Laski and Cole. If anything, the thrust was in the opposite direction. If the progressive historians harked back to an inverted Hamilton, the pluralist political scientists harked back to a semi-inverted Madison. The group concept was hailed as a scientific and realistic category for analysis, but the role of groups in politics was seldom viewed as better than ambiguous and was often viewed as nefarious. The machinations of interest groups were exposed. The extent to which organized groups threatened the rights of the individual and the power of the majority was emphasized.

At times the analytical and descriptive elements of the model were tangled together. The usefulness of the group concept when applied to American politics often led to the assumption, not generally tested until much later, that it would be equally appropriate to the study of other polities, an assumption which could be far from the truth. "Had the disciples of Bentley," as Hartz observes, "tried to apply his analysis to the Dreyfus Affair as they did to the Smoot-Hawley Tariff, they would hardly have found the procedure so easy. . . ."[13] The pluralist political scientists were thus using a category of limited territorial applicability to analyze American politics, often implicitly assuming that that category and analysis could also be applied equally well to other political systems. The progressive historians, on the other hand, were using categories of much more general applicability (elite-mass; class) and implicitly assuming that they were useful and relevant to the analysis of the American political system.

The emergence of political science was thus part of a broad movement of Progressive reform in American intellectual and political life. The nature and focus of the discipline plus the critical role of the pluralist paradigm also reflected the extent to which political science in some measure was a substitute for political theory in America. The discipline's empiricism and realism and the assumption that facts exposed became evils reformed were themselves evidence of the extent to which, despite the progressive and pluralist paradigms, there did indeed exist a consensus on basic political values. In its scope, sophistication, and general scholarly achievement, American political science soon easily exceeded the much more primitive levels which continued to prevail in Europe. American

[13] Hartz, *Liberal Tradition*, p. 30.

political theory, on the other hand, remained as underdeveloped and primitive as European political science. Political theory is most likely to flourish where there is a need to rationalize some forms of authority and to invalidate others; it normally flourishes during periods of intense conflict and controversy over fundamental issues of political and social organization. If, however, there is a relatively broad-gauged consensus on basic political values, there is little need for political theory. There is, however, a need for an empirically oriented political science to analyze and to expose the extent to which political institutions and practices in the society are in fact congruent with its political values. This process of exposure, of establishing the gap between the ideal and reality, is also both a cause and a consequence of the low status which politics itself has in such a society. In this context, to study politics is almost necessarily to criticize it.

The Consensus on Consensus

Until World War II, the progressive paradigm was thus preeminent among historians and the pluralistic paradigm among political scientists. The years after World War II saw the rise of the consensus paradigm as an intellectual construct. It reflected a focus on issues which had been almost totally absent from the intellectual world prior to World War II: How unique is the American experience? How relevant is the American experience?

The consensus interpretation of American politics was a product of the absence of social revolution in the 1930s, the success of the New Deal, and the development of the cold war. If Hamilton was the devil figure for the progressive historians and Madison the patron saint of the pluralists, Tocqueville was, of course, prophet of the consensualists. The central thesis of the consensus argument was advanced in most blatant form in Boorstin's *The Genius of American Politics* (1953) and in its most sophisticated form in Hartz's *The Liberal Tradition in America* (1955). The latter remains probably the most significant interpretation of the American experience written since World War II. Hartz's analysis is outstanding among the consensus writings for three reasons.

First, while the consensus theorists were generally much more comparatively inclined than either the progressive or pluralist theorists, Hartz made the comparison with Europe the central theme of his analysis. He viewed the American experience from a European vantage point and argued, persuasively, that from that vantage point the dualism which had been the central theme of the progressives shrank almost to insignificance. Unlike Europe, America lacked both feudalism and socialism. The controversies of American history were simply between different variants of liberalism. Subsequently, Hartz elaborated his concept of the "fragment" to view the United States not just in comparison with Europe but also in comparison with the other societies created by European colonization and settlement.[14]

Second, Hartz married Marx to Tocqueville. His basic categories of analysis were Marxist, much more explicitly so, indeed, than those of the progressives. Viewed in class terms, the United States, except in the South, had lacked an aristocracy; because of this, it also lacked a class-conscious proletariat. Instead, the middle class had from the first predominated; liberalism, the political philosophy of the middle class, had been unchallenged. In a brilliant manner, Hartz thus used Marxist categories to arrive at Tocquevillian conclusions. Hofstadter once called Calhoun "the Marx of the Master Class"; Hartz could equally well be described as "the Marx of the middle class."

Third, unlike many other consensus writers, Hartz also saw that consensus was not simply a cause for celebration; it was an ambivalent legacy. The absence of class conflict might be a blessing, but it was gained at the price of liberalism turning in and shadow boxing against itself. Unchallenged liberalism became irrational liberalism. America's "colossal liberal absolutism," Hartz concluded, "hampers creative action abroad by identifying the alien with the unintelligible, and it inspires hysteria at home by generating the anxiety that unintelligible things produce."[15]

Probably the most important contribution of the consensus theorists was to place the American experience in some form of comparative perspective. The issue of "American exceptionalism," of what is different or the same about American life and thought, was at the heart of this theory. As Marcus Cunliffe has argued, "the assumption that the Americans were set apart from other peoples was taken almost axiomatic."[16] In a sense, the consensus theorists took the dichotomy which the progressive historians saw within

[14] Louis Hartz et al., *The Founding of New Societies* (New York: Harcourt, Brace, 1964).

[15] Hartz, *Liberal Tradition*, p. 285.

[16] Marcus Cunliffe, "New World, Old World: The Historical Antithesis," to

American experience and transformed it into a dichotomy between America and Europe. America was defined as the antithesis of Europe; the theme was, of course, an old one which could be formulated in a variety of ways to serve a variety of purposes. In the years after World War II, the scope of the argument was also broadened to encompass not just the difference between America and Europe but the uniqueness of America with respect to all the rest of the world. Was the American Revolution a real revolution or something different from those of Europe, Asia, and Latin America? Was the United States the "first new nation" whose experience had parallels with and lessons for the new nations of the twentieth century? Could Americans transcend their limited experience to understand and to act effectively with people of other societies and cultures? If the American experience was unique, it was irrelevant to the rest of the world; if it was relevant, it could not be unique. The preoccupation with this set of issues implied that there was indeed something different about the United States. In how many other countries have scholars and intellectuals debated the historical experience of their society in terms of its uniqueness or relevance? The very fact that this issue was debated was, in some measure, evidence if not of American uniqueness at least of American hubris. Implicit in the argument for uniqueness was the assumption that no other society was as good as the United States; implicit in the argument for relevance was the assumption that every other society should be like the United States. Each side of the argument had its own form of national pride. Lost in the debate was the chastening possibility—which, I would suggest, was closer to actuality—that the United States could well be neither unique nor relevant.

The consensus interpretation of American politics was elaborated and developed in a variety of ways by historians and sociologists. Within the historical fraternity, the progressives and their disciples had "pushed polarized conflict as a principle of historical interpretation so far that no one could go further in that direction without risking self-caricature."[17] There was a need for a fresh start. While historians rode off in a variety of directions after abandoning the progressive interpretation, the major stream, insofar as there was one, clearly flowed from the springs of consensus.

---

be published in Richard Rose, ed., *Lessons from America* (London: Macmillan, 1974).

[17] Hofstadter, *Progressive Historians*, p. 439.

In sociology the "end of ideology" school plus the popularity of structural-functionalism and equilibrium models all tended to parallel, supplement, and reinforce from other methodological directions the message of the consensus school.

Within the discipline of political science, consensus did not play quite the same role as it did within sociology and history. It did not lead to the displacement of the earlier pluralist paradigm; rather it led to its reformulation and redefinition in conservative rather than radical terms. In history, Hofstadter argues, the last two major works clearly in the progressive tradition were Schlesinger's *The Age of Jackson* (1945) and Jensen's *The New Nation* (1950). In political science, however, the main stream of pluralist analysis, which had flowered earlier in the writings of Bentley, Merriam, Herring, Holcombe, and Schattschneider, was carried forward and given a new lease on life in the works of Key, Truman, Dahl, and many others. Earlier the "discovery" of pluralism in American politics had been "shocking" in that it meant that American politics was not contained simply in the concepts of majority rule and individual rights. Organized groups, not popular majorities or individual citizens, were the hard reality of American politics. By the 1950s, however, pluralism was redefined from a bad thing to a good thing: it was a way of dispersing power and of insuring (through cross-cutting cleavages) moderation in politics. In the first decade of the century, the pluralist paradigm had been born of the same impulse to exposure and reform which produced the progressive interpretation: Beard could be indulgent toward Bentley.[18] In the 1950s, on the other hand, the pluralist interpretation became a corollary of the consensus model: Hartz could be indulgent toward Truman.[19] Within the basic ideological consensus of American politics, the only conflicts which could take place were the relatively minor ones among interest groups over their marginal shares in the economic pie. The pluralist interpretation was used to defend American politics against the C. Wright

[18] Beard praised Bentley for his efforts "to put politics on a basis of realism where it belongs" and for making "effective use of the idea of 'group interests,' as distinct from class interests in the Marxian sense." *Political Science Quarterly*, 23 (December 1908), 739-41, quoted in Hofstadter, *Progressive Historians*, p. 186n.

[19] In Hartz's words, "Bentley went deeper than Beard, for the free and easy play of pressure groups was a real characteristic of the American liberal world, inspired by the moral settlement which underlay it and hence obscured class lines." *Liberal Tradition*, p. 250.

Mills and Floyd Hunters who argued that power was concentrated at the national and local levels. Its political and ideological functions shifted from the exposure of the evils of American politics to the celebration of its virtues. In due course, of course, this pluralistic celebration itself came under attack with the familiar arguments, first, that not all sectors of the population are equally represented in the group process and hence the interaction of groups produces a skewed and biased result in public policy, and second, that there are public interests which transcend group interests and which do not receive appropriate recognition in the group process.[20]

Tests of Paradigmatic Usefulness

To be accepted and useful, a paradigm has to meet two tests. First, in one way or another it has to be meaningful and relevant; that is, it has to make sense to people in terms of what they see about them and what they feel they need. The progressive and then the pluralist paradigms met these tests during the reformist years of the early part of this century; the consensus and the redefined conservative pluralist paradigms met the tests in the cold war years of the mid-twentieth century. During the late 1960s and early 1970s, domestic upheaval—racial conflict, student unrest, political controversy—combined with subsequent international detente to make consensus make less political sense than it did a decade earlier. Second, every paradigm also has to "make sense" in terms of the historical and political experience it purports to explain. It cannot be way off the scholarly mark no matter how useful it may be politically and ideologically. More specifically, in terms of explaining the principal characteristics of politics in a society, a paradigm should do three things: (a) It should highlight some aspect of social reality; it should distinguish what is of critical importance in the political experience of the society from what is of peripheral significance. (b) It should be comparative; it should call attention to the principal similarities and differences between the politics of the society and those of other societies. (c) It should be dynamic, in the sense that it should account for change (and continuities) in the political experience of the society. As they have been developed by histo-

[20] See Henry S. Kariel, *The Decline of American Pluralism* (Stanford: Stanford University Press, 1961); Grant McConnell, *Private Power and American Democracy* (New York: Alfred A. Knopf, 1966); Theodore J. Lowi, *The End of Liberalism* (New York: W. W. Norton, 1969).

rians, political scientists, and American civilizationists, the three paradigms we are considering differ considerably in the extent to which they meet these criteria. The progressive paradigm makes somewhat more provision than the others for change: it is rooted in a theory of conflict which, like the Marxist class struggle, can be interpreted as looking forward to the progressive victory of one party over the other. On the other hand, the sandwiching of the complexity of American political struggle into a dualistic framework scarcely did justice to the complexity of that struggle, and the progressive theory had virtually nothing to say about the similarities and differences between American politics and other politics. The pluralist paradigm, on the other hand, came to grips with a critical reality of American politics, but had no theory of change (except in terms of the replacement of one interest group by another) and also shed little light on the comparisons and contrasts between American politics and that of other societies. Finally, the consensus theory was very much a product of an explicit comparison of the American experience with Europe, but it also had little to say about change and obviously failed to account for the conflict and violence which had taken place in American history. In this respect the Marxist categories of the consensus theory, at least as it was formulated by Hartz, became blinders. Implicitly it was assumed that the only real conflict was class conflict, and hence the absence of class conflict meant the presence of consensus. The United States, however, may well have had less class conflict but also more social and political violence than many European countries. "Americans," as Hofstadter neatly put it, "do not *need* ideological conflict to shed blood on a large scale." And, as Dahl has argued, the case can be made that the United States has experienced relatively severe conflict about once every twenty years.[21]

While the paradigms of the one, two, and the many may differ in their particular strengths and weaknesses, they also have one important characteristic in common. Each explains politics in terms of social structure. The decisive influence on the nature of American politics is held to be the nature of American society: it is not political values, or institutions, or practices, or the nature of development and change. It is whether American society can best be understood in terms of one consensus, two classes, or many groups.

[21] Hofstadter, *Progressive Historians*, p. 461; Robert A. Dahl, *Pluralist Democracy in the United States: Conflict and Consent* (Chicago: Rand McNally, 1967), p. 283ff.

The social structure also shapes the nature of the values, interests, and ideologies which are manifest in politics. There is a presumption of congruence between social unit and political outlook. The consensus is liberal; the classes are conservative and progressive; the groups are materialistically self-interested. In addition, the picture of society and hence of politics is, by and large, a static one. The progressive interpretation does hold open the possibility of the eventual victory of the popular party, but even with it and to a much greater extent with the consensus and pluralist schools, there is little provision for change. How will American society and politics in the future differ from what they have been in the past? At best, consensualists, progressives, and pluralists all suggest more of the same.

The Comparative Context of Modernization

For a good part of this century American political science was political science of America. The strand of parochialism which developed in the 1890s remained strong; it coincided with the noncomparative, if not isolationist, inclinations of the progressive and pluralist paradigms. With a few exceptions comparative government (which, in any event, meant European government) was not at the center of the discipline. Even in the late 1930s, the two outstanding texts on comparative government were the products of two recent immigrants: Carl Friedrich and Herman Finer. After World War II, however, the expansion of American influence throughout the world created the environment and the impetus to develop foreign area studies programs and to attract political scientists to the analysis of what had been rather esoteric regions of the world. For political scientists, this work was originally and in larger part the study of foreign governments and then subsequently and in smaller part the study of comparative government. Comparative government, in turn, came to be defined as a subfield within the discipline distinct from American government, thus tending to separate the political science analysis of comparative politics from that of American politics.

This tendency was in some measure tempered by the fact that the study of comparative politics requires typologies for the classification of political systems. In the years after World War II, two such typologies successively played critical roles. The first, the distinction between constitutional and totalitarian regimes, was an obvious product of World War II and the early cold war. It provided a neat way of collapsing two enemies, Hitler's Germany and Stalin's Russia, into one intellectual pigeonhole. It also brought the United States together in a single category with Western Europe, minimizing the differences in political institutions and practices between the two. In a sense, by stressing the similarities between America and Europe, these political science categories provided an intellectual rationale for post-World War II foreign policy.

In the late 1950s the distinction between constitutionalism and totalitarianism in the study of comparative politics was supplemented and, in large part, supplanted by the distinction between modern and traditional societies and developed and underdeveloped political systems. "The field of comparative politics," as Lucian Pye observed, "has suddenly stopped being merely the study of the major European powers and has become the analysis of political development, one of the most youthful and vigorous subfields of the entire discipline of political science."[22] As the central concerns in the study of comparative politics, modernization and political development provided a more or less common intellectual framework for analyzing and comparing the politics of Asian, African, and Latin American countries. In due course, they also were seen to provide a framework within which the earlier experience of Western Europe and North America might be compared with the contemporary experience of Third World countries. Political scientists studying developing countries developed concepts, hypotheses, and theoretical frameworks which could be applied back to the historical analysis of more familiar societies.

Inasmuch as the United States was clearly the most modern society in the world and inasmuch as, in many dimensions, it was also one of the most politically developed, did it not make great good sense to look at American politics in terms of a paradigm of modernization? Such a paradigm would clearly provide the basis for the comparative analysis of similarities and differences with other societies, as, for instance, in Lipset's The First New Nation.[23] It also clearly would provide a framework for analyzing continuity

[22] Lucian W. Pye, "Advances and Frustrations in Comparative Politics," in Fred W. Riggs, ed., International Studies: Present Status and Future Prospects (Philadelphia: American Academy of Political and Social Science, Monograph no. 12, October 1971), p. 94.

[23] Seymour Martin Lipset, The First New Nation (New York: Basic Books, 1963).

and change within American society. Why could we not learn a lot more about American politics by looking at it within a modernization framework and in comparison with the experience of other countries? The "modernization" and "political development" of America seemed to offer fertile fields for such scholarly exploration.

Alas, it has not exactly worked out that way. To the best of my knowledge only one recent volume had been written with this goal explicitly in mind, and that, Clinton Rossiter's last book, *The American Quest* (1971),[24] leaves one with the undeniable feeling that the concepts of modernization and the experience of America do not really fit together. The reason is a familiar one which flows in part from the valid insights of the consensus theory. The United States was in many critical senses "born modern" as well as "born equal." Consequently, it has not had to modernize in the way in which most European and Third World societies have had to, and hence the concepts and themes of modernization are not all that relevant to its history. In other societies, the critical issues have been whether, how, and under whose leadership modernization occurs, how the traditional elites take the leadership in the process or attempt to oppose it. The central feature is the conflict between old and new values, leaders, social forces. It is, however, precisely this sort of conflict which has, with one notable exception, been almost entirely absent from American history. It has generally lacked the tensions and traumas of modernization which have been central to the experience of other societies.

At its most fundamental level, modernization involves changes in human attitudes, which, in turn, requires conflicts within men and among men over traditional versus modern values. The modern syndrome of attitudes has perhaps been well summed up by Alex Inkeles in his "OM" (Overall Modernity) scale which includes: openness to innovation and change; wide-ranging interests and empathy; a tolerance of differences of opinion; present and future rather than past orientation; a belief in planning and organization; a sense of efficacy, that is, a belief that men can learn from and dominate their physical environment; a freedom from fatalism; an awareness of the dignity of others and a willingness to respect that dignity; a faith in science and technology; and a faith in

[24] Clinton Rossiter, *The American Quest, 1790-1860: An Emerging Nation in Search of Identity, Unity, and Modernity* (New York: Harcourt Brace Jovanovich, 1971).

distributive justice: to each according to his contribution or work.[25] Traditional man would have just the opposite views. But the question then is: When were there traditional men in America? One cannot administer questionnaires to an eighteenth-century sample of Americans, but all the descriptions of American attitudes in the eighteenth and early nineteenth centuries highlight precisely those attitudes which Inkeles has defined as modern. When Crevecoeur asks who is this American, this new man, the answer is Alex Inkeles' "OM" man. The central problem of modernization, that of making men modern, was never much of a problem on these shores, and hence theories which see that as the central problem of development are of only dubious relevance.[26]

What is true of man is also in large part true, as Hartz has argued, of society. And as I have pointed out elsewhere, because there were no traditional or feudal institutions to be overthrown, there was no need to create a modern system of government to carry out that purpose.[27] Modernization theories are thus irrelevant because American society was born modern without having to be modernized and American government could be left as it was because its society was modern. The concept of modernization has, however, had a demonstrated usefulness in the analysis of the one segment of American society, the South, where there was something which could be called a fully developed traditional social order. The actors in Southern history clearly have their counterparts in eighteenth- and nineteenth-century Europe and in twentieth-century Latin America. There is a land-owning aristocracy, commercial oligarchs, foreign capital, a poor peasantry, slaves, politico-economic entrepreneurs, and populist demagogues. (To understand Huey Long, as Arthur Schlesinger has said, think of him as a

---

[25] Alex Inkeles, "The Modernization of Man," in Myron Weiner, ed., *Modernization* (New York: Basic Books, 1966), p. 138ff.; David Horton Smith and Alex Inkeles, "The OM Scale: A Comparative Socio-Psychological Measure of Individual Modernity," *Sociometry*, 29 (December 1966), 353ff.

[26] That is, they are of limited relevance so far as understanding the American past is concerned. They may be considerably more useful in understanding the transition which appears to be taking place in America and some other affluent societies from industrialization to postindustrialism. The parallels of this transition with the earlier transition from agrarianism to industrialism are at times rather striking. See my "Postindustrial Politics: How Benign Will It Be?," *Comparative Politics*, 6 (January 1974), 163ff.

[27] Samuel P. Huntington, *Political Order in Changing Societies* (New Haven: Yale University Press, 1968), p. 125ff.

Latin American populist dictator.)[28] Modernization concepts illuminate Southern experience precisely because it is different from other American experience, and hence H. Douglas Price, Lester Salamon, and others have been able to analyze aspects of Southern development in much the same way as other social scientists have analyzed development in the Middle East, Latin America, and Asia.[29]

While the concept of modernization generally is not of much help in understanding American development, other more specific, functional concepts and theories may be drawn from the comparative study of political development and applied usefully to the American experience. There is, moreover, still the need to reintegrate American politics into comparative politics, which was where it was in the 1880s, and from which it was dislodged by the parochialism of the Progressive movement.

The Conflict of Ideals vs. Institutions

The problem then remains: How to capture the valid elements of the unity, dualism, and diversity of the American experience embodied in the consensus, progressive, and pluralist paradigms and also take into account the changes and continuities within the American political system and the similarities and differences between that system and other systems? More fundamentally there is the whole question of the relation between socioeconomic interests and politics. All three familiar paradigms rested on the assumption that political behavior and political ideas were outgrowths of socioeconomic interests. That this is often and, indeed, generally

[28] Arthur M. Schlesinger, Jr., *The Politics of Upheaval* (Boston: Houghton Mifflin, 1960), p. 68: "At bottom, Huey Long resembled, not a Hitler or a Mussolini, but a Latin American dictator, a Vargas or a Perón. Louisiana was in many respects a colonial region, an underdeveloped area; its Creole traditions gave it an almost Latin American character. Like Vargas and Perón, Long was in revolt against economic colonialism, against the oligarchy, against the smug and antiquated past; like them, he stood in a muddled way for economic modernization and social justice; like them, he was most threatened by his own arrogance and cupidity, his weakness for soft living and his rage for personal power. And, like them, he could never stop."

[29] See H. Douglas Price, "Southern Politics in the Sixties: Notes on Economic Development and Political Modernization" (Paper presented at the Annual Meeting, American Political Science Association, September 1964); Lester Salamon, "Protest, Politics, and Modernization in the American South: Mississippi as a 'Developing Society'" (Ph.D. diss., Harvard University, 1972); and idem, "Leadership and Modernization: The Emerging Black Political Elite in the American South," *Journal of Politics*, 35 (August 1973), 615-646.

the case is clearly true. But the assumption of the correspondence between economic interests and political behavior—so dramatically reflected in their different ways in Beard, Bentley, and Hartz—also may leave much of politics unaccounted for.

This paper presents no paradigmatic panacea, but it does seem to make some sense to suggest at least two other lines of approach to American politics which may in some small way supplement those of the one, the two, and the many. The first involves the relation between political ideas and political institutions in the United States. All three familiar paradigms tend to minimize the autonomy of politics and particularly the independent role which political ideals may play as a stimulus, guide, and shaper of political action. They have generally, and correctly, assumed that political theory has been relatively underdeveloped in comparison with Europe. The highly systematized ideologies rooted in social classes have been notably absent from the American scene. But it is a mistake to move from this truth to the assumption that political ideals have played a less important role in the United States than in Europe. In fact just the reverse may be true. American politics has been characterized by less sophisticated political theory and more intense political beliefs than most other societies.

Political ideals have played a critical role in the American experience in two ways. First, more so than in any other major society apart from the Soviet Union, political ideas have been the source of national identity. In Europe political ideology and nationalism crossed each other. Ideologies expressed and shaped the interests of "horizontal" units, social classes, while nationalism, in its various manifestations, expressed and shaped the interests of "vertical" units, ethnic and linguistic communities. This produced a system of cross-cutting cleavages. In nineteenth-century Europe, it was not immediately clear who had more in common: two aristocrats (or two bourgeoisie or two socialists), one of whom was a Frenchman; or two Frenchmen, one of whom was an aristocrat (or bourgeois or socialist). This interplay between nationalism and ideology led each to be expressed in more extreme form but also meant that each exercised a restraining effect on the political manifestations of the other. In the United States, on the other hand, nationalism was defined in terms of a set of political beliefs, a political creed, which formulated in imprecise but highly meaningful fashion the basic ideals of the American way of life. From Crevecoeur to Tocqueville to Bryce to Myrdal to Brogan, foreign observers, as well as domestic ones, have not failed to comment on this striking phenomenon. A society produced by immigration needed such a way of defining its identity just as much as a society produced by revolution. If it were not for the "American creed," what, indeed, would Americans have in common?

Political beliefs thus played a necessary and positive role with respect to national identity and integration. They reinforced American nationalism and yet also in some respects moderated it. In this respect there was an American consensus. The consensus theorists, however, often tended to emphasize the *extent* of consensus over the *substance* of the consensus. The substance of that consensus was basically liberal, egalitarian, individualistic, populist. In 1889 Bryce summed it up in words which Tocqueville might have used fifty years earlier and which Myrdal did, for all intents and purposes, use fifty years later. The key dogmas of American thinking, according to Bryce, were: (1) the individual has sacred rights; (2) the source of political power is the people; (3) all government is limited by law and the people; (4) local government is to be preferred to national government; (5) the majority is wiser than the minority; and (6) the less government the better.[30] The distinctive thing about the substance of the liberal consensus or American creed was its antigovernmental character. Populism, individualism, egalitarianism formed the basis for a standing indictment of any political institutions including American ones. The political creed which formed the basis of national identity also was the threat to governmental legitimacy. The more intensely Americans committed themselves to their national political beliefs, the more hostile and cynical they became about their political institutions. The legitimacy of American government varied inversely with belief in American ideals.

The extent to which people take those ideals seriously changes from time to time and from group to group. Commitment to political beliefs will be particularly strong during periods of rapid social and economic change when the relations between social forces are changing, new groups are emerging on the scene, and old ones are fading. Certainly at times substantial groups of Americans have rededicated themselves to the creed, have been appalled at the gap between their ideals of how government should operate and the ways in which it actually does operate, and have made

[30] James Bryce, *The American Commonwealth* (London: Macmillan, 1891), I: 417-418.

vigorous efforts to bring reality into conformity with the ideal. At other times, Americans have mouthed the rhetoric and clichés of the creed but have not been intensely concerned about the extent to which political practice measured up to these political ideals. Americans take pride in their governmental institutions only when they do not believe very deeply in American political ideals.

In this sense the dualism of American politics between American political ideals and American political institutions is rooted in the broad consensus on political ideas which has existed in America. This consensus has, in turn, furnished the basis for alternating periods of institutional stability, on the one hand, and ideological renewal, on the other. Until the present, the reaffirmation of American political ideals has taken place in four major historical instances: the Revolution against British imperial institutions; the Jacksonian movement against the undemocratic and elitist aspects of the established political and economic order; the struggle culminating in the Civil War to restrict and eventually to eliminate the "peculiar institution" of slavery in the South; and the Populist and Progressive movement at the turn of the century to impose limits on the emerging concentrations of corporate economic power. In these invocations, American ideals of equality, individualism, and popular sovereignty have been used for anti-imperial, antielitist, antislavery, and antibig-business purposes. The principal invokers of the creed have been the spokesmen for yeoman farmers and independent entrepreneurial and professional types. Their relative success in challenging hierarchical institutions has declined steadily with each successive invocation. British imperial rule was effectively eliminated in the 1770s and 1780s. The existing political and economic system was in large part, but not entirely, democratized in the 1820s and 1830s. In the 1860s and 1870s the legal basis of slavery was eliminated, but the social, economic, political, and even legal basis for a caste system in the South remained for almost another century. Finally, the Populist-Progressive effort to curtail and break up corporate power had, in many respects, the air of a movement reacting against the mainstream of historical development; it was a partial success at best.

Political ideas have thus had a role in America, albeit a purgative role which is not characteristic of other societies. In countries in which there are a variety of ideologies and belief systems, there are a variety of sources of challenge to governmental institutions but also almost invariably a variety of defenses for major institutions. Tradition and social structure furnish a basis for the legitimacy of some institutions, and particular ideologies and political theories can be utilized to legitimize individual institutions. Attacks on one set of institutions from the perspective of one ideology generate equally intense defenses of that institution from the perspective of other ideologies. In the United States, on the other hand, the consensus is basically antigovernmental. What justification is there for government, for hierarchy, discipline, secrecy, coercion, the suppression of the claims of individuals and groups, within the American context? In terms of American beliefs, government is supposed to be egalitarian, participatory, open, noncoercive, and responsive to the demands of individuals and groups. Yet no government can be these things in any wholehearted way and still remain a government.

The ideological challenge to American government thus comes not from abroad but from at home, not from the conspiracies of anarchists but from the idealism of liberals. To the extent that Americans become carried away by their political ideals, they are in danger of doing away with their political institutions. In this conflict and interaction between ideals and institutions, between the invocation of the former by some social forces for an attack on the latter, lies a critical dimension of American politics which reflects its consensual, dualistic, and pluralistic quality, distinguishes it from most other political systems, and throws some light on both the cyclical and secular trends in American political evolution.

The Conflict of Generations

American society has been distinguished by an unusual degree of consensus. It has also been characterized by an unusual amount of social and economic change. Change, however, usually involves conflict. How can large amounts of change coexist with large amounts of consensus? Part of the answer, of course, lies in the extent to which the opportunities for mobility and expansion have permitted social-economic change to be carried out apart from the political realm. And another part of the picture concerns the relative preeminence of a type of group cleavage in America which is closely associated with the tensions between its political ideas and political institutions.

Conflict and change in Europe have normally been analyzed in terms of the rise and fall of social classes. Class analysis clearly has some relevance to the American experience, but also considerably less than to the European experience. Much more important in America than in Europe has been the role of generations and generational differences. In this sense, one can argue that a consensus has existed in the United States and its fundamentals have remained relatively stable, but its particular manifestations in attitudinal outlooks and public priorities and policies have changed from one generation to another. In Great Britain, for instance, the middle-class ethos and the working-class ethos (including in each social values, life styles, political attitudes, and speech) are relative constants of the social structure. In the United States, on the other hand, classes are less sharply differentiated and generations more sharply differentiated than they are in Europe. This is true both in terms of the leading elements of particular age groups— those who articulate and express its values in literature, art, politics—and even, in a different way, for the mass of the public as a whole. The massive swings of public opinion from the progressivism of 1912 to the stand-pattism of 1920 to the reformism of 1932 clearly cut across class lines and, while the evidence is inconclusive, are yet susceptible of interpretation in terms of generational changes. More recently, survey data have revealed marked differences in outlook among generations, which can, in varying degrees, be explained as much by the interaction and experiential theories of generational differences as by the maturation theory.[31]

[31] The *maturation* theory holds that intergenerational differences are the result of differing positions in the life cycle, and that each generation in effect repeats the cycle of earlier generations (e.g., each moves from youthful liberalism to elderly conservatism). The *interaction* theory holds that the outlook of a later generation is a reaction to that of the earlier generation (e.g., if one generation values economic success, the next generation will assign low priority to that value and instead pursue cultural achievement). The *experiential* theory holds that a generation is produced by a shared historical experience at a formative time in its development (late teens or early twenties) which shapes its outlook and distinguishes it from earlier and later age cohorts whose views were the product of different experiences (e.g., Munich and Pearl Harbor shaped the outlook of one American generation on foreign policy which remained dominant until an equally traumatic event—Vietnam—generated a different outlook in another generation). On the role of generations in political analysis, see Karl Mannheim, "The Problem of Generations," *Essays on the Sociology of Knowledge* (New York: Oxford University Press, 1952), pp. 276-322; Marvin Rintala, "A Generation in Politics: A Definition," *Review of Politics*, 25 (1963), 509-522; Norman B. Ryder, "The Cohort as a Concept in the Study of Social Change," *American Sociological Review*, 30 (1965), 509-522;

"Among democratic nations," Tocqueville argued, "each new generation is a new people."[32] In some measure, American history is divisible into phases, or "peoples," which more or less coincide with different generations: the Founding Fathers; the new generation of Western political leaders which emerged in and after 1810; the generation focused on sectionalism and slavery which emerged in and after 1840; the post-Civil War generation of politician-plutocrats; the populist-Progressive generation; the stand-patters of the 1920s; the New Deal generation; and the cold war generation which emerged after World War II. During each phase, leaders sprang from a different age cohort and embodied a different set of values and policies which came to reflect a high degree of popular consensus. The major political struggles took place between the advance guard of the new generation and the rear guard of its predecessor. The extent to which conflict has been intergenerational also explains why conflict in the United States has so often had such a fleeting quality. By its very nature, inter-generational conflict tends to be intense but brief, as in due course the consensus of one generation supercedes that of the earlier generation.[33] The shift in consensus pioneered by one generation, however, often means an abrupt and vicious turning on those' associated with the consensus of the earlier generation. In the 1940s the Red scare and McCarthyism produced the capture of some Soviet spies, but also the pillorying of many well-meaning liberals of the New Deal generation as security risks and subversives. By 1970, the latter (in almost classic Soviet fashion) were being resur-

---

Philip E. Converse, "Of Time and Partisan Stability," *Comparative Political Studies*, 2 (1969), 139-171; Neal E. Cutler, "Generation, Maturation, and Party Affiliation: A Cohort Analysis," *Public Opinion Quarterly*, 33 (1969-70), 583-588, and "Generational Analysis in Political Science" (Paper presented at the Annual Meeting, American Political Science Association, September 1971).

[32] *Democracy in America* (New York: Vintage Books, 1955), 2, p. 62.

[33] For a striking recent illustration of this point, see Graham Allison, "Cool It: The Foreign Policy of Young America," *Foreign Policy*, (Winter 1970-71), pp. 144-160. Allison contrasts ten "axioms of the postwar era" of foreign policy with their opposites which were the "axioms of elite young Americans" under thirty and argues that there is a fundamental generational difference on foreign policy. And, indeed, there was—for all of about five years in the 1960s. It is quite clear that an overwhelming consensus exists now among elite Americans in their fifties on the validity of Allison's "axioms of young Americans."

rected and rehabilitated as heroes and martyrs, while a new generation was, in turn, denouncing the foreign policy leaders of the intervening years as imperialists and war criminals.

The relevance of generations to American politics is also underscored by the extent to which various aspects of American experience have been interpreted in terms of cycles which normally approximate a generation in longevity: Schlesinger's liberal and conservative tides, Klingberg's introversion and extroversion moods, Burnham's party realignments, and Harris' oscillations in social mobility serve as examples.[34] Has the history of any other modern society been so frequently interpreted in such generational cycles? In addition, of course, the generational notion has been explicitly applied to the differences between first, second, and third generation immigrants; to the nature of the leadership during the Revolution by Elkins and McKitrick; and to the populist-Progressive era by Hofstadter.[35]

Like classes, generations have objective and subjective existences. Objective existence exists in part simply from age differences, but also from the facts of generational interaction and differences in generational experience. Generational consciousness, however, is a rarer phenomenon and only such consciousness turns the generation from a categoric group into an interaction group and a meaningful political actor. Generational consciousness is not constant: some age cohorts in some places are much more conscious of themselves as a cohesive unit than are others. The generation as a source of political action is also one whose interests cannot normally be defined in familiar economic terms. The generation is an experiential and attitudinal group, not an economic interest group. And, as has been suggested, one of the most significant

[34] Arthur M. Schlesinger, "The Tides of National Politics," *Paths to the Present* (Boston: Houghton Mifflin, 1964), pp. 89-103; Frank L. Klingberg, "The Historical Alternation of Moods in American Foreign Policy," *World Politics*, 4 (January 1952), 239-273; and Samuel P. Huntington, *Military Intervention, Political Involvement, and the Unlessons of Vietnam* (Chicago: Adlai E. Stevenson Institute of International Affairs, 1968); Walter Dean Burnham, *Critical Elections and the Mainsprings of American Politics* (New York: W. W. Norton, 1970); P. M. G. Harris, "The Social Origins of American Leaders: The Demographic Foundations," *Perspectives in American History*, 3 (1969), 159-344.

[35] Margaret Mead, *And Keep Your Powder Dry* (New York: William Morrow, 1943); Stanley Elkins and Eric McKitrick, "The Founding Fathers: Young Men of the Revolution," *Political Science Quarterly*, 76 (June 1961), 181-217; Hofstadter, *The Age of Reform*, pp. 165-168.

differences which can exist between generations is precisely the extent to which they have serious commitments to American political ideals. In addition to the other phases and cycles in terms of which American history can be interpreted along generational lines, the cycle of political idealism and institutional stability clearly plays a major role.

Beyond the One, the Two, and the Many

Contrary to the implications of the consensus thesis, conflict has played a significant role in American political development. Contrary to the images of the pluralist and progressive paradigms, the most significant forms of conflict have not been simply between upper and lower classes or among economic interest groups. They have instead been the product of differing degrees of intensities of belief in American political ideals and of commitment to American political institutions. They have also reflected the differing experiences and priorities of successive generations. The predominant role of these types of conflict helps to differentiate American politics from those of other societies. It also helps to explain some of the patterns of continuity and change which have characterized American politics. In the development and refinement of other comparative, dynamic, and realistic concepts, of which these are only limited specific examples, new paradigms of American politics may eventually emerge which will be more illuminating, useful, and relevant than those of the one, the two, and the many.

2 The Impact of Watergate on Children's Attitudes toward Political Authority

F. CHRISTOPHER ARTERTON

The question of how children acquire their opinions about their government and the political system in general has been of great concern to political scientists. One of the persistent findings of this research in political socialization has been that an American child's first awareness of the political system is of the president of the United States, and that the role and occupant are idealized to an overwhelming degree.[1] Especially at early ages (grades three, four, and five), the president is seen as benevolent, omniscient, omnipotent, protective, infallible, diligent, likable, and so on. In a 1969 study, after having interviewed more than 12,000 children, political scientists David Easton and Jack Dennis re-

[1] The literature on this point is extensive. For the early discussions see Robert D. Hess and David Easton, "The Child's Changing Image of the President," *Public Opinion Quarterly*, 14 (Winter 1960), 632–644; Fred I. Greenstein, "The Benevolent Leader: Children's Images of Political Authority," *American Political Science Review*, 54, no. 4 (December 1960), 934–943; Fred I. Greenstein, "More on Children's Images of the President," *Public Opinion Quarterly*, 25 (Winter 1961), 648–654; David Easton and Robert D. Hess, "The Child's Political World," *Midwest Journal of Political Science*, 6 (August 1962), 229–246; Judith V. Torney, "The Child's Idealization of Authority," M.A. thesis, University of Chicago, 1962; Robert D. Hess, "The Socialization of Attitudes Toward Political Authorities: Some Cross-National Comparisons," *International Social Science Journal*, 14, no. 4 (1963), 542–554.

The more recent literature treats the topic in considerably more depth; see David Easton and Jack Dennis, "The Child's Image of Government," *Annals of the American*

F. CHRISTOPHER ARTERTON is an assistant professor in the Department of Political Science at Yale University.

marked, "In all our testing and interviewing, we were unable to find a child who did not express the highest esteem for the President."[2]

The potential importance of this finding cannot be overstated, because, it is argued, adult perceptions of the legitimacy of the political system as a whole flow directly from this early tendency to idealize presidential authority. From approximately the sixth grade onward, the child's knowledge of the political system rapidly becomes more extensive and complex. He or she learns to differentiate between the president and the presidency; presidents receive less favorable ratings in personal qualities and attractions, while awareness of the power and importance of the "performance capabilities" of the office remains high.[3] Rather than viewing other institutions and political participants as subordinate to the president,[4] the older child begins to understand the interplay between the president, the Supreme Court, and Congress; to recognize the importance of different levels in the political system; and to differentiate theoretically the processes of legislation from administration and from adjudication. Along with this knowledge comes a more critical awareness of the conflictive nature of politics in the United States (and elsewhere). The president begins to be perceived as a political participant who stands for certain policy positions and maneuvers to attain his desired ends.[5] Nevertheless, Easton and Dennis have argued that from the earlier reservoir of idealism personalized around the president springs a diverse sense of the legitimacy of our political institutions:

> Even though the older child may see authority in more critical and less enthusiastic terms, early idealization may create latent feelings that are hard

---

Academy of Political and Social Science, 361 (1965), 41–57; David Easton and Jack Dennis, *Children in the Political System: The Origins of Political Legitimacy* (New York, 1969); Fred I. Greenstein, *Children and Politics* (New Haven, Conn., 1965); Fred I. Greenstein, "Popular Images of the President," *American Journal of Psychiatry*, 122 (November 1965), 523–529; Robert D. Hess and Judith Torney, *The Development of Political Attitudes in Children* (Chicago, 1967); and Roberta Sigel, "Image of a President: Some Insights into the Political View of School Children," *American Political Science Review*, 62, no. 1 (March 1968), 216–226.

[2] *Children in the Political System*, p. 177.

[3] This distinction was recognized quite early in the study of children's attitudes toward the president. See, for example, Hess and Easton, "The Child's Changing Image of the President," p. 636ff.

[4] The president is generally the first political authority recognized by children, followed by the policeman. Thus they are said to first become aware of the head and the foot of the political system. When other participants—senators, congressmen, mayors, etc.—are recognized, they are at first seen as subordinate to the president, in the sense that the president tells them what to do. See Greenstein, "The Benevolent Leader."

[5] Sigel, "Image of a President."

to undo or shake off. This is the major significance of the first bond to the system through the Presidency. The positive feelings generated there can be expected to have lasting consequences.[6]

This proposition should be taken as a theoretical hypothesis to be established by future research, for Easton and Dennis offer no supporting evidence.[7]

The present article examines the contention that legitimacy derives from the early idealization of the presidency. It does so by exploring the ramifications of recent political events in the United States upon the attitudes of children toward the president. Specifically, our point of departure will be an examination of whether the idealistic regard with which children view the president has been shattered by the revelations brought to public attention during the so-called Watergate crisis. If so, we may well have established a nonobtrusive, quasi-experimental, critical test of the Easton and Dennis theory in which the president becomes the variable.

In the first place, we would like to determine whether this pervasive finding of socialization research is susceptible to alteration by actual political events. There is some evidence that subgroups of our population (blacks, Appalachian poor, etc.) may not be as prone to this idealism as the dominant cultural group,[8] yet we do not know whether these attitudes may be epiphenomenal or developmental in the sense of being learned within a whole cultural complex. In other words, we would like to draw some conclusions as to whether these perceptions of the president as benevolent, infallible, protective, and omnipotent are part and parcel of the child's developmental process and therefore fairly impervious to influence from contemporary events or whether they are dependent upon a state of "politics as usual." Second, after determining the answer to this prior question, we should be able to discuss the substantive importance of this theory in relation to the long-range effects of Watergate for

---

[6] *Children in the Political System*, p. 207.

[7] This assertion has been strongly questioned by Dean Jaros in "Children's Orientations Toward the President: Some Additional Theoretical Considerations and Data," *Journal of Politics*, 29, no. 2 (May 1967), 368–387.

[8] The literature on subgroups of the population developed during the late 1960s as a critique of the assumption of cultural homogeneity of the "main line" studies of socialization. See Edward S. Greenberg, "Political Socialization to Support the System: A Comparison of Black and White Children," Ph.D. dissertation, University of Wisconsin, Madison, 1969; Dean Jaros, Herbert Hirsch, and Frederic J. Fleron, Jr., "The Malevolent Leader: Political Socialization in an American Subculture," *American Political Science Review*, 62, no. 1 (March 1968), 64–75; Sandra Kenyon, "The Development of Political Cynicism: A Study of Political Socialization," Ph.D. dissertation, Massachusetts Institute of Technology, 1970.

our polity. Given the Easton and Dennis proposition, at stake may well be the extent to which a future generation weighs the legitimacy of our political system's predominant authority structure. While such important considerations cannot be explored empirically today—being "time-lagged"—the injection of current politics as a variable into the measurement of this well-established observation should help determine the certainty with which the Easton and Dennis proposition can be advanced.

CONDUCT OF THE STUDY

On December 5, 7, and 10, 1973, questionnaires were administered to 367 children in grades three, four, and five of the public school system of a high socioeconomic-status suburb of Boston, Massachusetts. Forty-nine items were replicated from the national study undertaken in 1961 and 1962 by researchers at the University of Chicago. Accordingly, in the results reported below, data gathered in the Watergate environment are juxtaposed with data collected during the Kennedy administration, hereafter referred to as the 1962 study.[9] Half of the questionnaire was devoted to the child's cynicism concerning politics, general political awareness, specific knowledge of Watergate personalities, source of information concerning Watergate, and political opinions about the personal involvement of the president in wrongdoing, the role of the press in either fomenting a crisis or bringing malfeasance to light, and the question of impeachment.

FINDINGS

Attitudes toward the President

In the fall of 1973, children express attitudes toward the president of the United States that are not only much less positive (as has been found before only in certain population subgroups),[10] but can be more accurately described as wholly negative. The once benevolent leader has been transformed into the malevolent leader by the impact of current events; and there can be little doubt that these children have come to view the president as a figure to be strenuously rejected.

Easton and Dennis rely heavily upon an item in which children are asked if the president is a favorite of theirs;[11] the comparative percentage answers appear in Table 1. As can easily be seen, the two distribu-

[9] The data from this large research project have been reported in the publications of Easton and Dennis and Hess and Torney; see footnote 1 for citations.

[10] Greenberg, "Political Socialization"; Jaros, Hirsch, and Fleron, "The Malevolent Leader."

[11] Unresolved in any of the materials from the 1962 study is the question of the

TABLE 1

Comparison of 1962 and 1973 Studies in Rating of the President for "Is the president your favorite?"
(Percent of children responding)

	Mean	1 He Is My Favorite of All	2 He Is Almost My Favorite of All	3 He Is More a Favorite of Mine than Most	4 He Is More a Favorite of Mine than Many	5 He Is More a Favorite of Mine than a Few	6 He Is Not One of My Favorites	N
3rd, 1962	2.36	39%	27%	14%	8%	7%	6%	1,667
3rd, 1973	4.44	8	15	11	4	15	47	111
4th, 1962	2.60	28	30	17	11	7	7	1,732
4th, 1973	5.36	2	5	2	8	13	70	124
5th, 1962	2.83	21	29	21	13	9	8	1,787
5th, 1973	5.21	2	3	8	13	11	64	132

tions of responses are practically mirror images of each other. In 1962, anywhere from 50 to 66 percent of the children responded that the president was their favorite of all or of almost all; but, in 1973, the range responding in this positive fashion varied from 5 to 23 percent. In both studies, the older the children the less positive the assessment.

On the other hand, looking at the negative attidudes expressed in response to the same item, the results are even more striking. In 1962, even at the fifth-grade level, only 17 percent of the children rated the president as "not one of my favorites" or only as "more a favorite of mine than a few." In 1973, this figure jumped to 63 percent in the third grade, 82 percent in the fourth, and 75 percent in the fifth. Treating these responses as a scale, the differences in mean scores between the two studies are large and significant ($p < .01$) for each grade.

The 1962 study asked children to rate the president on a variety of indicators which Easton and Dennis argue can be grouped into five dimensions of the child's image of presidential authority: attachment, benevolence, dependability, power, and leadership.[12] In turn, these five dimensions are said to vary from highly affective in content (e.g., attachment or affiliation) to a high cognitive content (e.g., leadership). The data in Table 1 refer to indicators ("Is he your favorite?") which Easton and Dennis believe to contain the highest degree of affect. Therefore, strong attachment has been transformed into strong rejection on an affective level. But what of the other dimensions of the child's image? Do they also show the impact of Watergate revelations?

Table 2 presents a comparison of the mean responses for twelve different indicators grouped by the five dimensions of authority image. The higher the rating (choices were allowed from six increasingly less positive responses), the more unfavorable the evaluation of the president.[13]

An inspection of these data reveals that under the impact of Watergate, children have come to reject the figure of the president in its affective components but still rate very high the performance capabilities of his office. In attachment, benevolence, and dependability, the president does not merely receive less positive ratings than in 1962, but he receives *negative* ratings. The differences are less pronounced, however, for scales of perceived power and leadership; in these indicators the president still receives positive ratings, though less positive than in 1962.

---

meaning of this item to the respondents; that is, favorite what? President? Authority figure? Easton and Dennis appear oblivious to this ambiguity. See *Children in the Political System*, chaps. 7 and 8.

[12] Ibid., p. 188.

[13] Levels of significance were computed by Z-tests, which were based on a reconstruction of the variance of the 1962 data from the relevant tables found in Easton and Dennis, *Children in the Political System*, chap. 8.

TABLE 2

Comparison of 1962 and 1973 Studies in
Mean Ratings of President on Twelve Scales

	3rd Grade 1962	3rd Grade 1973	4th Grade 1962	4th Grade 1973	5th Grade 1962	5th Grade 1973
Attachment						
1. Is he your favorite?	2.36	4.44	2.60	5.36	2.83	5.21
Benevolence						
2. Would he want to help you if you needed it?	1.81	3.83	2.09	4.56	2.70	4.96
3. Does he protect you?	—	4.09	3.10	4.61	3.27	4.52
Dependability						
4.[a] Does he keep his promises?	1.69	3.37	1.85	4.06	1.90	4.30
5. Does he make mistakes?	—	3.10	1.97	3.81	2.16	4.11
6. Does he give up when things are hard to do?	—	2.17	1.19	2.20	1.18	2.19
Power						
7. Can he make people do what he wants?	2.47	2.93	2.55	2.94	2.67	3.06
8. Can he punish people?	—	3.10	2.85	3.17[b]	2.97	2.83[c]
Leadership						
9. How much does he know?	2.07	2.76	2.18	3.19	2.22	3.29
10. Does he make important decisions?	1.71	2.26	1.60	2.18	1.57	2.45
11. Does he work hard?	—	2.24	2.03	2.46	2.04	2.58
12. Is he a leader?	—	2.07	1.69	2.01[b]	1.71	2.16

[a] Scale inverted for comparison.
[b] Significant Z-test at $p < .025$.
[c] Not significant difference.

Furthermore, we find evidence of a small but persistent residue of antagonism toward the president which spills over from the negative affective assessments to those of performance capabilities. This can easily be seen in Table 3, which presents the percentage distribution for ratings of the president as a leader. At least in the third and fifth grades, approximately 10 percent of the students gave the president the most negative rating; and leadership was the indicator which exhibited the *smallest* percentage in the highly negative column. Ratings of power have up to 20 percent of the children in all classes expressing hostile attitudes toward the president. We have opted to present in detail here only the leadership scale because it offers the greatest contrast with the affective scale (Table 1) both in data and content.

Referring back to Table 2, one remaining inconsistency ought to be

TABLE 3

Comparison of 1962 and 1973 Studies in Rating
of President for "Is he a leader?"
(Percent of children responding)

Grade, Study	Mean	1 Always Leader	2 Usually Leader	3 More Often Leader	4 More Often Follower	5 Usually Fol- lower	6 Almost Always Follower	N
3rd, 1962	–	–	–	–	–	–	–	–
3rd, 1973	2.07	57%	17%	10%	4%	–	12%	110
4th, 1962	1.69	52	34	10	1	–	2	1,730
4th, 1973	2.01	44	31	13	6	2	3	124
5th, 1962	1.71	48	39	11	1	1	1	1,794
5th, 1973	2.16	48	26	11	2	2	10	127

cleared up. The sixth indicator, "Does the president give up when things are hard to do?" stands in contrast to the other items in the dependability dimension. While the president's rating has diminished from 1962, it is still quite positive in the sense that children believe the president does not easily give up. This can be accounted for in two ways. The less interesting observation is that the indicator may actually belong in the leadership dimension, being undoubtedly a characteristic of what children would think of as a leader. The other element is that quite clearly Mr. Nixon's stand on this particular concern has come through to the children; again and again he has stated that he will not give up, and the children have come to accept that fact.

The 1962 study asked children what they thought was the president's job. Very few differences were observed in the 1973 replies except that they were much less oriented toward the foreign-policy aspects ("to keep us out of war" and "to make friends with other nations"). Only 25 percent of the children mentioned these in 1973, as opposed to approximately 40 percent in 1962. This finding is particularly interesting in view of the fact that the incumbent's most prominent successes have been precisely in these two areas.

Finally, while the children studied in 1973 rated the president almost as powerful as did those in 1962, there is some indication that they have considerably diminished their expectations of what the power of the president *ought* to be. In both studies, children were asked to agree or disagree with the following statement: "If the president does not approve of a law, it should not be passed." Table 4 contains the percentage agreeing with that statement in the three grades. In addition to

TABLE 4

Comparison of 1962 and 1973 Studies in Agreement with Statement, "If the president does not approve of a law, it should not be passed," by Grade (Percent of children responding)

	3rd Grade	4th Grade	5th Grade
1962 study	83	68	42
1973 study	45	47	34

giving some indication of the inaccuracy of knowledge surrounding the president's prerogatives, these data do show a considerable difference in the lower grades which appears to narrow by grade five. This raises the possibility that the impact of Watergate has been merely to make children aware of the political nature of our system at an earlier point in their lives. We shall return to this in the discussion below.

Systemic Generalization

As one might anticipate, attitudes toward the president cannot exist in a vacuum, and thus it is not surprising to learn that in the fall of 1973 children respond in much less positive ways to items dealing with many aspects of our political system. The results in 1973 uniformly give the impression of cynicism and rejection.

In the 1962 study, children were asked to rate political candidates— "those who try to get elected to public office"—on different scales indicating their relative powerfulness, selfishness, intelligence, honesty, and trustworthiness. The response categories were much like those dealt with above for the rating of the president. As compared to the data reported by Hess and Torney,[14] today's children rate candidates in less approving fashion on every scale except power. Table 5 contains the comparative percentages of children giving the two most favorable replies.

In both studies, approximately one-third of the children believe candidates to be more powerful than almost anyone or than most people. The 1973 results do show that this percentage decreases among older children, a trend which appears later in fifth- through seventh-grade children in the 1962 study. It is remarkable, however, that just as with the ratings of the president, the results in 1973 only approximate those of 1962 when aspects of power are being considered. Children have separated the performance capabilities of the president and politicians in general from their personal qualities. In the latter, enormous differences emerge.

[14] Development of Political Attitudès, p. 76.

TABLE 5

Comparison of 1962 and 1973 Studies in Ratings of Political
Candidates as Two Most Positive Answers on Five Scales[a]
(Percent children responding)

	3rd Grade 1962	3rd Grade 1973	4th Grade 1962	4th Grade 1973	5th Grade 1962	5th Grade 1973
1. Candidates are *more powerful* than almost anyone or than most people.	—	43.9	29.6	35.0	30.2	33.3
2. Candidates are *less selfish* than almost anyone or than most people.	—	42.7	57.7	22.0	54.1	19.8
3. Candidates are *smarter* than almost anyone or than most people.	—	33.0	45.6	32.2	45.1	35.2
4. Candidates are *more honest* than almost anyone or than most people.	—	39.8	60.8	30.6	59.0	29.6
5. Candidates always or almost always keep their promises.	—	38.5	56.4	17.7	51.7	23.8

[a]Data from the 1962 study cited from Robert D. Hess and Judith Torney, *The Development of Political Attitudes in Children* (Chicago, 1967), p. 76.

Comparing 1973 and 1962, politicians are seen as more selfish, less intelligent, more dishonest, and less likely to keep their promises. The largest differences were found for selfishness and trustworthiness; the differences were less pronounced for intelligence. Unlike the ratings of the president, however, the responses to these items tend to be normally distributed about the middle of the scale rather than skewed toward a negative (in 1973) or positive (in 1962) assessment. This indicates that there has not been a wholesale shift in children's attitudes toward the referent actor (candidates), but rather that the effects of Watergate (and/or the intervening eleven years) have been a diminished respect for the personal characteristics of individuals who run for public office. Thus, in the transference from president to politicians in general, the negative effects apparently are not as severe as they might have been. However, ultimately, they may be a good deal more serious than is evident at first glance (see the discussion below).

TABLE 6

Responses to Political Cynicism Items in 1973 Study
(Percent of children responding)

1. "Most politicians are mainly out for themselves."

	Agree	Disagree	Don't Know	Total	N
3rd grade	31%	24%	45%	100%	111
4th grade	35	31	34	100	124
5th grade	44	31	25	100	132

2. "Dishonesty seems to be more common in politics than in most other careers."

	Agree	Disagree	Don't Know	Total	N
3rd grade	34%	19%	46%	99%	108
4th grade	43	32	24	99	123
5th grade	56	21	23	100	131

In 1973 the children were asked to respond to two rather standard questions which purport to measure political cynicism. The percentage replies to these items appear in Table 6. In both cases, responses indicative of political cynicism (agreement) increase with the school grade: more than 30 to 40 percent agree that politicians are mainly out for themselves; and 34 to 56 percent agree that dishonesty appears more commonly in politics than in other careers. It is also interesting to note that when given items that lead toward a negative assessment of the political system, younger children exhibit a good deal of confusion, as evidenced by the high number responding "don't know." The increase in the percentage of replies indicating political cynicism is accompanied by a decline in this confusion.

Comparative data also were gathered on the child's attitude toward the policeman, a topic given considerable attention in the socialization literature, but which is only tangentially related to our present concerns. The data in this regard show some of the same trends as those for politicians. Ratings of the policeman are less favorable in 1973 than they were in 1962, a deterioration which showed up on all dimensions, including those relating to performance capabilities. The policeman was not seen as unfavorably as the president on indicators of affective content, but certainly he has slipped in the child's estimation since 1962. Again, political disputes have intervened, affecting children's responses. Like the ratings of candidates, the responses for policemen tended to be normally distributed or not skewed as were the president's ratings.

As a final set of data indicating the generalization of negative attitudes to the entire political system which may have come about as a result of Watergate, let us turn to the children's agreement with three

TABLE 7

Comparison of 1962 and 1973 Studies in Agreement
with Three Statements about the Government
(Percent of children responding)

	3rd Grade 1962	3rd Grade 1973	4th Grade 1962	4th Grade 1973	5th Grade 1962	5th Grade 1973
1. "The government has too much power."	36	34	19	35	22	42
2. "The government meddles too much in our private lives."	28	42	21	42	17	35
3. "The government should have more power over the people."	22	16	33	7	24	5

broad statements made about the government in general. The comparative percentages of those agreeing with assertions about the power of our government appear in Table 7.

The beliefs that the government has too much power and that it meddles too much in our private lives have become more widespread among children since 1962, and, among today's children, these beliefs gain increasing acceptance with age. These responses should be interpreted with the knowledge that there has not been a great decline in the power of political participants (president and politicians) as perceived by children in 1962 and 1973. Thus, the concern of many adults that, at the very least, Watergate indicates that governmental power has grown beyond reasonable bounds is not lost upon children. They appear to be aware of this as a serious problem.

The Specifics of Watergate

How aware of Watergate events are children of ages seven to ten? What opinions do they hold? How have they learned of the people and actions which make up what the news media has branded the "Watergate crisis"? Partial answers to these questions can be gathered from our data.

In order to obtain an indication of what factual knowledge children possessed about Watergate, we asked five questions in which a major participant was to be identified by the best description from among the following: senator, lawyer, friend of the president, or judge. The coded data from these questions appear in Table 8. A seemingly rather low percentage of children are able to identify correctly the major figures of

TABLE 8

Political Information: Responses to Five
Identification Questions in the 1973 Study
(Percent of children responding)

		Correct Answer	Incorrect Answer	Don't Know	Total	N
1. Who is Samuel Ervin?						
	3rd grade	8%	15%	77%	100%	105
	4th grade	24	18	58	100	120
	5th grade	31	27	42	100	132
2. Who is H. R. Haldeman?						
	3rd grade	6	22	72	100	107
	4th grade	10	26	63	99	123
	5th grade	29	26	45	100	132
3. Who is John Sirica?						
	3rd grade	10	19	68	100	107
	4th grade	31	17	52	100	123
	5th grade	36	20	44	100	129
4. Who is Archibald Cox?						
	3rd grade	6	42	52	100	106
	4th grade	18	47	35	100	124
	5th grade	31	40	29	100	130
5. Who is Howard Baker?						
	3rd grade	6	18	76	100	105
	4th grade	18	24	58	100	124
	5th grade	25	18	57	100	130

the Watergate events. It is difficult to interpret these results in the absence of comparative data from an adult population group, but, given the fact that we are dealing with a high socioeconomic-status population, we might conclude that concrete knowledge is quite low. It appears to be somewhat lower than general political knowledge which was measured in part by a request to identify the governor of Massachusetts. Percentages of correct replies to that question for grades three, four, and five respectively, were 8, 40, and 45 percent.[15]

One interesting aspect of the identifications can be uncovered by comparing the responses for Archibald Cox with the other political participants. While the percentage of correct identifications was not greater for Cox than for the others, more children felt they had heard of Cox and so could take a guess at his identification; the percent of "don't knows"

[15] The percentages of correct identifications for the president and vice-president were in the high nineties, even though the latter was in a state of flux. Gerald Ford had been nominated when data collection began, and he was confirmed and sworn in by the time it ended. Even young children were quite aware of this.

is persistently smaller for Cox. The reader will no doubt recall the inundation of letters and telegrams which reached Washington after Cox's dismissal. Those events may have transformed Cox into something of a hero and boosted his name-recognition above the other Watergate participants. That Cox has become an ephemeral hero is not inconsistent with the data to be presented next.

The opinions of this group of children toward major aspects of Watergate were measured by three questions. In no other part of the question-

TABLE 9

Responses to Three Opinion Items about Watergate Grouped by Class
(Percent of children responding)

	3rd Grade	4th Grade	5th Grade
1. Some people believe that the newspapers and television are trying to make Watergate sound worse than it really is, while others believe that they were right in making the American people aware of everything that has gone on. Which do you think is closer to the truth?			
a. The newspapers and television have made Watergate sound much worse than it really is.	20	17	18
b. The newspapers and television were right in making the people aware of everything that has gone on.	40	65	56
c. I don't know which to believe.	22	13	21
d. I don't really know what Watergate is.	17	5	4
	99	100	99
2. Some people say that the president has done some very bad things, while others say that he is being blamed for the things his friends did. Which side do you agree with?			
a. The president did some very bad things.	38	53	42
b. The president is being blamed for things his friends did.	25	21	29
c. I don't know which to believe.	37	26	23
	100	100	100
3. Do you think the president should be impeached?			
a. Yes.	31	49	58
b. No.	15	22	18
c. I don't know what impeach means.	40	18	0
d. I don't know whether he should be impeached or not.	14	12	24
	100	101	100

naire is the exact wording of the questions so important. For this reason, Table 9 contains the precise format in which the questions were asked together with the various percentage responses for the three classes.

Overwhelmingly these children take an anti-Nixon stand. By a two-to-one margin they believe the president to have been involved in wrong-doing rather than being guilty merely through association with the misdeeds of his staff. By three-to-one in grades four and five, and two-to-one in grade three, children believe that the press has played a valuable role rather than that of manufacturing a crisis in order to "get Nixon." In each of these areas supporters of the president have explicitly attempted to defend him by arguing that he is being blamed by association and that the crisis is a manufacture of the news media. Their arguments have not had much impact, at least on these children.

By margins of two-to-one in the third grade, two-and-a-half-to-one in the fourth, and three-to-one in the fifth grade, today's children believe that the president should be impeached. These are remarkable figures given the fact that these children's parents voted two-to-one for Nixon only a year earlier.

A final set of interesting data can be presented on how children come to learn of major political events. They were asked to remember how they first heard about the Watergate crisis. Approximately 45 percent in all three classes named the news media as their first source of information about Watergate; parents were named in about 30 percent of the cases. All other possible sources (siblings, peers, relatives) were named infrequently; teachers were named by approximately 8 percent of the children. In addition, the children were asked to name the source of information that had been "most important" to them in finding out about the Watergate events. In response to this question the impact of the news media was even greater, and its reported effects increased in percentage with the children's grade: 55, 66, and 72 percent in the three grades respectively. It is also pertinent that among those children naming one form of news media, television was mentioned in about two-thirds of the cases. Yet, among the older children, newspapers command increased attention: of the fifth graders who answered that the news media was most important to them, 40 percent mentioned newspapers.

IMPLICATIONS

Several alternative explanations for the discrepancies between the 1962 data and that collected during the Watergate revelations need to be considered. It is possible that the differences may be attributed to differences in the respective sample: 1962 was a national sample of all socio-economic-status levels and the data reported here was derived from an upper-income community in Massachusetts—i.e., a liberal, Democratic environment. Greenstein reports that children from lower socioeconomic-status families have a greater tendency to idealize the president.[16] Although this finding has been somewhat contradicted by the research in specific cultural subgroups which are predominately lower status,[17] we should explicitly note this lack of correspondence between the 1962 and the 1973 respondents. It is difficult, however, to estimate the quantitative effect of this upon the results reported here. First, while both Easton and Dennis and Hess and Torney mention social-class differences to the effect that upper-status children tend to be less favorable in their ratings of the president, nowhere do they present a detailed description of the quantitative differences which emerge in their data.[18] Second, Hess and Torney and Easton and Dennis acknowledge that these differences may in part reflect some partisan feelings;[19] Kennedy, a Democrat, was more likely to appeal to lower-class children and to be rated less positively by children who identified themselves as Republicans. We do know that children are vaguely aware of salient policy positions of the incumbent.[20] Therefore, a Republican administration advocating policies more to the liking of upper-class individuals may partially affect potential differences in approval caused by differences in social class. These children are demonstrably aware of the political positions of their families. Only 21 percent of the children were unable to say how their parents had voted in the 1972 election. Of those who knew, the children reported that 61.8 percent of their parents had voted for President Nixon and 38.2 percent for McGovern (a figure which closely parallels the Nixon national percentage of 61.3 percent). These reports of parental voting appear to be quite valid when compared to the actual percentage of votes for Nixon in the community as a whole (58.4 percent) and in the precincts in which the schools were located (63.8 percent). While it is unlikely that these children are aware of how their precincts or community voted, they are certainly aware of the outcome of the election and the unique position of Massachusetts in that result. Even in the absence of Watergate, the effect of these factors would have to be considered before one could make a judgment of the quantitative differences in results stemming from social-class background.

Nevertheless, the magnitude of the differences in presidential ratings

[16] *Children and Politics*, chap. V.

[17] See footnote 8.

[18] Easton and Dennis, *Children in the Political System*, pp. 343–349; Hess and Torney, *Development of Political Attitudes*, pp. 150–159.

[19] Hess and Torney, *Development of Political Attitudes*, p. 135; Easton and Dennis, *Children in the Political System*, p. 197.

[20] Sigel, "Image of a President."

allow us to reject this hypothesis. The differences due to social class reported by the Chicago researchers are on the order of 4 or 5 percent, or a difference in mean ratings of around .40 on the six-point scale.[21] Variations of this size are quite marginal compared to the vast differences in children's affective attitudes toward the president when we contrast the 1973 data to that of 1962. The differences in mean ratings in Table 2 for attachment, benevolence, and dependability are on the order of two full points on the six-point scale. Percentage shifts in Tables 1 and 4 are approximately 40 percent or greater.

It may well be, on the other hand, that the differences in mean ratings for the president's performance capabilities (power and leadership) are attributable to the differences in socioeconomic status between the two samples; at least statistical tests were unable to rule out that possibility. But, this does nothing to weaken the interpretation presented above, namely, that the effect of Watergate has been to transform the president into the malevolent leader.

A second possible interpretation of these differences could be based upon the assertion that the effect of Watergate has been to speed up the process of political socialization. Grades three through five were deliberately chosen for this study because earlier research indicated that the idealization of the president would be at its highest level among third-grade children and that the trend toward a fading of the optimistic picture would be clearly apparent by the fifth grade.[22] One might argue that the process has merely been compressed, so that children, observing an enormous crisis of political malfeasance, learn earlier what they would have eventually discovered. Yet, for two reasons, the negative attitudes toward the president displayed by children in 1973 cannot be interpreted merely as a telescoping of the process of a gradual awakening to healthy adult cynicism. First, at no age do the children in 1962 reject the president as a negative affect symbol, but this clearly happens in 1973. Second, we find the same trend toward increasingly negative attitudes in higher grades evident in the 1973 sample alone. In fact, the differences between the 1962 and the 1973 attitudes become more pronounced in the fourth and fifth grades. The responses of children in 1973 indicate an entirely different experience in political socialization from the reports of earlier research. Political events and indeed the president himself do become important variables in the socialization equation, and their present impact should give us cause for great concern. The president

[21] See Easton and Dennis, *Children in the Political System,* pp. 342–346; and Hess and Torney, *Development of Political Attitudes,* pp. 135–137.

[22] Hess and Easton in "The Child's Changing Image of the President," first reported the effects of increased age, and it has been noticed in all the research published since.

is viewed as truly malevolent, undependable, untrustworthy, yet powerful and dangerous. If the president is the image of political authority and the central mechanism for building diffuse support of a political system, as Easton and Dennis argue, then for this generation of children, conceptions of authority and the political system which they underpin will be markedly different.

A More Optimistic Interpretation

If we accept the Easton and Dennis theory, we find the implications of the 1973 data for the future legitimacy of our political system to be disturbing indeed. Our data, however, provide for a less pessimistic outlook since they also question some major aspects of the Easton and Dennis model of socialization. First, Easton and Dennis argue that children are unable to differentiate between the occupant and the role of the presidency,[23] a proposition which seems less tenable given the marked differentiation we have found between affective responses and perceptions of performance capablities. Second, they propose a "vulnerability" hypothesis,[24] which amounts to a weaker form of the psychological defense mechanism of identification with an overwhelmingly powerful authority.[25] Helplessness produces anxiety which is reduced by idealization. But, in this instance, identification should produce a heightening of the president's positive ratings, since a president exercising his capability of doing great harm should produce ever increasing anxiety. Finally, Easton and Dennis argue that the idealism expressed toward the president is a transference of perceptions of the father to the national collectivity.[26] This "family writ large" hypothesis[27] is not supported by our data. No discernible differences appear between ratings in 1962 and 1973 for "your father" on any of the scales which measured significant changes in attitudes toward the president (data not shown).

There is, of course, the likely possibility that parents have explicitly

[23] *Children in the Political System,* pp. 193–198 and *passim.*

[24] Ibid., pp. 177, 205, and *passim.*

[25] The best statement of this mechanism as used in the study of political socialization is provided by Jaros in "Children's Orientations," p. 373: "The child is patently inferior; the President is a super-power. Such a relationship is potentially dangerous, for the super-power has the capability of doing great harm. This helplessness and vulnerability thus creates an anxiety drive. In order to avoid this anxiety, the child responds by idealizing the President, for a benevolent President will not manifest his harmful potential; anxiety is reduced and psychic tranquillity reigns." Jaros goes on to criticize sharply this proposition.

[26] *Children in the Political System,* p. 372.

[27] I believe Greenstein has coined this' term which he probes in *Children and Politics.* For an earlier statement see Easton and Hess, "The Child's Political World."

commented upon current events, thereby designating the present occupant as an inappropriate model for either transference or identification. But, if these hypotheses lose their inevitability which has been tied to the power of the president, they also lose their explanatory power, for they then lead to the proposition that children idealize only ideal authority figures.

It can be argued that a more satisfactory accounting for both the 1962 and 1973 data can be derived from the moral development work of Lawrence Kohlberg.[28] Children aged six to ten would most likely exhibit the first stage of what Kohlberg calls "preconventional moral thinking," in which actions and actors are evaluated by stark, categorical labels of "good" or "bad" without any grey areas in between. Past studies have been made of children who have seen the president as a morally good authority figure, and, therefore, good without exception on a whole range of evaluative dimensions. In the light of the Watergate revelations, children have placed the president squarely into the "bad" category, and, thus now rate him as completely negative. The effect of Watergate has been to transform the president from a positive, morally good symbol into a negative object to be affectively and morally rejected. If through resignation or impeachment, Nixon were replaced in office, one would anticipate, according to this explanation, that the response patterns would return to something approximating the 1962 distribution, for the president would again become a correct moral symbol.

Can political legitimacy be built on a cognitive structure so susceptible to such variation? It seems more plausible to suggest that the 1962 and 1973 questionnaires are measuring surface-level cognitions rather than basic orientations.

The Kohlberg-derived explanation does have difficulty, however, in accounting for the smaller, but significant, decline in affective ratings toward politicians, policemen, and "the government"; we would have anticipated either no change or a similar massive swing toward negative assessments. Inevitably, we are forced to conclude that the legitimacy of the political system has been impaired by events in the intervening years, to which Watergate, given the 1973 attitudes expressed toward the president, has certainly contributed. It is in this regard that the moderate deterioration in attitudes toward other parts of the political system poses a more serious question for the future stability of our political institutions than does the rapid and complete shift in attitudes toward the president.

[28] Lawrence Kohlberg, "The Development of Moral Character and Moral Ideology," in M. L. Hoffman and L. N. Hoffman (eds.), *Review of Child Development Research*, Vol. 1 (New York, 1964); and Lawrence Kohlberg, "The Child as Moral Philosopher," *Psychology Today*, 1, no. 4 (September 1968).

We have been able to establish that current events do have an impact upon the political socialization of children, at least in terms of their attitudes toward political authorities. Whether or not one wishes to argue that these attitudes become the origin of beliefs in the legitimacy of the political system, one must recognize that politics do have an impact on the attitudes children hold. In some sense then, in accounting for the views children have of the president, the incumbent himself is a relevant variable to consider. We do not find a spontaneous and automatic mechanism whereby children idealize all authority simply because it is powerful. Still to be established is the relevance of the attitudes of children—positive or negative—to their political behavior as adults; but that is a connection which has not yet been demonstrated by any research in the political socialization field.

Conclusion

The political scandals collectively called Watergate have provided researchers with a critical test of a major tenet of political socialization. Only the passage of time can resolve the question of whether these instruments are measuring merely a surface manifestation of an underlying developmental process which will in the long run produce much the same result as would have occurred in the absence of the Watergate events or rather a fundamental change in children's images of political authority which will find ramifications in the absence of adult political legitimacy. The beginnings of an answer to the contradictions our data provoke between Easton and Dennis, on the one hand, and Kohlberg, on the other, may become evident shortly after the Watergate crisis is resolved. If the Kohlberg-based explanation holds true, we should see a rapid turnaround in the assessments of the president back to pre-Watergate conceptions. In that case we will have lost one of our most firmly supported hypotheses in political science. On the other hand, should Easton and Dennis' arguments prove the more adequate explanation of children's attitudes in the long run, then for a generation we should see a substantial impairment of the legitimacy upon which the stability of our political system is based. We will have upheld a social science theory, but the costs of Watergate will be with us for a very long time.*

* The author would like to express his appreciation to Stephen Chilton, Michael Lipsky, and Jeffrey Pressman who read and commented on an earlier draft of this article.

Part II.

Parties
and
Elections

3 Whither the American Party System?

JAMES L. SUNDQUIST

The Republican mayor of New York City, John Lindsay, becomes a Democrat. Two ambitious young Republicans in the House of Representatives, Ogden Reid of New York and Donald Riegle of Michigan, do likewise. A former Democratic governor and prospective presidential candidate, John Connally, becomes a Republican. Another former Democratic governor, Mills Godwin of Virginia, leaves his party and accepts the Republican nomination for that same office. Meanwhile, two states of the once-solid Democratic South, Tennessee and Virginia, elect a majority of Republicans in their delegations to the House of Representatives. And four states of the former Republican heartland of the upper Midwest—South Dakota, Minnesota, Iowa, and Wisconsin—send to the Senate eight Democrats and not a single Republican.

What does it all mean?

Political scientists and journalists have been speculating for a decade that a major realignment of the American two-party system may be taking place. Every presidential election during that period

JAMES L. SUNDQUIST is a senior fellow at the Brookings Institution. He is the author of *Politics and Policy: the Eisenhower, Kennedy, and Johnson Years, Making Federalism Work, and Dynamics of the Party System*, from which this article is adapted.

has brought a spate of comment that this election might be the one
—the long-awaited "critical election" of the kind that V.O. Key
Jr. first wrote about, that results in a significant and durable shift
in strength from one party to the other, that creates a wholly new
structure of party competition. In 1964, a shift occurred in favor of
the Democrats; would it prove transitory or lasting? In 1968 and
1972, the speculation ran the other way. Observers wondered if
this was "the final breakup of the Roosevelt coalition" and the
beginning of "a new cycle of Republican hegemony."

Aftershocks of the New Deal Earthquake

In attempting to interpret the shifts of party strength in the past decade, the first question to be asked is whether those shifts record
the rumblings of a new political earthquake or merely the aftershocks of an old one. And to answer that question requires an examination of what has happened to the party system during the
whole of the forty-year period since the last great political
upheaval, the realignment of the 1930s.

It was during Franklin Roosevelt's New Deal that the present
party system came into being. In the 1930s, as in the 1890s and the
1850s, millions of voters made a permanent change of party identification; the country's previously normal Republican majority,
established in the critical election of 1896, gave way to a new
Democratic majority (or, perhaps more accurately, a strong plurality if independents are not allocated), which has proved equally
lasting.

The rationale of the new party system was one of ideology. The
overriding issue of the time, that precipitated the realignment, was
whether the government should pursue an activist or conservative
course in coping with the Great Depression—in relieving the des-
titute, reforming the economic system, and stimulating recovery.
That issue was powerful enough, in its manifold aspects, to shatter
the traditional party ties of millions of voters and impel them to
re-identify according to how they felt on the question of governmental activism, as represented in the Roosevelt New Deal. Traditional Republicans, especially in the cities of the Northeast, became
Democrats on that issue. A smaller number of traditional Democrats, largely in rural areas, became Republicans. The resulting party

system, basically ideological, also had a class aspect because the lower-income strata of the population, as the potential beneficiaries of governmental intervention in the economy, were the ones that rallied in overwhelming numbers behind the philosophy of the New Deal.

But the distinguishing feature of the realignment of the 1930s was that it did not take place in a single critical election, or even two or three of them. In some communities, like Chicago and Pittsburgh, the pro-Democratic shift was abrupt and solid, and the realignment could be considered complete by 1936. But in others, the realignment set in motion in the critical presidential elections of the New Deal period was completed only later—sometimes much later.

People do not change parties readily. As Angus Campbell has written, "partisan identification is remarkably resistant to passing political events and typically remains constant through the life of the individual."[1] These identifications could be so firmly fixed that even the cataclysmic events of the Great Depression and the New Deal could not upset them. So the realignment of the New Deal period altered voting behavior in presidential elections more than it altered party identification—and it is the latter, of course, that one must consider in a study of the structure of the party system. Millions of northern Republicans who, according to the new rationale of ideology and class, should have become Democrats did not change parties; they simply deviated in their vote for president. They rejected Hoover and Landon in favor of Roosevelt but continued to support their party in state and local politics—attempting, though, to liberalize it. And in the South the reverse of that phenomenon took place. Conservative Democrats remained in their party despite their abhorrence of the New Deal and all it stood for, but they voted for Republican presidential candidates in increasing numbers, especially with the nomination of Dwight Eisenhower in 1952 and 1956.

The result was a persistent pattern of split-ticket voting—something new in American politics. In some of the states that Roosevelt carried, he polled several times the vote of his running mate for

[1] "Voters and Elections: Past and President," *Journal Of Politics*, 26 (1964), 747.

governor (in 1936 in Wisconsin, 64 per cent against 22; in 1940 in Minnesota, 51 per cent against 11; in 1936 in North Dakota, 60 per cent against 30). That kind of divergence persisted in at least some degree for a long series of elections. It was not until the 1950s and even the 1960s that the Democratic party in many northern states finally succeeded in translating its presidential-level voting strength into equivalent strength in state and local voting and in party registration.

In the South, where one-party politics was even more deeply entrenched, split-ticket voting has persisted even longer. The region as a whole has become as Republican as the nation as a whole in presidential voting—more so in 1964 and 1972—but the Democrats are still dominant in most of the state capitols and county court houses.

Yet divergence between national and state-local political behavior is inherently unstable. A voter who identifies with one party nationally and another locally enters into such a contradiction with reluctance in the first place; once in it, he normally feels some degree of pressure to resolve it. He can resolve it, obviously, in either of two ways. He can return to his original loyalty at the national level, in which case he will have simply deviated for a time in his voting behavior. Or he can change his loyalty at the local level to accord with his new national identification, in which case he will have "realigned." Both kinds of resolution, of course, occurred. After 1936, the Roosevelt majorities declined, as deviating Republicans returned to the G.O.P. But the Democratic state and local vote also rose in the North as Roosevelt Republicans realigned or were replaced in the electorate by new pro-New Deal voters who were not inhibited by old allegiances from identifying as Democrats at all levels. And, somewhat later, the Republican state and local vote began its steady rise in the once-Solid South, as conservative Democrats changed parties or were replaced by a new generation willing to identify as Republicans.

In a party system based upon ideology and class, there is no room, obviously, for one-party states. The distribution in the population of basic attitudes toward the realigning issue of the 1930s —activism versus conservatism in domestic policy, to state it in somewhat oversimplified terms—is not likely to differ greatly from region to region or from state to state. And if the activist-conservative cleavage in the general population is somewhere near 50-50, then a 70-30 or even a 65-35 division in any state or community of normal socio-economic makeup can only reflect the persistence of old patterns protected by some artificial barrier against conformity with the national party system.

The barriers are of two kinds. The first consists of all the factors that make for the positive attachment of voters to their parties referred to earlier—sentiment, habit, inertia, family or community or group tradition, hope of office or preferment or reward. The other consists of all the factors that make for negative associations with the opposition party, at the state and local level. In the case of the predominantly Republican states of the North, the Democratic party might appear to Roosevelt Republicans as too Catholic, too ethnic, too urban, too labor-dominated, too corrupt, too poorly led, or too disreputable and discredited for any of a wide variety of reasons to make it an appealing political vehicle for them. In two cases, Minnesota and Wisconsin, the mass of the pro-New Deal forces even chose to express themselves through third parties for a time in preference to joining forces with the existing local Democratic organizations. Conservative Democrats of the South saw a Republican party that, besides bearing its ancient stigma, was led by tiny cliques of patronage-oriented "palace politicians" who had no tradition or hope of victory and no desire or competence to build a mass political organization.

To break these barriers necessarily required time. In the case of the positive attachments, those that were not broken in the politically heated New Deal era were not likely to be severed afterward; those barriers had to gradually erode as the voters with the fixed attachments passed from the electorate and new voters free of such attachments took their place. The second set of barriers could be broken only by the remaking of the minority party in each region. This had to await the rise of new and appealing leaders who could capture nominations for office and control of party machinery, thus giving to the minority party a new and attractive image.

In the North, then, the conversion of a one-party Republican state into a two-party battleground in the national pattern typically occurred when the Democratic party came under the control of fresh, reformist leadership—the "programmatic liberals" (typified perhaps by Hubert Humphrey of Minnesota and G. Mennen

Williams of Michigan). This kind of leadership gave the party its program in the postwar years. Similarly in the South, the establishment of two-party politics occurred when the spiritless "palace politicians" were displaced by dynamic and ambitious leaders, who were also, characteristically, ideologically motivated. Many of them were drawn into active politics during the Barry Goldwater conservative crusade of 1964.

But sooner or later, the barriers did come down and each of the former one-party, or one-and-a-half-party, states moved toward conformity with the national pattern of two-party competition. This movement toward conformity, or *convergence*, is by far the most conspicious influence upon shifts in party strength in the whole forty-year life of the New Deal party system. Most of what has appeared as party realignment throughout the entire period can be explained simply as convergence, as a delayed settling into place of the alignment created in the 1930s—as, in short, the aftershocks of the New Deal earthquake.

Crosscutting Issues Since the New Deal

Yet the aftershock interpretation may not account for all that has happened to party attachments during the past forty years. New issues have arisen of the type that produce political realignments: They cut across the existing party structure; they dominated political debate; they were powerful and emotional in their impact; they polarized large segments of the electorate; and strong political groups formed at the poles. To what extent did they set in motion realigning forces?

Four such new issues can be identified. The first, in the early postwar years, was communism. When the established Republican leaders straddled that divisive issue, a freshman GOP senator, Joseph R. McCarthy, stepped forward to exploit it. Ultimately, the issue failed because both major parties were on the same side. But the issue did hasten the convergence of the Catholic voting pattern with that of the nation by making it respectable for anti-New Deal Catholics, who had been bound to the Democratic party by tradition, to become Republicans.

A second crosscutting issue was Vietnam, in the late 1960s. When neither of the major parties would respond to the rising sentiment for extrication from the war, another back-bench Senator McCarthy, Eugene J. this time, undertook to mobilize it. Soon he had competition from Senator Robert F. Kennedy. But before the issue could tear the major parties apart, both yielded. President Johnson retired, his successors in the party leadership shifted to the antiwar position, and President Nixon led his party to the same side. As he began a gradual disengagement, the issue faded, with little realignment consequence.

A third, in the same period, was a cluster of related issues that centered on crime, or "law and order," but spread out as a broader "social issue" that also embraced drugs, student and youth rebelliousness, poor people's marches, welfarism, pornography and a host of related problems that could be attributed to "permissiveness." This cluster of issues was exploited by the Republicans as early as 1964, but when the GOP in 1970 made a deliberate attempt to achieve what Vice President Agnew termed "positive polarization" of the electorate around these issues, it failed. Essentially, the social issue lacked realigning power for the same reason that the communism issue had lacked it two decades earlier: both parties were on the same side, both against crime now as they had been against communism then.

The fourth, which is the only one of the four that still retains vitality, is race. That explosive issue showed its realignment potential as early as 1948, when it gave rise to the Dixiecrat third-party movement that shattered the Democratic Solid South. Many state and local elections since that time, and some national elections, have seen a high degree of polarization on the race issue. Political forces have formed at each pole, gaining strength particularly after the black ghetto riots of 1965-68. One polar group has been dedicated to advancing the demands of the black minority and the other has organized to resist at least some of those demands. And both have been ready to disrupt the existing major parties if that becomes necessary as a means to their respective ends.

If the polar forces formed around the race issue were to continue to grow, then conceivably the two-party system could shift on its axis and organize at the two new poles—the definition of a realignment. Either the major parties could move to the two poles, in which case an existing party—presumably the Republican party, since it has no significant black voting strength—would adopt the position of the polar group opposing the demands of the blacks. Or the strong third-party movement that has risen intermittently on the race issue since 1948—most recently in George Wallace's American Independent party of 1968—could continue to grow until it supplanted one of the major parties.

Neither of these eventualities is at all likely. As for the Republican prospects, it is true that President Nixon has taken positions and actions that have appealed to the white resistance—particularly his Supreme Court nominations and his stand on busing. But he has also supported some of the demands of blacks, and many Republicans in Congress have done so even more vigorously. So the national party as a whole continues to span the spectrum of views on racial questions.

An even more significant indicator of the Republican direction is what has happened at the local level. Rarely in the North has the Republican party become the instrument of the "white backlash," despite the obvious opportunities that have existed. Liberal forces in the GOP, including many big contributors and the press, have had sufficient influence to keep their party from any overt and widespread exploitation of racial antipathy. Indeed, the politicians who have become the symbols of white resistance to black demands in the major northern cities have more often been Democrats—in New York City, Philadelphia, Boston, Cleveland, and Los Angeles, as examples. To a considerable extent the same has been true in the South. There the Republican party has been torn between those who would seize openly upon race issues as the means for absorbing the Wallace following, and those who are moderate or even liberal on racial questions. But the former have suffered enough electoral defeats and the latter enough successes to keep the southern Republican party as a whole moving, if at all, in a direction away from racism.

The chances for a third-party movement based upon race to attain the status of a major party is equally remote. At the high point of that movement in 1968, when Governor Wallace won almost 10 million votes as the strongest third-party candidate in nearly half a century, the existing major parties may have had genuine cause for alarm. But Wallace himself did not even try to keep his American Independent party alive; instead, he ran for governor of Alabama as a Democrat and by 1972 was a leading competitor in Democratic primaries. Without him as its leader, the American Independent party amounted to nothing in 1972, and since then Wallace has shown no sign of intending to revive it.

So the one crosscutting issue of consequence in the current political scene—race—does not now appear to be leading toward a major realignment of the two-party system. The polar blocs remain, particularly the anti-civil-rights, anti-integration protest bloc that was dislodged from its Democratic moorings in 1948 and has floated with no fixed attachment ever since. But the short-term prospect is only for the continuing instability occasioned by those floating voters as they threaten the major parties and bargain with them. If one makes the optimistic forecast that the United States will move steadily, if slowly, toward solution of its race problems, then one may also predict that this remaining unsettling influence in the political system will weaken correspondingly.

Current Trends in Party Strength

If the crosscutting issues of the last half of the 1960s had had any realignment impact, one would expect to see the results in a net shift to the Republicans, since all of the issues worked against the Democrats. That shift would be reflected in the available statistics —election returns, voter registration figures, and public opinion polls. But none of these show any distinct or measurable new pro-Republican trend during the last decade. All that clearly appears is a continuance of the convergence movement that has been going on throughout the postwar period.

The one region showing a clear pro-Republican shift in the last half of the decade is the South, but there is nothing in the trend line to suggest any factors at work beyond convergence. If significant new realigning forces were being felt, the pro-Republican drift would presumably have been speeded. But as measured by Paul David's Composite B index (which averages the vote for senator, governor, and members of the House of Representatives) the period of sharpest Republican gains was 1958-62, before the new issues developed. Since then, the rate of convergence has markedly slowed down. Figure 1 shows the trend line.

Eighteen northern and western states identified by David as pre-

FIGURE 1

Convergence of Party Strength, as Shown in Democratic Proportion of Vote for Governor, U.S. Senator, and U.S. Representative, 1926–70

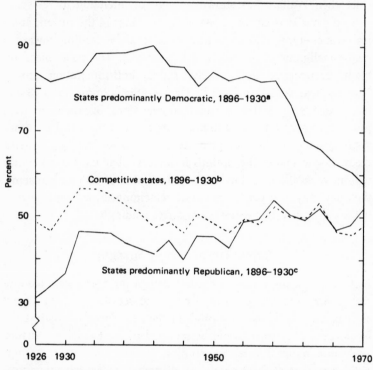

Source: Paul T. David, *Party Strength in the United States 1872–1970* (University Press of Virginia, 1972). Composite B index.
a. Alabama, Arizona, Arkansas, Florida, Georgia, Louisiana, Mississippi, North Carolina, South Carolina, Tennessee, Texas, Virginia.
b. California, Connecticut, Idaho, Illinois, Iowa, Kansas, Maine, Massachusetts, Michigan, Minnesota, New Hampshire, North Dakota, Oregon, Pennsylvania, South Dakota, Vermont, Washington, Wisconsin.
c. Colorado, Delaware, Indiana, Kentucky, Maryland, Missouri, Montana, Nebraska, Nevada, New Jersey, New Mexico, New York, Ohio, Oklahoma, Rhode Island, Utah, West Virginia, Wyoming.

dominantly Republican before the New Deal realignment experienced only a temporary interruption in their pro-Democratic convergence trend, as the figure indicates. They showed greater Democratic strength in 1970 than at any previous time except the party's peak years of 1958 and 1964. The remaining northern and western states, the traditionally competitive two-party states, do show a Democratic falloff between 1964 and 1966 that had not been recouped by 1970. But some of the decline, at least, appears to be simply a correction from the abnormally high Democratic vote of the 1958-64 period. This vote was marked by a Democratic landslide resulting from an economic recession at the beginning of the period and another landslide in the Johnson-Goldwater election year at the end. In any case, the Democratic strength remained stable during the 1966-70 period when the crosscutting issues were being exploited most vigorously. What stands out in Figure 1 is not change but continuity.

The absence of new and upsetting forces is indicated also by the party registration figures for five northern states which regularly compile and publish their totals on a state-wide basis. Two of these —Pennsylvania and Oregon—are former predominantly Republican states that have been part of the postwar pro-Democratic convergence movement; that trend showed no break during the political turmoil of the 1960s. West Virginia's long-term shift toward the Democrats likewise continued unabated. The long-term gradual decline in California's Democratic majority from its peak in the 1930s continued through the 1960s with no noticeable rate change. The pro-Democratic convergence trend in upstate New York leveled off after 1967 but it did not turn down sharply, as would be the case if a significant realignment were under way. As for New York City, the late 1960s was a period of Democratic gains at the expense of the Republicans. In sum, there is no indication anywhere in these northern states of a permanent, pro-Republican realignment in the 1960s.

Alienation and Independence

That brings us to the third set of statistics available—the data from public opinion polls. Here quite a different picture emerges. In the polls, a voter does not have to choose between two parties and their nominees; he can call down a plague on both the party houses. And this is increasingly what he has been doing.

Between the mid-1960s, when the Vietnam war, race, and social issues rose to their dominant position, and 1973, the Democratic party lost the allegiance of a net 5 to 7 million voters. *But those voters did not become Republicans. Indeed, since the late 1950s the*

FIGURE 2

*Party Identification of the Electorate, According to
Two Public Opinion Surveys, 1952–70*[a]

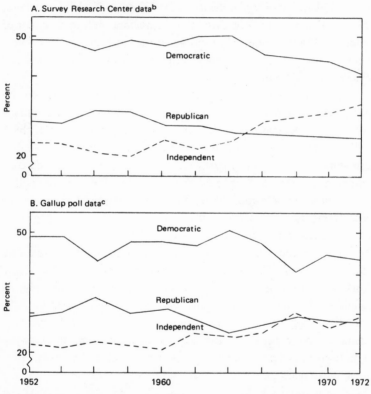

A. Survey Research Center data[b]

B. Gallup poll data[c]

Sources: Top panel, University of Michigan, Survey Research Center, Ann Arbor, Mich. Bottom panel, American Institute of Public Opinion, Princeton, N.J.

a. Plotted biennially. All figures exclude those who failed to respond to the question or who gave an answer classified as "apolitical," "don't know," or "other party."

b. Each entry based on election survey taken in October or November, except 1956, which averages two surveys in April and October; 1962, which averages two in May and November; and 1964, which averages three in January, May, and October.

c. Each entry based on the average of three surveys taken during calendar year, except 1970 figures, which average polls taken in October 1970 and April and October 1971; and 1972, which represents a single poll (these trend lines were, however, confirmed by 1973 Gallup surveys).

GOP has lost the support of about an equal number. As shown in Figure 2 opposite, the gain has been in the ranks of those who call themselves independents. On election day, these independent attitudes are reflected in a greater amount of ticket-splitting than at any time in the country's history.

An analysis of who made up the ten-million-voter exodus from the major parties in the 1960s may give some clues not only to their motivation but also to whether the major parties will be able to win them back. A comparison of the party identification of various population groups at the beginning and end of the decade, as reported in two Survey Research Center polls, provides some indication of who the ten million defectors were. The principal findings are given in Table 1 (pp. 572-73).

The first thing that stands out in an analysis of the makeup of the two blocs of independent voters is that the increase was entirely attributable to whites (section 2 of the table). Indeed, the white exodus from the major parties was greater than the net movement of both races, for the decade saw a pronounced solidification of party attachment on the part of black voters. Even though the samples of black voters are small, the swing shown is of sufficient magnitude to confirm the evidence from the election returns and from political observers that the Democratic party solidified its hold on the black segment of the electorate during the Kennedy and Johnson years. The remainder of this analysis will, therefore, disregard the blacks and attempt to further identify the white voters who are the new independents.

A comparison of the two surveys shows the Democrats-turned-independents as being mainly in the alienated South (section 3 of the table). Whatever loss the Democrats suffered among some voting groups in the North and West is offset by a corresponding gain in others, leaving their hold on 39 percent of white voters outside the South unchanged. The growth in independent political attitudes in the South is entirely among those opposed to government action to enforce school integration, or without an opinion (section 4 of the table). Southern integrationists show no increase in independent voting.

Another group can be identified among the Democrats-turned-

TABLE 1

Changes in Political Affiliation of Various Population Groups, 1960 and 1970

Identification of Group	1960[a]				1970[a]				Change[a]		
	N	D	R	I	N	D	R	I	D	R	I
1. Gross shift in party identification											
All voters	1,864	46	30	23	1,490	44	25	31	−2	−5	8
2. All voters, by race											
Whites	1,700	46	31	23	1,324	40	27	33	−6	−4	10
Blacks	147	50	19	31	144	78	. 4	18	28	−15	−13
3. Whites, by region											
South	542	61	21	18	430	44	18	38	−17	−3	20
Rest of country	1,158	39	36	25	894	39	31	30	0	−5	5
Northeast	(431)	(37)	(39)	(24)	(299)	(35)	(31)	(34)	(−2)	(−8)	(10)
Midwest	(476)	(36)	(38)	(26)	(390)	(38)	(33)	(29)	(2)	(−5)	(3)
West	(251)	(47)	(28)	(25)	(205)	(46)	(26)	(28)	(−1)	(−2)	(3)
4. Southern whites, by attitude on school integration issue[b]											
For integration	118	53	20	27	114	47	26	26	−6	6	−1
Against government action to enforce integration	332	65	22	13	204	46	19	35	−19	−3	22
Not sure, no opinion	92	58	19	23	80	38	13	50	−20	−6	26
5. Whites, by religious affiliation											
Protestants	1,170	39	38	23	912	37	32	31	−2	−6	8
Catholics	335	64	18	18	270	52	18	30	−12	0	12
Jews	57	61	9	30	42	55	5	40	−6	−4	10
6. Whites, by age group											
20–29	228	45	29	26	277	36	19	45	−9	−10	19

TABLE 1 *Continued*

30–39	384	49	27	24	239	33	27	40	-16	0	16
40–49	384	46	29	25	241	42	24	34	-4	-5	9
50 and over	704	45	36	19	567	45	32	23	0	-4	4
7. Whites, by place of residence											
Central cities in 12 largest metropolitan areas	186	54	22	24	106	52	25	23	-2	3	-1
Suburbs of 12 largest metropolitan areas	212	32	44	24	218	39	26	35	7	-18	11
Other cities (over 2,500)	628	48	31	21	558	38	28	34	-10	-3	13
Rural	554	49	28	23	442	41	27	32	-8	-1	9
8. Whites, by education											
Some college	392	33	46	21	352	32	34	34	-1	-12	13
No college	1,307	50	27	23	968	43	24	33	-7	-3	10
9. Whites, by social class [c]											
Working class	1,047	51	26	23	655	44	22	34	-7	-4	11
Middle class	595	37	42	21	627	37	31	32	0	-11	11

Source: University of Michigan, Survey Research Center, 1960 and 1970 polls. Percentages may not add to 100 because of rounding.

a. N = number of respondents. The apolitical, "don't know," "no answer," and other-party respondents are excluded. They amounted to 4.6 percent of the 1960 sample and 1.1 percent of the 1970 sample. The number of respondents in the different sections of the table are further reduced by eliminating those who did not respond to particular questions or whose responses were not recorded, as well as by those (as in sections 2 and 5) who would be classed as "other."

D = Democrat; R = Republican; I = independent. The numbers under each of these designations are percentages of the number of respondents in the same line.

b. The 1960 survey asked whether the respondent agreed or disagreed with the proposition: "The government in Washington should stay out of the question of whether white and colored children go to the same school." A "disagree" answer is classified as pro-integration. The 1970 question was: "Do you think the government in Washington should: see to it that white and Negro children are allowed to go to the same schools or stay out of this area as it is not its business?"

c. As self-identified.

independents. The proportion of independents among Catholic voters rose in the decade from 18 to 30 percent, all at the expense of the Democrats (section 5). Since relatively few Catholics live in the South, the defection of that religious group appears to account for a large share of total Democratic losses in the North and West.

People over forty were virtually undisturbed in their party allegiance by the total turmoil of the 1960s. But many younger voters were detached from prior allegiances or were reluctant to form any allegiance at all. Since polling began, younger voters have invariably shown looser party ties than their elders,[2] and this is still the case in our 1960 and 1970 samples. But the significant fact is that, apparently for the first time, individual voters under the age of 40 have actually shown a weakening of party attachment rather than the usual solidification as they have gotten older. Thus 26 percent of the voters who were in their twenties in the 1960s, as shown in section 6 of the table, were independents then, but the proportion had risen to 40 percent ten years later, when they were in their thirties. The proportion of independents in the group that was between thirty and forty in 1960 increased from 24 to 34 percent. Only those over forty maintained the same proportion of party identification. Each age group shows a greater proportion of independent voters than the corresponding age group a decade earlier, and the disparity in the younger age brackets is especially high.

While the Republican losses are distributed among all regions (see section 3 of the table), they are most heavily concentrated in the Northeast, which has also been the region of the GOP's most conspicuous electoral decline, especially in 1964, the Goldwater year. It should be noted that a Republican loss of party identifiers has also occurred in the South, which contradicts the sharp GOP gains in state and local elections. (If the total sample, rather than the white component, is used, the Republican loss in the South is even greater, 5 percentage points instead of 3.) This loss of identifiers confirms the evidence from other polls that most of the new GOP voters in the South still have not crossed the realignment threshold. They consider themselves "independents," not yet

---

[2] See, for example, the tabulations of various Gallup and SRC polls in Everett C. Ladd, Jr., Charles Hadley, Lauriston King, "A New Political Realignment?" *The Public Interest*, 23 (Spring 1971), 60-61.

"Republicans."

The Republicans-turned-independents are less easily identified than the former Democrats. But an examination of the many categories of voters into which the Survey Research Center respondents can be divided reveals three groups where independent gains of more than ten points have been made preponderantly or wholly at the expense of the GOP. These groups are identified by place of residence, education, and social class (sections 7, 8, and 9).

The figures show heavy Republican losses in the suburbs of the country's largest cities, among the college educated, and among voters who consider themselves middle class. If these data are combined with those from the other sections of the table and from Figure 2 the prototypical Republican-turned-independent can be described. He or she is a young, middle-class, college-educated, Protestant suburbanite in a large metropolitan area of the Northeast who left the party sometime between 1960 and 1964. Along with "southern-segregationists" and "northern-Catholic-former Democrats," "northern-suburbanite-Protestant-former Republicans" take their place as a third identifiable, substantial element among the ten million new independent voters who appeared in the 1960s.

The movement of all three groups again illustrates the principle of convergence discussed earlier. Over the years each of these three groups has been an anchor of one of the major parties, tied to it by bonds of regional patriotism, of family-community tradition, of class consciousness, of religious or ethnic group identity. With the fraying of some or all of those bonds at an accelerating pace in the postwar years, younger voters in particular have been set free from the party allegiances of the past. Many of these younger voters, who belong to a mobile, better-traveled, better-educated generation, have simply not formed the traditional allegiances at all.

So a growing body of millions of voters remains independent, detached, atomistic, floating. Moreover, party members as well as independents split their tickets with increasing freedom. "I vote for the man, not the party" has become the political norm. David Broder and Haynes Johnson of the *Washington Post* in interviewing voters in twenty precincts around the country in 1970 "found it rare to encounter a voter—anywhere—who thinks of politics in terms of political parties."[3]

Long-term and Short-term Influences

Walter Dean Burnham suggests that what has happened since the 1950s, and especially since the mid-1960s, is merely the latest phase in "a secular trend toward the gradual disappearance of the political party in the United States."[4] Burnham dates the beginning of that trend at about the turn of the century. Certainly, at the time of the progressive movement, the political party was in disrepute. The muckrakers condemned it. Political reformers rose up against the party bosses. Many of the reforms they espoused were deliberately designed to weaken the "political machines"; others, if not so intended, had that effect. Ballot reform, nonpartisan elections, replacement of patronage with civil service—all undermined the party machines. Civic groups like the League of Women Voters spread the gospel that it is the "independent" voter who is the watchdog of the political system, who holds the balance of power between two more-or-less corrupt party organizations. This doctrine found its way into high school civics courses. At the same time, the party newspapers, characteristic of the nineteenth century, gave way to the independent press that prevails today. Rare, nowadays, is the metropolitan newspaper that endorses a party slate without deviation; a self-respecting editor feels obliged to advise his readers to split their tickets. The same is true of "good government" groups, ethnic political associations, farm organizations, and even many labor unions. All these influences toward independent politics have had their greatest influence on the more highly educated and economically secure, and the proportion of these citizens has been rising constantly.

With the realignment of the 1930s the parties became more salient, but not to the degree of the nineteenth century. The "onward march of party decomposition," in Burnham's phrase, resumed in the 1950s. By this time, public assistance programs had largely

---

[3] *Washington Post*, October 9, 1970.
[4] *Critical Elections and the Mainsprings of American Politics* (New York, 1970).

superseded the parties' welfare activities, and rising pay levels plus improved job security in the private economy had lowered the value of their remaining patronage jobs. Then came a revolution in political campaign techniques that helped to rob the party of one of its basic functions—the organization and management of campaigns. Television became, almost overnight, the principal channel of communication between the candidate and the voter. A party structure might have been needed to stage rallies and torchlight parades and to distribute literature from door to door. For television, however, one needed not political organizers but film makers and advertising specialists. Candidate-marketing firms sprang up and began to crowd the traditional party organizations out of campaign management. Also, professional fund raisers appeared, to challenge the role of the party as an organization for campaign financing.

The party organization lost control not just of campaigning but of the candidate selection process. As the voter lost touch with the party organizations, aspirants for office came to ignore it. Money, media, and marketing could build a political following for an ambitious unknown in the same way and about as quickly as they could build the sales of a new deodorant. Rich men, or men with access to money, could defy the established political organizations and win the party nominations. Some state and local party organizations ceased to even try to influence the party nominating process.

These long-term trends are surely irreversible: the old fashioned, closed political system is not going to be reestablished, the old-style bosses restored to power, media campaigning outlawed, or the levels of affluence and education that make for independent politics reduced. Nevertheless, it is easy to overestimate the degree of change. Insurgents found ways to beat party organizations long before television was invented. The whole progressive movement grew by toppling one entrenched machine after another. Robert La Follette, Sr., Ben Tillman, and Hiram Johnson were able to create powerful personal political organizations even before the days of radio. And George McGovern's success in winning the Democratic presidential nomination in 1972, which was attributed more to superb organization than to superior use of the media, shows that even in the age of television, meticulous old-style organization in the precincts is still important, although it may have to be done by new-style people.

If the indicators show a phenomenal growth in ticket-splitting and rejection of the major parties in the 1960s, so do they show a remarkable stability until ten or fifteen years ago. If there was a long-term trend toward party decomposition before the middle or late 1950s, it was so slow as to be at times imperceptible. The party identification data from the polls show nothing like a gradual, steady increase in the proportion of independents; rather they show an essentially level line until the upheaval of the 1960s. Even Burnham's analysis covering ninety years of ticket-splitting in five states[5] shows no increase in one state, Indiana; less ticket-splitting in Michigan in the 1950s than in any decade in this century; and less in Wisconsin in the 1950s than in any decade since 1910. Rhode Island showed very little ticket-splitting before 1956. Only Massachusetts, among the five states, displayed a clear secular trend. Even if one concedes the existence of long-term influences, the sharp, abrupt departures from party regularity that marked the 1960s have to be explained by short-term factors.

The nature of these factors has been suggested. The rise in independent attitudes in the 1960s coincided with the rise to a dominant position of the three powerful and related issues mentioned earlier—race, Vietnam, and the social issue. By cutting across the existing line of party cleavage, these issues blurred the distinction between the major parties and created polar forces that found no satisfactory expression through those parties. Identifying the population groups most affected by the new crosscutting issues also identifies a large proportion of the added millions of voters shown in Table 1 who are rejecting the major parties and calling themselves independents. One group of new independents is the young, the group most alienated by Vietnam. Another consists of southern segregationists, the group most stirred by the race issue.[6] Still another is made up of Catholics, who along with Southerners comprise the blocs most aroused by the social issue. A fourth consists of northern middle-class, well-educated suburbanites of Re-

[5] *Critical Elections,* 111-18, 195-203.

[6] More than half the southerners who voted for Wallace in 1968, reported Gallup, called themselves "independents" in 1969. American Institute of Public Opinion release, July 19, 1969.

publican antecedents. These latter are the Republicans probably most offended by their party's exploitation of the race issue, particularly during the Goldwater campaign, and its subsequent position on law and order. One cannot say with certainty just why any particular group of voters left their party to take an independent stand, but the coincidence of those who *did* leave their party and those who would be *expected* to leave because of the new issues is strong circumstantial evidence that those issues were the cause.

The party system is always thrown into turmoil when powerful, crosscutting issues are at work. Fluidity, independence, and party switching are characteristic of the prerealignment and realignment periods that such issues generate. The present time—when millions of voters have been jarred loose from past allegiances and are floating unattached in political space—has all the characteristics of a prerealignment period. But, as suggested earlier, race, the one current issue that has the potential to bring about the reidentification of the floating voters in a new alignment, appears highly unlikely to do so.

Alternatively, party systems weakened by the passage of time can be reinforced if powerful new issues arise that run along, rather than across, the existing line of party cleavage. As during a realignment period, parties become relevant again and new and durable party attachments are formed, but this time they are formed on the rationale of the existing party system. Whether a reinforcement of the New Deal party system is likely to occur to arrest the onward march of party decomposition remains to be examined.

A Rebirth of the New Deal Party System?

If the next set of issues to dominate American politics is in the tradition of the activist-conservative and class conflicts of the last four decades, the New Deal party system can be reborn. Just as the crosscutting issues of the 1960s have blurred that line of cleavage, so issues that run along the line, which may be called "coincident" issues, would redefine and sharpen it. Crosscutting issues weaken the attachment of voters to the existing parties; coincident issues reinforce attachments. If the party system seems meaningless when crosscutting issues dominate political debate ("There is no difference between the parties," "Neither party takes a clear stand," "Neither party represents my point of view"), it takes on meaning when coincident issues dominate. This was demonstrated most recently in the late 1950s, when the coincident issues of government activism and government spending were the center of party conflict and the proportion of independents in the electorate (see Figure 2) for a time declined.

In the first year of the second Nixon administration, a set of domestic issues squarely coincident with the line of cleavage of the New Deal party system has been rapidly moving back to the center of public and political attention. On the assumption that the country's disengagement from hostilities proves durable and that attention turns away from Watergate, it appears likely that President Nixon's second term—like President Eisenhower's— will be dominated by the same fundamental dispute over the role of government that defined a new party alignment in the 1930s and has reinforced that alignment on so many occasions since.

It was the Republican President who chose the issues when he set out to liquidate through administrative action, in defiance of the Democratic Congress, not only much of what the New Frontier and the Great Society had created, but even programs that had their origin in the New Deal itself. And it was for the activists to defend, and to counterattack.

Responding to the coincident issues, the parties have been taking their familiar stance. Fellow partisans who have been divided by crosscutting issues like Vietnam and busing have drawn together again. Cohesion within the parties has increased, the distance between them has widened, party rhetoric has renewed old themes. The always difficult problem of the out-party in attaining unity has been eased, in this case, by the fact that the President's attack on Democratic programs appears also to be an attack on the powers of the Congress as an institution. (Watergate, of course, has helped to unify it too.) Conservative senators and representatives who might share the President's disdain for the programs their party colleagues have enacted still spring to the defense of the Congress's right to determine when and if those programs are to be dismantled.

Certainly there have been some within the Democratic party, chastened by the events of 1972, who have sought to hold the party back from open conflict with the President over the issues of government spending and economy. But the dynamics of the party system suggest that they will not prevail—not for long, at least. If somewhere near half the electorate is activist by philosophy and temperament (the polls suggest that more than half of it is activist on major domestic problems most of the time), the Democrats, as the party on the activist side of the line of party cleavage, are bound to reflect the attitude of that segment of the population. Party leaders who fail to articulate the activism of the party's rank-and-file will not remain leaders. Indeed, the prospect is that those who speak for the Democratic party in the Congress will not only resist the President's proposals to cut back the role of government but will also come up with initiatives of their own to expand that role, as they did during the Eisenhower years, to their political gain. So new issues will be added from both sides to the cluster centered on the question of governmental activism, and as the debate progresses the old line of cleavage between the parties will be sharpened and deepened. The New Deal party system will take on a fresh significance as it copes with the kind of issues for which it was designed.

In the long run, the prospect may well be for a further gradual decomposition of the party system. But there is at least as much reason to believe that in the short run the headlong march toward decomposition that marked the late 1960s will be checked and reversed, that the New Deal party system will be reinvigorated, and that most of those who ceased identifying with one or the other major party in the recent turmoil will reidentify. The parties may not regain the degree of voter loyalty that was accorded them in the crisis days of the Great Depression. But the bonds between voters and party would be restored to something like the strength of the late 1950s and the early 1960s—before Goldwater, Vietnam, Watts and Hough, campus riots and draft card burning, and the Chicago Democratic convention of 1968.

4 1972 Democratic Convention Reforms and Party Democracy

JUDITH A. CENTER

The Democratic National Convention of 1968 already has settled into the folklore of American politics. Its mere mention evokes the vision of tumultuous floor debate, bloodshed and tear gas in the streets, demonstrators and delegates standing together, arm-in-arm, in confrontation with the police. To some it also evokes the image of rigged procedures, of a political party assembled to reach predetermined decisions. The convention became the shame of the Democratic Party, and in all likelihood assured its defeat in the November following. Wherever politicians meet—wherever Americans meet—they agree that the Convention imposed such a strain on the democratic system of government that a repetition would be intolerable.[1]

This description and warning appeared in a January 1970 *Harper's Magazine* article by Senator George McGovern. Entitled "The Lessons of 1968," the essay was both a comprehensive indictment of the rules governing delegate selection and convention procedure in the Democratic party in 1968, and a brief catalogue of the reforms initiated by the Commission on Party Structure and Delegate Selection (popularly known as the "McGovern Commission"). At the center of McGovern's argument was the explicit assumption that the reforms which would so profoundly transform the party in the next few years had been prompted—even necessi-

---

[1] George McGovern, "The Lessons of 1968," *Harper's Magazine*, January 1970, pp. 43–47. All McGovern quotes used in this article are taken from this source.

JUDITH A. CENTER is a Danforth Fellow in Yale University's Department of Political Science.

tated—by the dissent, the fratricidal violence, the bitter disharmony that was Chicago 1968. This idea was echoed in *Mandate for Reform*, the official report of the McGovern Commission, which declared that "the 1968 Democratic National Convention in Chicago exposed profound flaws in the presidential nominating process; but in doing so it gave our party an excellent opportunity to reform its ways and to prepare for the problems of a new decade."[2]

And the party did indeed reform its ways between 1968 and 1972. We can take the reformers at their word that the events of the 1968 convention stimulated their efforts; but this does not mean that we must accept the belief, expressed in a September 10, 1970, *New York Times* editorial, that the McGovern Commission "grew out of the debacle of Chicago."[3] Was Chicago really a debacle? We can ask this question not simply for purposes of iconoclasm, but rather as a point of departure to examine the philosophy, motivations, goals, and the immediate and long-term consequences of the Democratic party reform movement.

The 1968 Democratic National Convention nominated a candidate who very nearly won the presidency in November. Since the *raison d'être* of American political parties has always been the election of its candidates to public office, and the traditional function of national party conventions has been the selection of candidates most likely to win office, then the 1968 convention cannot be considered an abysmal failure in this regard. The reformers, however, declined to judge the party's experience in 1968 in terms of the usual criteria of political success and failure, for they held radically different ideas about what ought to be the nature, purposes, and operating principles of a political party. This study examines the meaning and implications of post-1968 Democratic party reform from the perspectives of these differing conceptions of American politics and party democracy.

The Strange Case of 1968

Certainly the demographic composition of the 1968 Democratic National Convention appeared to reinforce the traditional image of national convention delegates as a convocation of middle-aged, white, upper-income males. *Mandate for Reform* noted that at the 1968 convention, sixteen state delegations contained no voting members under the age of thirty, and thirteen others had only one delegate each from that age group. Eight states claimed an average delegate age of over fifty years. According to the commission report, only 5.5 percent of the 1968 delegates were black (although figures from the *Joint Center for Political Studies Guide to Black Politics '72* indicate that blacks numbered 209 out of 3084, or about 6.7 percent of the total convention delegates).[4] Median delegate income was over $15,000, and only 13 percent of the voting delegates were women.

Such a cursory appraisal of demographic data can easily yield up an unsavory specter of cigar-smoking Elks Clubbers (epitomized forever in the minds of most reformers—and most television reviewers—by Mayor Daley and his Illinois chorus) gathered in Chicago in the name of conviviality, self-interest, and political expediency. But these statistics deserve closer examination; indeed, they are particularly uninformative when pulled out of the general context of pre-1968 Democratic party reform, or divorced from the actual events and issues of the 1968 convention.

Consider, for example, one of the several demographic categories that the reformers have deemed "critical." It is easy to overlook, from within the crucible of debate over current reform, the very significant progress the Democratic party achieved in securing greater black participation and representation within its ranks by the end of the 1960s. The 1952 convention was only 1.5 percent black, and by 1964 that percentage had not substantially increased: at Atlantic City blacks held only 2.2 percent of the full delegate positions, and seven southern and border states had no black delegates at all.

The dramatic and conscience-pricking challenge of the Mississippi Freedom Democratic party, however, stirred the 1964 convention to append an antidiscrimination requirement to the call for the 1968 convention, demanding that each state party "assure that voters in the state, regardless of race, color, creed or national origin, will have the opportunity to participate fully in Party affairs."[5] This commitment to equal opportunity was more than mere rhetoric or campaign atmospherics. In January 1965 the Democratic National Committee (DNC) created the Special Equal Rights Subcommittee in order to implement the 1964 convention's directive.

After receiving testimony and considering a number of proposals for increasing black delegate representation, the subcommittee (chaired by New Jersey Governor Richard Hughes) issued some vigorous directives to the state parties. Violation of the 1964 convention's equal opportunity

---

[4] Joint Center for Political Studies, *Joint Center for Political Studies Guide to Black Politics '72. Part I: The Democratic National Convention* (Washington, D. C., 1972), p. 73.

[5] *Congressional Quarterly*, Weekly Report, XXVI, no. 23 (June 8, 1968), 1343.

mandate in the 1968 delegate selection process of the Democratic party of any state, warned Hughes, would prompt his subcommittee to "recommend that the Credentials Committee declare the seats to be vacant and fill those seats with a delegation broadly representative of the Democrats of that State."[6] Hughes also distributed among the state organizations a list of six general principles to guide their efforts in eliminating discrimination in their party affairs. The DNC gave some authority to the Hughes guidelines by adopting them as a policy statement and including them in the official 1968 Convention Call.

Brooding upon the lessons of the 1968 Democratic convention, Senator McGovern noted correctly that "this Convention was governed essentially by the same rules which nominated Woodrow Wilson, Franklin Roosevelt, and John F. Kennedy." Which is to say, there were very few rules, at least rules formulated by the national party and binding upon the various state organizations. The delegate selection process in the Democratic party, particularly since the institution of the first primary in 1904, has been extremely complex and recondite. Most states selected all or part of their delegations at state conventions; others chose their representatives by party committees; while at least two states allowed their governors to name their delegates. Still other states directly elected their delegations in primaries. And in 1968 there was a profusion of traditional state party practices, usually couched in state law (which *Mandate for Reform* would later dryly christen "procedural irregularities"), such as the unit rule, proxy voting, and arbitrary quorum requirements.

Pre-1968 reform had not appreciably disturbed the idiosyncratic, labyrinthian character of the delegate selection institutions and processes of the Democratic party; the party remained essentially a confederation of more-or-less distinctive and autonomous state parties. The Hughes subcommittee guidelines were designed to correct discriminatory abuses, and state parties needed only to take measures to promote equal opportunity for participation within their existing delegate selection frameworks, or to be prepared to lose their convention seats.

The credentials of fifteen state delegations were in fact challenged, in whole or in part, at the 1968 Democratic National Convention. The antidiscrimination provision of the 1968 Convention Call requiring the "opportunity to participate fully in party affairs," provided a major basis for two kinds of challenges: southern delegation disputes squarely raised the issue of black participation and representation in the party systems of those states; and a number of McCarthy supporters argued for proportional delegate representation on several northern delegations, challenging certain methods of allocating delegate votes within the states and ways of selecting delegates at the state and local levels.

[6] Ibid.

Although the convention seated the challenged delegations in all but the Mississippi, Georgia, and Alabama cases, the northern challengers nevertheless secured a significant advantage from the proceedings, for the convention eventually adopted a Credentials Committee resolution that the 1972 Convention Call instruct state parties to guarantee that all Democrats in their states have a "meaningful and timely opportunity" to participate in the delegate selection for the 1972 convention. The majority report concluded that "the deliberation of this Committee suggests that we can and should encourage appropriate revisions in the delegate selection process to assure the fullest possible participation and to make the Democratic Party completely representative of grass-roots sentiment."[7] Furthermore, the committee recommended the creation of a special committee under the aegis of the DNC to study state systems and suggest changes in them to the 1972 convention.

Meanwhile, the Committee on Rules and Order of Business was also grappling with the issue of reform. The full Rules Committee accepted a subcommittee's recommendation not to enforce the unit rule at the 1968 convention, but rejected two other subcommittee proposals to prohibit the use of the unit rule at all levels of the Democratic party in 1972, and to guarantee that all national convention delegates would be selected within the convention calendar year.

A covey of Rules Committee liberals, however, submitted a minority report to the convention, which adopted it by a narrow roll-call vote of 1350 to 1206. The resolution specified that the 1972 Convention Call declare that:

> It is understood that a State Democratic Party, in selecting and certifying delegates to the National Convention, thereby undertakes a process in which all Democratic voters have had full and timely opportunity to participate. In determining whether a State Party has complied with this mandate, the Convention shall require that:
>
> 1) The unit rule not be used in any stage of the delegate selection process; and
>
> 2) All feasible efforts have been made to assure that delegates are selected through Party primary, convention, or committee procedures open to public participation within the calendar year of the National Convention.[8]

This, then, was the "mandate for reform"—the only one of the many mandates and resolutions adopted since 1964 which explicitly required certain changes in delegate selection practices and procedures. The adoption of the minority report of the Rules Committee formalized the shift of emphasis that had profoundly transformed the nature and purposes of the Democratic party reform movement.

[7] *Mandate for Reform*, p. 52.
[8] Ibid., p. 53.

Increasingly, in the years between the 1964 and 1968 conventions, the attention of party reformers turned from the issue of racial discrimination toward the more general subject of the procedural and structural aspects of delegate selection. The nuances of phraseology reflect this change. For example, the 1968 Convention Call demanded that all Democrats "have the opportunity to participate fully in Party affairs," but the 1972 Convention Call required that each state party establish "*a process* in which all Democratic voters have had a full and timely opportunity to participate." The Richard Hughes special subcommittee's guidelines designed to end discrimination and achieve "broadly representative" delegations were followed by the 1968 Convention Credentials Committee's appeal for measures "to assure the fullest possible participation," which was, in turn, almost immediately succeeded by the minority report of the Rules Committee's outright abolition of the unit rule and mandate for more extensive reform of delegate selection systems. There was a shift in conception and policy from a negative to a positive emphasis. Just as desegregation and integration are two fundamentally different ideas, so it is one thing to mandate or legislate the absence of restraint, to open up a system to the free flow of people, but quite another to change that system so as to secure, or at least greatly facilitate the participation of those previously excluded.

But it was obvious that most of the liberal, antiwar, McCarthy-supporting reformers ultimately were concerned not about people, but rather about ideas and issues. The matter of the protection of the political rights of racial minorities had dissolved into the consideration of candidate and issue minorities. McGovern said it himself: "The issue which brought the convention to the edge of chaos . . . was not race but Vietnam." The reformers desired more blacks, more Chicanos, and more Puerto Ricans at the next national convention. But more important, they wanted more antiwar delegations, more antiwar candidates, more antiwar planks and resolutions—and more antiparty-establishment delegates.

Many McCarthy, McGovern, and Kennedy delegates seemed hell-bent on viewing the turmoil of the Chicago convention as the inevitable consequence of rigged preconvention and convention procedures. The Harold Hughes Commission, an ad hoc study group of prestigious liberals assembled by the then-governor of Iowa, urged on reform by citing "widespread cynicism about the capacity of the parties, especially the Democratic Party, to accommodate the aspirations of emergent social forces."[9] McGovern concluded that "the Convention imposed such a strain on the democratic system of government that a repetition would be intolerable." The McCarthyites and their antiwar brethren seemed to have assumed

[9] *The Presidential Nominating Conventions* (Washington, D. C., 1968), p. 195.

that they were the only legitimate representatives of the party rank-and-file, and that their inability to determine the outcome of the convention could best be explained in terms of the corruption of the democratic process.

McGovern's analysis of the 1968 convention illustrates this conviction. "In the primaries," McGovern maintained, "Democrats had spoken out unmistakably against the war, yet now the party machinery was treating them with contempt. No wonder so many of them felt that the party had lost touch, perhaps forfeited its very right to exist. . . ." He conceded that "if anything, the rules in 1968 provided for more popular participation than in 1964, when the delegates were warned that delegations would not be seated unless chosen without regard to race"—a remark that is somewhat ironic in light of McGovern's enthusiastic support of the quota system. Yet the senator insisted that "the war exposed the profound flaws in the American convention system. It showed that institutions which work satisfactorily in times considered normal may be unequal to periods of stress."

What exactly did McGovern mean by these statements? Perhaps he believed that the majority of Democratic party voters agreed with the McCarthy position on the war. No one could deny that Democrats registered a good measure of genuine antiwar sentiment in their presidential primaries. But primary results may have offered up a distorted impression of the magnitude, pervasiveness, and nature of antiwar, antiadministration feeling. For one thing, the American electorate does not vote at primaries; voting studies indicate that primary vote averages about 51 percent of a party's general election vote for president.[10] Moreover, this small primary electorate possesses special characteristics: primary voters tend to have higher levels of political interest, and they appear to be more concerned with issues and ideology than are nonvoters.[11] One might expect, then, that voters who held deep and active convictions about Vietnam would exert a disproportionate influence at the primary polls.

One could argue, however, that the primary results did not even provide an accurate index of the views of the primary voters themselves. Richard M. Scammon and Ben J. Wattenberg, in their book *The Real Majority*, suggest several reasons why the 1968 primary electorate may not have been as dovish as it appeared to be. For example, a University of Michigan Research Center poll taken at the time of the New Hampshire primary sheds revealing light upon the nature of the voters' perceptions of policy alternatives. The results of that poll, Scammon and Wattenberg

[10] Harry Zeidenstein, "Presidential Primaries—Reflections of the Peoples' Choice?" *Journal of Politics*, 32 (November 1970), 827.

[11] Frank Sorauf, *Party Politics in America*, 2nd ed. (Boston, 1972), p. 224.

report, "show that three out of five *of the McCarthy supporters* in New Hampshire believed that the Johnson administration was wrong in Vietnam because it was not hawkish *enough*, not because it was *too* hawkish."[12] Although the Johnson candidacy seemed to offer voters a choice between things as they were, or against things as they were:

> Even that choice was not a clear and simple sort of choice: Johnson did not actively campaign, and the non-Democratic candidates who were also against things as they were were not really yet in the race; Wallace was not in the primaries, and Nixon was running unopposed in Republican, not Democratic primaries. But when Johnson announced his decision not to run, McCarthy and Kennedy essentially were fighting it out only for those who would hold the "against" banner on the left side of things as they were....[13]

Scammon and Wattenberg emphasize that the McCarthy-Kennedy confrontations were essentially "intramural" matches, for Humphrey's name did not appear on any presidential primary ballot.

Neither did national public opinion polls support the conclusion that Democrats "had spoken out unmistakably against the war." Gallup polls conducted in March, in the aftermath of the Tet offensive, indicated that the doves and the hawks were then flying neck and neck; a concurrent Harris poll showed that 54 percent of the American people favored the administration war policy.[14] Harris polls of two candidate nominee preferences among Democratic voters revealed that Humphrey gained popularity as the convention approached (from 48 percent in June to 56 percent in August).[15] Gallup's results indicated that Humphrey lost ground during the summer, but still remained four percentage points in front of McCarthy at convention time.[16]

It might be interesting, in light of this evidence, to examine the delegate vote on the hotly debated Vietnam plank. The 1968 convention rejected the antiwar minority report (which called for an immediate cessation of bombing in North Vietnam and the negotiated withdrawal of troops) by a vote of 1567¾ to 1041¼; that is, the McCarthy-McGovern plank received the support of 39 percent of the convention.

McGovern's observation that "institutions which work satisfactorily in times considered normal may be unequal to periods of stress" suggests that the reformers, in their outrage and frustration, appeared to have confused the right to be heard with the right to determine outcome. More-

[12] Richard M. Scammon and Ben J. Wattenberg, *The Real Majority* (New York, 1970), p. 91.
[13] Ibid., pp. 122–123.
[14] Ibid., p. 28.
[15] Ibid., p. 327.
[16] Ibid.

over, McGovern seems to have intimated that effective democratic processes should work to forestall a rancorous convention. One might ask: Should not stressful times, times of challenge and dissent, produce in a democratic milieu situations of civilized confrontation and debate? But the reformers consistently condemned Chicago as a perversion of democracy, even as they were successfully bringing attention and action to some of their protests and demands.

The 1968 convention was bitter, convulsive, and violent; but 1968 was a bitter, convulsive, and violent year. The paroxysms of Chicago more faithfully mirrored the divided temper of the nation than did the halcyon aura of the Republican beachfest. And the party had done much to execute the mandate that had been forged in the struggle to extend equal opportunity to all Democrats. The percentage of black delegates had almost tripled since 1964; 6.7 percent (or 5.5 percent, for that matter) is not a particularly impressive figure, unless one recalls that just four years earlier, only 2.2 percent of the national convention delegates were black.

In 1964, the issue was race. In 1968, the issue was war. In both years, the Democratic party confronted itself, debated, deliberated, and resolved. But in authorizing the transformation of delegate selection systems, the 1968 convention set the party on a new course. This reform was not to be simply more of the same; it was something radically different in conception, scope, strategy, and purpose from previous reform.

The New Rules

Early in 1969, in accordance with the narrow mandate of the convention, DNC chairman Fred Harris appointed two twenty-eight-member commissions to consider reforms. Harris named George McGovern chairman of the Commission on Party Structure and Delegate Selection (McGovern resigned from this post in January 1971 upon announcing his presidential candidacy, and was succeeded by liberal Minnesota Representative Donald M. Fraser). Michigan Representative James G. O'Hara, another congressional liberal, became head of the parallel Commission on Rules.

The McGovern Commission was the body most directly concerned with developing, issuing, and implementing the rules that would govern the processes of delegate selection for the 1972 convention. Although one might think that a group assuming such broad-ranging responsibility should reflect fairly the diverse major interests of the party constituency —including labor, moderates, and conservatives as well as liberals and New Politics advocates—the commission was top heavy with liberals, reformers, and grass-roots political activists. Chairman Harris gave labor a few token voices in the persons of I. W. Abel, United Steel Workers president, and William Dodds, United Auto Workers community action director, but Abel, at least, rapidly became disenchanted with the commission work.[17] And interestingly enough, the group that would later approve quotas for female representation was itself surprisingly free of women; there were only three women on the McGovern Commission.

The reforms, which had been formulated in less than nine months, were specific and comprehensive measures designed to introduce some degree of uniformity into the crazy-quilt pattern of delegate selection systems and increase decisively the political influence of those who in the past had had only marginal impact upon party policy making and candidate selection. The commission divided the guidelines into two groups: one group consisted of eighteen specific changes that would be required of state parties, while the other included several steps that the commission deemed "desirable" and "urged" the state parties to take.

The first guideline ordered the state parties to "adopt explicit written Party rules governing delegate selection." It was followed by eight "procedural rules and safeguards" which the commission demanded be applied in the delegate selection process. Specifically, the states were henceforth to forbid proxy voting; forbid the use of the unit rule and related practices such as instructing delegations; require a quorum of not less than 40 percent at all party committee meetings; remove all mandatory assessments of delegates and limit mandatory participation fees to no more than $10; ensure that party meetings in nonrural areas were held on uniform dates, at uniform times, and in places of easy access; ensure adequate public notice of all party meetings concerned with delegate selection.[18] For the most part, these changes were of a limited nature and consistent with the moderate suggestions of the Special Equal Rights Subcommittee.

The unit rule was a particular *bête noire* of the reformers, who were fond of hailing its abolition as a great victory for more democratic party government. The unit rule, which *Mandate for Reform* defines as "a practice by which a majority of a meeting or delegation can bind a dissenting minority to vote in accordance with the wishes of the majority,"[19] has had a long and controversial association with the Democratic party. But by the time the 1968 convention formally expunged the unit rule from all phases of the party's delegate selection process, the device had already lost favor among most state party organizations. *Mandate for Reform* estimates that only fifteen states used one form or another of the unit rule in delegate selection for the 1968 convention.[20]

[17] R. W. Apple, "Democratic Panel Changes Plot for Making of President 1972," *New York Times*, December 8, 1969, p. 40.

[18] *Mandate for Reform*, p. 34.

[19] Ibid., p. 22.

[20] Ibid.

If the abolition of the unit rule was somewhat superfluous, it was also irrelevant in one very important respect. The object of unit rule reform was to bring to the surface—to provide for the representation of—submerged minorities. Another of the commission's "participatory" reforms, however, managed to choke voting minorities much more effectively than did the archaic and enfeebled unit rule.

Alexander Bickel has observed that "to permit successive majorities to govern the process is to achieve precisely the effect of the unit rule."[21] That is, instead of *forcing* all of the delegates from a county or congressional district to vote the same way, the party can simply allow local majorities under winner-take-all rules of the game to *elect all* of the delegates to the national convention in the first place. The commission did not require that all of the delegates be chosen at the local level (although it did recommend this), but commission guideline B-7 did direct that the state parties, "in convention systems, select no less than 75 percent of the total delegation at a level no higher than the congressional district."[22]

The commission was apparently convinced that taking delegate selection decision making down to the "grass roots" would produce fairer representation of candidate preferences. This happy result, however, would not necessarily be the case. Paul David, Ralph Goldman, and Richard Bain note that "the selection of delegates through procedures that maintain district autonomy has the effect of permitting a series of small all-or-none contests. . . . Separate district elections avoid the high stakes inherent in state-wide winner-take-all elections, but offer potential rewards for those who mobilize and campaign actively."[23] A hegemonic majority, mustering the most votes at party meetings or primaries, can walk away with the whole clutch of district delegates. This "participatory" reform, therefore, possesses an inherent majoritarian bias, even though it admittedly was exquisitely designed to promote the interests and representation of activist minority groups.

The commission also demanded that the state organizations "select no more than 10 percent of the delegation by state committee," "prohibit the ex-officio designation of delegates to the National Convention," and "designate the procedures by which slates are prepared and challenged."[24] These guidelines specified conditions for delegate selection which magnified the influence of those groups most motivated and most able to participate, namely, the activist groups within—and outside—the party. One

[21] Alexander Bickel, *Reform and Continuity: The Electoral College, the Convention, and the Party System* (New York, 1971), p. 61.

[22] *Mandate for Reform*, p. 35.

[23] Paul T. David, Ralph M. Goldman, and Richard C. Bain, *The Politics of National Party Conventions* (Washington, D. C., 1960), p. 201.

[24] *Mandate for Reform*, p. 45.

of the reform's effects was to divest elected party officials and representatives—men and women by pragmatic necessity responsive to a broad party constituency and responsible for the party's success or failure—of all prerogatives in the delegate selection process. The McGovern Commission, in an ostensible effort to "open up" the system, stated that "Party membership, and hence opportunity to participate in the delegate selection process, must be open to all persons who wish to be Democrats and who are not already members of another political party."[25] Thus the 1972 convention replaced Mayor Daley's Illinois delegation with a set of challengers led by the Reverend Jesse Jackson, who was not a registered Democrat (although neither was he a registered Republican). Ironically, the reformer emphasis upon "openness" seemed to slam the door on those who lacked the time, resources, or motivation to sustain an activist campaign. For example, Penn Kemble and Josh Muravchik, in their December 1972 *Commentary* article, pugently describe some aspects of slate-making reform that seemed to sanction disruptive tactics and mischievous horseplay:

> [T]he reformers' remedy exceeded the proper cure. It required that no group or individual could devise a slate to be submitted to the electorate without holding a publicly announced slate-making meeting in which anyone could participate, whether or not he shared the political outlook of those advancing the slate and, in fact, even if he was not a Democrat! A labor slate, by this logic, could not be formed without a public meeting allowing participation by management, a liberal slate without permitting the participation of conservatives, or a law-and-order slate without the meeting being open to H. Rap Brown and Jerry Rubin.[26]

The commission's apportionment requirements also reflected the reformers' inability to answer two hard questions: What is a political party, and who composes it? Not able to embrace fully, at least for apportionment purposes, the notion of the "open party," the commission announced that henceforth delegate apportionment within the states was "to be based on a formula giving equal weight to total population and to the Democratic vote in the previous Presidential election."[27] Apparently, by this logic, everyone is (potentially at least) a Democrat, but some people are more Democratic than others.

These guidelines, however, represented but one prong of the commission's design for the establishment of a "full and timely" opportunity to participate. Harking back to the antidiscrimination resolution of the 1964

[25] Ibid., p. 47.
[26] Penn Kemble and Josh Muravchik, "The New Politics and the Democrats," *Commentary Magazine*, December 1972, p. 82.
[27] *Mandate for Reform*, p. 45.

convention, the National Committee's adoption of the Special Equal Rights Subcommittee guidelines, and the incorporation of the 1964 resolution into the 1972 Convention Call, the commission declared that "these actions demonstrate the intention of the Democratic Party to ensure a full opportunity for all minority group members to participate in the delegate selection process." Whereupon the commission ordered the state party organizations to "overcome the effects of past discrimination by affirmative steps to encourage representation on the National Convention delegation of minority groups, young people and women in reasonable relationship to their presence in the population of the State."[28] Clearly cognizant of the implications of such a requirement, the commission included in the guidelines a footnote emphasizing that "It is the understanding of the Commission that this is not to be accomplished by the mandatory imposition of quotas."[29] Many of the subsequent actions of the commission, however, appeared to belie this disclaimer.

The commission adopted the "reasonable representation" guidelines in November 1969 by the margin of a single vote. Following the narrow decision, commission chairman McGovern revealed his strategy to a reporter from the *National Journal:* "The way we got the quota thing through was by not using the word 'quotas.' We couldn't have gotten quotas."[30] Whatever the subtle semantic distinctions involved, the compliance directives of the commission indicated that the state parties would be expected to show the results of their efforts to "overcome the effects of past discrimination." For example, on October 15, 1971, the commission issued a notice to all state party chairmen which, in the words of the commission's final report, "suggested examples of 'affirmative steps' that state parties could take to encourage the participation of women, young people and minority group members in the delegate selection process," such as the "balancing" of delegate slates.[31]

The following month, in a letter to national chairman Lawrence O'Brien, new commission chairman Fraser explained the possible consequences of a state party's failure to assemble a "representative" national convention delegation:

> We believe that state parties should be on notice that whenever the proportion of women, minorities and young people in a delegation offered for

[28] Ibid., p. 34.
[29] Ibid., p. 40.
[30] Judith G. Smith (ed.), *Political Brokers: People, Organizations, Money, Power,* by the editors and reporters of *National Journal Magazine* (Liveright, N. Y., 1972), p. 244.
[31] The Commission on Party Structure and Delegate Selection to the Democratic National Committee, Final Report of the Commission, *The Party Reformed* (Washington, D. C., July 1972), p. 6.

for seating in Miami is less than the proportion of these groups in the total population, and the delegation is challenged on the grounds that Guidelines A-1 and A-2 are not complied with, such a challenge will constitute a *prima facie* showing of violation of the Guidelines, and the state Democratic Party along with the challenged delegation has the burden of showing that the state party took full and affirmative action to achieve such representation including an *effective* affirmative action program along the lines outlined in our policy statement adopted on October, 1971.[32]

O'Brien included the Fraser letter in a December memorandum to the state chairmen and other party leaders, declaring that he wished to "underscore those points in Congressman Fraser's letter that emphasize the importance of each state taking specific, affirmative action to encourage the representation and involvement of women, minorities and young people in the selection of delegates."[33] Obviously, then, to require the state parties to "*encourage* representation on the National Convention delegation of minority groups, young people and women" meant, according to the commission's interpretation of its guidelines, to *require* such representation.

The increasingly forceful interpretation of the quota guidelines reflected the commission's—and the reformers'—definition of the legal status of the guidelines as a whole. Although the majority report of the Credentials Committee adopted by the 1968 convention had ordered that the "Special Committee" to be established by the DNC "report its findings and recommendations to the Democratic National Committee," the official report of the Commission on Party Structure and Delegate Selection maintained:

> Because the Commission was created by virtue of actions taken at the 1968 Convention, we believe our legal responsibility extends to that body and that body alone. We view ourselves as the agent of that Convention on all matters related to delegate selection. Unless the 1972 Convention chooses to review any steps the Commission has taken, we regard our Guidelines for delegate selection as binding on the states.[34]

Democratic National Committee counsel Joseph Califano advised Chairman O'Brien that the commission was correct in assuming that only the national convention could amend the guidelines. Thus the Democratic National Committee's unanimous adoption in February 1971 of the guidelines into the 1972 Preliminary Convention Call was of only ritualistic significance. According to *New York Times* correspondent R. W. Apple, "The party conservatives said nothing as the McGovern proposals were

[32] Ibid., p. 8.
[33] Ibid.
[34] *Mandate for Reform*, p. 36.

approved. In fact, many of those at the meeting, which was held at the Mayflower Hotel, were unaware that they had been voted on."[35] Twenty-eight men and women, deriving their authority from a self-defined and unlimited mandate, had created an entirely new structure of party law, and it was extremely unlikely that the 1972 convention delegates—the great majority of whom would owe their seats to the reforms—would substantially modify the commission's handiwork.

The controversial quota guidelines, however, provoked many more questions besides those concerning legality or legitimacy. One of the most important arose from the fact that the commission did not choose to elaborate on just how the institution of quotas would work to create more participation and representation. Several observers perceived a quandary in the quota requirements and the reformers' emphasis upon increased participation. Will Davis, former chairman of the Texas State Democratic Committee, reminded the commission that "it's not possible to have such a provision and still maintain the mandate to elect more delegates."[36] Similarly, Judith Parris has written that "demographic demands may clash with the objective of wide participation. In order to achieve descriptive representation of social groups, each state party would have to draw up a balanced ticket of delegates; but this would violate the principle of broad participation by ordinary partisans in delegate selection." It may also conflict with the principles of fair representation of voter preferences, because "at any political level, it is impossible to ensure that the convention delegation simultaneously will reflect the presidential preferences of the party rank-and-file and be a perfect microcosm of the state's population or of its party voters."[37]

One of the most immediate issues that sprung from the commission's quota requirements was a widespread confusion about what exactly constituted a "reasonable relationship." The commission declined to provide a precise definition, and seemed content to leave the problem to the 1972 Credentials Committee, which in turn simply concluded that the great majority of the state parties had complied satisfactorily. One could argue, however, that most of the states sent more representative delegations— at least with regard to race—to Chicago in 1968 than to Miami Beach in 1972. Twenty-eight states in 1968 assembled delegations whose percentages of black delegate strength corresponded more closely to the states'

[35] R. W. Apple, "Democrats Reform Rules on Convention Delegates," *New York Times*, February 20, 1971, p. 1.

[36] John S. Saloma, III, and Frederick H. Sontag, *Parties: The Real Opportunity for Effective Citizen Politics* (New York, 1973), p. 21.

[37] Judith Parris, *The Convention Problem: Issues in Reform of Presidential Nominating Procedures* (Washington, D. C., 1972), p. 76.

black population figures than did those of their reformed 1972 delegations. For example, 3 percent of Arizona's delegation at the 1968 convention was black; in 1972, 8 percent of the Arizona delegates were black.
Massachusetts is also 3 percent black, and in 1968, 3.1 percent of its delegation was black; by 1972, its black delegate representation had soared
to 11.8 percent.[38] As the *Joint Center for Political Studies Guide to Black
Politics '72* noted approvingly a month before the 1972 convention, "In
over 30 states black delegate representation is proportionately greater
than the state's total black population."[39]

The commission had established a quota system, but it was amorphous
and exceedingly ill defined; if anything, the criteria seemed to suggest
that overrepresentation was acceptable evidence of "reasonable representation," whereas underrepresentation (and possibly even nearly proportional representation) was not. Those who challenged Mayor Daley's
Illinois delegation called attention to the fact that the state's black delegate percentage fell below that of the population—Illinois is 12.8 percent
black, and Daley's dismally unrepresentative delegation was only 10
percent black. Oregon, on the other hand, was frequently praised by the
reformers as a "model" delegation; with a 1.3 percent black population,
Oregon had selected a delegation which was 5.9 percent black.

The quotas were meant to prove a point, to lend credence to the rhetoric
of the "open party." A number of delegates thus won their seats primarily
by virtue of the color of their skin, or their sex, or their age; how representative they were of the candidate preferences of the party members of
their district or state was but a secondary consideration. The reformers
apparently lost little sleep pondering the possibility that a superabun-
dance of delegates chosen in compliance with quota requirements might
effectively deprive other groups, such as lower middle-class, blue-collar
citizens, of their rightful share of representation. The reformers—waist
deep in compliance charts and delegate demographic data—were intensely concerned with the *how* of delegate selection, and with *who* the delegates were in terms of biological categories. One wonders why they did
not judge worthy of their attention the questions: "*By whom* are the delegates selected?" and "*For whom* do they speak?"

More New Rules

Although the work of the Commission on Party Structure and Delegate
Selection seized most of the attention and controversy surrounding the

[38] *Guide to Black Politics '72*, p. 21.
[39] Ibid., p. 19.

party reform, James O'Hara's Commission on Rules was simultaneously formulating changes in convention preparation and practices.[40] The Rules Commission decided to increase convention size to 3000 delegate votes (there were 2622 delegate votes at the 1968 convention) and increase the size of the standing committees by 50 percent. Ostensibly these changes were intended to stimulate greater participation by and representation of the body politic, but they exacted a sacrifice in delegate participation and effectiveness. Procedural reforms included a ban on floor demonstrations, strict rules on the interruption of vote, and limitation of debate on any question to a total of twenty minutes. (The last was intriguingly similar to the "gag rule" so beloved by the conservative Rules Committee of the U. S. House of Representatives.) The new rules were designed to facilitate decorous and businesslike proceedings. They were, however, somewhat superfluous at the 1972 convention. The delegates came not to argue or harangue or protest; they came to ratify.

The Predictable Results

The Democratic party was indeed reformed. But what were the consequences of these changes? The convention whose delegates had been chosen under the provisions of the Commission on Party Structure and Delegate Selection, and whose procedures were governed by the rules of the O'Hara Commission was very different from its unreformed predecessor of 1968. The 1972 convention, compared to the 1968 convention, was remarkably homogeneous and tame, in spite of its touted diversity. There were more black and brown and young and female faces, of course, but the great majority of the delegates were well educated, relatively affluent, liberal, and pro-McGovern.

As Arthur Schlesinger observed with apparent satisfaction, "For a convention that threw out Mayor Daley and put down Governor Wallace, Miami Beach turned out to be a surprisingly amiable, even benign affair."[41] In 1968, there had been vigorous and substantive debate over platform and rules; in 1972, the platform was adopted with scant discussion (only the abortion and gay liberation planks provoked a measure of controversy), and consideration of rules was largely confined to the tactical context of McGovern's quest for California's and Illinois' disputed votes. And there was no meaningful contest for the presidential nomina-

[40] A description of the work of the Rules Commission is included in the commission report *Call to Order* (Washington, D. C., June 1972), p. 11.

[41] Arthur Schlesinger, Jr., "How McGovern Will Win," *New York Times Magazine,* July 30, 1972, p. 28.

tion at Miami Beach. (McCarthy, at least, had remained in the running to oppose Humphrey in the balloting at the 1968 convention.) The new delegate selection guidelines were admirably suited to an activist, issue-oriented campaign such as that of McGovern. The outcome of the convention was certainly a foregone conclusion by Tuesday of convention week, following the credentials vote on California.

It is ironic that the reform movement, ostensibly born out of dissent and debate, culminated in such a cut-and-dried affair. If one of the purposes of reform was, as *Mandate for Reform* claimed, to invigorate the convention, to produce "the face-to-face confrontations of Democrats of every persuasion, in a mass meeting . . . productive of healthy debate, important policy decisions . . . reconciliation of differences . . . ,"[42] then it failed utterly in this regard.

At the 1972 convention, there were not many differences to resolve. The reforms had succeeded in transforming 1968s substantial delegate minority into 1972s overwhelming delegate majority. Yet not only did that majority's candidate lose the presidential election by a large margin, but surveys taken after the November election indicated that as many as 36 percent of Democratic voters cast their ballots for Nixon.[43]

The 1972 delegates had been elected by Democrats who cared deeply about the issues of war and broad social change, who cared enough to make it to the primary polls, to the precinct, district, and county caucuses, to select delegates who would register these beliefs about the need for change in the political order. If Six-Pack Joe and the machinist's wife from Dayton preferred to stay home, so be it: they had forfeited their right to representation. But, so went the reformer rationale, at least the reformed Democratic process would offer them, and all Americans, a real choice in November.

Toward a More Responsible Party?

The McGovern-style reformer conception of democracy has much in common with certain precepts of the theory of responsible party government. The notion of effective party government—which is derived, in part, from the British parliamentary experience—has received a great deal of attention in the past few decades from a number of prestigious political scientists, including E. E. Schattschneider, Austin Ranney, and others. Ranney, in *The Doctrine of Responsible Party Government* (1954), discusses what he believes are the basic assumptions of responsible party theory. "The doctrine of party government," he writes, "rests upon the belief

[42] *Mandate for Reform*, p. 12.
[43] Jack Rosenthal, "Desertion Rate Doubled," *New York Times*, November 9, 1972, p. 1.

that, in a modern, thickly populated society like that of the United States, democracy should be conceived of as popular *control* over government, and not as popular *participation* in the day-to-day activities of government."[44] According to Ranney's interpretation, what is needed to achieve this democratic control is popular choice between two more-or-less ideological and sharply differentiated political parties.

Before parties can clarify and promote certain policy positions, however, they must achieve "sufficient coherence and discipline for their members to display solidarity on all great questions of public policy."[45] Just how this consensus is to be realized has been a matter of debate among party government theorists. The late E. E. Schattschneider, for example, maintained that ideas of mass participation in party affairs must be discarded if a party is to be able to assert unified, coherent positions on the issues.

Other party theorists have disputed Schattschneider's thesis. *Toward a More Responsible Two-Party System*, a report prepared in 1950 by the Committee on Political Parties of the American Political Science Association, agreed that responsible parties demand a great deal of internal cohesion, but argued that "such a degree of unity within the parties cannot be brought about without party procedures that give a large body of people an opportunity to share in the development of the party program."[46] The committee thus concluded that intraparty and interparty democracy, far from being irreconcilable, are necessarily complementary, and that party discipline can be enforced only when there is widespread democratic consensus within the party electorate.

The committee report in turn has not been without its critics.[47] A host of political scientists have conducted empirical studies that demonstrate conclusively that only a small minority of citizens are motivated to participate actively in political affairs, and indeed, only a bare majority of those eligible bother to vote in general elections, let alone vote in primaries or attend party caucuses. However, an even thornier problem for the responsible party theorists who view the legitimacy of party policy in terms of democratic consensus arises from the question of majority rule versus minority rights.

[44] Austin Ranney, *The Doctrine of Responsible Party Government*, Illinois Studies in the Social Sciences, Vol. XXXIV, no. 3 (Urbana, Ill., 1954), p. 10.

[45] Ibid., p. 16.

[46] The Committee on Political Parties of the American Political Science Association, *Toward a More Responsible Two-Party System* (New York, 1950), p. 1.

[47] One interesting assessment of the committee report is former committee member Evron M. Kirkpatrick's retrospective critique, " 'Toward a More Responsible Two-Party System': Political Science, Policy Science, or Pseudo-Science?" *American Political Science Review*, 65 (December 1971), 965–990.

The essence of responsible party theory lies in the principles of majoritarian democracy. Responsible party theory, if it is to be clear and explicit, must not incorporate and reflect a significant measure of concession and compromise. In the words of the committee, "A stronger party system is less likely to give cause for the deterioration and confusion of purposes which sometimes passes for compromise but is really an unjustifiable surrender to narrow interests."[48] And this strict majoritarian intraparty democracy is echoed in the majoritarian interparty democracy that operationalizes responsible party government: if half-plus-one of the voters are dissatisfied with the performance of the party in control of government, they can replace that party in the next election. Ranney writes that this conception of democracy:

> is concerned only with the location of ultimate political power in the community and with the process by which that power is made effective. The nature of the particular decisions made by such a government do not make it more or less democratic so long as the framework within which they are made exhibits the same characteristics. In short, party government is a proposal for implementing majority rule, no matter what the majority may decide to do with its power. Any decision made in accord with the majority's wishes is, by definition, a "democratic" decision. . . .[49]

This procedural majoritarianism seems to be responsible for several of the paradoxes and unresolved dilemmas of post-1968 reform. For instance, is the reformed party really "open" to all Democrats, or only to the small percentage of Democrats who are willing and able to participate in the currently in vogue delegate selection process? McGovern appeared to realize that participation is not an automatic thing, conceding in "the Lessons of 1968" that "there is a long way to go. I know that the vitality of the Democratic party will probably involve more than mere structural changes. Participation will increase only as people see the political parties as responsive to their needs and concerns." But, in the meantime, according to McGovern's grass-roots prescription, "as a first step, we must immediately open the door to all those people who are or may be inclined to use political parties to serve the ends they seek." There was scant possibility, however, that the activists would make the party more responsive to the needs and concerns of those who preferred not to participate in the first place.

By securing majorities, or at least pluralities, in county and district caucuses and primaries, by virtue of much hard work and inspired organization, McGovern activists won control of the party they had helped

[48] *Toward a More Responsible Two-Party System,* p. 20.
[49] Ranney, *Responsible Party Government,* p. 11.

reform. Because the legitimacy of their majority rested upon a procedural, one-half-plus-one of those who participated definition of democracy, and not upon the breadth of interests it encompassed and served, it should not be surprising that the 1972 convention was so incomparably lifeless and dull. In past campaigns, candidates had arrived at conventions with delegate majorities, but these were often fragile, tenuous things pieced together with promises, bargains, and barter, susceptible to flux and erosion in the supercharged convention atmosphere. Most pre-1972 delegates were not elected directly by partisans of particular candidates or policy views; more likely, they won their seats by virtue of party loyalty, service, and diligent personal efforts. And because of their manners of selection, they were usually not bound—either by law or by conviction—to the outcome of a preconvention decision-making process. These delegates were not greatly concerned about how the party voted in March or April, but rather about how the national electorate would vote in November. In 1972, however, the delegate majority was solid, committed, and immovable; there was very little place for the traditional processes of national convention consensus building. As the reformers saw it, the will of Democrats (at least of Democrats who counted, i.e., those who could be counted) was self-evident, and that mandate was not to be sullied by crass political expediency.

Larry O'Brien was probably right when he pronounced the work of the reform commissions to be "the greatest goddamn change since the two-party system."[50] Reform had shucked away the complexes of party traditions, old saws, and unwritten bylaws that had evolved and persisted since Andrew Jackson's time, and replaced them with a streamlined package of national party decision-making rules. And in doing so, it challenged the ancient wisdom that has held that the purpose of a political party is to mobilize majorities to win general elections, and that compromise and accommodation are eminently acceptable and valuable means to that end. The Democratic reformers—like all reformers—were obsessed with rules, imbued with the notion that if you can change the rules, you can cure the beast. They therefore seized upon the most obvious and most sanctified tool of democracy, majority or plurality vote, and applied it everywhere within the party, sincerely convinced that they were bringing the party closer to true democracy.

But democracy, as is any idea that addresses itself to the needs and desires of human beings, is a complex thing. As Carl Cohen has written,

> Good decision-making rules serve and support the democratic process by making it effective, but they are not the whole of that process. This may be shown by considering the relations of the rules to dimensions of democracy

[50] Smith, *Political Brokers*, p. 253.

other than breadth. The employment of any decision-making rule is, at best, only the culmination of a participatory process that is continuing rather than intermittent, involves discussion and debate as well as commitment, and is manifested in a host of ways only one of which is the casting of votes. The desire for specificity, and the impelling need to make some verifiable judgments, results in a widespread tendency to identify democracy with its decision-making rules. This is a mistake, reducing democracy to only one of its dimensions, breadth, simply because it is breadth that lends itself to quantitative analysis.

At the stage of the democratic process when decision-making rules are applied, the question has become, in effect: "Now that we have discussed the matter, what actions shall we take?" Proposals are made, and a vote in some form is taken. Reaching decisions demands some definite and publicly verifiable measurement of community opinion, so there must be resort to what is measureable—ballots cast, hands raised. We hope the rule will be fair, wise, justly administered. But no rule, however wise and consistent with democracy, can measure all aspects of the democratic process; its application can never reflect the depth of the participation of those voting.[51]

Commission chairmen O'Hara and Fraser's proposed "Charter for the Democratic Party of the United States," showed how intent many of the reformers were upon creating a nationalized, policy-oriented party. The charter, which urged the restructuring of the Democratic party along the lines of the responsible party model, recommended that the national party set up "categories" of formal dues-paying membership, and permit only enrolled members to participate in party affairs. It also suggested doubling the size of the Democratic National Committee, and proposed that a 3000-delegate National Policy Conference meet in even-numbered years between presidential elections to formulate explicit policy programs and elect the national chairman. A National Executive Committee would carry on the real work of the party in off-years.[52]

The 1972 convention, although it did not endorse the document in toto, adopted several provisions of the O'Hara-Fraser charter; for example, it called for "additional National Committee members with a total vote of 150 apportioned to each state on the basis of that state's representation on the Standing Committees of the 1972 Democratic National Convention."[53] The convention authorized the new Democratic National Committee to appoint a special commission to recommend a permanent party charter, and suggest the size, composition, and manner

[51] Carl Cohen, *Democracy* (Athens, Ga., 1971), p. 64.

[52] A copy of the O'Hara-Fraser charter is included in the Rules Commission report *Call to Order,* pp. 133–143.

[53] The Democratic National Committee, "Resolution Adopted by the 1972 Democratic National Convention" (mimeographed), p. 1.

of delegate selection to a 1974 national policy and organization conference.

Neither did the subject of national convention delegate selection escape the convention's attention; presumably in response to the confusion surrounding the interpretation and implementation of the 1972 reforms, the 1972 delegates mandated the creation of a new commission to "review the guidelines for delegate selection incorporated into the Call of the 1972 Democratic National Convention, for the purpose of making appropriate revisions of such guidelines after due consideration of their operations in 1972. . . ."[54]

In October 1973 this new commission—christened, in a curious inversion of its predecessor's title, the Commission on Delegate Selection and Party Structure—unanimously approved and submitted to the DNC a new set of delegate selection guidelines that contained several revisions of the McGovern-Fraser reforms. For example, the commission dropped the infamous "reasonable representation" guideline, and replaced it with a provision stating that the party's goal is to encourage the participation of women, youth, and minority groups "as indicated by their presence in the Democratic electorate." The new guideline declared that the fuller participation "shall not be accomplished either directly or indirectly by the party's imposition of mandatory quotas at any level. . . ." (The language is strikingly reminiscent of the McGovern Commission's solemn disavowal of a quota system.) Compliance under the revised rules would not be determined by the presence or absence of a "reasonable number" of women, young, or minority delegates, but rather upon how "vigorously" state parties attempted to increase the participation of these groups.[55]

Despite these changes, an examination of the new rules suggests little more than token retrenchment from the McGovern-Fraser reforms. The revised guidelines, for example, may remove some features of the quota system most objectionable to party moderates and conservatives. But the compliance activities of the McGovern Commission demonstrated what flexible interpretations can be given to such difficult concepts as participation and representation. It is not inconceivable that the new commission would conclude—like its forebear—that the most convenient way of assessing the "vigor" of state party efforts to ensure greater participation is to look at the results they produce, in the form of more delegate repre-

---

[54] The Commission on Delegate Selection and Party Structure to the Democratic National Committee, Final Report of the Commission, *Democrats All* (Washington. D. C., December 1973), p. 5.

[55] Ibid., p. 21.

sentation of women, young people, and minorities (and perhaps certain socioeconomic groups as well).

The new commission also endorsed a system of proportional representation of candidate preferences, in keeping with the 1972 convention's decision to ban winner-take-all primaries. According to the new formula, a candidate who obtains an electoral majority or plurality in a precinct, congressional district, or state would not win all of the delegates, but would share them proportionately with other candidates receiving at least 10 percent of the vote. The provisions of this guideline, however, apply not only to primary states, but also to those that select their delegates through caucus and convention systems. Penn Kemble has predicted that local-level proportional representation will either force local party leaders to commit themselves to a candidate very early in the election year, or organize into independent "constituency" slates—into labor or black caucuses, for example—that "will increase the tendency toward ideological and group conflict within the party" and produce a "political convention which is made up of an array of hardened minority factions. . . ."[56]

The Commission on Delegate Selection and Party Structure reaffirmed most of the "participatory" McGovern guidelines, including those requiring local selection of delegates and prohibiting ex-officio representation. Although state committees were given the right to elect up to 25 percent of their state delegations, the commission attached severe limitations to this prerogative: members of state committees so selecting delegates were required to be elected through "open processes in conformity with the basic procedural guarantees utilized for delegate selection," and delegates elected by state committees had to "reflect the division of preference of the publicly selected delegates."[57]

On March 1, 1974, the Democratic National Committee officially adopted the commission report with only minor revisions. The DNC did, however, raise the cut-off threshold for proportional representation from 10 percent to 15 percent of the votes cast in primaries, caucuses, and conventions.

Significant as the implications of the delegate selection reform are, the most important discussion of the long-term goals and purposes of the Democratic party has been focused on the work of the Charter Commission, charged with preparing a formal constitution to be submitted for ratification at the party's December 1974 Charter Conference. The debate over the content of the charter has crystallized into two broad alternatives: should a new national party structure be created which would derive its

[56] Penn Kemble, quoted in David S. Broder, "Democrats: The Unquota," *Washington Post*, February 10, 1974, p. B6.

[57] *Democrats All*, pp. 18–19.

authority directly from Democratic voters, or should the traditional federative, coalitional processes of the party be cultivated more effectively? The reformers, for instance, have argued that a mid-term policy conference would be a valuable injection of participatory democracy, providing Democrats with a direct opportunity to influence party policy formulation. Others have questioned the wisdom of incorporating a policy conference of popularly elected delegates into the charter; the Coalition for a Democratic Majority has maintained that:

> The genius of the Democratic Party has lain in its frequent ability to put forward national leaders who, by stressing those particular issues which appeal to a broad variety of constituency groups, and by seeking compromises among such groups on the issues that may divide them, have been able to win national elections. It is hard to understand how this difficult process would be served by bringing large numbers of the representatives of such groups together at a time when there is no national campaign to unify them, for a mid-term convention which will be tempted to hammer out positions by majority vote on a wide range of public issues.
>
> This is assuming, of course, that the authentic representatives of the major Democratic voting blocs would be chosen to such a mid-term policy conference in the first place. The likelihood is that they would be gravely underrepresented. The elections for delegates to a mid-term convention would simply not attract the ordinary voter. . . . The mid-term convention would probably be dominated first by the more affluent, educated voters with strong patterns of participation, and second by activist, ideologically committed minorities. . . .[58]

The subject of Democratic party reform is not simply a matter of alternative models of delegate selection, or differing conceptions of party structure and policy making. It is, rather, a sustained, critical dialogue that attempts to resolve which of two political ideals—participation or representation—should be the primary criterion of legitimacy in American party democracy.*

[58] The Coalition for a Democratic Majority, *Unity Out of Diversity: A Draft Position Paper on a New Charter for the Democratic Party of the United States* (Washington, D. C., 1973), p. 7.

* This paper owes much to the patient advice and helpful criticism of Dr. Herbert Waltzer, of Miami University's Department of Political Science.

5 Convention Reform and Conventional Wisdom: An Empirical Assessment of Democratic Party Reforms

JEFFREY L. PRESSMAN
AND DENIS G. SULLIVAN

For the past six years, the Democratic party has been implementing a number of significant changes in the process of selecting delegates to its national nominating conventions. The party's Commission on Party Structure and Delegate Selection headed by Senator George McGovern, which grew out of the turbulent 1968 convention, put forward a list of wide-ranging reforms in its 1970 report.[1] These recommendations, which have stimulated an ongoing controversy within the party, were designed to achieve two goals: to increase participation by groups previously underrepresented in party affairs, and to make the delegate-selection process itself more open. Addressing itself to the group-representation goal, the commission declared that blacks, women, and youth should be represented in each state delegation in "reasonable relationship to their presence" in the population of the state.[2] And with

[1] The Commission on Party Structure and Delegate Selection to the Democratic National Committee, *Mandate for Reform* (Washington, D.C., April 1970). Senator McGovern resigned from his position as commission chairman when he announced his presidential candidacy in January 1971, and he was replaced by Minnesota Congressman Donald Fraser.

[2] Ibid., p. 34.

JEFFREY L. PRESSMAN is associate professor of political science at the Massachusetts Institute of Technology. DENIS G. SULLIVAN is professor of government at Dartmouth College. They are coauthors (with others) of a book on national convention behavior entitled *The Politics of Representation: The Democratic Convention 1972*.

reference to the openness goal, the commission set down requirements for timeliness in delegate selection, publicized and accessible party meetings, abolition of the unit rule, and the banning of proxy voting.[3]

Somewhat to the surprise of both regulars and reformers within the party, compliance with the changes was widespread at state and local levels. Young people, blacks, and women, who had been severely underrepresented at the 1968 convention, increased their participation in 1972. Table 1 shows how marked this increase was.

TABLE 1

Increase in Representation of Blacks, Youth, and Women at the 1972 Convention

	1968 Convention	1972 Convention	Population Percentage
Blacks	6%	14%	11%
Under thirty	2	23	30
Women	14	36	51
Total number	2,528	3,100	

At the same time state parties revised their rules to comply with the commission's recommendations for making delegate selection more open.

Especially in the aftermath of 1972, the Democratic convention reforms have been subjected to attack, primarily from party regulars who felt shut out of the 1972 convention. Critics have concentrated their fire on the group-representation provisions, declaring that such "quotas" constituted reverse discrimination and helped to turn "middle Americans" against the Democrats in 1972. The openness provisions have also been subject to attack on the grounds that such provisions made it too easy for inexperienced amateurs—not dedicated to the party or to the goal of winning elections—to take over a national convention.

A recent example of the criticism of the 1972 reforms is Judith A. Center's article on "1972 Democratic Convention Reforms and Party Democracy," which appeared in the June issue of this journal.[4] Although Center does not make explicit the causal relationships she believes are involved in the impact of the reforms, she appears to make three important assumptions which are widely shared among the reforms' critics:

1. The reform rules were responsible both for producing a nominating con-

---

[3] Ibid.

[4] Judith A. Center, "1972 Democratic Convention Reforms and Party Democracy," *Political Science Quarterly*, 89, no. 2 (June 1974), 325–349.

vention that was ideologically far to the left of the Democratic party as a whole, and for the nomination of George McGovern for president.

2. The delegates to the convention were uncompromising amateurs who cared more about issue purity than about winning elections.

3. The Democratic convention of 1972 contributed importantly to the party's massive defeat in the presidential election of that year.

In the following discussion, we will examine these assumptions in the light of available empirical evidence. Much of the data we will use comes from a Dartmouth College study of the 1972 convention which we helped to direct. Our research in that study was based on (1) structured interviews with a randomly selected sample of 234 delegates over the five-day period of the convention, (2) first-hand observation of caucuses, state-delegation meetings, and convention-floor proceedings, and (3) the results of a preconvention CBS poll of all delegates.[5]

While examining the key assumptions of reform critics, we will address ourselves to political scientists' continuing concern with the explanation of decision making at nominating conventions and with the analysis of delegate style. Given the changed selection rules and demographic composition of the 1972 convention, what changes could be observed in traditional patterns of decision making and in the orientations of delegates?

Finally, in considering the future course of party reform, we will speculate on the implications of the 1974 rules modifications and also identify some of the reourring dilemmas of nominating conventions.

THE RULES CHANGES AND THE SELECTION OF McGOVERN DELEGATES

One of the most persistent assertions made by opponents of the 1972 rules changes has been that those changes were responsible for the selection of very liberal delegates and the nomination of George McGovern. Center, for example, declares: "The reforms had succeeded in transforming 1968s substantial delegate minority into 1972s overwhelming delegate majority."[6] Indeed, some party regulars have voiced the suspicion that Senator McGovern deliberately designed rules to enhance his pros-

---

[5] A full treatment of the results of this study is contained in Denis G. Sullivan, Jeffrey L. Pressman, Benjamin I. Page, and John J. Lyons, *The Politics of Representation: The Democratic Convention 1972* (New York, 1974). The present article does not examine the hypothesis that the reform rules widened the gap between the liberalism of convention delegates and that of party rank and filers. Although our book does present some relevant data, a definitive treatment must await future research. See *Politics of Representation*, pp. 30–34.

[6] Center, "1972 Democratic Convention," p. 342.

pects for the nomination. As one of the non-McGovern delegates we interviewed put it, "McGovern is a bastard . . . changed the rules to suit his own candidacy."[7] The argument of the reform critics is that the open state caucus procedures enabled committed ideologues, who felt intensely about issues and were willing to spend time fighting for them, to dominate the delegate-selection process.

Although it is true that McGovern supporters were in a stronger position at the convention than in the rank and file of the party as a whole, their success in the nomination process can be traced to factors other than the new reform rules. The image of McGovern fanatics running roughshod over party regulars in state conventions is simply not supported by the facts. Actually, the bulk of McGovern's support came from his victories in primary elections. Over 51 percent of the delegates elected in primaries supported McGovern, while the combined opposition of Humphrey-Muskie-Jackson received only 21 percent. Thus, McGovern was a typical insurgent in the sense that he established his base in the more open forum provided by the primary elections. The picture is somewhat different when we turn to delegates selected in state conventions. In 1972 there were roughly 1009 delegates selected at such conventions, approximately one-third of the overall total. The new rules on open procedures surely helped McGovern in wresting delegates away from party regulars who wanted to travel to Miami uncommitted. And in some cases, amateur McGovernites did replace local and state party leaders on state delegations. But as Figure 1 shows, the new rules on procedures and group representation did not result in McGovern's domination of state conventions; by June 3, 1972, McGovern held only a slight edge in support among delegates elected in state conventions. Even though his margin of support increased through June, the difference by convention time was not large; McGovern was supported by 32 percent of state convention delegates, while 20 percent supported Muskie, Humphrey, or Jackson. Following the top line in Figure 1a, which traces the growth of delegate support in primary elections, it appears that the narrow McGovern victory in the California winner-take-all primary (271 votes) on June 6 accelerated McGovern's inroads into state convention delegates.

A major factor in McGovern's success was the fragmentation of the Democratic "center" and the weakness of the so-called center candidates—Humphrey, Muskie, and Jackson. Organized labor divided its support among these three candidates, as the AFL-CIO executive board was split on the question and George Meany declined to make a decisive move.[8]

---

[7] Sullivan et al., *Politics of Representation*, p. 17.

[8] For a good analysis of the collapse of the center, see David S. Broder, "The Democrats' Dilemma," *The Atlantic*, 233 (March 1974), 32–33.

FIGURE 1

Delegate and Rank-and-File Support for Leading Democratic Candidates

a. Cumulative Percentage Among Delegates

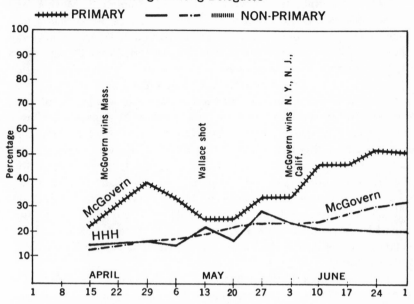

b. Percentage Among Democratic Rank and File —
Public Opinion Polls

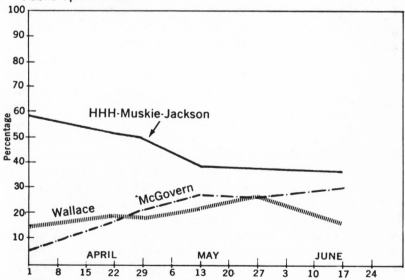

Source: Delegate data from *National Journal* April 15 through July 1, 1972. Public opinion data from Gallup Opinion Index with the exception of a May 9-10 Harris Poll including Independents as well as Democrats. Gallup question reads as follows: "Which one of the men on this list would you like to see nominated as the Democratic candidate for President in 1972?"

Also contributing to the weakness of the Humphrey, Muskie, and Jackson efforts was the candidacy of George Wallace, which had a profound effect in the preconvention period. Although Figure 1a does not show it, Wallace was gaining in delegate strength, from 13 percent on April 29 to 27 percent on May 20, one week after the shooting. By July 1, his delegate support from primaries had slipped back to roughly 18 percent. Yet, despite the attempted assassination of Wallace, rank-and-file support for Wallace continued to increase, as Figure 1b shows, through June. Moreover, support for Wallace increased at the same time it increased for McGovern, suggesting that Wallace was gaining at the expense of more centrist candidates. A Gallup poll, released just before the New Hampshire primary, suggests precisely that.[9] Gallup shows, assuming the Democratic center to consist of Humphrey-Muskie-Jackson, that 68 percent supported a center candidate while only 7 percent supported McGovern. But with Wallace included in the list of possibilities, support for the center declines by 11 percent whereas McGovern loses only 1 percent.

The Democratic center was badly hurt by the Wallace candidacy. The shift in attention from the insurgency of Wallace to that of McGovern, as a result of the assassination attempt, may have heightened the impression that McGovern was gaining at the expense of support for the center. But the shift in attention did not slow the growth in support for Wallace, and by June 16, the combined support for the two insurgents represented a majority of rank-and-file Democrats, at least in terms of measured support in public-opinion polls. By June, the center was in disarray; the preconvention process did not, as Figure 1b shows, result in a convergence of public support around one candidate. The party was truly divided.

If public opinion among rank-and-file Democrats was divided, so was delegate support. As a comparison of Figure 1a and 1b reveals, the percentage growths in delegate strength through the medium of state conventions and favorable public opinion are roughly equal. Figure 1a also shows that McGovern's moderate surge in delegate support came as a result of the California primary. It is somewhat ironic that the effect McGovern's California victory seemed to have had on the remaining state conventions was precisely what J. P. Maloney, the Humphrey strategist, had forecast for Humphrey if he won the primary. Victory in the primary, Maloney said, would "be the most meaningful influence on delegates chosen in non-primary states."[10] So it was, as Figure 1a shows.

Of all the factors contributing to McGovern's success—the weakness

[9] See Congressional Quarterly, March 25, 1972, 657.
[10] Quoted in National Journal, 4 (July 1, 1972), 1086.

at the party's center, the Wallace candidacy, the intensity of McGovern's support, the impact of his narrow California victory, and the reform rules—the center's weakness relative to the intensity and capability of the McGovern organization seems most important.[11] Of course, it was possible that the intense, well-organized McGovern movement could take advantage of rules changes, but we think that the commitment and organization of the McGovernites, when compared to the Muskie and Humphrey efforts, was far more decisive.

Again, this is not to deny that there are ways in which the rules changes might have helped McGovern. The reform rules might, for example, have served as a useful symbol for organizing liberal activists.[12] And the changes may also have spread uncertainty among party regulars who were used to long-established patterns of behavior in the nominating process. Ironically, the rules changes might have helped McGovern most by leading state party officials to abandon caucuses and conventions in favor of primaries—as a means of avoiding the rules changes. David Broder has written that:

In 1969–70, the McGovern commission set out to "clean up" the presidential nominating process by scourging its most questionable machinery—the party caucuses and state conventions, where organization leaders frequently railroaded through handpicked delegate slates. The rules adopted for "opening up" the caucuses and the conventions were quite effective—so effective, in fact, that several states thought better of continuing to use the caucus-convention system for choosing national convention delegates. Since the question of the presidential nomination is of secondary importance to many state and local professional politicians, several states decided to separate the decisions on presidential politics from their own district and state conventions, where more important matters like nominations for sheriff and state treasurer are settled. The upshot was that after a long period of years in which the presidential primary had fallen into increasing disfavor and disuse, seven additional states—for a total of twenty-three—adopted or reactivated presidential primaries for 1972.[13]

Thus, the McGovern commission—which had preferred state caucuses and conventions to primaries—ended up stimulating a return to the primaries. And it was the primaries that overstrained Muskie and gave

[11] Politicians tend to simplify arguments in order to favor their own power positions. Thus, conservative Democrats drop all factors from the list except the reform rules.

[12] William Cavala makes this point in "Changing the Rules Changes the Game: Party Reform and the 1972 California Delegation to the Democratic National Convention," *American Political Science Review,* 68 (March 1974), 27–42.

[13] Broder, "The Democrats' Dilemma," p. 36.

McGovern his greatest success. In this roundabout way, then, the reform rules may be said to have been of benefit to McGovern.

Even with the collapse of the center, the Wallace candidacy, and the McGovern organizational effort, Senator McGovern's triumph was by no means easy. In her article, Center declares that "the great majority of delegates were . . . pro-McGovern"[14] and that "there was no meaningful contest for the presidential nomination at Miami Beach."[15] But the crucial vote of the convention, on the California credentials challenge, was decided by only 173 votes; the convention could hardly be called a closed one.

DELEGATE STYLE AT THE CONVENTION: TRIUMPH OF THE PURISTS?

Another common belief of the critics of reform has been that the McGovern delegates, who dominated the 1972 convention, were ideological activists who were unwilling to compromise in the interests of party unity and victory in November. Supporters of the "regular" candidates, who controlled the 1968 convention (and earlier ones), but lost out in 1972, are seen as pragmatic professional types who put the interests of party and electoral victory over those of ideological purity. Thus, it is argued, the 1972 convention represented a sharp—and disturbing—break with the past traditions of conducting party business.

The distinction between issue-oriented (ideologically pure) and party-oriented activists has been utilized in a variety of different studies of political participation and, especially in the 1960s, in studies of national nominating conventions. The arrival of "purists" as a significant element in nomination politics was noted by Aaron Wildavsky in his commentary on the 1964 Republican convention,[16] and the issue-oriented style was also noted by James Q. Wilson in his book on the emergence of amateur Democratic clubs in three cities in the late 1950s.[17] Wilson's analysis revealed a recurring conflict between Democratic regulars and issue-oriented amateurs. In his view, the issue orientations of the amateurs are connected, not to self or narrow group interest, but to a larger public interest. For the amateur, participation in politics becomes an extension of private morality into the public sector. In his analysis of Goldwater delegates at the 1964 Republican convention, Wildavsky

---

[14] Center, "1972 Democratic Convention," p. 341.

[15] Ibid., pp. 341–342.

[16] Aaron Wildavsky, "The Goldwater Phenomenon: Purists, Politicians, and the Two-Party System," *Review of Politics*, 27 (July 1965), 386–413.

[17] James Q. Wilson, *The Amateur Democrat* (Chicago, 1966). See especially Chapter 12, "The New Party Politics: An Appraisal."

spoke of the distinction between purists and politicians in much the same way as Wilson did for that between amateur and regular Democrats. Wildavsky continued the purist-versus-professional theme in his study of the 1968 Democratic convention, casting the young McCarthyites in the role of purists, and the Humphrey supporters in the role of professionals.[18] In another study of the same convention, Soule and Clarke developed a measure of purism or, as they called it, amateurism, that separated quite nicely the McCarthy supporters from the Humphrey delegates.[19] It seemed, then, that purism was not the sole property of the right; it could serve to distinguish rightist Goldwater delegates from more centrist party regulars as well as leftist McCarthyites from more centrist professional Democrats.

In 1972, the conflict between opposing styles could again be seen. The McGovern surge in the primaries and state conventions in that year was in many ways a continuation of the earlier McCarthy movement. And the same themes of political reform and purism dominated the rhetoric of the McGovern organization. Again, as in 1968, the conflict between the insurgent organization and the regulars was as much a clash of styles as it was a conflict over policy.

It would be a mistake, however, to divide the 1972 convention too neatly into camps of "purist" and "professional," and to argue that the convention itself constituted a radical break with past behavior. Although it is unquestionably true that McGovern delegates had many purist attributes, our evidence showed that these people were also willing to compromise repeatedly to advance the interests of their candidate. As in previous conventions, delegates directed their behavior toward the nomination of their preferred candidate rather than the expression of group interest through identification with special group causes. And in this way, their behavior conformed to patterns of decision-making observed in other conventions. Finally, there is some evidence that the "regular" delegates took on some purist attributes of their own during the course of the convention.

Platform

Although the McGovern delegates were very much concerned with issues —Vietnam, social programs, racial justice, environment, and many

[18] Aaron Wildavsky, "The Meaning of 'Youth' in the Struggle for Control of the Democratic Party," in Aaron Wildavsky, *The Revolt Against the Masses* (New York, 1971), pp. 270–287.

[19] John Soule and James Clarke, "Amateurs and Professionals: A Study of Delegates to the 1968 Democratic National Convention," *American Political Science Review*, 64 (September 1970), 888–899.

others—they recognized that, in order to enhance their candidate's prospects both at the convention and in the general election, they might have to compromise on the presentation of those issues in the party's platform. The McGovern organization played a central role in the Platform Committee's proceedings—not so much in writing platform language as in monitoring it, modifying it, and exercising occasional veto power. McGovern's representative in the committee's proceedings, Ted Van Dyk, declared: "We hope to see a platform that will be liberal, unite the party, and defeat President Nixon in November."[20] Toward this end, Van Dyk carefully shepherded the drafting process, working with the drafting subcommittee throughout its labors and striving to avoid language that might be construed as needlessly controversial.

The McGovernites' willingness to put the interests of electoral victory ahead of inflexible ideological purity was shown by their behavior with respect to the more radical "minority reports" of the Platform Committee. These included Senator Harris' redistributive tax reform, the National Welfare Rights Organization's $6500 guaranteed income plan, and the plank guaranteeing homosexuals protection from job discrimination and other harassment. Although many McGovern delegates were personally in sympathy with these planks, the candidate's organization was concerned that such stands might cause problems in November—and this concern was communicated to the delegates. The minority planks were defeated.

According to our interview evidence, and in apparent contradiction to the conventional wisdom, McGovern delegates did not tend to be ideological purists about the platform any more than did backers of the "regular" candidates. Table 2 shows that only the Wallace delegates tended to ignore completely the matter of winning votes; as many McGovernites as regulars cited this function of the platform as one of their concerns. As in conventions before 1972, the delegates bent their ideological preferences to attempt to write a platform with broad appeal.

Arenas of Decision

Other similarities in behavior between the 1972 convention and previous ones are evident when we examine patterns and arenas of decision making.

According to the classic model of convention decision making, the key units for bargaining are the state delegations. This model assumes

[20] New York Times, June 24, 1972.

TABLE 2

McGovernites and Regulars on "Purist" Attitudes Toward Platform*

Goal for Platform	Candidate Commitment			
	McGovern	Wallace	Regulars	Total
Winning votes	24% (18)	0% (0)	24% (7)	21% (25)
Ideological purity	41 (31)	58 (7)	48 (14)	44 (52)
Both of the above	24 (18)	0 (0)	21 (6)	21 (24)
Other	12 (9)	42 (5)	7 (2)	14 (16)
	100 (76)	100 (12)	100 (29)	100 (117)

*Entries are based on delegates' explanations of why they wanted particular planks (or none) excluded from or included in the platform. The 40 percent who did not answer this question are excluded from the analysis, and those predominantly concerned with winning or correctness, are combined with those who were exclusively concerned with these effects. "Regular" candidates are Muskie, Humphrey, and Jackson. The values are significant at $p < .10$.

that such delegations, operating under the unit rule,[21] bargain with each other and with candidate organizations. The rank-and-file delegates are manipulated by hierarchical leaders holding important roles in national, state, or local party organizations.[22]

But the 1972 rules changes appeared to falsify some of the assumptions of the classic model. Because of the abolition of the unit rule and the requirements for opening up the delegate-selection process, it could be expected that party leaders or high elected officials would have a harder time controlling the votes of a state delegation. Thus, the importance of hierarchical state delegation leaders in the bargaining process would be reduced. With decision-making power at the convention more widely dispersed, there would be an increase in the number of groups to be consulted and this would strain an already burdened information system. Therefore, there would be strong incentives to find ways to assemble the smaller groups into more manageable bargaining units.

The expected desire, and need, to develop new kinds of bargaining units appeared to coincide with the new forms of group representation

[21] The Democratic unit rule required that the entire vote of a state delegation be cast as the majority of the delegation desired, if the state delegation had been so instructed by the state convention.

[22] For further discussion of this model, see Paul T. David, Ralph M. Goldman, and Richard C. Bain, *The Politics of National Party Conventions* (Washington, D.C., 1960); Nelson W. Polsby and Aaron B. Wildavsky, "Uncertainty and Decision-Making at the National Conventions," in Nelson W. Polsby, Robert A. Dentler, and Paul A. Smith (eds.), *Politics and Social Life* (Boston, 1963); and Nelson W. Polsby and Aaron B. Wildavsky, *Presidential Elections* (New York, 1971).

at the convention. With the increase in participation by women, youth, blacks, and nonparty activists of all kinds, state delegations would be subject to even more factionalization than might be predicted by the change in the unit rule. It became clear that interest-group representation at the convention would go beyond the traditional testimony on the platform and the holding of labor union receptions. In the spring of 1972, there were calls for black caucuses, women's caucuses, youth caucuses—the formation of new arenas for bargaining. With strong loyalties to their race, sex, or age groups, the participants in such new caucuses might be expected to take these meetings very seriously.

Thus, it appeared that in 1972, convention decision making might conform to a somewhat different model. According to this model, the importance of state delegations as arenas of decision would be decreased, and the need for new bargaining units would be met by the emergence of group caucuses of blacks, women, and youth. Before the convention began, both journalists and political activists expected the group caucuses to be important arenas of decision.[23]

The experience of the caucuses, however, did not justify their organizers' optimism or the observers' expectations. Although there were meetings during convention week of a Black Caucus, Women's Caucus, and Youth Caucus (as well as a Latin Caucus, Senior Citizens' Caucus, and Jewish Caucus), none of these groups was able to become a major arena of decision making at the convention; most could not even make a sustained claim on the attention of their potential members. A number of caucus leaders had hoped to draw up lists of issue positions and then bargain with candidates to secure their support for such positions, but this never occurred. Although the liberal McGovern delegates were somewhat more likely than others to feel that the caucuses were important, Table 3 shows the general decrease over time in delegates' estimates of the potency of group caucuses.[24]

The group caucuses' failure to meet expectations can be explained by reference to a number of recurring organizational problems. One of these was the problem of time. Because of the fast pace and heavy workload of the convention itself, delegates were often in a rush, and they could not afford the time to go to special caucus meetings. Caucus leaders and participants found that there was not enough time to carry out the grand strategies that some of them had planned. Some members

[23] For example, see "Caucus Calling Meeting July 9 of Black Democratic Delegates," *New York Times*, June 14, 1972.

[24] Delegates were asked: "Where do you think the most important decisions were made or will be made concerning [delegate's convention goal]?" Respondents were permitted to check the names of as many different arenas as they wished.

TABLE 3

Delegates' Changing Estimates of Group Caucuses' Importance*

	Black Caucus		Women's Caucus		Youth Caucus	
	McGovern	Non-McGovern	McGovern	Non-McGovern	McGovern	Non-McGovern
Sunday–Monday	41% (19)	16% (5)	30% (14)	9% (3)	28% (13)	9% (3)
Tuesday–Wednesday	15 (5)	26 (8)	18 (6)	16 (5)	17 (6)	19 (6)
Thursday–Friday	23 (9)	7 (1)	18 (7)	7 (1)	22 (9)	36 (5)

*Number of cases upon which percentage is based is included in parentheses. Chi-square probabilities are:

McGovern delegates–Black Caucus: .021
Non-McGovern delegates–Black Caucus: .286
McGovern delegates–Women's Caucus: .259
Non-McGovern delegates–Women's Caucus: .601
McGovern delegates–Youth Caucus: .539
Non-McGovern delegates–Youth Caucus: .099

of the Black Caucus had sought to hammer out a common program, see who the front runners were, and then bargain with them in the interests of black people. All this was to be done at the convention, but as District of Columbia delegate Walter Fauntroy told a news conference: "We looked and saw we couldn't wait that long."[25] Closely related to the problem of time was that of distance. The public transportation facilities in Miami were criticized by many delegates, some of whom cited lack of transportation as the reason why they did not attend group caucus meetings.

Another organizational problem for the caucuses was that of self-definition; it proved difficult for these groups to set and maintain their own boundaries. Who, for example, should be allowed into a Women's Caucus: All women delegates? Members of the National Women's Political Caucus? Women who subscribed to certain goals, such as easing of abortion laws? The Black Caucus tried to restrict its membership to delegates and alternates but found it impossible to keep nondelegates out. Finally, the decision was made to let any black person into the meetings of the Black Caucus, with full voting privileges. A broad definition of the group, while increasing membership, can lead to other difficulties. For the heterogeneity of the group can result in so much internal bickering that action is effectively impeded.

A final, critical problem for the special caucuses was that other organizations—notably candidate organizations—felt their own goals might be threatened by the existence of strong, independent group caucuses. The McGovern organization, for example, had serious reservations about an active Youth Caucus, and McGovern aides tried to discourage the senator's young delegates from building an independent youth group. There were also some clashes between the McGovern organization and the Women's Caucus, over a strong abortion plank and other issues. For delegates with multiple group identities, there were internal strains. Those who had a stake in the nomination of a particular candidate proved to be unwilling to drop their commitment to that candidate in favor of loyalty to a group caucus. McGovern delegates, many of whom had played a leading role in the development of the caucuses, were willing to subordinate caucus loyalty to candidate success. This strategy was in the best tradition of the professional who understands the role of compromise in the political process. And such behavior suggests once again that the McGovern delegates were not undiluted purists.

The special group caucuses were thus confronted with a number of

---

[25] "In Waning Hours, Mrs. Chisholm Courted 1st Ballot Support," *Washington Post,* July 13, 1972.

serious organizational problems: time, distance, group self-definition, internal disunity, and conflict with the goals of other organizations. It is not surprising that they found it difficult to promulgate common lists of demands and then bargain with candidates and party leaders to further the acceptance of those demands.

In contrast to these caucuses, the state delegations had some significant advantages as arenas for delegate activity and decision making. Members of state delegations were housed together in Miami Beach; they had been selected at common conventions or in the primaries back home; and the delegates had often known each other prior to the national convention.

Furthermore, delegates had to attend state caucuses to receive their floor credentials and guest passes for the gallery—items of considerable importance. But state delegations were more than just dispensers of credentials and guest passes. In a number of cases, they provided the sites for discussion and planning of state political campaigns. Vermont's delegates spent considerable time in Miami Beach planning what turned out to be the successful Democratic campaign for the governorship. And various Connecticut political leaders sought backing from members of that state's delegation for their 1974 statewide races.

A final, and crucial, function performed by state delegations was the transmission of messages from candidate organizations to delegates. Delegates who already were committed wanted information on what issues would come before the convention and how their candidate felt about those issues. State delegations, not group caucuses, were the sites where delegates could gain information and instructions. The candidate organizations listed delegates by state and contacted them in their state delegations. State delegation chairmen, in turn, organized delegation meetings around presentations by candidate representatives. In this way, delegates were able to obtain the information they wanted.

It must be noted that the importance of candidate organizations at the convention was considerable. Among decision-making arenas at the convention, the McGovern organization was perceived by the delegates to be the most important. Over 50 percent of the delegates viewed the McGovern organization as the site of the most important decisions at the outset of the convention, and that figure rose to over 70 percent by Thursday and Friday. Table 4 shows that delegates who were not supporters of McGovern were even more likely than McGovernites at the end of the convention to view the McGovern organization as the most important arena.

The 1972 rules changes, combined with changes in the group composition of delegates, had led some observers to predict that special group

TABLE 4

Delegates' Changing Estimates of the McGovern Organization's Importance *

	McGovern Delegates	Non-McGovern Delegates
Sunday–Monday	67% (31)	38% (12)
Tuesday–Wednesday	77 (26)	52 (16)
Thursday–Friday	68 (27)	86 (12)

*Number of cases upon which percentage is based is included in parentheses. Chi-square probability for McGovern delegates is .629; for non-McGovern delegates, .011.

caucuses would replace the traditional state delegations as the focus of delegates' attention. But the delegates' overriding purpose, as in the past, was to nominate a candidate—and candidate organizations continued to work through state delegations. Dramatic changes in the arenas of convention decision making never took place. The "New Politics" convention of 1972 utilized decisional structures which were similar to those found in its "Old Politics" predecessors.

POLITICAL STYLE: INHERENT CHARACTERISTIC OR RESPONSE TO ORGANIZATIONAL SITUATION?

The clear distinction between issue-oriented purists and party-oriented professionals is complicated further when we look more closely at delegates' political styles and changes over time in those styles. In the literature, political style has usually been treated as an enduring characteristic of the person rather than of the particular political and organizational situation in which that person finds himself. But this may be an oversimplification. It is easy for the party regular to be a professional in a process of mutual adjustment when the center of gravity in the party reflects his issue position. The insurgent purist, on the other hand, worries more about issues precisely because the center of gravity of the party is so far removed from his issue preferences.

Other elements of the purist-professional dichotomy lend themselves to the same analysis. The rallying cry of the purists for intraparty democracy is also a request for reduction in the power of the regulars relative to that of insurgents. The reiteration of themes of moral purity is also a device for maintaining incentives for participation where there are no material rewards. Insurgents demand policy-making arenas where rational discussion and open debate predominate; from another perspective this is a demand that skills possessed by a middle-class insurgent group be weighted more heavily in policy making.

If style is partially a response to one's fortunes in the organization, a reversal of roles might be expected as the purists approach positions of leadership responsibility and as the regulars are displaced. Yesterday's regular is tomorrow's purist worried about the issue integrity of a party he no longer owns. And yesterday's purist is today's professional worried about organizational unity, incentives, and winning elections.

Regardless of which perspective we adopt in considering political style, almost all commentators agree that the McGovern and Wallace organizations were more purist in style than were the Humphrey-Muskie-Jackson delegates. When we look at how the delegates change over the course of the convention, the relevance of the differences between these two perspectives on style becomes apparent. If political style is independent of winning and losing, then we should expect no pronounced changes in orientation among McGovern supporters as they move into positions of leadership in the party. And those who are professionals on Monday should be professionals on Friday. On the other hand, if political style responds to winning and losing, then we should expect the McGovern forces to become increasingly pragmatic over the course of the convention and the Humphrey-Muskie-Jackson delegates to become increasingly purist.

To test the competing interpretations of political style, we developed a measure of the delegates' purist or professional perspectives from our interview data. Each delegate was asked to state what he really wanted to see done at the convention and the reasons for his preference. Using guidelines drawn from the previously mentioned work of Wildavsky, Wilson, and Soule and Clarke, we classified delegates according to the code set out in Table 5.

Thus, of the 234 delegates interviewed, we were able to classify 187 or 80 percent. In all our subsequent discussions of purist versus professional perspectives, we shall be using this measure. Of course, the validity of a measure of purism-professionalism would be in doubt if it did not differentiate McGovern supporters from those supporting Humphrey-Jackson-Muskie. Our measure does so quite nicely in Table 6.

But when we examine the results on change over the course of the convention, some interesting differences begin to emerge. As Figure 2 illustrates, the hypothesis that McGovern delegates would grow increasingly pragmatic as their organization assumed a position of leadership in the convention was not confirmed. The delegates, it seems, were willing to accept the discipline imposed upon them for the sake of a McGovern victory in the convention, but they were not willing to surrender their belief in the importance of correct issue stands and intraparty democracy.

TABLE 5

Classification of Delegates as Either Purist or Professional

A. Nomination of candidate	If delegate goal was nomination of preferred candidate because his candidate could win in in November	= Professional N = 11*
	If delegate goal was nomination of preferred candidate because candidate was correct on the issues, or correctly represented new groups or party reform	= Purist N = 76
B. Issue preference and platform	If delegate goal was party unity because of need to win in November, or if delegate goal was issue in platform because it would aid winning in November	= Professional N = 27
	If delegate goal was correct issue in platform for any other reason	= Purist N = 19
C. Convention decision process	If delegate goal was representation of new groups in convention decision making and party decision making, or party reform	= Purist N = 26
D. Party orientation	If delegate goal was nomination of winner to unify party, express traditional issues dividing Republicans and Democrats	= Professional N = 28

*N is the number in the sample.

Thus, the "organizational situation" hypothesis—that winning converts purists into professionals—does not receive support from our data. The reverse, however—that losing turns professionals into purists—is supported by the data. Whereas on Sunday and Monday Democratic regulars were thinking as professionals are reputed to think, on Thursday

TABLE 6

The Delegates' Purism and Professionalism, by Candidate Preference *

	Purist	Professional	Total
Preference for McGovern	83% (98)	17% (11)	109
Preference for Wallace	65% (11)	35% (6)	17
Preference for HHH, Muskie, or Jackson	45% (22)	55% (27)	49
Total	70%	30%	175

*Candidate preference was assessed by asking each delegate the name of the candidate he most preferred for the nomination regardless of how he had voted or intended to vote. The results are roughly the same as the preconvention vote preference recorded by CBS for each delegate.

FIGURE 2

Changing Purist Orientation Among McGovern and Non-McGovern Delegates

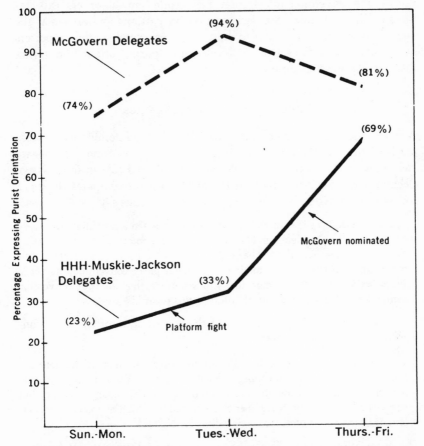

For the HHH group the change in the purist percentage is statistically significant by chi square with probability less than .012. Candidate preference is candidate most preferred at time of interview.

and Friday they were almost as purist as the McGovern supporters. What we seem to see here is a process of radicalization. When party control shifts to an insurgent group, the issues assume as great an importance for the regulars as they formerly held for the insurgents. And the contrast between purists and professionals becomes blurred.

Thus, the evidence gleaned from the 1972 Democratic convention raises some serious questions about the assertion that the dominant group of delegates there were uncompromising ideologues who wrested control of the party from their pragmatic, "party regular" opponents and changed the nature of the convention process itself. Interview results and other data show that: (1) McGovern delegates were willing to yield on ideological purity when such yielding would help their candidate's prospects in the convention and election; (2) despite some observers' expectations of sharp changes, the decision-making patterns and arenas at the 1972 convention were similar to those of the past; and (3) the supporters of "regular" candidates actually developed a "purist" orientation during the course of the convention.

THE CONVENTION AND THE ELECTION

A third article of faith among the critics of the 1972 nomination process has been that the Democratic convention of that year—and the delegate -selection process that preceded it—played a crucial role in the massive electoral defeat in November. In her article, Center compares the 1972 convention unfavorably with its 1968 predecessor. She says:

> The 1968 Democratic National Convention nominated a candidiate who very nearly won the presidency in November. Since the *raison d'etre* of American political parties has always been the election of its candidates to public office, and the traditional function of national party conventions has been the selection of candidates most likely to win office, then the 1968 convention cannot be considered an abysmal failure in this regard.[26]

In contrast, consider her dim view of the contribution of the 1972 convention:

> The reforms had succeeded in transforming 1968s substantial delegate minority into 1972s overwhelming delegate majority. Yet not only did that majority's candidate lose the presidential election by a large margin, but surveys taken after the November election indicated that as many as 36 percent of Democratic voters cast their ballots for Nixon.[27]

The implication is clear: The 1968 convention was more successful than that of 1972, because Hubert H. Humphrey, the candidate it produced, came much closer to victory than did George McGovern.

This comparison between the "success" of 1968 and the "failure" of 1972 must be called into some question, for it omits a number of important differences between the two elections which worked against the Democratic candidate in 1972. One of these differences was the incumbency of Richard Nixon. In 1968, Nixon was a former vice-president; in 1972, he was an incumbent president who had just completed popular trips to China and the Soviet Union. Another difference was the absence of

---

[26] Center, "1972 Democratic Convention," p. 326.
[27] Ibid., p. 342.

George Wallace in the 1972 general election. The University of Michigan's postelection analysis found that almost eight out of ten individuals who voted for Wallace in 1968 cast their ballots for Nixon in 1972;[28] with Wallace in the race, the election would have been much closer.

One common item of conventional wisdom has been that it was the convention itself—featuring televised views of young people, blacks, activist women, and assorted nonregular politicians—that cost the Democrats the 1972 election. But the Michigan study found that the "data strongly suggest that the popular myth has overestimated the importance of the Democratic convention as an explanation of the election outcome."[29] It appears that the 1972 convention did not play the decisive and disastrous role that some have attributed to it.

Looking toward the Future

The struggle over delegate-selection rules in the Democratic party has continued. It is interesting that so much of the conservatives' anger has been directed at the group "quota" provisions, for it would be hard to argue that those provisions had an effect on the convention's outcome. (After all, Humphrey, Jackson, and Muskie could all recruit women, minorities, and young people to serve as their delegates.) In view of the opposition these group-representation rules engendered, it is not surprising that a new party delegate selection commission recommended in late 1973 the abolition of the "reasonable representation" guidelines. Instead, the commission's report put forward an "Affirmative Action" program to ensure participation by women, youth, and minority groups "as indicated by their presence in the Democratic electorate." The new commission report, which was endorsed with only minor changes by the Democratic National Committee in March 1974 declared: "This goal shall not be accomplished either directly or indirectly by the Party's imposition of mandatory quotas at any level of the delegate selection process or in any other Party affairs."[30]

While Center professes to see in these changes "little more than token retrenchment from the McGovern-Fraser reforms,"[31] a somewhat dif-

[28] Arthur H. Miller, Warren E. Miller, Alden S. Raine, and Thad A. Brown, "A Majority Party in Disarray: Policy Polarization in the 1972 Election." Paper delivered at the 1973 Annual Meeting of the American Political Science Association, New Orleans, p. 62.

[29] Ibid., p. 42.

[30] Report of the Commission on Delegate Selection and Party Structure as Amended and Adopted by the DNC Executive Committee, March 1, 1974.

[31] Center, "1972 Democratic Convention," p. 347.

ferent answer is suggested if we focus on the provisions for compliance in the new guidelines. It is important to note, for example (as Center herself does), that compliance this time will not be determined by the presence of a "reasonable number" of young, women, or minority delegates, but rather by the vaguer standard of a state party's effort in encouraging participation by these groups. It is also important to keep in mind that party chairman Robert Strauss and the "regulars" prevailed over the "reformers" in determining the size of the compliance commission and in the choice of that commission's chairman (Robert Wagner, former mayor of New York).[32]

Another of the 1974 reforms, the provision for proportional representation of candidate preferences, may well have some significant effects. According to the new rules, winner-take-all primaries are banned, and delegate places in the relevant states are to be allocated proportionally on the basis of the vote (to those candidates having more than 15 percent of the total). In nonprimary states, proportional representation will operate at every stage of the selection process; any candidate receiving 15 percent of the votes at a particular level will be entitled to his proportional share of delegates at the next higher level.

The effect of this rules change will surely be to encourage candidates to mount campaigns in a larger number of states, for partial victories are possible—and necessary. No longer can a candidate afford to concentrate on a few large primaries and ignore the other states.[33] And without the bandwagon effect of the winner-take-all primaries, it will be harder for any one candidate to establish an overwhelming lead. Thus, the prospects for a multiballot, bargaining convention are enhanced. Penn Kemble, a critic of recent convention reforms, has predicted that proportional representation could have a fragmenting effect within the party and could lead to the formation of "constituency" slates such as labor or black caucuses.[34] But the 1972 experience of group caucuses indicates that there are limits to caucus loyalty in the presence of strong candidate organizations. As to the major participants in 1976, it is quite possible, we think, that the bargainers at the 1976 convention may be the very party regulars championed by critics of reform. Indeed, despite some predictions to the contrary, the evidence so far indicates that Democratic regulars are doing well in the delegate-selection process for the party's 1974 midterm convention.[35]

---

[32] See "Democrats Approve New Rules to Select Convention Delegates," *New York Times*, March 2, 1974.

[33] See Broder, "The Democrats' Dilemma," p. 38.

[34] See David S. Broder, "Democrats: The Unquota," *Washington Post*, February 10, 1974.

[35] "Democratic Regulars Controlling Selection of Delegates to Mini-Convention," *New York Times*, May 23, 1974.

SOME CONTINUING DILEMMAS

Regardless of short-run changes in convention rules and party-power relationships, the Democrats will continue to face a number of fundamental dilemmas with respect to the nomination process. The first dilemma arises from the issue of deciding who is entitled to participate directly in that process. Not all citizens who declare themselves in support of a candidate can be considered members of that candidate's party. But who is to decide where the boundary between member and supporter lies? Political parties are not private organizations that can easily refuse freely offered services. Moreover, in periods of dissatisfaction with political parties, amateur activists often demand that the scope of participation in the parties be widened to include them. Center speaks warmly of the "complexes of party traditions, old saws, and unwritten bylaws that had evolved and persisted since Andrew Jackson's time."[36] But these traditions operated to limit participation by young people, women, and minority groups. It should not be assumed that, in the absence of group-representation guidelines, some sort of open party merit system prevails, in which competence and experience are the criteria of success. For, like other kinds of organizational leaders, party officials often subordinate other goals to the maintenance of their own places in the organization.

A second dilemma lies in the party's necessary division of its attention between past and future constituencies. In its choice of leaders and platforms, a party may indicate a responsiveness to what has been "tried and true"—to the nurturance of old constituencies—or it might look to new constituencies in exchange for new support. And a party may, in its platform and choice of candidates, contribute to the development of new constituencies, creating sources of future support. The dilemma is, of course, characteristic of all organizations: as their political environments change, or seem to change, parties run the risk of losing the old while attracting the new.

Finally, there is a dilemma central to political life—the balance between issue purity and organizational power. Parties are organizations that must attract votes to survive. Yet they also exist as instruments to achieve issue goals. Awareness of this dilemma on the part of a party's members creates a profound organizational tension. And this tension has been increased by the high degree of issue polarization currently found in the Democratic party.[37] In such a situation, it becomes much harder for a nominating convention to perform its traditional functions of unifying the party and legitimizing the choice of nominee. And

[36] Center, "1972 Democratic Convention," p. 345.
[37] See Miller et al., "A Majority Party in Disarray," for a full discussion of this polarization.

this polarization is unlikely to be summarily abolished by any combination of rules changes.

Given the deep divisions within the Democratic party and the continuing controversy over delegate-selection rules, it is perhaps inevitable that evaluations of convention reforms will reflect current political preferences. The McCarthy supporters overemphasized the closed nature of the 1968 convention, and non-McGovernites have exaggerated the exclusionary impact of the 1972 reform rules. But surely it is not unreasonable to request that those who analyze the effects of rules changes should base their evaluations, to the extent possible, on empirical evidence.

6   Insulation and Responsiveness in Congressional Elections

WALTER DEAN BURNHAM

The 1974 congressional election is part of a crisis sequence in the current history of the American political system. The tremendous upheaval which has been going on in our electoral politics since 1964 has had a number of remarkable by-products. Chief among these has been the progressive weakening of the hold which party loyalties have had upon the voters in channeling their voting decisions. This growing dissolution of party-in-the-electorate entails a serious erosion of political parties as basic institutional components of the political system. Closely associated with this, a profoundly important electoral reinforcement of the constitutional separateness of our national policy-making institutions has occurred. The 1974 election has made its own contribution to these trends, and it seems clear that the policy-making vacuum which dramatically emerged in the spring of 1973, when the Watergate cover story fell apart, will continue unabated at least until 1977. Yet this election has some features which do not easily fit a simple model of party decay; and it has had consequences of importance, both substantively and analytically. There is justification, therefore, for giving it a close study.

RECENT CHANGES IN CONGRESSIONAL-ELECTION PATTERNS

Recent analyses of American elections have made discoveries which are of direct concern to this study. We now know that the portrait of the

WALTER DEAN BURNHAM is professor of political science at Massachusetts Institute of Technology. He is the author of *Critical Elections and the Mainsprings of American Politics* and numerous articles on American electoral politics.

American electorate which was laid down by the Michigan survey-research group in the early 1960s must be very significantly modified when voting behavior and attitudes in the late 1960s and early 1970s are evaluated.[1] It is now quite clear that the pressure of political events during the past decade has produced levels of attitudinal constraint and issue-oriented voting behavior which were largely unsuspected in an earlier period.[2] Not surprisingly, much of this literature has been concerned with attempting to assess the prospects for a critical party realignment as a resolution of the current crisis sequence.[3] Whatever such prospects may be, the dislocation of voting coalitions which has developed during this crisis sequence has had major effects on the structure of congressional-election outcomes, and on the relationship between congressional and other elections. The 1974 election requires detailed analysis in this context.

Two scholars, David Mayhew[4] and Edward Tufte,[5] have addressed themselves to certain basic and very recent changes in the aggregate profile of congressional-election outcomes. Since about 1956–1960, incumbent members of Congress of both political parties have become increasingly invulnerable to defeat in their districts, more or less regardless of the fate of their party's candidates for other offices in the same election. Incumbents have become quite effectively insulated from the electoral effects, for example, of adverse presidential landslides. As a

[1] See, e.g., Gerald Pomper, "From Confusion to Clarity: Issues and American Voters, 1956–1968," *American Political Science Review*, 66 (June 1972), 415–428, as well as the contributions of John Kessel, Richard Boyd, and Richard A. Brody and Benjamin I. Page to this symposium issue; Arthur H. Miller, Warren E. Miller, Alden S. Raine, and Thad A. Brown, "A Majority Party in Disarray: Social and Political Conflict in the 1972 Election," paper presented at 1973 meeting of the American Political Science Association, New Orleans, September 1973; and Norman H. Nie and Kristi Andersen, "Mass Belief Systems Revisited," *Journal of Politics*, 36 (August 1974).

[2] Except, perhaps, by the late V. O. Key, Jr. See his *The Responsible Electorate* (Cambridge, Mass., 1966).

[3] One recent analysis of this literature is contained in Walter Dean Burnham, "American Politics in the 1970s: Beyond Party?" appearing as the final chapter of William N. Chambers and Walter Dean Burnham (eds.), *The American Party Systems*, 2d ed. (New York, 1975).

[4] See David Mayhew, "Congressional Elections: The Case of the Disappearing Marginals," paper presented at 1973 meeting of the New England Political Science Association, Boston, April 1973. A more general discussion of his thesis that congressional behavior is shaped by the rational desire to be reelected is found in his *Congress: The Electoral Connection* (New Haven, Conn., 1974); but the book contains surprisingly little information on actual electoral patterns.

[5] Edward Tufte, "The Relationship between Votes and Seats in Two-Party Systems," *American Political Science Review*, 68 (1973), 540–554. See also his *Data Analysis for Politics and Policy* (Englewood Cliffs, N. J., 1974), pp. 91–101.

result, a once-notable phenomenon, the so-called coattail effect, has virtually been eliminated.[6]

A profound change has occurred in the shape of congressional-district outcomes as the influence of party in shaping voting decisions has decayed. At one time (say, around 1900), the percentage distribution of the vote between the two parties was very similar, or unimodal, tending to coincide with a usually competitive national partisan percentage. These distributions also tended to converge, whether one looks at outcomes involving incumbents running for reelection, contests without incumbents, or the presidential vote at the congressional-district level. In particular, there was little or no difference between the concentration of cases in the competitive range for congressional races with or without incumbents. Somewhat later (most notably, perhaps, in 1924, 1952, and 1956) these distributions began to diverge, but all of them remained unimodal. At some point after 1956, however, the pattern of outcomes involving incumbents running for reelection began to change dramatically. Since then, the concentration of cases somewhere within the competitive range has been "hollowed out," and replaced by two modes or peaks. One of these is occupied by Democratic incumbents and the other by Republican incumbents, and both are normally located quite far from the competitive center. As a result, the proportion of all incumbents running for reelection who lose their contests has tended to decline sharply, while the proportion of incumbents running to all contests has tended to increase. But while this has been going on, the distribution of outcomes for both presidential elections at the district level and for congressional contests without incumbents has remained heavily concentrated in a single mode which tends to coincide with the national partisan percentages for the two offices.[7] It seems clear that electorally decisive minorities of voters have increasingly been voting for incumbent representatives as incumbents during the past two decades.

These changes in distributional patterns, so obviously favorable to incumbents of both parties, are of large significance. In evaluating their causes, both Mayhew and Tufte have stressed the importance of efforts

[6] For an effort to analyze this phenomenon, see Malcolm Moos, *Politics, Presidents and Coattails* (Baltimore, 1952). In retrospect, it seems probable that the "coattail effect" was part of an intermediate stage in the historical decomposition of American parties as electoral mechanisms. Prior to about 1900, near-identity of results at most or all levels of election tended to be the rule; but since the early 1960s, the dissociation of electoral coalitions for various offices has become increasingly complete.

[7] See the charts in Mayhew, "Congressional Elections," and in Burnham, "American Politics in the 1970s."

by elites to control and enhance the predictability of congressional-election outcomes. Incumbent members of Congress, with rapidly growing resources of staff, free publicity through the frank and other resources at their disposal, do what they can to entrench themselves personally in their districts. These efforts become increasingly successful the more available such resources become and the more skillfully and single-mindedly the legislator uses them. Additionally, as Tufte points out, many if not most state legislatures prefer the "collusive gerrymander" —the protection of incumbents of both parties—as a conflict-minimizing device when the time comes for them to redraw congressional-district boundaries.[8]

There is no question that these explanations are valid as far as they go. But it is very likely that the phenomena with which they deal are more significantly rooted in major changes which have developed in the behavior of voters.[9] The newer literature has clearly identified many of these changes. It is now pretty certain, for example, that the shift toward the professionalization of House careers—including the emergence of the seniority norm—occurred not later than the 1894–1910 period. One assumes an enduring interest after 1910 in a lifetime career on the part of incumbents; yet we need to wait half-a-century to see the decisive distributional breakthrough which Mayhew and Tufte identify. We need to wait, in short, until the current crisis of party decomposition intersects with a major increase in the availability of resources for incumbents seeking to be reelected. Of course, we do not know nearly enough about the history of reapportionment to be sure as to when "collusive gerrymanders" became common. But we do know that there are a number of states—among them, New Hampshire and West Virginia—where no such device was ever needed because of one-party control of the state legislature, but where the shift toward landslides favoring congressional incumbents can easily be traced anyway.

In the early 1960s Warren E. Miller and Donald E. Stokes pointed out that few voters know very much about congressional candidates. What little they know normally tends to favor the incumbent, who has some visibility in the district.[10] This creates a kind of "breakage effect" favoring incumbents, roughly similar to the steady percentage advantage which the owners of an honest gambling house have over the players

---

[8] Tufte, *Data Analysis for Politics and Policy*, p. 99.

[9] See the communication of Walter Dean Burnham to the editor, *American Political Science Review*, 68 (1974), 207–211.

[10] Warren E. Miller and Donald E. Stokes, "Party Government and the Salience of Congress," in Angus Campbell, Philip E. Converse, Warren E. Miller, and Donald E. Stokes, *Elections and the Political Order* (New York, 1966), chap. 11.

as a whole. One is probably right in assuming that this breakage effect is now considerably greater than it was when Miller and Stokes first described it. But if so, it would be reasonable to assume that the erosion of party-in-the-electorate—an alternative cue-giver to voting decisions —occurs at a time when the incumbent's available publicity resources are increasing. Of course, in such circumstances the "collusive gerrymander," if used, will tend to be increasingly successful. Added together, the effects of party decomposition in the most recent period would also necessarily erode the quantitative basis for any hypothesis that "nationalization of political effects" was increasing across time.[11]

Instead, we can summarize what we could expect to happen under these circumstances:

> The number of incumbents seeking and winning reelection will tend to approximate an actuarial maximum.
>
> Heterogeneity will massively increase across both time (as measured by partisan swing) and space (as measured by electoral outcomes).
>
> The aggregate relationship between congressional and all other elections will systematically decrease, which entails the proposition that the pattern of electoral coalitions will become increasingly discrete by office, with one predominant in a presidential election, another in a congressional election, and so on. This will finally reach the point where the separateness of these coalitions becomes decisive in both electoral and policy terms, above all providing an immense behavioral reinforcement of the separation of powers which the Constitution prescribes.

The structure of American electoral politics came quite close to approximating these conditions in the 1966–1972 period. It becomes of some importance to analyze if, and to what extent, the 1974 election has maintained these trends.

A PROFILE OF THE 1974 ELECTION

The 1974 election was fought under notoriously abnormal circumstances. It was part of a drama of high constitutional politics ending in Richard Nixon's resignation in disgrace. As it happened, the congressional election can really be said to have begun early in 1974, when six seats in the House which Republicans had won in 1972 became vacant.[12] Most

---

[11] Donald E. Stokes, "Political Parties and the Nationalization of Electoral Forces," in Chambers and Burnham, *The American Party Systems*, chap. 7. It must be emphasized that the incumbent-insulation pattern fully emerges only *after* the latest decade of Stokes's analysis (1952–1960).

[12] In order of their occurrence: Pennsylvania twelfth, Michigan fifth and eighth, Ohio first, and California fifth and nineteenth, with only the last retained by the

of these were supposedly safe bastions for the GOP, but five of them elected Democrats between February and June. Moreover, these by-elections were subjected to the most intense scrutiny, by politicians and analysts alike, of any since Franklin Roosevelt's attempted purge of conservative Democrats in the 1938 primaries. They thus made their own contribution to the politics of presidential impeachment and resig-nation. Among other things, they projected a nationwide Democratic swing of between 8 and 10 percent in November, and produced the first Democratic victory in President Ford's old Grand Rapids district since 1910.

It was anticipated both before Nixon's resignation and after his par-don by Ford that the Republican party would suffer major losses in 1974. Throughout the year, the Gallup Poll projections indicated that the Democrats would win at least 60 percent of the national congressional vote. In the event, they did somewhat less well than this; but, with 59.2 percent of the two-party vote, they still won the largest share of the two-party and total vote in their entire history, and the second largest congressional popular-vote landslide of all time. The Republi-cans lost forty-eight seats net over 1972, five of them during the by-election sequence in the spring of 1974.

The situation for Republicans was manifestly poor throughout the year, and it was widely argued that this had contributed to a heavy re-tirement rate among Republican incumbents. Viewed in terms of *two* transitions, 1970–1972 and 1972–1974, there is clearly something to this argument. The total attrition rate for 1970 incumbents after the 1974 election was 17.6 percent for the Democrats but 31.1 percent for

TABLE 1

Incumbents and Nonincumbents in House Elections, 1972 and 1974[a]

| Year | Incumbent Democrats | | | Incumbent Republicans | | | Nonincumbents | | | Total House | |
	Won	Lost	Total	Won	Lost	Total	D	R	Total	D	R
1972	216	7	223	149	4	153	24	35	59	243	192
1974	210	3	213	124	36	160	45	17	62	291	144

[a]Both years' figures are based on treating all winners of preceding by-elections as nonin-cumbents. If the winners of 1973–1974 by-elections are regarded as incumbents, the figures change marginally:

1974	216	4	220	127	36	163	39	13	52	291	144

GOP and the Ohio first recaptured by it in November. The mean percentage Demo-cratic of the total vote in the five districts won by the Democrats had been 37.3 per-cent for the House in 1972 and 39.0 percent for president.

the Republicans. But the attrition resulting from retirement or other preelection causes was 12.5 percent in 1972 and 12.3 percent in 1974 for Democrats, and 15.0 and 17.1 percent respectively, in 1972 and 1974, for Republicans—certainly a small absolute difference.

There was a relatively intense participation of Republican incumbents in the 1974 congressional election. As Table 1 indicates, the bulk of the GOP attrition in 1974 is accounted for by the electoral defeat of an abnormally large number of these incumbents. In November 1974, a total of fifty-five seats changed party hands.[13] Of these, forty were lost by incumbents of both parties, while only fifteen involved contests between nonincumbents.[14] It is obvious, then, that this election did not conform in this vitally important respect to the incumbent-insulation model which we have discussed above. Nevertheless, as we shall see, the outcome of this election much more closely resembles the *recent* large-swing results of 1964 and 1966 than those of earlier "landslide" congressional elections.

Among other things, the distribution of outcomes and vote swings involving Republican incumbents was anything but what a nationalized-effects model might predict. The 1972–1974 shift—a swing of 6.0 percent to the Democrats nationwide—was made up of extremely complex elements at the district level. Two things emerge with crystal clarity at the outset. First, the Democratic seat gain was not won by anything remotely approximating a uniform swing, for example one which might have tipped over most Republican incumbents who had won relatively close contests in 1972. Second, incumbent Republican

[13] All comparisons between 1972 and 1974 are affected by the judicially ordered redistricting of California's forty-three seats in the interim. One entirely new seat was created and was won by a Democrat (the twenty-fourth). Of the forty-two others, four had no incumbents; two of these were held by Democrats and two were won by Democrats from the GOP. Of the thirty-eight seats with incumbents running for reelection, twenty-one were defended by Democrats, all of whom won, and seventeen by Republicans, of whom two lost (the seventeenth and the thirty-fifth). In a number of cases, specified where they occur, it has been necessary to exclude California from data presentations.

[14] On the basis of incumbency as of November 1974, we find:

Category	Incumbents		Nonincumbents		Total	
	N	%	N	%	N	%
Unchanged R	127	33.2	11	21.2	138	31.7
From D to R	4	1.0	2	3.8	6	1.4
From R to D	36	9.4	13	25.0	49	11.3
Unchanged D	216	56.4	25	48.1	241	55.4
New seat (D)	..	..	1	1.9	1	0.2
Total	383	100.0	52	100.0	435	100.0

TABLE 2

Party and Policy: Composite Policy Scores of Reelected and Defeated Republican Incumbents, 1974

Score[a]	Reelected	Defeated	% Defeated
+40 and over	5	0	0
+30 to +39	2	0	0
+20 to +29	3	0	0
+10 to +19	4	0	0
+0 to +9	2	0	0
–0 to –9	5	1	16.7
–10 to –19	1	0	0
–20 to –29	5	1	16.7
–30 to –39	8	1	11.1
–40 to –49	8	1	11.1
–50 to –59	13	4	23.5
–60 to –69	18	6	25.0
–70 to –79	22	5	18.5
–80 to –89	15	10	40.0
–90 to –100	16	7	26.1
–49 and above	43	4	8.5
–50 to –79	53	15	22.1
–80 to –100	31	17	35.4
TOTAL	127	36	22.1

[a]This index is based on a composite of ratings by Americans for Democratic Action (liberal) and Americans for Constitutional Action (conservative). It varies over a range of 200, from –100 (most conservative) to +100 (most liberal).

losses in 1974 were not randomly distributed across the wide policy spectrum which exists within the congressional Republican party. Using a simple policy-score index based on votes during the 1971–1974 period, Table 2 provides a stratification of winning and losing Republican incumbents along this policy dimension.

Very clearly, Republican losses were concentrated at the conservative end of the party's policy spectrum. As the journalists' accounts of the election pointed out, the conservative Republican Steering Committee lost thirty of its seventy members, including its chairman, Lamar Baker of Tennessee (—96 on our index). In this respect too, it would appear that the 1974 election presents similarities to the 1964 situation: in both cases there was a visible relationship between the policy liberalism of Republican incumbents and their relative success at the polls.

This suggests the existence of policy voting among some 1974 voters. Unfortunately, the analysis of aggregate data alone is inadequate to permit solid inference on this point. But it does reveal—quite graphically

—the complexities. As in the past, one of the chief elements of complexity is the persistent deviation of the South as a region from national norms. It is not necessary for the purposes of this analysis to do more than point out that this region is asymmetrically conservative. This conservatism is manifested not only in presidential elections such as 1968 and 1972, but in the policy scores of its representatives as a whole, and of its Republican representatives in particular.[15] Thus, any study of the relationship between the policy stances of members of Congress and what happened to them electorally between 1972 and 1974 must take account of this southern regional deviation.

Another complicating factor can be derived almost deductively from the incumbent-insulation model discussed here. It can be expected that, all other things being equal, first-term representatives running for reelection will do markedly better in any trend situation than older incumbents of the same party. The rationale here is that there is an upward trajectory today in an incumbent's career at the polls. The first election (as a nonincumbent) would be relatively close, but margins thereafter would increase until they reached a point somewhere near the noncompetitive mode established for all incumbents of the party. Moreover, we might expect that a very large fraction of this upward shift from competition to electoral insulation would occur between the representative's first and second election campaigns. In the specific situation before us, this implies that Republican first-termers in 1974 should show little or no pro-Democratic swing as a group, and Democratic newcomers should enjoy a much larger swing than their older incumbent party colleagues.

Table 3 demonstrates that the pattern of the data is consistent with these expectations. In fact, the first-generation or "new incumbent" Republicans as a group actually *improved* their position very slightly in the face of an exceptionally large national shift toward the Democrats.[16] This generalized pattern captures a trend which is reflected in extreme form by the showings of three 1972 freshmen in the 1974 election: Joel Pritchard, a liberal Republican from Washington (a shift from 49.4 to 29.4 percent Democratic); Trent Lott of Mississippi, a Nixon supporter on the Judiciary Committee and a conservative Republican (a shift from 44.4 to 16.9 percent Democratic); and Gerry Studds, a liberal

[15] Outside the South and border states, the mean score for Democratic incumbents was +59, and for Republicans was −48. The mean score in the South was −32 for Democrats and −82 for Republicans; the latter, it should be noted, with a much smaller standard deviation than for any other party/regional grouping in the House.

[16] Nevertheless, 11 of the 45 Republicans first elected in 1972 (24.4 percent) lost their seats, compared with 25 (21.2 percent) of the 118 older Republicans.

TABLE 3

New Incumbents versus Old Incumbents: Partisan Percentages and Swing, 1972-1974[a]

		Mean Percentage Democratic 1972	Mean Percentage Democratic 1974	1972-1974 Swing toward Democratic Party
		(N)		
Democratic	NI (13)	60.8	73.1	+12.4
districts	OI (114)	65.8	70.7	+ 5.1
t		(-1.69)	(+0.87)	(+2.95)[b]
Republican	NI (42)	43.4	43.2	- 0.2
districts	OI (96)	33.6	44.2	+10.6
t		(+7.88)[c]	(-0.63)	(-7.44)[c]

[a]Mean percentage swing among all incumbents, +6.6; standard deviation, 9.0. Total number excludes all incumbents without major-party opposition in 1972 or in 1974, and all incumbents from California.
[b]t significant, d.f. = 120, at .005 level.
[c]t significant, d.f. = 120, at .0005 level.

Democrat from Massachusetts (a shift from 50.2 to 74.8 percent Democratic). Whatever else may have been going on in 1974, the electoral careers of at least some new legislators were following the pattern which the incumbent-protection model presupposes.

A congressional election is supposedly a national event, an event whose outcome has been thought to depend at the margins upon the presence or absence of compelling short-term forces of national scope.[17] One would have thought that such national forces were particularly salient in 1974; and indeed they were to some extent influential, as we have pointed out. Yet one obvious inference to be drawn from the party-decomposition model of contemporary American electoral politics is the expectation that diversity of outcomes, influenced by a host of factors peculiar to each individual contest, will become increasingly important as party-in-the-electorate fades. An overview of the 1972–1974 swing as a whole does nothing to challenge this proposition. As Figure 1 makes graphically clear, the 1972–1974 swing outside the South was vastly more heterogeneous than the 1966–1970 swing in Great Britain, and considerably more so than the 1862–1864 swing in the United States.[18]

[17] This is the rationale behind Stokes's argument in "Political Parties and the Nationalization of Electoral Forces."
[18] The variance in the former case was 11.7 times as large as in the latter. Similarly —and excluding the South for both elections—the variance in the 1972–1974 swing was 3.6 times as great as was the variance of the 1862–1864 swing.

FIGURE 1

Comparative Heterogeneity of Partisan Swing: United Kingdom, 1966–1970; and
United States, 1862–1864 and 1972–1974*

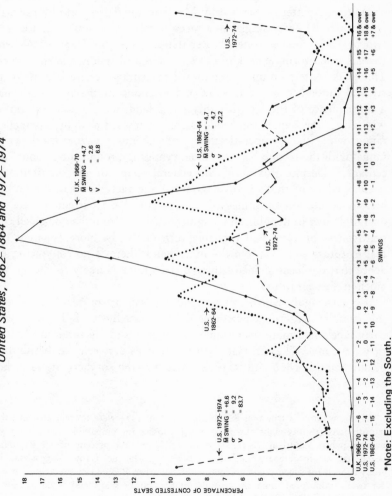

*Note: Excluding the South.

There is a degree of diversity in this swing which, at other times and places, has been curbed by the central importance of party in shaping electoral outcomes. It follows, of course, that any effort to explain the determinants of the 1972–1974 vote swing would require a model of truly formidable complexity.[19]

The distribution of partisan percentages in 1974 is very similar in shape to the pattern described by Mayhew and Tufte; and by now, this should not be surprising.[20] For races involving incumbents, there are two peaks or modes—one for Republicans, one for Democrats—while there is a sharp single peak of cases in the set of nonincumbent contests. This peak centers around the national percentage. There is a major positional difference between 1974 and elections in the immediate past, a consequence of the fact that this was a landslide election. By contrast with 1972, the Republican mode is shifted toward a highly competitive range, while the Democratic mode moves into the 70.0–74.9 percent range, with the trough between them centering around the national percentage.[21] Despite this shift, the general shape of the distribution is unchanged from that of 1972. Granted the fact that nationwide congressional-election outcomes of 59–41 have been extremely rare, the overall danger to Republican incumbents arising from the one-sided competitiveness of 1974 will probably turn out to be more apparent than real in future elections. On the other hand, there is no convincing evidence that the basic shape of these distributions is likely to change very much in the near future.

It is once again worth emphasizing, by way of contrast, how sharply this complex pattern of outcomes differs from those of the past, when party labels had more operational meaning in our electoral politics than they have now. The contrast chosen here is as between the distributions of outcomes in 1866 and in 1974, excluding the southern states in both cases.[22]

---

[19] Thus, while it is true that Republican *losses* in 1974 were concentrated in suburban districts (twenty-eight out of forty-eight losses in comparable districts, or 58.3 percent, while suburban districts constituted only 42.8 percent of all Republican seats), the *swing* data are much less compelling. The mean 1972–1974 swing was +8.3 percent for seventy-one predominantly suburban Republican seats, +5.7 percent for twenty-nine predominantly central-city Republican seats, and +7.9 percent for sixty-six nonmetropolitan Republican seats; and the dispersions around these measures of central tendency are very large in all three cases.

[20] The basic bimodal shape of 1974 outcomes involving incumbents is substantially the same as that graphed for 1972 in Burnham, "American Politics in the 1970s," and quite different from the 1952 distribution presented there.

[21] I.e., in the 55.0–59.9 percent range, precisely the area of *maximum* concentration of outcomes for contests with no incumbents running.

[22] Apart from the need for comparability with Civil War elections, the exclusion

TABLE 4

A Study in Contrast: Distribution of Percentages Democratic by Incumbency and Party, 1866 and 1974

	Percentage of Seats by Category							
	1866				1974			
Percentage	Incumbents			Nonin-	Incumbents			Nonin-
Democratic	R	D	All	cumbents	R	D	All	cumbents
0.0–19.9	5.4	0	4.4	0	0.8	0	0.3	0
20.0–29.9	11.7	0	9.6	9.2	4.7	0	2.1	0
30.0–39.9	24.5	0	20.2	12.3	26.4	0	12.1	0
40.0–44.9	18.1	0	14.9	16.9	20.6	0.7	10.3	8.7
45.0–49.9	34.0	15.0	30.7	27.7	25.6	2.0	12.8	15.2
50.0–54.9	5.3	45.0	12.3	12.3	14.7	4.6	9.3	17.4
55.0–59.9	1.1	15.0	3.5	7.7	3.1	4.6	3.9	28.3
60.0–69.9	0	10.0	1.8	6.1	3.1	25.0	14.9	13.0
70.0–79.9	0	5.0	0.9	6.2	0	35.5	19.2	8.7
80.0–100.0	0	10.0	1.8	1.5	0	27.6	14.9	8.7
N	94	20	114	65	129	152	281	46

What Table 4 stresses most fully is the severe decline in competitiveness and the association of this decline with incumbency. Taking the 40.0–59.9 percent range as broadly competitive, we can actually see marginal improvement in the nonincumbent sets: 64.6 percent of such contests fell within this range in 1866 and 69.6 percent fell within it in 1974. For contests with incumbents running for reelection, however, there is a decline from 61.4 percent in the former year to 36.3 percent in the latter. The effect of this change is magnified by the professionalization of House careers over a century: while nonincumbents contested 36.3 percent of the nonsouthern seats in 1866, they contested only 14.1 percent of them in 1974.

1974 IN LONG-TERM PERSPECTIVE

If we are more fully to appreciate the place of the 1974 election—and its immediate aftermath within the House—in the context of contemporary American politics, we need to see it in its broader historical setting. The time is more than ripe for a detailed quantitative history of congressional elections and of the internal processes of the House of Representatives. This, however, must await another occasion; what is

---

of the South emphasizes the universality of this trend in areas of the United States which did not undergo the massively deviant political evolution found in the ex-Confederate states.

offered here is a summary statement of trends over the past century and their relationship to the outcome of the 1974 election.

1. The competitiveness of congressional elections has been declining persistently ever since the turn of the century, even while the national vote as a whole has remained competitive between the major parties. The South has, of course, been a deviant case. In the aftermath of the region's massively successful movement toward disfranchisement seventy-five years ago, the proportion of seats in southern and border states which were won by 60 percent or less of the total vote declined abruptly from 64.0 percent in 1896 to 20.8 percent in 1902.[23] It has remained below one-third of the total in the ex-slave states ever since. Accordingly, this decline has been particularly marked as a secular trend in the North and West. Between 1874 and 1892, the proportion of contests which were won with 60 percent or less of the total vote in these regions was always more than four-fifths of the total, and was sometimes over nine-tenths.[24] After the critical realignment of the 1890s, a decline set in until, by 1926, competitively won congressional seats reached a low of 35.2 percent of the total.[25] This decline was abruptly and massively reversed with the critical realignment of 1932. But once again, decline in competitiveness reasserted itself: while three-quarters of the seats in the North and West were won by broadly competitive margins in 1932, only half were in 1964.

The bimodal pattern of outcomes favoring incumbents which we have discussed above has been superimposed on this longer-term trend. As a result, the decline in competitiveness since 1964 has not only continued but accelerated. By 1972, only 32.5 percent of the seats in the North and West were won with less than 60 percent of the district vote, the lowest figure since the beginning of the series in 1824. Of course, as the massive Democratic swing ate into the Republican mode in 1974, such seats increased to 43.5 percent of the total; but this remained markedly below the 1964 figure of 51.5 percent and vastly below the 66.1 percent registered in the 1948 election. The improvement in the proportion of competitive seats in 1974 was thus tightly constrained by historical standards. Indeed, this proportion has been *lower* than in 1974 on just six

---

[23] The data for this discussion is from a much larger file, provided by courtesy of the Inter-University Consortium for Political Research.

[24] The 1874–1892 mean was 85.7 percent of all seats in the North and West; the standard deviation was 3.9.

[25] There was a temporary reversal of trend in 1912 and 1914, a result of Progressive and Socialist candidacies in these House elections. But the downward trend resumed dramatically in 1918, an election whose characteristics reveal it to be one of the most important in this century.

occasions in our history. These characteristically occurred in 1926, 1928, and 1966–1972: the former two at the trough of the semioligarchic fourth-party system, and the latter four in the years of party decomposition immediately preceding 1974.

2. As Professor Tufte has demonstrated, the emergence of a bimodal pattern of outcomes favoring incumbents is naturally associated with a sharp drop in the responsiveness of party representation in the House to shifts in the popular vote. The reader can visualize this for himself. If the distribution of outcomes has a cluster or peak centering around the 50 percent mark, small shifts in aggregate vote percentages will produce considerably larger shifts in seats toward the party enjoying a vote swing in its favor. The steeper the peak is, the larger will be this seat turnover for any given size of vote swing. If, on the other hand, the national percentage approximates 50 but there are *two* clusters or peaks far away from this point and a shortage of cases near the competitive center, a relatively wide shift in the vote will produce only very limited gains for the advantaged party.[26]

In the late nineteenth century, the sensitivity of turnover to changes in the major-party vote was extremely high; very often, a shift of 1 percent in a party's vote won it an additional 4 percent or more of seats in the House. Since about 1896 these swing ratios have undergone a generalized but undulating downward trend which closely parallels our other indicators. At the same time, it is clear that as late as 1948, a large swing in the vote could produce a turnover in seats which was higher than the 2.8:1 swing ratio suggested by the so-called cube law, or the rough 2.5:1 ratio suggested by Professor Tufte. The ratio in that year was 3.1:1, for the Democrats gained 7.2 percent of the two-party vote outside the South over 1946, and fully 22.5 percent of the seats.[27] By 1966, on the other hand, the Republicans could gain only 11.9 percent of the nonsouthern seats with a vote shift of 7.3 percent in their favor; the swing ratio was only 1.6:1. As one might expect, 1974— with its swing *away from* competitiveness nationally—stands some-

[26] An unusually good example is the 1968–1970 relationship. The popular-vote swing to the Democrats was 4.0 percent (51.1–55.1 percent of the two-party vote), but they gained only an additional 2.7 percent of the seats for a swing ratio of 0.68. The Democrats gained twelve seats; had the distribution been unimodal and the system otherwise unbiased, they could have expected to gain thirty-nine according to the so-called cube law.

[27] Calculations of swing are of course affected by many possible sources of bias. One of the most important is the concentration of uncontested (usually Democratic) seats in the eleven ex-Confederate states. Removal of this region from analysis provides a rough but fairly effective correction for this factor, particularly when dealing with long time series.

where between the two, but much closer to 1966. The 6.1 percent pro-Democratic swing outside the South produced a seat swing of 12.8 percent, and thus a swing ratio of 2.1:1. It is worth noting that in fifteen of the past sixty congressional elections, a vote swing of 5 percent or more has occurred; of these fifteen, only one—1966, of course —showed a *lower* ratio than 1974. Despite the special factors which led to the defeat of so many Republican incumbents in 1974, this damping down of responsiveness held their losses down. In all probability, considerably more than a dozen Republican incumbents survived the 1974 tide who would have lost under pre-1960 conditions.[28]

3. It is fascinating to observe that aggregate policy differences between the two parties in the House have followed a pattern of decline in the past century which is very similar to those described above. Moreover, this decline has also speeded up very considerably since the early 1960s; in the Ninety-first Congress (1969–1970) the global differences between the parties on roll-call votes reached the lowest point since the creation of the Republican party in the 1850s. The policy measure used here is, of course, a very gross one, an Index of Party Dissimilarity taken across all nonunanimous roll calls in each Congress.[29] Accordingly, it cannot take account of differences in the substantive political importance or weight of any given issue domain. It is nevertheless a useful measure of a very important, and a very long, secular trend.[30] Table 5 summarizes two aspects of change: a general downward trend, but punctuated by upsurges in party polarization or distance. These upsurges chiefly occur in the immediate policy aftermaths of the critical realignments of 1896 and 1932.

In this series too, there has been a speedup over the past decade in a

---

[28] If one uses large-swing election pairs as a criterion—those where the swing was 5.0 percent or more either way—this gain would have ranged from 5 (using the 1918–1920 swing ratio) to 31 (using the 1936–1938 swing ratio) more seats than actually won in 1974, with a mean of 17.

[29] Data courtesy of Inter-University Consortium for Political Research.

The original data are reported in terms of the Index of Party Likeness, a standard roll-call measure and corresponding to the formula

$$1 - \frac{(D_{yes} - R_{yes}) - (D_{no} - R_{no})}{2}$$

where, e.g., D_{yes} is the proportion of Democrats voting yes on an issue. This measure varies from 1.0 (identical) to 0 (total dissimilarity). The Index of Party Dissimilarity simply removes the term $1 -$, so that it ranges from 0 (identical) to 1.0 (total dissimilarity).

[30] A regression of this index on time from the Forty-third Congress (1873–1875) to the Ninety-second (1971–1973) gives an equation of $Y = .624 - .062X$, an r of $-.698$ and an r^2 of .487.

TABLE 5

The Case of the Disappearing Party: Index of Party Dissimilarity in the House, 1873–1973

Period	Congresses	Mean Index of Party Dissimilarity [a]	(Standard Deviation)
1873–1881	43–47	.583	(.019)
1883–1893[b]	48–50, 52–53	.438	(.042)
1895–1911	54–62	.625	(.087)
1913–1931	63–72	.424	(.059)
1933–1939	73–76	.529	(.038)
1941–1951	77–82	.397	(.020)
1953–1963	83–88	.357	(.030)
1965–1971	89–92	.250	(.049)

[a]The higher the mean score, the more dissimilar the voting of the two parties in roll-call votes.

[b]The index of .713 for the fifty-first Congress (1889–1891) is abnormally high; the explanation for this is to be found in the large number of procedural votes taken during Speaker Reed's struggle to establish centralized House rules over bitter Democratic opposition. If it is included, the mean for the period becomes .484 and the standard deviation becomes .109.

longer-term trend toward the erosion of party in the political process. To say the least, this forms an arresting context for the 1975 effort by House Democratic liberals to restore the importance of party in that body's decisional structure.

4. All of the long-term trends discussed so far are associated in time with another which promises to be of very great importance to the workings of the American policy process as a whole in the near future. Put at its simplest, there has been greater and greater divergence in presidential and congressional voting coalitions since the turn of the century. One way of measuring this phenomenon is to test the state-by-state relationships between the Democratic percentages of the vote for the two offices in presidential years, when both offices are voted for at the same time. Table 6 summarizes this twentieth-century trend, partitioning the country into southern and nonsouthern regions. As is obvious, the trend is broadly downward, but with many countervailing movements in the nonsouthern states. The lag in reintegrating the party system after the New Deal realignment in these states is conspicuously evident. More to the immediate point, this trend toward divergence of electoral coalitions, like so many others, has markedly accelerated in the past fifteen years.

It is particularly worthy of note that the proportion of the variance in the nonsouthern congressional vote which can be explained by the

TABLE 6

Party Decomposition, 1900–1972[a]

		United States				Nonsouthern States		
		Correlation between Percentage Democratic of the Congressional and the Presidential				Correlation between Percentage Democratic of the Congressional and the Presidential		
Year	N	Vote (r)	(r²)	(Sy · x)	N	Vote (r)	(r²)	(Sy · x)
1900	45	+.978	(.956)	(3.33)	34	+.984	(.968)	(1.30)
1904	45	+.973	(.946)	(4.77)	34	+.874	(.763)	(3.92)
1908	46	+.928	(.861)	(7.33)	35	+.870	(.757)	(3.64)
1912	48	+.961	(.923)	(5.78)	37	+.824	(.679)	(4.76)
1916	48	+.931	(.867)	(7.03)	37	+.663	(.440)	(6.94)
1920	48	+.950	(.903)	(7.29)	37	+.857	(.735)	(6.38)
1924	48	+.930	(.865)	(8.70)	37	+.758	(.574)	(9.16)
1928	48	+.810	(.656)	(12.36)	37	+.490	(.240)	(8.37)
1932	48	+.907	(.822)	(7.20)	37	+.555	(.308)	(6.96)
1936	48	+.908	(.825)	(7.24)	37	+.634	(.402)	(7.37)
1940	48	+.920	(.846)	(8.19)	37	+.692	(.478)	(8.47)
1944	48	+.941	(.885)	(6.69)	37	+.819	(.671)	(4.90)
1948	48	+.941	(.885)	(6.32)	37	+.812	(.659)	(5.56)
1952	48	+.861	(.742)	(9.96)	37	+.871	(.758)	(3.96)
1956	48	+.717	(.514)	(11.77)	37	+.755	(.570)	(4.28)
1960	50	+.368	(.136)	(14.83)	39	+.651	(.424)	(5.36)
1964	50	−.265	(.070)	(10.37)	39	+.579	(.335)	(5.62)
1968	50	−.274	(.075)	(12.27)	39	+.470	(.221)	(7.14)
1972	50	−.071	(.005)	(11.54)	39	+.335	(.112)	(9.24)

[a]In the South, 1948, the figure is based on combined presidential percentages for Democratic and Dixiecratic candidates.

presidential vote has declined from over one-half in 1956 to little more than one-tenth in 1972. Viewing the national system as a whole, however, the impact of the South's secession from the presidential Democratic coalition since the 1950s is of at least equal political importance.

Much has been written about split-ticket voting and the newer independent element in the electorate. But this partisan decay cannot fail to have massive effects on the political system at the center as well. As Republicans have come to win the White House more often than Democrats in the past two decades, so their base of support in Congress has become increasingly eroded. The dissolution of the partisan nexus that used to link the two branches of government involves an enormous and very recent reinforcement of the separation of powers, and of the mutual conflicts between persons in office, which the drafters of the Constitution sought to prescribe two centuries ago. The result of the 1974 election sharpens the basic problems of governing which this situation presupposes. Despite the large Democratic victory, this pattern of coalitional dissociation also means that the outcome of the 1974 congressional election tells us precisely nothing about which party's candidate will win the presidency in 1976. It would seem more likely than not that this dissociation at the base will be linked at the center with an ongoing concern of presidents of either party: how to get and maintain an adequate base of support in Congress.

5. In one crucial respect, 1974 reflects not merely similarity to trends of the immediate and more remote past, but their extension. For some years past the rate of participation in American elections has been declining in both presidential and off years. This decline accelerated dramatically in 1974. National turnout, at 37 percent for House contests, fell very nearly to the all-time lows registered in the 1920s and in the wartime election of 1942. Even this low national turnout does not tell the whole story. Recent southern elections, stimulated by the Civil Rights Acts of 1965 and 1970, have seen increases in off-year congressional turnout to levels not reached since the early twentieth century. When the South is excluded, the 41.0 percent participation rate in 1974 becomes the second lowest since the creation of the party system in the Jacksonian era. For many states such as Indiana, the 1974 turnout was the lowest of all time.

As the introduction of women's suffrage cannot account for the steep drop in participation in 1918, so the enfranchisement of eighteen- to twenty-year olds in 1971 cannot begin to account wholly for the 1970–1974 decline. Similarly, despite some Republican claims to the contrary, there is no very good reason to suppose that the abysmal participation rate in 1974 was the result of one-sided abstentions of GOP supporters in the wake of Watergate. On the contrary, it is much more likely that the recent decline in voting participation is part of a current syndrome of party decomposition and widespread, generalized public dissatisfaction with politics as such.[31] To the extent that this is so, it would follow that Republican prospects, if any, for recovering the bulk of their con-

---

[31] The evidence for this growing disillusionment is now quite impressive. For one example, see the first survey ever commissioned by the Congress, Louis Harris' *Confidence and Concern: Citizens View American Government*, Committee on Government Operations. U. S. Senate, 93d Congress, 1st Sess. (December 3, 1973).

gressional losses must lie elsewhere. The year 1974 resembles the immediate past closely enough to permit the prediction that many of the seventy-five Democratic newcomers will have begun successfully to entrench themselves by 1976.

This decline in voting participation is a massive political fact. In the 1870–1894 period, outside the South, off-year participation averaged 68.1 percent; as late as 1914, it was 59.6 percent. More recently, it has been poor but stable, averaging 51.3 percent between 1950 and 1970. Whether the drop to 41 percent in 1974 is temporary only the future will show. But insofar as it is associated with major increases in levels of public alienation, this colossal abstention rate intrudes an element of uncertainty into any predictions. It also, of course, raises serious questions about "American democracy" as a whole. It would be reasonable to suppose, on past form, that the system can remain both stable and electorally demobilized. But it would have taken the participation of 11 million more voters than actually came to the polls in 1974 to return participation even to its mediocre 1970 level. One wonders what conditions might stimulate them to enter, or return to, the active electorate.[32]

The Present and the Near Future

So it is that a complex system behaves like a system. As party erodes both in the electorate and in the House, divergence in the electoral coalitions of president and Congress increasingly reinforces the separation of powers; incumbents tend increasingly to be protected or insulated, except to some extent in abnormal cases like 1974; the responsiveness of the representational system to electoral change declines; and abstention from the polls becomes the largest mass movement of our time. To this one may add that the events of the past decade have produced a new institutional balance between executive and legislature, and a larger autonomous importance for Congress than it has had in many decades.

In this context, the immediate aftermath of this election almost startles the observer. The greatest reorganization of power within the House has occurred since the great anti-speaker revolt of 1910. The importance of central party mechanisms in the majority's decisional processes has been strikingly reasserted. It is just possible that the first steps may have been taken to develop a collective will which alone can

---

[32] Of course, if the mean 1838–1894 off-year turnout rate had been realized in the 1974 congressional election, the added increment would have been on the order of 38 million.

permit a serious competition for influence over policy with the executive. Very clearly, the new Democratic freshmen have taken a central part in all this. From the viewpoint developed here, this is the more remarkable, since the proportion of freshmen is not much different than in 1965, and is very much smaller than it was in 1949. To be sure, the totals of newcomers become more impressive when one adds reelected 1972 freshmen to the 1974 newcomers. These constitute 129 members of the House (29.7 percent of the whole), a respectable rate of turnover by contemporary standards. Even so, one would have thought that an antiseniority generational interest has always existed among newcomers to Congress. Why the change in 1975?

Of course, we do not yet possess a complete voting profile on the 1974 newcomers, but the probabilities are that most of them entered the House on the "left" end of the Democratic policy spectrum. It is fair to assume that these newcomers in the main reflect a new politics, a new age generation and, in some measure, a public dissatisfaction with the older political styles of the Johnson and Nixon years. But another factor is the long-term regional transformation in party coalitions in Congress; and the cumulative effects of this change are very likely of crucial importance for the events of early 1975. The revolt of 1910 against Speaker Cannon had been preceded by both a long-term solidification of the seniority norm within the House and by the replacement of conventions by direct primaries for congressional nominations outside of it. The current change appears to reflect not only the increased importance of the "new politics" in the House, but also a recent and rapid decline in the South's relative weight in the congressional Democratic party.

After the 1974 election, southern representatives constituted only 27.8 percent of the total House Democratic membership, and 18.8 percent of all House Republicans. This is the lowest proportion of southerners to all Democrats since 1870, and the highest proportion of southerners to all Republicans since 1872. Moreover, there has been a persistent pro-Democratic countervailing trend elsewhere over the past generation, especially in the Northeast and the Midwest. These movements parallel, at a much slower pace, well-known changes in the regional bases of party support in recent presidential elections. Assuming that these trends continue, at some point between 1980 and 1985 the South will be represented in both congressional parties in proportion to its share of the whole House for the first time since the 1840s,[33] though this may be only the prelude to an eventual one-party Republicanism outside the region's metropolitan areas (see Table 7).

[33] In the 1972–1980 period, 24.8 percent of the whole House.

TABLE 7

Shifting Party Bases in the House by Region, 1940-1974 [a]

Region	Percentage Democratic Seats			Y_c		(r^2)	$(S_{y \cdot x})$
	1948	1964	1974	a	b		
Northeast	46.7	66.1	67.6	33.99 + 1.55X		(.543)	(7.84)
Midwest	36.4	49.6	54.1	20.32 + 1.34X		(.443)	(8.26)
West	49.0	68.1	65.8	46.62 + 0.64X		(.106)	(10.30)
Border	88.1	80.6	82.9	73.50 + 0.31X		(.033)	(9.23)
South	98.1	84.9	75.0	105.55 − 1.74X		(.841)	(4.16)
U.S.A.	60.6	67.8	66.9	52.76 + 0.47X		(.167)	(5.84)
	Percentage Democratic and Republican Seats from Given Regions						
	A. Democrats						
North and West	46.8	59.7	62.2	38.03 + 1.24X		(.709)	(4.36)
South	39.2	30.5	27.8	48.25 − 1.04X		(.619)	(4.49)
	B. Republicans						
North and West	95.9	83.6	77.1	98.48 − 1.04X		(.783)	(3.02)
South	1.2	11.4	18.8	−3.78 + 1.10X		(.863)	(2.40)

[a]Biennial series, based on percentage Democratic of the two-party total of seats.
Regions: Northeast—New England, Middle Atlantic, Delaware; Midwest-East North Central, West North Central except Missouri; West—Mountain, Pacific; Border—Kentucky, Maryland, Missouri, Oklahoma, West Virginia; South—eleven ex-Confederate states.

In connection with these trends, it is important to point out that southern Democrats are today the most heterogeneous regional grouping in the House, so far as policy scores are concerned. On the other hand, the growth of the southern Republican contingent has involved the entry of people who are overwhelmingly and cohesively on the far right of the congressional GOP. There are two apparent reasons for this. First, the growth of urbanism in the South has brought with it an influx of moderate and liberal Democratic representatives in such areas, including the three black representatives first elected in 1972 or 1974. Second, ultraconservative Democrats have been increasingly replaced by ultraconservative Republicans. There are some interesting recent examples of this. In 1972, Trent Lott and Thad Cochran won the fourth and fifth Mississippi districts, once held for many years by John Bell Williams and William Colmer, when their incumbents chose to retire. The sixth Louisiana district had been held since 1966 by John Rarick, a Democrat whom the authors of *The Almanac of American Politics* flatly describe as "the most rabidly right-wing member of Congress."[34] Rarick lost the 1974 Democratic primary to a more moderate Democrat, who in turn lost in November to W. Henson Moore, III, a Republican, by an apparent majority of fourteen votes. Moore then resigned, a new election was held, and he won easily.

Perhaps an even more interesting case is that of Congressman John Jarman, who from 1950 to 1975 represented the fifth Oklahoma district (Oklahoma City) as a Democrat. Jarman is a conservative, and appeared to fit the district: it gave Nixon 76.0 percent of its presidential vote in 1972. But the congressman encountered more than usual difficulty that year, winning only 60.4 percent of the vote. Still worse was the result in 1974, when he won reelection with only 51.7 percent, a swing of -8.7 percent in a Democratic year. Following the caucus votes which removed Representatives Hebert, Patman, and Poage from the chairmanships of the Committees on Armed Services, Banking and Currency, and Agriculture, Jarman announced in January 1975 that he was joining the Republican party. He gave as his reason the view that the Democratic party in the House was being captured by the same elements that had nominated George McGovern in 1972. There is no doubt that, with a -76 score on our index, Jarman will feel more at home in the ranks of congressional Republicans. At the same time, he may well improve his chances of reelection in this conservative district.

Such cases may prove to be as isolated as that of Strom Thurmond, who joined what he called the "Goldwater Republican" party in 1964. But there has been an interesting trickle of defections in recent years. These have also included Ogden Reid of New York and, most recently, Donald Riegle of Michigan—both liberal Republicans who crossed the aisle to join the Democrats. It may well be argued that the chief motivating force which has bound conservative southerners to the congressional Democratic party recently has been the disproportionate power over the legislative process which was given to them by seniority and associated norms of committee activity. The congressional power game is more complex now. Seniority has by no means been wholly abandoned as a selection device. But it prevails only so long as the policy stance and personality of the chairman involved do not deviate too widely from the majority's preferences. The implications of this for the motivations of conservative southerners to remain Democrats are obvious.

Leaving aside newcomers, there are forty House Democrats—thirty-seven southerners and three others—who have scores of -40 or lower on

[34] Michael Barone et al., *The Almanac of American Politics 1974* (Boston, 1974), p. 398.

our index. Were they all to defect to the Republicans, the Democratic gains of 1974 would be virtually wiped out and a new balance of 255 Democrats to 185 Republicans would be created. But there would be other consequences as well. In the first place, the liberal policy majority in the Democratic caucus would become overwhelmingly large. Secondly, the minority of liberal Republicans would become even more hopelessly isolated within the congressional GOP than it is now; and this could well prompt other Riegles to join the Democrats. The end product of any such large-scale movement would be, presumably, the creation of a "more responsible two-party system" in Congress and the realization of the dreams of many programmatic reformers. On past form, one would have to suppose that such a shift will tend to remain relatively gradual in the very near term rather than abrupt or massive, but there is very little reason to suppose that the coalitional trends underlying it will be reversed. A necessary paradox of this movement, so far as programmatic liberals are concerned, is that it constitutes the only significant chance the Republicans have to capture the House of Representatives at all within the foreseeable future.[35]

The entire context of the 1974 election, no less than the striking mixture of diverse movements in its result, suggests that it marks a turning point in the current crisis sequence which has been affecting American electoral politics as a whole. Moreover, it is associated with a swing in the institutional balance between president and Congress toward the latter, the first such swing in many decades. For many quite deterministic reasons, this will not mean the emergence of anything approximating "congressional government" even in the short term. But for some time to come, the autonomous policy importance of the legislative branch will probably be enhanced to a degree scarcely imagined by political analysts of even a few years ago. It would seem very probable, therefore, that scholarly attention in the field of electoral politics will also shift toward Congress. To be sure, much important work has been done on congressional elections, both by the Michigan survey research center group and by others.[36] But there is little doubt that the lion's share of

[35] A shift of forty conservative Democrats into the Republican party in the House, retrojected into the recent past, would have given control of that body to the GOP in four of the last eight congressional elections (1966, 1968, 1970, and 1972), assuming no countervailing defections from the extreme left of the congressional Republican party.

[36] See, for example, the articles on congressional elections and electorates in Angus Campbell et al., *Elections and the Political Order*; Stokes, "Political Parties and the Nationalization of Electoral Forces"; Milton Cummings, *Congressmen and the Electorate* (New York, 1966); and, perhaps especially, William McPhee and Bernard Berelson (eds.), *Public Opinion and Congressional Elections* (New York, 1962).

analysis has hitherto been devoted to presidential electorates and elections. As it becomes clearer that electoral coalitions are increasingly diverging on office-specific lines, and that Congress will retain considerable importance in its own right, it can be hoped and expected that more scholarly effort will be made in this area. A great many lacunae still exist in our knowledge of the past development and present structure of American congressional elections.

7 Election Campaign Financing: The 1974 Reforms

DAVID ADAMANY
GEORGE AGREE

The Federal Campaign Act of 1974[1] marks a major turning point in the regulation of political finance in the United States. First, it implements to an unprecedented degree the principal reform approaches born in the Progressive era, by placing ceilings on campaign expenditures, by setting low limits on contributions and imposing strict limits on the aggregate donations of individuals, by strengthening already sweeping requirements for full disclosure of campaign finances, and by establishing an independent agency to enforce political finance regulations. Second, as a major innovation, the act introduces public financing of campaigns—a step taken earlier by other democracies and by the American Commonwealth of Puerto Rico, widely debated in the United States, but not enacted on the state or national level until the Watergate era.

---

[1] Federal Election Campaign Act of 1974, Public Law 93–443, 93d Cong., 2d Sess., 1974.

DAVID ADAMANY is professor of political science at the University of Wisconsin-Madison and is presently serving as Wisconsin's secretary of revenue. He is the author of *Financing Politics; Campaign Finance in America;* and *Campaign Funds as an Intraparty Resource.* GEORGE AGREE is director of the Committee for the Democratic Process. He formerly served as executive director of the National Committee for an Effective Congress, and he was active in developing the 1967 voucher plan for publicly financing presidential campaigns. David Adamany and George Agree are also coauthors of the book, *Political Money.*

Whether the 1974 Campaign Act will ever be fully implemented is an open question: a number of original supporters of campaign finance reform are having second thoughts about the policy implications of some of the act's features. Its very constitutionality is being challenged in a lawsuit brought by an unlikely coalition including Senator James Buckley, former Senator Eugene McCarthy, the New York Civil Liberties Union, and the Conservative party of New York. The Supreme Court is expected to decide their case before the end of 1975; and, whatever their decision, the justices will thereby delineate important new parameters for the conduct of American elections.

THE BACKDROP

Congress first began to regulate the aspects of campaign financing covered by the 1974 act in 1910. That year, legislation was enacted that required candidates for senator and representative and political committees operating in two or more states—i.e., committees for presidential candidates—to file with the clerk of the House of Representatives reports of contributions of over $100 received and of persons to whom payments of more than $10 were made. Over the years these reports were fragmentary and incomplete; the law did not provide effective enforcement machinery for ensuring the disclosures mandated, nor did it require reports on contributions or payments made for primary campaigns. With the passage in 1925 of the Corrupt Practices Act, Congress set ceilings on campaign spending at $2500 to $5000 for a House candidate and at $10,000 to $25,000 for a Senate candidate.

In 1940, amendments to the 1939 Hatch Act set ceilings of $3 million on spending by political committees operating in two or more states. The Hatch Act amendments also prohibited contributions of more than $5000 a year by an individual to a candidate for an elective federal office or to a committee campaigning on behalf of such candidates. These limitations were all easily evaded, both by candidates proliferating the number of committees making expenditures on their behalf and by wealthy individuals making a multiplicity of contributions in the names of different members of their families.

Since 1907 Congress has also placed prohibitions on the sources from which political contributions may come. In that year, corporations were prohibited from making political contributions and expenditures. This ban was extended to public utility holding companies and their subsidiaries in 1935 and to labor unions by wartime legislation in 1943 and then permanently by the Taft-Hartley Act in 1947. The law, however, does permit expenditures by corporations and unions to communicate to stockholders, union members, and their families, to sponsor nonpartisan registration and get-out-the-vote drives, and to operate segregated voluntary political funds. These prohibitions and exceptions were left unchanged by the 1974 act.

The modern thrust toward reform of national political financing practices dates from the report of President Kennedy's Commission on Campaign Costs in 1962, which urged full disclosure of campaign financing, with a separate agency to enforce the laws.[2] Following the pattern established in 1952 by Florida's "sunshine law,"[3] the commission urged that disclosure would sufficiently regulate political money and that "the present meaningless ceilings on individual contributions and on total expenditures . . . be abolished." If other measures failed to curb abuses, the commission suggested that the government match private contributions to candidates up to $10 with federal tax funds. In the meantime, the commission suggested a more modest government role: federal tax deductions and credits for modest campaign gifts.

In 1966 President Johnson recommended tax incentives for small political contributions and sweeping full disclosure of political finances. His proposals were overshadowed, however, by Senator Russell Long's bolder move to allow citizens to check off $1 of their income taxes to finance presidential general election campaigns.[4] Long's masterful advocacy, his influence as chairman of the Senate Finance Committee and as assistant majority leader, and his superior parliamentary skills helped steer this pioneering measure through the Senate, then through the conference committee, and finally into law.

In 1967, however, Republicans and disaffected liberal Democrats—some moved by opposition to the president's foreign policy, others by fear that public financing would strengthen the president's hand politically— joined to suspend operation of the check-off, which Mr. Johnson had heartily endorsed. The debate stretched over five weeks and required thirteen roll calls. In defeat, Senator Long and the president demonstrated that public financing of campaigns commanded undreamed of support in the Senate.

In September 1970, Congress moved in a wholly different direction, re-

[2] President's Commission on Campaign Costs, *Financing Presidential Campaigns* (Washington, D.C., 1962).

[3] See Elston E. Roady, "Florida's New Campaign Expense Law and the 1952 Democratic Gubernatorial Primaries," *American Political Science Review*, 48 (June 1954), 465–476. For a more comprehensive survey of the law's operation see Roady, "Ten Years of Florida's 'Who Gave It—Who Got It' Law," *Law and Contemporary Problems*, 27 (Summer 1962), 434–454.

[4] For an extended description of the maneuvering surrounding the Long Plan, see Herbert E. Alexander, "The Presidential Election Campaign Fund Act: The American Subsidy that Wasn't," *Jahrbuch Des Öffentlichen Rechts Der Gegenwart*, Neue Folge/ Band 17, pp. 597–614.

sponding to the emergence of television advertising as a major force in campaigns. The Political Broadcast Act of 1970 limited radio and television spending by candidates for federal offices and for governor and lieutenant-governor in both primaries and general elections.[5] It also repealed the equal-time provision of the Federal Communications Act in presidential campaigns, opening the way for media debates between major party candidates in 1972. The act fell victim to President Nixon's veto, which was sustained by the Senate.

In 1972, Congress again passed campaign finance legislation and the president reluctantly approved it. The Federal Election Campaign Act of 1971 required the most comprehensive disclosure of campaign contributions and expenditures in American history.[6] It also imposed limits on spending for media advertising and on expenditures by candidates and their families. While the Senate secretary and House clerk continued as depositories for finance disclosures by candidates for the respective houses, the comptroller-general was given those duties for presidential candidates and national committees. His vigorous discharge of those responsibilities in 1972 was instrumental in persuading Congress that independent enforcement should be included in the 1974 act. The 1971 act repealed the spending limits and the $3000 contribution limits of the Corrupt Practices Act of 1925. Like the President's Commission, Congress apparently believed such limits were unworkable and that full disclosure would adequately police campaign financing.

In the Revenue Act of 1971, Congress went further.[7] It enacted tax deductions and credits for small campaign contributions. Faced with a national committee debt of $9 million on the eve of the 1972 campaign, national Democratic party leaders renewed their push for a tax check-off and Senate Democrats added this feature as an amendment to the act. Fearful that the president would veto the whole measure, which was intended to spur the lagging national economy, Representative Wilbur Mills and the other House conferees insisted the tax check-off be deferred. As passed, the act provided only that taxpayers could begin

[5] The legislative politics and the provisions of the Broadcast Act are detailed in Robert L. Peabody, Jeffrey M. Berry, William G. Frasure, and Jerry Goldman, *To Enact a Law* (New York, 1972).

[6] The Federal Election Campaign Act of 1971, Public Law 92–225, 92d Cong., 2d Sess., 1972. The politics, provisions, and early administration of the act are described in Jeffrey M. Berry and Jerry Goldman, "Congress and Public Policy: A Study of the Federal Election Campaign Act of 1971," *Harvard Journal on Legislation*, 10 (February 1973), 331–365; also, Herbert E. Alexander, *Money in Politics* (Washington, D.C., 1972), pp. 305–312.

[7] The Revenue Act of 1971, Public Law 92–178, 92d Cong., 2d Sess., 1972, Title VII (tax deductions and credits) and Title VIII (the Presidential Election Campaign Fund Act of 1971).

checking off for the Presidential Election Campaign Fund on their 1973 tax returns; appropriation of the money for campaigns would require further congressional action.

New Impetus for Reform

The aftermath of the 1972 election made comprehensive campaign finance legislation inevitable. First, the full disclosure provisions of the 1971 act revealed campaign financing patterns that startled and shocked public officials as well as citizens and the press. Campaign expenditures for all nomination and election contests at the local, state, and national levels rose from an estimated $300 million in 1968 to about $425 million in 1972.[8] The Nixon presidential campaign managers spent a staggering $56 million—more than double the previous high of $25 million reached in the 1968 Nixon-Agnew canvass. The McGovern-Shriver ticket spent $49 million, more than four times Hubert Humphrey's 1968 costs. Congressional campaign spending rose from an estimated $71.6 million in 1970 to more than $77.2 million in 1972.[9]

It also became clear that the media-spending limits enacted in 1972 had little or no effect on campaign outlays.[10] While presidential media spending was down, this apparently stemmed from changing political strategies rather than legal limitations. Few congressional candidates were affected by the limits, as several analysts showed. And in rare instances where the limits were reached, campaign money was displaced to other purposes.

Revelations about fund raising were even more striking. The Nixon campaign desperately attempted to conceal its money sources by collecting vast sums before the effective date of the 1971 act. Forced to disclose

---

[8] The expenditure estimates from 1952 to 1968 are reported in Alexander, *Money in Politics*, p. 34. The 1972 estimate is by David Adamany and George Agree, *Political Money: A Strategy for Campaign Financing in America* (Baltimore, 1975), p. 19.

[9] Presidential campaign expenses for 1968 are found in Herbert E. Alexander, *Financing the 1968 Election* (Lexington, Mass., 1971), pp. 80 (Nixon), 84–85 (Humphrey), 89 (Wallace). Those for 1972 are based on Office of Federal Elections, *Report of 1972 Presidential Campaign Receipts and Expenditures* (Washington, D.C., 1974). The 1970 congressional figures are from Alexander, *Money in Politics*, p. 24. The 1972 data are reported in Common Cause Campaign Finance Monitoring Project, *1972 Congressional Campaign Finances*, 10 vols. (Washington, D.C., 1974), p. vii. The 1972 congressional figures probably understate true expenditures, because they are based on official reports filed under the 1971 act, which did not go into effect until April 7, 1972. The 1972 presidential spending statements have been supplemented to include pre-April 7 outlays.

[10] Adamany and Agree, *Political Money*, chap. 5. Also, Comment, "Campaign Spending Controls under the Federal Election Campaign Act of 1971," *Columbia Journal of Law and Social Problems*, 8 (1972), 309–312, 317–319.

by Common Cause lawsuits, the president's men acknowledged raising $16.8 million (28 percent of all funds) from 124 contributors of $50,000 or more.[11] Studies by Representative Les Aspin showed that the Committee for the Re-Election of the President obtained $5.4 million from officials of the 100 largest defense contractors and almost $5 million from officials of 178 leading oil companies.[12] Dozens of corporations and corporate officers would ultimately be found criminally guilty of using company funds for political donations.[13]

Second, despite the most extensive media and mail appeals in history, only 12 percent of Americans contributed to politics in 1972— the same percentage that gave in 1960 and 1964.[14] The newly enacted tax incentives did not expand political giving; only 2.5 percent of taxpayers took the credit and only 1.3 percent used the deduction.[15] Treasury figures reveal that high-income taxpayers used tax incentives very disproportionately.

Further, the Internal Revenue Service, apparently reflecting the Nixon administration position, buried the 1973 tax check-off option on a separate schedule deep in the tax booklet. Only 3 percent of taxpayers checked off. In the summer of 1973, however, Congress forced the IRS to put the check-off option on the front of the 1974 returns, and participation leaped to 15 percent (compared to a previous high of citizen giving in congressional years of 9 percent).[16] The 1974 experience encouraged further experimentation with the check-off.

Third, public attitudes toward reform were changing dramatically. In 1964, opinion polls showed Americans rejected public financing of presidential campaigns by a lopsided 71 percent to 11 percent. By the fall of 1973, the public mood had reversed itself: 65 percent favored tax support for both presidential and congressional campaigns; only 24 percent opposed it. A year later public support had increased to 67 percent.[17]

---

[11] Adamany and Agree, *Political Money*, p. 32.

[12] Office of Representative Les Aspin, "Study Shows Defense Contractors Gave $5.4 Million to Nixon Campaign" (Washington, D.C., 1972). "Oil Companies: $5-Million in Donations to Nixon," *Congressional Quarterly Weekly Report*, 32, no. 3 (January 19, 1974), 113–115.

[13] Center for Public Financing of Elections, *Progress Report No. 8* (Washington, D.C., May 17, 1974), pp. 2–3.

[14] The 1972 figure is from a nationwide poll conducted by the National Opinion Research Center of the University of Chicago for the Twentieth Century Fund Project on Campaign Financing. The earlier years are reported in Alexander, *Money in Politics*, pp. 335–336.

[15] Adamany and Agree, *Political Money*, chap. 7.

[16] "Campaign Fund Tax Check-Off Gains in Users," *Congressional Quarterly Weekly Report*, 32, no. 27 (July 6, 1974), 1742–1744.

[17] The 1964 figures are from a nationwide poll by the Survey Research Center of

Fourth, an effective lobby for campaign finance reform, especially public financing, emerged for the first time. The spearhead was Common Cause, which brought to the fray substantial resources—a relatively large, well-educated, and attentive membership; ample funds; a skilled Washington staff; and a genius for winning media attention. In addition to the usual techniques of legislative lobbying, Common Cause used meticulous research and relentless litigation to good advantage. Its 1972 congressional campaign finance monitoring project revealed the amounts spent, the size of gifts, the special interest contributions, and the money edge of incumbents in every congressional race in the country.

Joined with Common Cause were the Center for the Public Financing of Elections, union labor, the National Committee for an Effective Congress, the League of Women Voters, the National Women's Political Caucus, and others. The center reported in December 1973 that eighteen groups were coordinating legislative strategy to enact public financing. Most important, the nation's leading newspapers overwhelmingly endorsed campaign reform, including public subsidies. Even those with strong conservative leanings, such as the *Los Angeles Times* and columnist James Kilpatrick, who had previously opposed public financing, now found it meritorious.

Fifth, Watergate greatly influenced the climate of opinion in which Congress acted. Watergate itself involved already illegal uses of money—unreported contributions and expenditures, illegal funding sources, financing of criminal activities, and the rest. Watergate's effect, however, was to arouse public opinion against current political practices of other kinds; the congressional response was reform in many quarters, often unrelated directly to any specific conduct surrounding the Watergate burglary.

Sixth, there was a host of reform precedents and examples for Congress to follow. Public sentiment was reflected first in the states, and more than forty legislatures enacted a rich variety of new campaign finance regulations before Congress and the president finally acted. Six states included public financing provisions in their statutory revisions: Iowa, Minnesota, Montana, Rhode Island, and Utah adopted tax check-off plans, and New Jersey enacted a system of public matching grants for private contributions.

Finally, presidential influence was eroded, and the opposition of Richard Nixon and then Gerald Ford to public financing of campaigns counted little in the legislative process. Nixon's weakness was Watergate and the

---

the University of Michigan. The 1973 and 1974 figures are found in George Gallup, "U.S. Financing of Campaigns," *San Francisco Chronicle*, September 19, 1974, p. 6.

rising impeachment tide. Despite a March 8 warning that he would veto any public financing measure, the Senate passed a sweeping bill on April 11, 1974. A Republican staffer then said, "The White House won't be an influence in the House among middle-of-the-road Republicans because it has totally lost credibility."[18] Furthermore, since members of Congress believe themselves expert in campaign financing questions, they were less reliant for information on the Executive and would give less weight to its opinions.

THE POLITICS OF ENACTMENT

Passage of the 1974 act was witnessed by the bitter and protracted legislative maneuvering that frequently signals changes in underlying rules of politics and therefore presages permanent shifts in political power. On July 30, 1973, the Senate passed S. 372, providing spending and contribution limits, strengthening full disclosure, and establishing an independent enforcement agency.[19] An amendment by Senators Edward Kennedy and Hugh Scott, providing public subsidies in general election campaigns for Congress, was tabled by a vote of fifty-three to thirty-eight.[20] But its proponents' strength suggested that for the first time a majority of the Senate might support public subsidies for congressional as well as presidential races.

Campaign reform was quietly stalled in the House, where Representative Wayne Hays, chairman of the Administration Committee and Representative John Dent, chairman of its Subcommittee on Elections, held protracted hearings through the end of the session.[21] Impatient with the House delay, the Senate, in November 1973 used a temporary debt ceiling extension bill as a vehicle to pass public financing for both presiden-

---

[18] "Campaign Reform: Public Financing Faces House Test," *Congressional Quarterly Weekly Report*, 32, no. 19 (May 11, 1974), 1213.

[19] S. 372, 93d Cong., 1st Sess., 1973. Both the Commerce Committee and the Rules and Administration Committee had considered S. 372, because its provisions overlapped their respective jurisdictions. See, U. S. Congress, Senate, Committee on Commerce, *The Federal Election Campaign Act of 1973*, 93d Cong., 1st Sess., 1973, Sen. Rept. 93–170; and U. S. Congress, Senate, Committee on Rules and Administration, *Federal Election Campaign Act of 1973*, 93d Cong., 1st Sess., 1973, Sen. Rept. 93–310.

Debate on S. 372 is found at U.S., *Congressional Record*, 93d Cong., 1st Sess., 1973, vol. 119, July 25, S14683–14717; July 26, S14782–14822; July 27, S14829–14832, S14838–14868; July 28, S14973–14980, S14982–15005; July 30, S15064–15097.

[21] The debate is found ibid., July 26, S14803–14816, and the roll call at S14816.

[21] The committee maneuvering by Representatives Hays and Dent is described in *Congressional Quarterly Weekly Report*, 31, no. 40 (October 6, 1973), 2666–2667 and no. 48 (December 1, 1973), 3147.

tial and congressional general elections and for presidential primary races.[22] A compromise worked out between Senate and House leaders to retain the presidential public financing provisions at final passage floundered when Senate opponents filibustered it to death.[23]

On April 11, 1974, the Senate passed S. 3044, which would ultimately become the 1974 act. It combined provisions of S. 372 with public financing of both primary and general election campaigns for both president and Congress. Senate action came after the bill's supporters overcame a filibuster by winning only the fourteenth of seventy-six cloture votes taken since the adoption of Rule 22 in 1917.[24]

The House continued its delay until August 8, 1974. Its bill added one new feature, public financing of presidential nominating conventions. But it rejected public financing of congressional campaigns and approved only a weak enforcement agency.[25]

Even the Conference Committee was the scene of bitter disagreement. The House objected to the Senate conferees, who were drawn not only

[22] H.R. 11104, 93d Cong., 1st Sess., 1973. The debate is reported in U.S., *Congressional Record*, 93d Cong., 1st Sess., vol. 119, November 27, S21148–21197, S21210–21125.

[23] Maneuvering in the House to save the public financing provisions of the bill is described in "Sen. Allen Delays Action on Campaign Reform, Debt Bill," *Congressional Quarterly Weekly Report*, 31, no. 48 (December 1, 1973), 3163. The House discussion and vote returning H.R. 11104 to the Senate is found in U.S., *Congressional Record*, 93d Cong., 1st Sess., vol. 119, November 29, H10312–10318.

The extended Senate debate is reported at U.S., *Congressional Record*, 93d Cong., 1st Sess., vol. 119, November 30, S21495–21505, S21575–21578; December 1, S21631–21634; December 2, S21638–21647; December 3, S21707–21726.

[24] S. 3044, 93d Cong., 2d Sess., 1974. U.S. Congress, Senate, Committee on Rules and Administration, *Federal Election Campaign Act Amendments of 1974*, 93d Cong., 2d Sess., 1974, Sen. Rept. 93–689. Extensive hearings had already been held by the committee. U.S. Congress, Senate, Subcommittee on Privileges and Elections, Committee on Rules and Administration, *Hearings on S. 1103, S. 1954, and S. 2417*, 93d Cong., 1st Sess., 1973.

The extended debate is found at U.S., *Congressional Record*, 93d Cong., 2d Sess., vol. 120, March 26, S4438–4441, S4454–4471; March 27, S4542–4560, S4565–4566, S4568–4574; March 28, S4702–4722, S4725–4727; March 29, S4799–4804, S4809; April 1, S4921–4942, S4944–4946; April 2, S5061–5064, S5066–5086; April 3, S5173–5196; April 4, S5271–5281, S5235–5298; April 5, S5326–5327, S5332–5340, S5341; April 8, S5411–5416, S5419, S5433–5434, S5439–5440; April 9, S5531–5565; April 10, S5646–5654, S5688–5709; April 11, S5829–5864.

[25] H.R. 16090, 93d Cong., 2d Sess., 1974. See, U.S. Congress, House of Representatives, Committee on Administration, *Federal Election Campaign Act Amendments of 1974*, 93d Cong., 2d Sess., 1974, House Rept. 93–1239.

Debate on H.R. 16090 in the Committee of the Whole and in the House is found at U.S., *Congressional Record*, 93d Cong., 2d Sess., 1974, vol. 120, August 7, H7806–7851; August 8, H7892–7947.

from the bill's parent committee but also from two other related committees and from among the bill's floor leaders who had no pertinent committee assignment.[26] The Senate's purpose was to bolster its position against the beligerent and obdurate tactics Wayne Hays had used in the conference over the 1971 act.[27] Faced with 138 points of difference, the conferees deliberated for thirteen days, until September 30, before the Senate gave way on congressional financing and accepted a weakened enforcement arm.[28] On October 15, President Ford reluctantly approved the act, expressing reservations about public financing and the First Amendment implications of contribution limits, but apparently fearful of vetoing a campaign reform bill on the eve of the 1974 congressional elections.

The protracted consideration of the 1974 act reflected deep reservations by many members of Congress. Its opponents feared that public financing would lead ultimately to government interference in free elections, perhaps by manipulating grants to advantage some candidates and parties over others. These fears may have been reenforced by the frequency with which proponents attempted to short-circuit usual legislative procedures by attaching their proposals to unrelated measures. This was the strategy of the original Long Plan in 1966, of the check-off attached to the 1971 Revenue Act, of the elimination of party choice in the check-off in the Debt Ceiling Act of 1973, and of the unsuccessful public financing plan advanced as an amendment to the debt ceiling revision act in November 1974. Proponents insisted, however, that public financing would promote free elections by eliminating the grip of big money and special interests on candidates and officeholders.

A second vew, strongly held by many fiscal conservatives, was that public financing would loot the treasury to promote politicians' careers. Proponents suggested, however, that public financing would ultimately benefit citizens by freeing government expenditure and regulatory policy from the influence of campaign contributors. Also, they pointed out, the cost of public financing would not be much more than $1 annually for every eligible voter.

A third objection, especially pervasive in the House, was that public financing of congressional campaigns would upset long-standing patterns of incumbency advantage. Most House districts are marked by

[26] "Campaign Spending Bill Delay," *Congressional Quarterly Weekly Report*, 32, no. 34 (August 24, 1974), 2305.

[27] See Berry and Goldman, "Congress and Public Policy," pp. 352–356.

[28] U.S. Congress, House of Representatives, *Conference Report, Federal Election Campaign Act Amendments of 1974*, 93d Cong., 2d Sess., 1974, House Rept. 93–1438.

electoral one-partyism; and House campaigns are frequently desultory affairs, because the opposition is unable to muster enough resources to challenge intrenched incumbents. Public financing would fuel a well-funded opposition in both primaries and general elections, jeopardizing the almost automatic reelection of incumbents. Senators, by contrast, are more accustomed to running in competitive constituencies. Their concerns tend to focus on the difficulty of raising money for these expensive campaigns and the danger to their independence implicit in heavy financing from special interests.

A fourth line of division also involved incumbency advantages, but it divided Congress along ideological as well as institutional lines. The low intensity of most House campaigns, caused by one-partyism and incumbency resources, requires very little spending. House members from such noncompetitive districts were shocked at proposals that public financing and spending limits should be as high as $90,000. Many insisted that expenditures should not exceed the $40,000 salary of representatives. Here the focus was on the private benefit to representatives of election, not on the public interest in vigorous competition in elections. Implicitly, this position maintained the status quo and handicapped effective opposition.

In the Senate, proponents endorsed both generous public grants and high spending limits to promote effective competition. Opponents divided, however. Some, like Senator James Buckley, took the ideologically conservative position that any limit on spending unconstitutionally invaded political freedom. Others, however, argued that low spending limits were an alternative to public financing as a means for reducing the influence of money in politics.

A similar controversy raged around contribution limits. Senator William Proxmire proposed that contribution limits in S. 372 be reduced from $3000 to $100. So low a limit "would free all of us from reliance on the fat cat, on the big contributor, on those who seek to buy laws that will favor their interests."[29] But Senator Alan Cranston warned that money was needed for vigorous campaigns. He would support a $250 contribution limit, but only if coupled with public financing. Otherwise, "the $100 limit would place an impossible obstacle on most nonincumbents."[30] Again, congressional debate implicated delicate questions of political freedom for individuals, the disproportionate political influence of big contributors, and the impact on incumbents of regulating campaign funds.

[29] U.S., Congressional Record, 93d Cong., 1st Sess., 1973, vol. 119, July 26, S14791.
[30] Ibid., July 26, S14795.

Provisions of the Federal Election Campaign Act of 1974
Expenditure Limits

The act, as finally adopted, limits spending by presidential candidates to $20 million in general elections and $10 million in nomination races. No candidate may spend more than twice the senatorial limit in any state. Candidates for senator are limited to the greater of 8 cents times the voting-age population or $100,000 in primaries and 12 cents times the voting-age population or $150,000 in general elections. House candidates are limited to $70,000 in each primary and general election. House candidates in states with only a single representative are governed by senatorial spending limits. Additional expenditures up to 20 percent of the spending limit are allowed for fund raising.

National party committees can spend an additional 2 cents times the voting-age population to support their presidential candidates; national and state party committees can separately spend up to 2 cents per eligible voter to aid their Senate and House candidates, with a minimum allowance of $20,000 and $10,000 respectively for those races. Independent individuals and groups may make expenditures up to $1000 to support candidates. And all spending limits are adjusted in each election to conform to changes in the consumer price index.

Contribution Limits

The 1974 act limits an individual's contributions to any federal office candidate to $1000 in each nomination and election contest and restricts him annually to $25,000 to all federal office candidates. A candidate's contributions to his own campaign cannot exceed in nomination and election contests together $50,000 for president, $35,000 for senator, and $25,000 for representative. Political committee gifts are limited to $5000 to each federal office candidate in each nomination and election contest. Earmarked or indirect contributions are counted against these limits; donations by foreign nationals are prohibited; and contributions (and expenditures) in cash may not exceed $100.

Public Financing

The act initiates public financing for presidential general elections, nominating contests, and nominating conventions. Major party general election candidates are given the option of receiving the full amount of the spending limit ($20 million) in public funds. Major party candidates seeking a presidential nomination may receive matching grants for each individual contribution up to $250, after qualifying by raising

$5000 in such contributions in each of twenty states. Matching grants are limited to a total of $5 million—one-half the statutory spending limit of $10 million. Major parties may draw $2 million in public funds for the expenses of their national nominating conventions.

Minor parties are eligible for proportional participation in all public financing formulas. Their grants are calculated as the percentage of major party subsidies that their vote in the prior election was of the average major party vote. New parties and minor parties may qualify for postelection public financing on the same proportional basis if their vote in a current election entitles them to larger grants than would their polling in the last balloting.[31]

The $1 tax check-off is retained, and checked-off dollars are automatically appropriated to the Presidential Election Campaign Fund. All public financing must be drawn from that fund. The act establishes priorities for payments from the fund, with amounts necessary for nominating conventions and general election grants set aside in that order and with nomination matching grants taken from any balance remaining in the fund. All grants are adjusted to conform to changes in the consumer price index.

Full Disclosure

The 1974 act made several changes in the sweeping disclosure provisions of the 1971 act. Reporting dates were changed from the fifteenth and fifth days before an election to ten days before and thirty days after elections as well as quarterly and annually; the new dates were generally regarded as easing the burden on political treasurers without significantly diminishing the availability of campaign financing information. Two other provisions with the same effect repeal the requirement that campaign committees keep a record of the occupation and principal place of business of contributors over $10 (but did not repeal the same requirement for those giving more than $100) and of those to whom expenditures are made.

The act strengthened auditing and disclosure by requiring each candidate to designate a single depository bank and to make all transactions through that depository, except that presidential candidates may designate a depository in each state. Each candidate must also designate a prin-

---

[31] Major parties are defined as those whose candidate received more than 25 percent of the popular vote in the previous election. Minor parties are defined as those receiving between 5 and 25 percent of the vote, and new parties as those which qualify neither as major nor minor parties. Revenue Act of 1971, Public Law 92–178, 92d Cong., 2d Sess., 1972, Title VIII, sec. 9002(6), (7), and (8).

cipal campaign committee, which shall be responsible for all financial transactions on the candidate's behalf. Other committees supporting a candidate must file their financial statements with the principal campaign committee, which compiles all reports and files them together. These provisions are intended to make information more readily available by centralizing all reports for each candidate in a single filing.

Enforcement

The 1974 act creates a Federal Election Commission consisting of the Senate secretary and House clerk, serving ex officio without vote, and of six appointed members. Two are named by the president; and in a sharp departure from the usual Executive prerogative to name agency members, two are appointed by the president pro tem of the Senate and two by the speaker of the House, upon recommendation of the majority and minority leaders in the respective houses. No pair of members may be from the same political party. And in a second break from other appointment procedures, commissioners must be confirmed by a majority vote in both houses, rather than just by the Senate.

The commission is given power to supervise the full disclosure provisions of the law, but the secretary and clerk remain the depository officials for the filings of candidates for the respective houses. The commission is given authority to investigate reported or apparent violations, to give advisory opinions, and to promulgate rules and regulations. It may seek civil remedies to prevent or correct violations of the law. But the Senate effort also to give it an independent power to bring criminal prosecutions failed, and its authority is limited to reporting apparently willful violations to the Justice Department. Also, the commission's rulemaking power is hobbled in a way dissimilar from any other federal regulatory agency: its proposed regulations must be submitted to each house, and either may veto them by majority vote within thirty days.

SECOND THOUGHTS

In some of its goals, the 1974 act seems a great advance over existing methods of financing campaigns.[32] The low contribution limits and public financing will reduce the special access of monied groups to the electorate and to the officeholders elected with their financial help. Further, in theory public financing provides adequate funds for vigorous competitive campaigning that allows candidates to communicate their stances

---

[32] The analysis in this section is drawn mainly from Adamany and Agree, *Political Money*, chap. 8.

to the electorate and voters to know their choices at the polls. The extension of the principle of public financing to primaries as well as general elections acknowledges the importance of nominations, the potential for financing abuses in those contests, and the special impact of money in primaries where voters do not have the party label to guide them. The public financing for new and minor parties at least recognizes the potential that they may become major contenders and honors their historic roles as vehicles for new ideas, voter protest, or charismatic leaders.

In other ways, however, the act falls short of respecting the realities of American politics and campaign financing. Most important is the act's failure to publicly finance congressional campaigns. Presidential candidates funded fully with tax dollars may use their awesome influence to solicit and channel private money for Senate and House races. This already happens in midterm elections, reaching a zenith in Mr. Nixon's White House, where key staffers secretly directed money in 1970 to help the president's friends in Congress and to punish his enemies. The deployment of even greater presidential influence in financing campaigns, in both midterm and presidential elections, will increase the president's clout in Congress and further undermine the already badly eroded separation of powers.

A shift in public confidence is also likely when presidential candidates are "cleanly" funded with tax money and congressional aspirants are still dependent on "tainted" private fund sources. Finally, of course, public financing of presidential elections makes candidates both more responsive and more visible to the public. Congress, meanwhile, remains in a shadowland, where financial undernourishment of challengers makes it less accountable to voters in elections and less visible to citizens.

Basing eligibility for presidential general election grants on past election results will produce distortions and unfairness in American politics. These are aggravated by the requirement that new party candidates must wait until after the votes are counted before receiving public grants, while others receive their grants for use during the campaign. Under these rules, formerly significant parties whose support has decayed may nonetheless claim full grants in later elections; the Whig party after 1852, the Bull Moosers in 1916, and the Wallace American Independents in 1972 come easily to mind as examples. By contrast, newly emerging parties or independent candidates, with strong citizen support in an election, may not receive grants in a timely or useful fashion. Neither the Bull Moosers nor the American Independent party would have received public grants during the campaign when it made its impressive showing.

The act's provision for postelection grants to new parties making a strong showing at the polls allows them, at best, to pay off election debts. But most insurgent parties will not be able to borrow large sums during the campaign, so postelection grants will do them little good in wooing votes. Indeed, the act's limit of $1000 on loans as well as contributions throws up a barrier to such borrowing by new parties.

The matching grant system for nominations seems to address many of these issues by basing public financing on a current rather than a past index of support. But the index is support by contributors, not by voters. And the $250 level for matchable grants appears to promote substantial inequality among citizens. Ironically, each citizen equally can allocate only $1 to the Presidential Election Campaign Fund; but in the distribution of these dollars citizens trigger very unequal grants to candidates, because a $250 contributor directs a like amount to his preferred candidate while a $1 contributor sends only a single public dollar to his favorite. The $250 maximum for contributions counting toward the eligibility threshold creates similar inequalities. A mere 4000 of these donors qualify a candidate for matching grants, but it would take 100,000 one dollar contributors to achieve that result.

The requirement that a candidate raise $5000 in each of twenty states to become eligible for nomination matching grants is apparently intended to discourage favorite sons or regional candidates. This is a doubtful goal, since these contenders have sometimes emerged as national leaders after starting in their home areas. Particularly, it discriminates against governors, whose initial constituencies for the presidency are likely to be local rather than national. In addition, the twenty-state rule ignores the distribution of voters in favor of a peculiar "state equality" theory of presidential politics. The Constitution does not require a candidate to carry, or even to run in, twenty states in order to be elected president. Indeed, the electoral votes of the eleven largest states are sufficient for victory. And, in 1972, fourteen state delegations in the Republican national convention and nine in the Democratic conclave commanded the majority necessary to nominate a presidential candidate.

Nomination financing raises an interparty distributional problem. Is it fair for a party with a heated nomination contest to draw most or all of the matching money? Since all the party's hopefuls are likely to campaign against the opposition party, especially against a sitting opposition party president, the nomination grants have general election implications. Yet during the nomination stage, one party's many contenders will claim vastly more of the available public funding than will the uncontested or weakly contested nominee of the other party.

Finally, the act's limits on expenditures and public grants are questionable. The $10 million ceiling for nomination contests seems reasonable; presidential hopefuls have seldom exceeded that amount. But the $20 million general election ceiling and grant appear too low; the Mc-Govern-Shriver campaign spent about $38 million in a canvass that few would describe as lavish. Measured against past spending levels, the senatorial limits appear adequate and the House ceilings are only slightly too low, even in competitive contests.

Any spending limits may be challenged, however, because they cannot take into account the great variations in campaign circumstances from one district to another—the number of voters, the density of the population, the strength of parties and interest groups, the availability of mass media for campaign advertising, the degree of competitiveness, the salience and importance of deeply felt issues, the traditions of the district, and other factors bearing on campaign spending.[33] A more theoretical objection holds that spending is related to vigorous competition, an essential element of electoral democracy.

Moreover, spending limits are almost unenforceable. Do expenditures supporting a candidate, but made by other citizens, count against his spending limit? Such independent expenditures could very quickly diminish a candidate's opportunity to spend money to emphasize the issues he believes are important. Even more troublesome is the allocation toward spending limits of outlays that do not support any candidate. Is spending by independent citizens or groups opposing a candidate a charge against his opponent's expenditure limits? Whose spending limit is affected by similar expenditures if they only mention a candidate, but do not endorse or censure him? And what about expenditures—such as those by the National Rifle Association or "right to life" (antiabortion) groups—which raise the salience of issues on which candidates have well-defined positions, but which do not mention either contender?

Expenditure limits also appear to curtail the freedom of speech and of association.[34] To prevent evasion of spending limits and to control the

[33] The study of variables affecting spending levels is still in a formative stage. See Alexander Heard, *The Costs of Democracy* (Chapel Hill, N. C., 1960), pp. 380–387; David Adamany, *Financing Politics* (Madison, Wis., 1969), pp. 61–107; and Adamany, *Campaign Finance in America* (Scituate, Mass., 1972), pp. 51–78. An important statistical analysis of the significance of several variables is John R. Owens, *Trends in Campaign Spending in California, 1958–1970: Tests of Factors Influencing Costs* (Princeton, N. J., 1973), pp. 70–80.

[34] One major court case has upheld spending limits on candidates to reduce pressures on them to seek money from special interests; but the justices refused to apply the limits to independent expenditures on behalf of the candidate. Most campaigns were subsequently financed by "voluntary committees" operating under the legal fiction that they were not directed by the candidate. *State ex rel. LaFollette* v. *Kohler*, 200 Wis. 518 (1930). A more recent and far more persuasively reasoned case holds, however, that all expenditure limits violate the First Amendment. *Bare* v. *Gorton*, —Wash. 2d—, 526 P. 2d 379 (1974).

kinds of borderline expenditures mentioned above, money must be channeled through a central campaign committee under the candidate's control.[35] Otherwise interest groups, parties, and separate campaign committees will simply take over the financing of a candidate's canvass when his own organization has reached the limit. But the central campaign committee imposes a form of censorship on citizens; they can spend money to express their opinions about candidates only if the candidate approves of their activities.

Further, when some citizens have contributed or spent money through the candidate's committee up to the spending ceiling, other citizens are entirely cut off from such activity. Citizen activity is abridged even more

---

Most commentators agree that expenditure limits invade First Amendment guarantees: Ralph K. Winter, Jr., "Money, Politics and the First Amendment," *Campaign Finances: Two Views on the Political and Constitutional Implications* (Washington, D.C., 1971), pp. 60–61; Joel L. Fleishman, "Freedom of Speech and Equality of Political Opportunity: The Constitutionality of the Federal Election Campaign Act of 1971," *North Carolina Law Review*, 51 (January 1973), 434–479; Martin H. Redish, "Campaign Spending Laws and the First Amendment," *New York University Law Review*, 46 (November 1971), 907–924; Irving Ferman, "Congressional Controls on Campaign Financing: An Expansion or Contraction of the First Amendment," *American University Law Review*, 22 (Fall 1972), 1–38.

One commentator has suggested that expenditure ceilings might be upheld to guarantee equality among candidates, but he follows the *Kohler* case, *supra*, by insisting these limits could not bar independent expenditures. Albert J. Rosenthal, *Federal Regulation of Campaign Finance: Some Constitutional Questions* (Princeton, N. J., 1972), pp. 32–39. A United States district court recently followed the reasoning of the *Kohler* case, *supra*, in a dictum sanctioning expenditure limits to permit candidates of modest means to seek office. The judge did not comment on the independent expenditures problem. *Abercrombie* v. *Burns*, 377 F. Supp. 1400 (1974).

The most forceful argument for the constitutionality of spending limits is "Common Cause Memorandum on the Constitutionality of Contribution and Expenditure Limitations" (Washington, D. C., 1973). It suggests that campaign spending is action, not protected speech; or that, if speech, it is in any case subject to regulation to effectuate the "compelling" public interest in equality among candidates and in preventing corruption of government.

[35] Two courts have disapproved central treasurer arrangements. *State* v. *Pierce*, 163 Wis. 615 (1916); *American Civil Liberties Union* v. *Jennings*, 336 F. Supp. 1041 (1973) (three-judge court). See also *Bare* v. *Gorton*, *supra*. Most commentators agree with this view. See, for example, Fleishman, "Freedom of Speech and Equality of Political Opportunity," p. 451; Rosenthal, *Federal Regulation of Campaign Finance*, pp. 34–38.

A more optimistic view about the constitutionality of the central treasurer is Theodore Mitau, "Selected Aspects of Centralized and Decentralized Control over Campaign Finance: A Commentary on S. 636," *University of Chicago Law Review*, 23 (Winter 1956), 630–635. Also, "Common Cause Memorandum on the Constitutionality of Limitations on Independent Expenditures Advocating the Election or Defeat of Candidates for Federal Office" (Washington, D.C., 1974).

sharply in presidential general elections where major party candidates are fully publicly financed, preventing all citizens from expressing views by contributing any funds to candidates.

Congress attempted to avoid these issues by allowing independent citizens or committees to spend up to $1000 (the same as the limit on contributions) outside the principal campaign committee. Even this resolution falls short, however. Those willing to contribute money through the candidate's committee can pool their resources for greater effectiveness; others are limited to spending $1000, raising the question of whether their freedom of association is infringed.

AFTERMATH

On January 2, 1975, Senator James Buckley took advantage of an amendment he had sponsored to the Federal Election Campaign Act, by filing suit in the United States District Court for the District of Columbia challenging the constitutionality of almost every major provision of the law.[36] He was joined by former senator and presidential candidate Eugene McCarthy, Representative William Steiger, millionaire philanthropist and political activist Stewart Mott, the Committee for a Constitutional Presidency, the Conservative party of New York, the New York Civil Liberties Union, the American Conservative Union, and *Human Events*. Among them, the plaintiffs represented candidates, parties, contributors, taxpayers, political committees, citizens, and the press.·

They challenged contribution and spending limits on First Amendment grounds; alleged that spending limits discriminated against challengers because of the perquisites available to incumbents; and asserted that the additional spending authorization for national and state parties discriminated against those with no national committees, those running in a single state, and those campaigning as independents. The qualifying requirements for general election public financing were challenged as discriminatory against minor and new parties and independent candidates. The plaintiffs also insisted that the tax check-off supported political causes in violation of the First Amendment, discriminated against candidates and parties which could not meet the qualification requirements, forced individuals to support parties and candidates they did not favor, and denied taxpayers' freedom of association by denying them the opportunity to designate their check-off dollar to parties of their choice.

The plaintiffs also attacked the Federal Election Commission. They

[36] The pleadings are reprinted in U.S., *Congressional Record*, 94th Cong., 1st Sess., vol. 121, January 16, H173–178.

argued that the method of appointment violated the separation of powers and denied minor parties representation. Further, the commission's composition denied those not affiliated with major parties a hearing before an impartial tribunal during the investigation of violations. The power to make rules was asserted to violate the separation of powers and the due process clause, while the commission's power to disqualify candidates was alleged to infringe the First, Fifth, and Sixth Amendments. The full disclosure provisions were challenged as invasions of the rights of privacy, speech, and association. Even the exclusion of news stories and editorials from the definition of expenditure, but not the definition of contribution, was the basis for constitutional argument—it purportedly restricts the freedoms of speech and press.

If the litigation was founded on alarm at the great sweep of the act, the first steps toward its implementation gave every sign that its real effect might be minimal. The president waited more than two months after the act's effective date on January 1, 1975, before nominating his commissioners. The Senate leadership named close political associates, while both the president and the House leadership nominated former congressmen. By early April no staff was assembled for the commission, and there was no indication of how candidates and parties should begin complying with the act's provisions. Those who had fought for the act —especially Common Cause and leading newspapers—bitterly denounced the method and quality of appointments as an attempt to gut the law.

Moreover, numbers of lawmakers who had voted for the act in Congress had begun to indicate misgivings about it. On March 26 Senator Lee Metcalf petitioned to join the pending litigation by filing an *amicus curiae* brief "in support of the constitutionality of the concept of public financing [but] also in concurrence with certain causes of actions stated in plaintiffs' complaint with respect to constitutional deficiencies in sections of [the act] pertaining to public financing procedures. . . ."[37]

Meanwhile, taxpayers showed that their sentiment was still favorable toward public financing. The Internal Revenue Service reported checkoff participation in mid-February at 26 percent, compared to 15 percent a year before. This level of involvement in a nonelection year was more than twice the contribution rate in high excitement presidential years and almost three times that in congressional election years.

[37] United States Court of Appeals for the District of Columbia Circuit, *James L. Buckley et al., Plaintiffs* v. *Honorable Francis R. Valeo et al., Defendants, Motion for Leave to File Brief as Amicus Curiae and to Participate in Oral Argument on the Merits,* p. 2. [On January 30, 1976, the Supreme Court struck down as infringements of freedom of speech the Federal Election Campaign Act's expenditure limits on indepen-

dent individuals and groups, on congressional candidates, and on presidential candidates who do not accept public funding; struck down the method of appointing the Federal Election Commission as contrary to the separation of powers; but upheld the Act's provisions on contribution limits to candidates, public financing of presidential campaigns, and full disclosure of contributions and expenditures. Ed.]

Part III.

The Presidency,
Congress,
and Bureaucracy

8   American Political Institutions after Watergate—A Discussion

DEMETRIOS CARALEY
CHARLES V. HAMILTON
ALPHEUS T. MASON
ROBERT A. McCAUGHEY
NELSON W. POLSBY
JEFFREY L. PRESSMAN
ARTHUR M. SCHLESINGER, JR.
GEORGE L. SHERRY
TOM WICKER

On September 13, 1974, the Editor and eight members of the Editorial Advisory Board of the *Political Science Quarterly* met to discuss what they believed would be the long-term implications for American political institutions of the Watergate events, including the resignation of the president. The group gathered in the Deanery of Barnard College, Columbia University. No written presentations were prepared so that the discussion could be spontaneous and free flowing. The transcript of that discussion follows:

CARALEY*: Perhaps it would be best to begin the discussion with a fairly specific question and then proceed to more general ones. So let me first ask Alpheus Mason whether or not Watergate has made important changes in what we understood to be basic constitutional law?

WATERGATE AND THE JUDICIARY

MASON†: There may have been a change, but I don't think it's a drastic change. I would like to address my remarks to the one decision of the Supreme Court—*U. S. v. Richard M. Nixon*, decided July 24, 1974. That decision reaffirmed and reestablished judicial review as an essential ingredient of a government under an overruling Constitution. The basic issue in this case, as argued by the president's lawyer, James St. Clair, was whether we live under a government of laws or of men. He put it almost categor-

---

* DEMETRIOS CARALEY, the editor of the *Political Science Quarterly*, is professor of political science at Barnard College and the Graduate School of Arts and Sciences, Columbia University. † ALPHEUS T. MASON is McCormick Professor of Jurisprudence Emeritus at Princeton University.

ically in those terms. So what was involved, I believe, was the viability of *Marbury* v. *Madison*. I think it significant that Chief Justice Burger quoted from the *Marbury* opinion that "it is emphatically the province and duty of the judicial department to say what the law is." In the chief justice's mind, St. Clair was claiming for the president, at least in this area, the power to say what the law is. In justification, St. Clair invoked the principle of separation of powers. Ironically, Burger, like Chief Justice Marshall, used the same principle to support judicial review against the claims of either Congress or the president.

Chief Justice Burger didn't use the term "executive privilege"—a striking omission, I think. He talked about "the privilege of confidentiality of presidential communications," and mentioned three areas—"military, diplomatic, or sensitive national security secrets." I hesitate to take any exception to Tom Wicker who has written an article on this subject in which he seems to think that somehow or other the president has gained a good deal as a result of this decision. For the first time, Tom tells us, the Court established "constitutional underpinnings" for executive privilege. And, as a matter of fact, Nixon, agreeing for once with Tom Wicker, was gratified "to note that the Court reaffirmed both the validity and the importance of executive privilege—the principle I have sought to maintain." It doesn't seem to me that this decision or the opinion quite bears this out. In the first place, the areas are specified in which the confidentiality of communications are deferred to by the Supreme Court. And, in the second place, the Court still reserves to itself the power to draw the line between those matters which are confidential and therefore beyond the control of the Court and those which are not within the president's power. So, I don't think anything has been changed as a result of this decision. Judicial review is still intact. The extraordinary thing about this case is the president's challenge of judicial review, in practice for nearly 200 years. The decision was unanimous. Not even Nixon appointees could be expected to sign their own judicial death warrants.

POLSBY*: Is it your view that by the act of defining executive privilege . . .

MASON: They didn't define it.

POLSBY: They circumscribed it.

MASON: They circumscribed it and specified three areas. Those areas had been recognized from almost time immemorial as within the province of the president. In these areas, Chief Justice Burger noted, the Court had "traditionally shown the utmost deference to presidential responsibilities."

---

* NELSON W. POLSBY is professor of political science at the University of California, Berkeley.

CARALEY: So are you saying there is nothing new in the upholding of the concept of executive privilege?

MASON: It's a reaffirmation . . .

SCHLESINGER*: It makes explicit what had been implicit in practice.

MASON: That's right.

WICKER†: That is precisely the point that was striking to me. Now you are better able to quote precisely the terms of the decision than I am. It is my recollection that the Court specifically cited military affairs, foreign diplomacy, and national security. I am stating to you that that Court in defining those three exceptions has defined an area of exception which is wide enough to drive through a whole Amtrack locomotive. Now if the Court had attempted, which it did not, precisely to specify what are military affairs, foreign diplomacy, and national security affairs and had they succeeded, as they could not have and the mind of man is not able to, in defining that into the narrowest limits, I would say you are correct. But what in fact they have done is to specify three areas in the most general terms which any clever president will be able to plaster over virtually any area of government activity. I am stating my view —not, of course, a flat fact. I am saying that somewhere in the future, in my judgment, we risk here the possibility that a president will be able to use one of those labels or perhaps all three on something that does not really inherently belong under any of them and cite the Burger decision as justification.

SCHLESINGER: Everyone's right. I mean what Tom says is quite true but this is what presidents have always done and they will now be able to cite the Supreme Court decision. On the other hand, Alpheus can reply that at the same time they acknowledge the right of the Court to decide, which means abandoning the claim that executive privilege is unreviewable.

POLSBY: More, they're inviting litigation on the case.

SCHLESINGER: I don't think the situation has changed so much as it has been raised to a higher level—and this I regret because all those things are better worked out informally rather than formally.

WICKER: There might be an area of difference. I think you are right Arthur, but there might be an area of even factual difference. I don't want to state a superior claim here but I read that decision—every man can read his own decision—I read that decision to mean that if the president asserted a claim of confidentiality in one of these three areas, that probably the Court would not even entertain review.

---

* ARTHUR M. SCHLESINGER, JR., is Schweitzer Professor of the Humanities at the City University of New York.   † TOM WICKER is associate editor of the *New York Times*.

CARALEY: That's not what it says . . .

POLSBY: Yes, I too think the opposite. In fact, what has happened is that the Court, by first taking a case of this character, has put itself in the business precisely of inviting litigation on the matter.

WICKER: But this decision simply stated that the president had not made any such claim on these tapes. Now suppose he had?

CARALEY: Let me read the key passage from the *U.S.* v. *Nixon* decision:

> The President's need for complete candor and objectivity from advisers calls for great deference from the courts. However, when the privilege depends solely on the broad, undifferentiated claim of public interest in the confidentiality of such conversations, a confrontation with other values arises. Absent a claim of need to protect military, diplomatic or sensitive national security secrets, we find it difficult to accept the argument that even the very important interest in confidentiality of presidential communications is significantly diminished by production of such material for *in camera* inspection with all the protection that a district court will be obliged to provide.

The Court is, in effect, saying here that this is the president's weakest case. They are not saying the opposite though—that if the claim had been made, they would not have even entertained review.

WICKER: This is the kind of language that can be read to say that if the president had asserted that his tapes in this case involved military, foreign diplomacy, or national security matters, it might have helped him.

POLSBY: Well, Tom, it wouldn't have helped him. That's very clear. I think it important that we not lose Arthur Schlesinger's point—that something which heretofore has been negotiated out has now been placed in the realm of litigation and that the Court has taken unto itself the right to decide cases where these sort of claims are controverted whereas until now it's been done as among politicians. And I think that is a significant difference.

WICKER: The Court has taken on that right "absent the claim."

SHERRY*: There is a respectable tradition in democratic thought to the effect that these three areas are in fact privileged in certain respects and it goes all the way back to Locke and before. So that there is a historical background to that . . .

SCHLESINGER: And a practical background.

SHERRY: And a practical background, of course, and there are reasons for it which cannot simply be dismissed.

WICKER: Of course, they cannot be dismissed.

---

* GEORGE L. SHERRY is Principal Officer, Office of the Undersecretaries General for Special Political Affairs, at the United Nations.

CARALEY: Let me ask if we had all been given an examination a year ago and required to say whether the Court would take on this kind of litigation or say that it was a political question and therefore not justiciable, how would we have answered? Would we have all said it was a political question?

POLSBY: I would have said the Court will take the case. I am sure we would have said that. Although I believe Alexander Bickel's argument is essentially correct: they were asked to give an advisory opinion and gave one.

SCHLESINGER: I would not have thought it was a political question. It is not one in the traditional sense of the political question.

CARALEY: That was because the courts were directly involved and were dealing with evidence in a criminal trial, so that it was really the conduct of the judiciary's own business that was involved. It wasn't an issue between the Congress and the president but had to do with the conduct of the judiciary's business, which is to try cases.

MASON: The Court in a way is saying that they are reinforcing, are making the president sensitive to his obligation in this particular case to take care that the laws be faithfully executed.

WICKER: That is a very generous interpretation.

MASON: I know you are on the other side.

WICKER: I'm sure we don't want to spend the evening on this point. The observed practice of presidents, and in fact of governors everywhere, is when given an inch they take a mile. I trust sincerely that I am wrong and that everyone else is right. But I think the net impact of the Pentagon papers decision and that of the Nixon tapes decision, read twenty years from now and outside the context of these circumstances we are in, is that there are certain cases in which, yes, the government can enjoin publication in advance and, yes, there are certain circumstances in which the president has an adequate claim of confidentiality. I predict, and I hope I am wrong, that twenty years from now we will see presidents acting on those assumptions.

CARALEY: Well, they can claim it but that claim would be based on language that is all dictum. The holdings in each case went against the president's claim so all the other paraphernalia is dictum.

WICKER: In most of those cases it went against specific facts. It did not necessarily go against theory.

CARALEY: Yes, but lawyers make this differentiation that anything that's said in an opinion which is inconsistent with the actual holding of the case, with what was actually decided . . .

SCHLESINGER: Beyond what's required to decide the case.

CARALEY: Beyond what's required to decide the case, that such language is not binding law. Therefore any language that appears to grant the president any rights was just obiter dictum, that is, "said in passing," since in both instances, the president lost the case.

MASON: There's a footnote that might be relevant here. I am thinking of the *Keith* case decided in 1972 [*U. S.* v. *U. S. District Court*, 407 U. S. 297], in which the Court said specifically that "domestic security" is too vague a concept to be reliable as a guide for presidential conduct. It tends to refute your idea that the Court will give carte blanche to any president asserting military and foreign affairs and national interest problems. Why do you assume that the justices would be so free? The Court was unanimous in the *Keith* case, too.

SCHLESINGER: I would agree . . . Let me say one thing, I think what Tom Wicker points to is a technically possible development of the opinion. On the other hand the results took another side which shows the basic point that the language of the opinion is less important than the context in which the opinion is made. What all this means is that once again the Court throws the ball back to the country. They maintain certain options which an antipresidential Court and country can move in one direction and a propresidential Court and country can decide to move in another direction. I continue to think that this is just raising to a different level a situation that always existed. In the end it is the political balance in which the judicial decision is made that is going to be critical. I think we ought perhaps to pass on from the actual decision which maintains potentialities in different directions, to see to what extent it can be said, first, that a deep political impression has been made by these events which is going to affect the political climate for some time—and if so, for how long—and second, since, however long it lasts, the impact will be transient, are there structural changes that should be made to prevent such events from recurring?

CARALEY: That's a good question.

WATERGATE AND THE POWER OF THE PRESS

McCAUGHEY*: I've been struck by the conversation so far perhaps because I fall too easily into the occupational fallacy of trying to identify comments according to how the commentators spend an eight or ten or twelve hour workday. But it struck me, Tom, that you believe that the Court had opened the door to a continuation—after a quiet lapse—to an expanding executive . . . that the particular holder of the crown had been

---

* ROBERT A. McCAUGHEY is associate professor of history at Barnard College, Columbia University.

displaced but the crown will come on shinier than ever, and that the Court perhaps didn't do in the crown. My own reaction to the events is that the Court all through the Watergate series may be seen as somehow strengthening itself; it was asked an advisory opinion and gave one. Perhaps this is a muscle flexing of a sort. But your concern seems to be it didn't flex enough to put the presidency back in its historical place, its appropriate place. My own sense of it is that the real winner in these events is the press. It has become, however unofficial, the most assertive branch of the government; it is not the president that comes out ahead and it is not the judiciary that comes out ahead but in an informal way the press. You are correct, I think, in saying that the Watergate and Pentagon opinions could be used later on to buttress an "imperial presidency," but I think for people who didn't read the Pentagon decision with the occupational concerns of a journalist, the exposé of the Pentagon papers constituted not a down-the-road challenge to the press but a successful assertion of the press. It strikes me that one of the structural changes we may be confronting is a press much bemuscled as a result of Watergate.

SCHLESINGER: But that's a political change not a structural change.

McCAUGHEY: Well I'm not so sure.

POLSBY: Why even a political change? Argue your case.

McCAUGHEY: Because we've made several decisions without resorting to the ballot box. We've been able to make several rather basic changes in executive personnel without having once gone to the public except through the press.

POLSBY: You mean the Twenty-fifth Amendment, somehow, is an illegitimate enactment?

McCAUGHEY: No, but we have in a series of events, I think—which in some ways precede Watergate, you may date it from the spring of 1968 with Johnson if you will—witnessed changes in the political arrangements in this country that have not come about essentially through the ballot box or, I would argue, through the courts.

SCHLESINGER: But there's nothing new about that surely.

McCAUGHEY: But the degree to which a string of successes has been put together, that's new.

SCHLESINGER: The press is not the cause. It was events that shocked public opinion.

McCAUGHEY: Well, certainly. But we weren't shocked in June of 1972 by the break-in.

SCHLESINGER: Nor was the press shocked. The *New York Times* carried the story on the back pages until after the election, as I recall.

McCAUGHEY: But the story was kept alive—and not by the 1972 Democratic candidate.

SCHLESINGER: He did his best to keep it alive.

McCAUGHEY: But he was unsuccessful in doing so.

POLSBY: Well for good reason; nobody knew what its dimensions were.

PRESSMAN*: Yes, part of the reason for the success of the press with respect to Watergate was that there was a lot to be uncovered. So we should keep those special circumstances in mind in assessing the future role of the press as a limitation on presidential power. And I certainly think that the demise or weakening of the executive shouldn't be too widely heralded before it happens. By the way, it's interesting to note that, soon after the Nixon resignation, the press was once again calling for executive leadership in foreign affairs and also in economic affairs— to do something about inflation. The press was right there, calling for strong action and saying that President Ford was the one person who could provide that action. I think that Ford's pardon announcement might have been the one event that could have dissipated some of this glow. But after a month—or maybe only two weeks—of talking about the need to limit the executive, people will point again to a crisis on Cyprus or the price of bread, and say that the president has to act. That all indicates to me a continuing feeling that there are world events which somehow cry out for executive leadership. And the press, for all of its good work on Watergate, has not exactly been at the back of the line of those calling very loudly for executive leadership. So I think your point about the press in this case being the effective opponent of the president is well taken, but I also think the Watergate case may be a very extreme example and the presidency might turn out to be as strong as ever. Watergate behavior is really an extreme; presidents can't do that sort of thing but most of them probably wouldn't want to do so.

WICKER: I agree with that profoundly. The tendency of the press in this country is, has been most of the time, and will be again to play on the team. The tendency of the press in this country is not to attack presidents and I think the Watergate case has proven that rather than refuted it. Most of us were dragged kicking and screaming into Watergate. And ultimately, it may well be, the press did play a substantial role, although I think that role is exaggerated considerably. Your point is beautifully taken about immediate reaction to Ford. The *New York Times* was out there within a week of Ford's accession calling for vast exertions of presidential power again by this new guy. I think that it is something that this panel might well deliberate and I don't quite understand it myself . . . that yearning on our part for a great leader.

* JEFFREY L. PRESSMAN is associate professor of political science at Massachusetts Institute of Technology.

SCHLESINGER: I think the presidency is indestructible—partly for good reasons, partly for foolish ones. The foolish reason is the great public desire to believe in and admire the president. This was shown in the immense euphoria which greeted Ford. One saw it in ourselves . . . I mean Ford was a very disarming figure and one wanted to think he was better than he is. And we owe it to Gerald Ford—and we ought to express our gratitude to him—that he reminded us so expeditiously of his fallibility. But, beyond the foolish reasons, there is, I believe, a functional necessity about the presidency. Take problems, Tom, that you've cared about through the years, like civil rights . . . where would we be in civil rights if it weren't for executive leadership? Historically, the office of the president has served the nation well. I think the crippling of the constitutional powers of the presidency would do the nation great harm. The problem is to combine rational beliefs in effective presidential power with skepticism and demystification about the institution.

PRESSMAN: That continues to be a critical dilemma for all of us who would like to see a strong president, but not an excessive president. We've got to figure out in what ways we could draw the line, what sorts of structural changes are possible. There are a lot of people who are quite willing to throw out the baby with the bath water and just tear down the presidency.

WICKER: Let me add a further impression that I have quite aside from editorial advocacy or even investigative reporting or exposure or anything of that sort. One of the great problems we face is the tendency of the press to glorify a president. It's what I call, with all due respect to a fellow I liked, "Merriman Smith reporting." Merriman Smith conceived of the idea that the public wanted to know what toothpaste the president uses. And over the years that's become our main coverage of the White House. You can see this in the first weeks of coverage of Ford, showing him on the trampoline, and cooking breakfast.

POLSBY: Well, now, Ford didn't put that in the paper, the newspaper people did that.

WICKER: That's what I'm saying. Aside from the questions of exposing Watergate or advocating policy decisions, the tendency of the press is to glorify this man out of all proportion, beyond anything that is rational. Whether it's Ford, or Nixon, or Johnson.

POLSBY: Why?

WICKER: This has to do with what's wrong with the press. On the other hand, I think if you took it deep enough you would find that the press was satisfying some instincts of the public or at least it thinks it is, and therefore is getting some lead from the public. So it's not institutional reform that has to do with government.

POLSBY: Let's discuss this some more. Why does the press behave in this fashion? In part I think it's because they really aren't very preoc-cupied with the activities of governing.

SHERRY: Perhaps because they are, because they realize that the only agency within our own or any other system of government that can carry out a coherent policy in any realm of endeavor is bound to be the execu-tive; the legislative by its very structure is not capable of carrying out any long-term policy either in domestic or foreign affairs.

POLSBY: Sure, but you look at a newspaper and you don't see them talking about what effects executive measures have on people, or at least this is a very small proportion of their coverage of the presidency. Tell me where I can find, for example, what the day-to-day effects were on the government of the changes in the Bureau of the Budget when it became the Office of Management and Budget. The only time we got that, as a mat-ter of fact, was when we had a changeover and everybody said now may-be they are going to do something about that terrible Office of Manage-ment and Budget which was messing up the whole of the United States executive branch.

SHERRY: Again the usual naive assumption that structural change will, of course, necessarily result in change in policy—that changing the name of the Post Office to the Postal Service will improve service.

POLSBY: In fact apparently there were significant changes in the way in which we were governed and yet there was no coverage. Instead we had the normal sort of preoccupation with personality and human in-terest.

SHERRY: The kind of reporting that you are calling for is extremely difficult and very rare.

HAMILTON*: To get back to Arthur Schlesinger's comment about executive leadership and civil rights, I think it is only recently that the presidency, under Kennedy, has become a major catalyst in civil rights. I would look to the courts as the major innovator in twentieth-century America.

SCHLESINGER: Truman's civil rights report really defined the issue. Eisenhower did not.

HAMILTON: Right. But I think there are two institutions that came late to the whole question that we are talking about now, the political party and Congress. They were late-comers to this particular crisis and maybe that's their role. It may well be their role and we will continue to see the need for a strong presidency to deal with not so much the ultimate traumatic crisis, but rather with long-term ongoing questions—inflation, foreign policy. I'm not sure that Congress or the political party can crank

---

* CHARLES V. HAMILTON is Wallace S. Sayre Professor of Government at Columbia University.

up to deal with those ongoing critical questions. But when it becomes a question of traumatic, immediate crises like those we faced in the last year, other institutions will move forward and take temporary leadership—the parties, Congress—as they did.

CARALEY: Or even the press. And what it may do is simply perform a catalytic function. I'd like to go back just another minute to Bob McCaughey's point about the press. I think it was downgraded a little bit too much. You are all right that the press doesn't take the initiative. It needs a source to bounce something off and then it will start talking about it. It will not talk about the Office of Management and Budget until there is a credible source, a newsworthy source already talking about it. But its major power comes from the ability to perform a catalytic function and crystallize latent discontents. When the press got disenchanted with the Vietnamese war, that, in my mind, caused Johnson's downfall. Before the press got converted . . .

SCHLESINGER: Wait, the press is only a medium. What destroyed support for the Vietnam war were two things: first, the Viet Cong; and second, the changes in the draft regulations that permitted the sons of opinion makers to be drafted. These were events. All the press did was to report and reflect them.

CARALEY: Yes, but it can report events widely and selectively. I think when Nixon released all those transcripts in April he did not take into account—and maybe he should have—that half an hour later the TV networks were going to broadcast the most damaging sentences and not report on all the material in the whole stack of volumes he made public. We had the sentences that were absolutely the most damaging to Nixon's point of view, and we had it from the commentators, within half an hour that night. Even I didn't realize as I was listening to the speech that the press could do it that quickly. Nixon also probably thought that the immense volume of the transcripts would simply overwhelm anybody's ability to find the relevant portions.

WICKER: The point coming out of this is that when the Vietnam war became an obvious failure, the press began to react to that. When Watergate became an obvious scandal, the press reacted to that, and only by those two routes did the press ever get into the question of executive power—and then almost by unavoidable coincidence. No one who criticized the Vietnam war, criticized the presidency as such. Then Bob Woodward and Carl Bernstein's book [*All the President's Men* (New York, 1974)] tells you that they were horrified—or at least they say they were—when they discovered that they had to get at the presidency if they were going to get at Watergate. I think that is a pretty true picture of the way the press felt about it.

McCAUGHEY: The trouble I have here is that when the Vietnam

war is a failure, when it's "obvious," then the press gets into it. Obvious to whom? To the two organizations to which Charles Hamilton refers? To the Congress or to the parties? They didn't announce it was obvious. Or obvious to Lyndon Johnson?

WICKER: To editorial writers, reporters, columnists, and so forth. They aren't really stupid men. When it became obvious to them, and when it became obvious how Watergate had been handled, then at some point it occurred to them as a result of both of those fiascoes that perhaps the presidential power here is open to question. But until you had the two fiascoes, you didn't get to the root question, and that's the point.

PRESSMAN: But also in each case it was important to have some recognizable political leaders saying that the Vietnam war was a failure or that Watergate was bad. That way the press would not just show college students having that insight, but also some senators and congressmen. It's important to remember that, after all of the press's revelations, if the Judiciary Committee had not managed to get itself together, the whole impeachment business would have been sidetracked. Remember, in July people felt that impeachment had a very good chance of failing even after all of the publicity had gone on. I think the press's role was extremely important, but we shouldn't minimize the contributions of, for example, congressmen in each of the cases you mentioned. That made it respectable and comfortable and believable for others to take a critical stand.

CARALEY: When we talk about the press, we of course also have television, and I assume we are using the word to include all the media. We saw the direct coverage of the Judiciary Committee in action where the media provided their communication function without their editorializing function. That kind of straight coverage probably had a great deal to do with forming public opinion.

POLSBY: I thought they were rather weak in their commentary on the Judiciary Committee meetings, and I was delighted that the House required them to simply show what was going on because if they had intervened more, I think it would have been worse.

WATERGATE AND THE STRONG PRESIDENCY

HAMILTON: We heard a lot of talk at the end of August that the "system worked." What we are talking about is precisely that, but I don't think it is what a lot of people meant. What they meant, I think, is that we can catch the bad guys when they get too far out of line. I'm still of the opinion that we're going to have to rely substantially on a rather strong presidency. That pains you a little bit doesn't it, Tom?

WICKER: No, I agree with that.

HAMILTON: And I think if the "system worked," it was precisely because the institutions, the media heads, the leaders of the two major political parties functioned when they had to function, at the last moment. And in the way they functioned, they played the role I suspect they could play under the circumstances. I don't think we are going to be able to get continuing ongoing government on many issues from those two arenas, and that's the point I'm making.

WICKER: I think this joins issue very clearly with the charge which I feel quite strongly without really having much detail to present to the group, that we go wrong if we think the solution somehow is to dismantle the presidency. And we go right if we say that somehow over a long period of time and out of mostly unnatural causes we have developed one institution which is unbalanced in terms of the others, that the problem is to find some new means—new by definition—of checks and balances to guard against this strong institution that indeed we need and, I think, none of us wants to dismantle.

SHERRY: And perhaps one of the principal effects of Watergate has been precisely that a quasi-institutional check on the presidency has been created and verified as being in existence and being capable of functioning, so that every president in the future will know in the back of his mind that if he steps too far out of line something can in fact be done to check him within the system. In that sense the system has "worked."

POLSBY: I think we ought to talk about the pardon at this point because it seems to me that the chief reason why the pardon was such an unfortunate event was precisely because it muddied those waters. That is to say, it made much more confusing and difficult over the medium run, the firm articulation of precisely what the norms are.

HAMILTON: Do you really want to codify it that way?

POLSBY: Yes, of course.

SHERRY: You can't avoid the operation of a political system and political forces . . .

HAMILTON: Don't try to codify too much.

SHERRY: You can't avoid politics.

POLSBY: What I'm thinking is, I would like this experience to have been sufficiently and thoroughly and officially explored so that people will know and understand what sorts of things are improper and unacceptable in a president.

HAMILTON: In other words you want your precedent to be clear when we have to return to it later. All right, fine.

PRESSMAN: That's an important point. It is not a question of asking for rigid rules. But the norms should have a certain clarity. Because of the pardon, the lessons of Watergate—in our discussion tonight, for instance —are a lot muddier than they would be otherwise. I think the sour taste that this leaves in the mouths of people who were feeling good for exactly one month is worth noting. And what implications does this have for people's views toward the criminal justice process? The pardon muddies the waters in what could have been a very important symbolic experience for the country.

SCHLESINGER: This also brings in that most disastrous of constitutional amendments, the Twenty-fifth Amendment. It's disastrous because it permits a president to appoint a vice-president and an appointed vice-president, whether out of prearrangement or out of sheer gratitude, can pardon the president who appointed him.

POLSBY: It seems to me that does scant justice to the confirmation process.

SCHLESINGER: The confirmation process is entirely nominal.

POLSBY: Well, I don't think it was nominal . . .

SCHLESINGER: It was nominal with Ford, it will probably be nominal with Rockefeller.

POLSBY: Well, I disagree entirely. It wasn't nominal because if it were, we would have gotten Connally.

WICKER: It's less nominal than Nixon's choice of Agnew or McGovern's choice of Eagleton.

POLSBY: Considerably. Oh, I think the confirmation process is very important—indeed, I think as we now can see, it is probably the only legitimizing aspect that remains, but nevertheless a very powerful one.

PRESSMAN: Can we just go back for a minute to George Sherry's point—which I think is an important one—that the lesson of Watergate is that there are limits to presidential power. Now, even without the question of the pardon, the limits of permissible activity were pretty wide. The focus in impeachment Article II was on abuse of power, but Article I was on the narrow grounds of criminal obstruction of justice. So rather specific criminal acts were being censured. Issues like Cambodia, war powers, and impoundment were dismissed by the committee as being relatively inconsequential. So a lot of high-handed presidential behavior does not seem to have been ruled out.

CARALEY: We also have to keep in mind that the articles were voted upon not only on their merits. Certain people had to vote "no" on some articles to stay politically alive.

POLSBY: Nevertheless they ended up with articles which seem to me are defensible on the grounds that they refer to offenses against the public order.

SCHLESINGER: Two criminal and one constitutional.

PRESSMAN: What could we say were the lessons regarding the limits of power? What is it the president can't do? We all feel the limits are important, but what is it that future presidents will refrain from doing because of Watergate?

WICKER: That's a very important question and I think one of the lessons of this impeachment process that we've been through with Nixon is that a president is not impeachable—I am stating it perhaps too flatly but I think it's true—for anything he does in the guise of commander-in-chief, no matter how reprehensible it may be.

POLSBY: That very well may be true. After all impeachment is a political process, it was confided by the founding fathers to a political body, and political judgments are being used here. I would argue that the central fact which made Mr. Nixon's acts scrutinizable with respect to impeachment was that he conducted a systematic campaign to cripple, weaken, and delegitimize all the other elites that are also legitimate and have powers to govern in this country. His attacks on the executive branch, on Congress particularly through the executive privilege and impoundment issues, the way he went after the press . . . not merely disagreeing with them or attacking them in the normal way but through the broadcast licenses, through the harassment of Daniel Schorr and people like that . . . it seems to me he made it very clear to everybody else in official and semiofficial Washington that the Nixon administration was out to delegitimize them. Then, in that context, to see that criminal acts and coverup were involved, raises the issue of impeachment squarely. Now, take away the systematic attempts to delegitimize the other elites and insert only the possible commission of criminal acts and coverup and I am not so sure that you would in fact move toward impeachment. So an extreme form of the statement that you make, but quite possibly a tenable one, would be that a president in the future can get away with damn near anything so long as he remains within the political process.

CARALEY: I take exception to that point, because I think there's a more serious lesson . . .

MASON: I was just going to raise the question of whether you feel this experience means that the impeachment process is just the way it was before it was tried against Richard Nixon. After the impeachment of Andrew Johnson, scholars seventy years apart agreed that impeachment was all over.

CARALEY: Henry Jones Ford in 1898 called impeachment "a rusted blunderbuss, that will probably never be taken in hand again."

MASON: Now it would seem to me that the experience of impeaching or starting to initiate the impeachment process has indicated that this whole provision of the Constitution is by no means moribund. It was effective. It drove Nixon out of office.

CARALEY: It drove him out of office but what scares me is—and I seem to have a disagreement with Nelson Polsby in that I think just the opposite of the lesson he draws—I think the impeachment proceedings show that the president can get away with trying to delegitimize all the other elites, can try and succeed in interfering with the nominating process of the "out party" and so in effect weaken the out party's chance to defeat him. As long as a president is going to be wise enough from now on not to keep tapes to show that he is committing a crime, a serious statutory crime like obstruction of justice, he can still get away with it.

POLSBY: That's too extreme. No, I don't think the tapes were crucial. Also the accusation that he interfered with the Democratic nomination is, I think, much too strong. I would simply say that whatever expenditure of money he put into interference with the Democratic nomination, the Democrats spent so much more money to ruin their own nominating process that it was derisory. I was merely attempting to respond to Tom Wicker's view that while impeachment was there and was used, it's still a highly chancy thing to rely on, and I was pursuing that point because it has got considerable merit. We can't fully, or even really begin to predict what the configuration of political forces might be in the future which would bring impeachment back on the agenda again. But we would be wrong in drawing a lesson, as some people were in fact doing, that it is readily usable, and I think that is just not true.

CARALEY: I certainly agree that it remains very chancy.

WICKER: I'm not prepared to do it at this moment, but I think with very little study I could make a pretty good case that the secret war in Cambodia was the most heinous offence charged to Nixon in terms of our Constitution, the abuse of power, the consequences of it, and yet that was the one thing quite clear from the start that they were not going to use as grounds for impeachment. They were not going to impeach the commander-in-chief for acting as commander-in-chief.

POLSBY: Also, Congress felt they had been implicated in it. They felt they had acquiesced in it. That's a very important point because it suggests that so long as the president gives Congress a piece of the action, that action can be as questionable as you like.

WICKER: Congress is always going to have a very difficult time not acquiescing in these things, which is the flaw in the War Powers Act, important as that was symbolically. Nevertheless, when the president comes down and says our boys are in danger and our national interest is in danger, we've got to act, it's going to be very hard for Congress to say no . . . we can't do that.

POLSBY: But what's your alternative?

WICKER: I don't have one. I'm simply saying we've got a tremendous hole in the War Powers Act.

POLSBY: But it's structural and the question is, is there a structural remedy that you can imagine that wouldn't make things worse in some way? I think the answer is no. Do you agree to that?

WICKER: Yes.

IMPUGNMENT AS A PRECONDITION FOR IMPEACHMENT

HAMILTON: Earlier I was suggesting to a few of us that what I saw happening in the last year was something I called impugnment of the president which preceded impeachment and I think impeachment is possible if it is preceded by this vague, but not too vague, process called impugnment. By this I mean, a process whereby a president's credibility and integrity are called into question in the most direct way. We began to see a number of events unfold which cut to the core of Mr. Nixon's personal character. And this was much more damaging than his simply becoming politically unpopular. You see, even if he had not resigned or been ultimately impeached, I suggest his impugned status had already rendered him finished as a leader. Clearly, Mr. Nixon had been impugned. I date it from Senator Baker's questions. What did the president know? When did he know it? What did he do about it? We had these three questions and all the time Mr. Nixon was telling us what he knew, that is— very little. The Saturday night massacre of Cox, Richardson, and Ruckelshaus contributed to the impugnment of the president. When the president of the United States has to go before the press and the public and say "I am not a crook," he is at that moment already impugned. I'm not talking about a legal concept here, I am talking about a political reaction, and the admission, of course, of lying which came in early August. Finally he was impugned with the revelation of his income taxes. I'm suggesting there's a distinct difference between unpopularity and impugnment. And when you get the occurrence of impugnment followed by the accumulation of evidence tending toward impeachment, a president is finished.

WICKER: I agree with that.

POLSBY: The distinction I think has to do with opinion at the elite and at the mass level. Truman was unpopular with the people when he fired Douglas MacArthur but General Marshall didn't resign, Undersecretary Lovett didn't resign, Dean Acheson didn't resign . . . as a matter of fact they breathed a sigh of relief. They were delighted and MacArthur came marching back and he walked into a Senate investigation by Richard Russell and Robert Kerr which was convened for the express purpose of letting the air out of his balloon. The difference I think is instructive. Now the elites who had been suffering this campaign of vilification from the Nixon administration turned on him and the masses came along afterward and it was the combination, in effect, which accomplished this impugnment that you are talking about, and it's a deadly combination.

HAMILTON: I accept that, and I would suggest it is still possible to launch impeachment proceedings, if you get that combination of forces.

WICKER: Chuck Hamilton's point about the taxes is well taken . . . because the elites turned on Nixon for many things but with that tax business, he also lost a lot of . . .

POLSBY: Mid-elites.

WICKER: The bowling crowd types.

POLSBY: Sure, the people out around the country who are very, very influential in their communities and, it wasn't just the taxes but the transcripts . . . it was that the whole spirit of the administration was seen by those people to be ugly.

WICKER: There is no income tax charge in the impeachment article voted by the Judiciary Committee. Nevertheless the income tax situation had a great deal to do with the votes on impeachment.

PRESSMAN: I think it helped make impeachment possible. When a congressman can say, now here are these fifteen terrible things, but I'm only going to vote for impeachment on the most serious of them, that helps him appear to be moderate about the issue. It helps somebody like Walter Flowers explain to people in Alabama what was going on, showing his moderation by pointing out the fifteen terrible things that he is going to overlook to concentrate on the two *really* terrible things. It seems to me that the tax situation, hovering in the background, played a very crucial role in that.

POLSBY: And the educational process . . . when the editor of the *Omaha World Herald* speaks to his people, and he did on the taxes and on the transcripts, that in effect lays down the base which makes it possible for Flowers and others similarly situated to make that statement.

HAMILTON: And the *Chicago Tribune.*

McCAUGHEY: Having retreated from the field earlier on the charge that the press could be conceded the winner, the statements just now bring me back. The Omaha editor is reading other papers that the Omaha readers are not. It seems to me that we can still come back to the process of impugnment as opposed to impeachment—which after all didn't take place in the case of Richard Nixon, who left the White House without being impeached. Nor did impeachment drive out his predecessor. Both of them were victims of impugnment undertaken by a multiple set of elites. But certainly one of the crucial elites here was the press.

POLSBY: But it is significant that Johnson was never close to impeachment. It was never in the cards at all.

McCAUGHEY: I don't think that is significant at all, because the argument I would make is that a successful impugnment makes impeachment unnecessary.

LIMITING THE IMPERIAL PRESIDENCY

CARALEY: Let's get back to the question of whether Watergate and the resignation are going to fundamentally weaken the presidency. In the concluding chapter of Edward Corwin's book on the presidency [*The President: Office and Powers*, 4th ed. (New York, 1957)], we remember he said that "by and large, the history of the presidency is a history of aggrandizement." And while Corwin conceded that not every president adds to presidential power he argued that "precedents established by a forceful or politically successful personality" are available to his successors so that a new assertive president takes off from the peak of his predecessors. Therefore if we read it that way and if we follow our discussion here that the presidency has not been irreparably weakened in any way at all—I think we are all agreeing to that—is the next president, the next assertive president, going to take off from the peak of Nixon's farthest extension of power rather than from the depths to which his power had fallen just before the resignation?

SCHLESINGER: In considering this question, we have to keep two things in mind. The founding fathers, I believe, intended to set up an energetic presidency. But they also wanted to make sure that presidents always operated under conditions of continuous accountability for their actions. I think we ought to focus on both aspects. The reason why the Constitution is out of balance is because of the erosion of the system of accountability. That system had one grave weakness—the realm of foreign affairs. Presidents not only necessarily ran foreign relations from day to day; but they also sometimes had to act, or believed they had to act, on their own—without the authorization of Congress—to protect the nation's interests or safety in the world. In responding to presidential initiatives in foreign affairs, Congress, the courts, and the people felt much less sure of their ground, much less confident of their information and their judgment, and therefore much less inclined to challenge and check and balance, as they did so freely in domestic affairs. As foreign affairs thus opened a breach in the historical system of accountability, so an extended international crisis widened the breach and began to weaken the whole system. The more active a role the United States took in the world, the more power flowed to presidents. It has been the unending international crisis in the thirty years since Pearl Harbor that has dangerously upset the balance between presidential power and presidential accountability and has created the imperial presidency. Congress itself was delighted in these years to get out of the line of fire and shift responsibility to the presidency. Then in time some president was bound to take the prestige, the initiative, the supremacy he had been granted so willingly in foreign affairs and try to use it to strengthen himself at home. That's what Nixon tried to do. It's not so much a matter of trying to cut back, wing-clip the presidency as it is to make the system of accountability effective.

POLSBY: How would you do that?

SCHLESINGER: I think the answer lies only marginally in structural changes. There are a certain number of things that might be done, such as a joint congressional committee on the CIA or congressional overhauling of the secrecy system and that kind of thing. But these things are essentially expressions of congressional will; and, if that will existed in Congress, Congress could easily restore the whole situation anyway. So my conclusion is that basically the answer is political not structural. Basically it requires in the phrase from the Women's Liberation Movement, "consciousness raising." It requires the raising of the consciousness of presidents so that they hereafter will respect the system of accountability; it requires the raising of the consciousness of Congress so that they will hereafter begin to acknowledge and meet some of their responsibilities; and it requires the raising of the consciousness of the press so that they will end this nonsense of president worship—I mean the primitive rites we are all going through now with Gerald Ford—he cooks his own breakfast, swims forty laps, the first family, and all this guff.

POLSBY: What about in foreign affairs? What are we going to do about Kissinger worship?

WICKER: There also has to be "consciousness raising" of the people, the voters, of course.

POLSBY: That's the hardest of all. Start with the way Congress deals with the secretary of state under current conditions . . .

SCHLESINGER: It's coming through though. I think in the first place we should be grateful for the pardon because the pardon destroyed the idea that the presidency had changed an ordinary politician from Michigan into an all-wise ruler like . . . Cinderella after she put on her glass slipper. The point is that we must have not "respect for the presidency," but studied disrespect for the presidency.

WICKER: If we're talking about change as a result of Watergate, I think that quite beyond the press and political figures, there has been one significant change. It is sheer apprehension on my part but I really do believe that the highest edge of mythology of the presidency has been dulled and I think it has been dulled and bloodied for years to come. While it is true that the press has attempted, rather unwittingly, to idolize Ford all over again, I don't think that went over too well with the public and it took this pardon to explode it.

POLSBY: Moreover, he didn't do anything wrong until the pardon, did he? In fairness . . .

CARALEY: In fairness, his jumping on a trampoline is not exactly page one . . .

POLSBY: Never mind that. The fact is he didn't do anything wrong for a whole month.

PRESSMAN: Which in the light of recent history, makes him a pretty good president.

POLSBY: That's right.

WICKER: I saw a TV film clip about six months ago, after one of the income tax revelations. They were filming in a bar in Grand Rapids. These guys were joking that Nixon is a crook . . . that they pay more taxes than Nixon. I don't think you can do that to a president without its having an impact on the presidency.

McCAUGHEY: I certainly agree with you. And the point you make about the regard for Ford during the first weeks is a function not of the way people are reading the paper but of the way that fifty-year-old night editor is telling his reporter and photographer to go to Alexandria and get him to jump, and the way Ford, a politician for forty years, willingly jumps. Yet those people who came of reading age—children who grew up during the period of Nixon's presidency—will never be able to understand the deference we as teachers and public commentators almost automatically bestow on the president and the presidential office. It is a difficult process; they have been educated in a very different way, and while the night editor may not have changed his tone and Ford won't have changed his tone, there are young people who have been, perhaps, permanently shaped by Watergate.

WICKER: I know my fifteen-year-old son is never going to have the attitude about the presidency that I had when I was twenty-eight or twenty-nine.

CARALEY: Like those of us who grew up when during our whole life the president meant Franklin Roosevelt.

SCHLESINGER: It's all going to come back, too quickly. One saw it coming back under Ford. Thank God for the pardon. I don't know when this instinct appeared . . . it wasn't true in the nineteenth century . . . we didn't have a cult of the president then. It may have something to do with the decay of the political parties. Loyalty in the nineteenth century went to the party more than the personality in the White House.

WATERGATE AND CONGRESS

POLSBY: There's a study by Elmer Cornwell ["Presidential News: The Expanding Public Image," *Journalism Quarterly*, 36 (Summer 1959), 275–283] of news coverage during the twentieth century. It was greatly in favor of Congress during the early period and this has been dramatically reversed in recent decades.

PRESSMAN: I would like to pick up on that. So far, our assessment of the imbalance among institutions seems to have been reflected in our discussion, in which Congress has probably received a minute and a half of attention. I wonder if we could turn to that now. Arthur Schlesinger had mentioned the necessity of "consciousness raising" for Congress to live up to what its role ought to be, and I was wondering what ideas people had about the effect of the Watergate experience on Congress and on its future role definition. Is this a brief moment of glory and courage for the Judiciary Committee, to be dissipated in a return to business as usual? Or is Congress going to go through some sort of resurgence?

SCHLESINGER: Nelson, you're the expert on Congress.

POLSBY: I will say I don't know. No, I assume not. I assume that there are very powerful organizational constraints that operate on congressmen which will in fact keep them from fulfilling Arthur's hopes.

PRESSMAN: Could you say what your hopes might be?

SCHLESINGER: I do not think that Congress has necessarily taken the right way to rejuvenate itself. I am skeptical, for example, about all assumptions of a congressional role based on a notion of a unitary congressional policy, such as the new Budget Act. Congress in exceptional situations may act as an institutional unit against an aggressive or unpopular executive but the notion that this is going to be the normal or appropriate role of Congress seems to me wrong. I do not think the Budget Act is going to work miracles nor do I think the War Powers Act will do much to restrain the presidency; quite the opposite, perhaps. Congress is not terribly inhibited in domestic affairs. In fact, it may have in some respects too much power to block the executive. The real place where the presidency has got its momentum is foreign affairs. There Congress has deferred—and wished to defer. It's hard to solve that. Providing better information to Congress isn't the answer. Lack of information is an alibi for the congressmen. Congress can get all the information it needs, one way or another—if it really wants to get that information.

POLSBY: You're absolutely right.

WATERGATE AND FOREIGN POLICY

SHERRY: May I comment on what Arthur Schlesinger has been saying about the relationship between the predominance of the presidency for a long time in foreign policy and its spillover into domestic policy. What has not been sufficiently remarked upon is the fact that, conversely, the weakening of the presidency domestically has had over the past year a very substantial spillover into foreign policy. There's a whole list of items which were ongoing problems, on which a policy had been initiated by Nixon and Kissinger in the past four years, and on which in the past year and a half of Watergate the president found himself gradually in a position in which he couldn't deliver. And I am not referring here in any way to the merits or demerits of a particular policy, but simply to the spillover in foreign policy of his domestic problems. He was unable to deliver to the USSR on trade and credit; he was forced into cosmetics during his visit to Moscow in 1974, unlike his visit in 1972 when important and hard agreements were arrived at. Policy with regard to China was impaired in order to maintain Nixon's credibility vis-à-vis his hardcore anti-impeachment one-third in the Senate, the conservative anti-impeachment one-third. He diluted his policy with regard to Peking by appointing, again on account of domestic considerations, a new ambassador to Taipei which infuriated Mao and Chou En-lai. With regard to Japan, he was unable to deliver on plans for joint enterprises in order to develop and exploit natural resources in eastern Siberia in which the Japanese were enormously interested because of their dearth of resources. Also, he was unable to resist protectionist pressures that made it very difficult for him to maintain normal economic relationships with Japan, a matter of vital interest to the Japanese. With regard to Western Europe, Nixon was unable, because of his weakened influence in Congress, to guarantee the maintenance of troop levels. Again I am not talking in favor or against the maintenance of troop levels in Europe. The fact of the matter is, he was unable to guarantee that, as other presidents might have, and as he himself might have been able, only a few years ago, when Watergate had not yet started. On Vietnam, he was unable to get approval of his proposals for increased military and financial support of South Vietnam. Again, I am not talking in favor or against, but this was a part of his policy that he was unable to implement. Cuba, European economic policy problems, there is a host of things which indicate the spillover of his domestic weakening on foreign policies.

POLSBY: Well now look, it seems to me that raises the question of whether in some respects congressional accountability was working. That is to say there are measures short of impeachment which Congress was taking.

SHERRY: Perhaps the impugnment stage, which Charles Hamilton was talking about.

POLSBY: All right, the threat to impeach meant not Congress as a whole surely, but people in Congress were exercising sizable influence over public policy. Now the trouble with that is of the sort your examples indicate: that in Congress they can always do a marvelous job of stopping something but the question is whether they can put something together. Clearly not.

SHERRY: Initiate and carry out a foreign policy? Out of the question.

WICKER: I think the question of the inability of the president to deliver on his promises is very important and we ought not to lose sight of it. Because when we talk about the immense power of the presidency, we begin to find that they tend to be policy powers, policy-setting powers, not administrative delivery powers, and the more you talk about them, as Arthur Schlesinger said, the more they tend to enter the foreign-policy area. And we find still further that they tend to come down to the war-making area, the national security area. In a sense these revelations we've been seeing about Chile—that's a form of warfare. But if the president, out of these immense powers, makes a policy and then finds that in the normal, legitimate workings of American government, he's unable to carry that policy out, he's frustrated. Congress won't authorize it, or the money is not there, or whatever it might happen to be—he can't deliver on the policy. Then we've seen time and again that presidents tend to short-circuit the system and put the policy into effect anyway. You can look at Vietnam, the modern history of our involvement in the world since Vietnam—that period of time—and you find that presidents if they don't in fact use totally clandestine methods as in the opening of the war in Cambodia, at least use extraordinarily devious methods as in the Gulf of Tonkin Resolution, and so forth. So I think that the inability of presidents to deliver straightforwardly through the system on the policy promises that they've made is one of the great spurs, you might say, toward the evolution of extraordinary presidential powers. That's why it's so important, I think, that we see in the Nixon impeachment proceedings that they shy away at every point from impeaching Nixon for anything he may have done in the area of foreign policy, national security, or as commander-in-chief. They wanted to find skulduggery of a lesser dimension, that is, in a lesser area, and they did find it and they wanted to impeach him for it. But if the only charge pending had been the secret war in Cambodia, there wouldn't even have been hearings.

PRESSMAN: We seem to have an inescapable problem here. Because what makes it hard for the president to deliver on policy promises is the dispersion of power in the American political system. And if we were to change things so the president could deliver on his promises without short-circuiting the system, that would make the presidency all powerful and lead to an even greater imbalance in the system. So I think we're still faced with a dilemma of wanting both governmental action and representation for a national presidential constituency, and also some limits of accountability on the presidency.

The Role of the Political Parties

POLSBY: Well then, does it not come down to a problem of the political parties? I must say I'm getting terribly pessimistic about the presidential-selection process because what we are losing—slowly, but at an accelerated rate it seems to me—is the ability of the party organizations to insert a screen which reflects elitist values about candidates. By that I mean simply whether people who know each of the various candidates intimately think that he can do a decent job, or that he's smart enough, or that he has enough character. My view is that more and more this screen has been pulled apart and disintegrated. Thus, we're in for a worse rather than a better time up ahead because of the weakening of the political parties. If Congress can't check or account or adequately oversee the conduct of foreign policy, I believe the political parties could at least insert that kind of a screen into the presidential-selection process, but that's going by the boards now.

SHERRY: Perhaps the parties might perform a function of that kind under optimum conditions, which obviously don't prevail now.

CARALEY: I also think we're in for more trouble. The question I would like to raise is how the Republican party leadership is being held accountable for Watergate.

POLSBY: Why should it be?

CARALEY: By the accession of Ford to the presidency and with his own choice under the Twenty-fifth Amendment of a person who then appeared to be a strong vice-presidential candidate for 1976, the Republican party looked as if it was in better shape to win than ever before. So only a single elective official would have been held responsible and removed from office, but the party leadership who put him there would be escaping injury . . .

POLSBY: I beg your pardon, the party didn't put him there, the electoral college put him there.

CARALEY: Yes, that's technically true. But in fact the party made him one of the two major nominees who had a chance to become president and the party's leaders who were close to him—it's the argument you were just making—and should have protected us, should have protected all the voters—Republicans, Democrats, independents—did not. The party leaders, who it could be argued knew what kind of person Richard Nixon was, did not prevent his nomination, gave him the nomination, and then the people and the electoral college made him president. But that party leadership hasn't been held responsible for this. Only a single individual has been held responsible. And can you have a democratic form of government without some better kind of party accountability? Don't we have to make the party more accountable also because now any particular president can serve only two terms in any event, even if they are good ones? Consequently, during the second term, the control that comes from the wish to be reelected vanishes.

POLSBY: No, there's something prior to that. Presidents must be made accountable to their political party and they are not.

SCHLESINGER: Even behind that, we must have political parties which are strong enough to deserve and enforce accountability. But our party system is in a state of crisis—maybe of dissolution.

POLSBY: Well, yes, but you see how the problems are intertwined. The parties are being pulled apart by the presidential nominating process which is being taken from their hands and placed in the hands of small primary electorates which means . . .

SCHLESINGER: In the hands of the people.

POLSBY: The people, yes—small primary electorates manipulated by money and publicity.

SHERRY: Evaluation of the nominating process depends on whose ox is gored. The primary system is a magnificent system when it results, as in the New Hampshire and West Virginia primaries in 1960, in the election of a Kennedy; and it's an appalling process when it results in the nomination of certain other people.

POLSBY: That was the year I was for Humphrey, so I don't happen to agree with you. Kennedy was too reactionary.

PRESSMAN: No wonder you've been against primaries for so long a time.

POLSBY: He was too reactionary for me, but not for Arthur Schlesinger.

SHERRY: But you see my point is that I am anti-institutionalist in this sense—that it is not the institutional structure that matters, it is the nature of the political process. And this political process can operate through primaries as well or as badly as it can operate through political parties, so I don't think it will make all that much difference.

POLSBY: No, I think that's naive.

SCHLESINGER: Look in New York . . . what our alternatives were for the 1974 statewide campaign. We had a large representative state committee that produced a ticket every member of which was repudiated in the primary. Yet by the normal criteria for ticket balance, in terms of geography, race, religion, and sex, the primary system produced a better balance than the state committee.

PRESSMAN: To return to Nelson's point, it seems to me that the whole notion of re-forming an elite screen would be a very difficult proposition right now. In the Democratic party, there is so much issue polarization and style polarization that the party "elite" probably couldn't even coexist in the same room together. And who knows what will happen at the mini-convention in Kansas City?

POLSBY: We're having what V .O. Key suggested to us in his *Southern Politics* [(New York, 1950)]. We're having what in the first place is the destruction of the minority party. It is sort of being handed over to its ideological diehards which in turn leads to the fragmentation . . .

PRESSMAN: Both sets of ideological diehards I might add.

POLSBY: . . . which in turn leads to the fragmentation of the majority party, as people busily search for the minimum winning coalition, and chuck one another out into the cold, thus ending up losing when they shouldn't. Nowhere, it seems to me in the process of so-called democratization are they doing anything about the problem of whether somebody has the character that you need. Now I am not saying that should be the only screen, but it seems to me it should be part of it.

WICKER: When did we ever have that screen?

POLSBY: I think one consequence of a smoke-filled room is that every once in a while—they don't need to surely—but every once in a while somebody can at least say this man can't do the job, and prevail.

SHERRY: Nobody said that about Harding . . .

POLSBY: I quite agree with you; they didn't with respect to Harding, but they could have said it. I don't know how you can say it when nobody at the point of decision making knows these people and all they get are in effect, manipulated images and name recognition.

HAMILTON: Well this is on the party system, but to get back to Jim Caraley's point . . . are you suggesting that the Republican party should have been held accountable for Watergate?

CARALEY: I'm suggesting that that party's leadership chose a presidential nominee whose track record clearly indicated to many people his capacity to engage in the Watergate kind of activity. Nevertheless the party leadership put him up as their nominee, twice, and I think the argument can be made by those who believe that popular control requires party accountability, that the Republican leadership should not be permitted—either by the Republican rank-and-file or by all the voters—totally to escape responsibility.

SHERRY: But whatever the track record may have been, Nixon was nominated among other reasons because people felt he was going to pursue a policy—not so much in foreign affairs because this was as yet an unknown quality, Kissinger had not yet entered the picture—but with regard to domestic affairs, with regard to economic matters and social policy, which they favored. Even though they knew there were questions raised, and perhaps legitimate ones, about his character, about his morality, and so on and so forth . . . they were confident that he would pursue the economic and other domestic policies which they wanted followed at the top and would do so effectively. For them this was more important than doubts about his character.

CARALEY: Well Machiavelli a long time ago explained about political leaders in *The Prince*. He wrote that the many can see only "what you appear to be" whereas the few can "feel what you are." In terms of presidential nominations, only the few who constitute the party leadership can "feel" what a candidate is really like and therefore can perform the "screen" function and if those few don't protect us from unsuitable candidates, I don't think there is anyone left to protect us at all. And I mean this to apply to both parties.

POLSBY: Not that they do protect us often, but the point is the difference between what is possible and what is impossible is what we've gotten to, not the difference between what used to be more or less probable.

CARALEY: Suppose I advance this proposition ... that there is a group to which a president is accountable for his conduct and tenure and that this group consists of the leading members of his party in Congress. When they turn against him, as the Democratic senators turned against Johnson and as finally the Republicans in the House and the Senate turned against Nixon, the president is in trouble and has to change his course of action.

POLSBY: Well clearly that's true because of the threat of impeachment. They are entitled to impeach and therefore when they turn against him in a very serious way which is not merely a matter of policy disagreement, then of course he's in trouble.

CARALEY: But it's more than just impeachment. Impeachment was never considered in terms of Johnson. It's a question of the president not having their voting support for his legislative initiatives or vetoes. It's also a question of not being able to count on them to obstruct hearings or special investigations aimed at shaping antipresidential public opinion.

THE PARDON

MASON: May I interrupt a minute? I have to leave but before I go I would like to have one question cleared up that Arthur Schlesinger raised in my mind. As I understand it, he said he thought the pardon served a very good purpose. Did you say that?

SCHLESINGER: I did. I'm not sure it outweighs the harm it has done. But it has its silver lining in halting for a moment the rush to return to president-worship.

MASON: I want to address myself to the cost. What was the cost that President Ford had to pay and the country had to pay for the advantage that you see in dispelling the euphoria surrounding the man in the White House? It seems to me the cost was very great. In the first place he pardoned a man who was almost certain to be impeached. The one exception to the president's power to pardon has to do with impeachment. I say that President Ford, at least, violated the spirit of that provision of the Constitution. But that's not all. Under the impeachment clause the president having been impeached is subject to the judicial process. Well, he short-circuited that too. He played rather fast and loose not with one provision of the Constitution but with two. And in so doing it seems to me he skirted the first article in the impeachment of President Nixon—that is, he obstructed justice. Ford, like Nixon, ignored the truth Brandeis highlighted in 1917: "Our government is the potent, the omnipresent teacher. For good or evil it teaches by example."

SCHLESINGER: I think you can make a case. Perhaps Ford should resign and then whoever is vice-president, upon succession to the presidency, could pardon him!

McCAUGHEY: It has struck me during most of the evening, and Alpheus Mason's point now brought it up, that the specter about the imperial presidency is not dead, at least down at the Wicker-Schlesinger end of the table. Alpheus' remarks about the Court suggest that the imperial presidency could come back stronger and fiercer shortly. You find a silver lining in the pardon because it pricks the balloon that, from both your views, seemed to fill up again with the same kind of hot air that the press had been generally inclined to blow in the direction of the White House. But Alpheus' point seems to be more telling . . . if what we would like is a strong president but one somehow desanctified. . .

SCHLESINGER: Within the Constitution.

McCAUGHEY: Within the Constitution. The imperial president which I take to mean one functioning "without," or outside of, the Constitution, has to be slain somehow, or brought back "within," but let's use the more mortal term. I think as Alpheus points out the imperial president that we're talking about in some ways has not been dealt a fatal blow. Congress will not make a move against Nixon now. The courts are not running out the executive. The crucial act concerning Nixon has already happened, and it happened because our presiding president acted in a way to preclude the acts of the other two branches. It seems to me the ball game is still within the White House. I mean we haven't done in the imperial president.

WATERGATE AND THE POWER OF THE BUREAUCRACIES

WICKER: I think that's a well-taken point coming out of the previous remarks, and it goes in other directions too. What part is played here by the bureaucracy in having a strong president representing its interests against Congress?

SCHLESINGER: A strong president doesn't represent his bureaucracies.

WICKER: Well, does he or doesn't he?

SCHLESINGER: Nixon did not represent his bureaucracies. A strong president represents the presidency which is a fourth branch of government, often against the interests of the permanent government—the people who stay in place while presidents and their appointees come and go.

WICKER: Here is Ford sending messages to Congress yesterday and today—they are very low down in the news play, but there they are—his legislative priorities of foreign aid and so forth. The language hasn't changed a bit. Now Ford didn't know anything about these things. In the general sense, it's not the kind of thing that he would have said to the legislature. He is sending along bureaucratic messages coming right out of the foreign-aid bureaucracy.

PRESSMAN: I think one gainer from all this may be—and will continue to be—the bureaucracy. The recommendations of the transition committee to decrease the role of OMB and increase the role of departments is, I am sure, good news for the bureaucracy. And if we're talking about permanent opponents of the presidency, we might rank the bureaucracy ahead of the press and Congress. Bureaucrats seemed to be doing quite well for themselves in the waning years of the Nixon presidency, in terms of following their own preferred patterns of behavior with their own clientele groups. And they got very little bother from people in the White House, who were worried about other things.

CARALEY: I think that is an excellent point—that we all tended to approve the president's dismantling of the OMB supervisory machinery. Normally people like ourselves would take the antibureaucrat point of view. But here it was the president's instruments for trying to deal with an unresponsive bureaucracy that was being dissolved, and we applauded.

PRESSMAN: It's sort of ironic that liberals, who have traditionally been worried about how to make disparate parts of government responsible to presidential will, are now moving in the opposite direction. When the transition committee told President Ford that he ought to downgrade OMB and let the cabinet departments go their own way, liberals said that it was a great idea, it prevents overcentralization, and so forth. But they've been profoundly against that in the past.

POLSBY: Well I think there are some good reasons other than happenstance for people to take that view. One of them is that it was not true when the earlier view was fashionable as it is now that a lot of the interests that liberals wanted to see gratified have been built into the bureaucracies.

SCHLESINGER: That's true.

POLSBY: Looking at the federal bureaucracy as a whole, then, the interests that a lot of us care about are getting greater support from them than was the case earlier.

SCHLESINGER: There was no claimant interest group for environment in the old days and therefore the president had to fight for it. Now these things are bureaucratized.

POLSBY: Urban development, transportation, HEW has the biggest budget . . . so I think there is some reason in it. Second, I think it is true whether liberals like it or not that bureaucracies embody certain patterns which are not altogether evil anyway. They embody expertise, they embody alliances with interest groups that have some legitimacy in the society, they embody alliances with Congress which is in turn a body that is entitled to have an imprint on public policy.

PRESSMAN: Besides which, and not unimportantly, most of the bureaucrats are liberal Democrats, as President Nixon understood.

POLSBY: I don't know if most of them are, but I think the general law is that whoever sets up the agency, staffs it, and gives it its mission in effect freezes the general character and composition of the people that run the agency from then on out, and of course mostly liberal Democrats did this.

PRESSMAN: That's right, and there are a number of reasons why liberal Democratic interests might be represented in a bureaucracy. One is that people who want to see more government intervention create a bureaucracy to do that. And, once they have been created, even someone without that ideological predisposition will pursue those goals just to advance his own organizational interests.

POLSBY: Right. Moreover, there are bureaucratic norms involved in resistance to illegal acts which we've just gone through, and in some of our least favorite agencies, I suppose—FBI and Internal Revenue Service. That means that bureaucratic norms of resistance to politically inspired illegality take on a glow.

CARALEY: They take on a positive function.

CONCLUSIONS

CARALEY: Perhaps at this point we should go around the table and in the way of trying to sum up, each of us should give what he thinks is the single most important lasting impact that Watergate and the forced resignation will have on our entire political and constitutional system. I don't know if that's possible, but it would be a good way to bring the discussion to a close.

SCHLESINGER: Perhaps we should consider putting it this way: To what extent is the impact of events sufficient in itself; or will we need constitutional or structural changes of some significance if the impact is to last?

HAMILTON: I don't think it will be on the level of a major structural change in the sense that we think of developing or establishing new institutions. But it is very clear to me that there is going to be a rather substantial interest as a result of the Watergate phenomenon in trying to devise new ways to finance our campaigns, particularly at the national level. Whether this takes the form of some sort of public financing of campaigns or whatever that should be, could well be a major spinoff of the Watergate phenomenon.

CARALEY: Anybody else ready?

WICKER: I'll just expand a little bit. I really don't believe you can consider Watergate quite in isolation, but if you take Watergate and Vietnam and Nixon and Johnson—granted even the good things you can perhaps say about Johnson or Nixon or Vietnam—if you take all of that together I think there is a very important consequence the end of which we can't forsee. That is just the sort of thing we're doing here tonight. For the first time in my life really, people are willing to call into question the most cherished institution of our government—the presidency and the way it works—and to raise questions about them . . . to ask what are we going to do? Do we need reform? Should we change the Constitution in fundamental ways? I think that's very important . . . it's a kind of self-questioning process that I think in the late fifties and early sixties this nation simply wasn't undergoing. We had arrived at a point and seemed fixed in time. So I think that self-questioning mood is a major consequence of Watergate and could be very important—which is not to say that it will be.

McCAUGHEY: I can follow Tom in that sense. I think the self-questioning process is well underway and it strikes me, perhaps because I remain an unreconstructed strong president man, that the dangers which have been very pointedly expressed about the strong imperial presidency have essentially been made in the area of foreign affairs. Our problems on the near horizon, however, are not likely to be in foreign affairs but in domestic matters. They are likely to relate to the economy and to take the form of some kind of belt-tightening and it seems to me that such an undertaking, if it is to be equitable, calls for the kind of leadership that can probably only come from the White House and only from a White

House filled with a good deal of mythology. We must actually believe Ford is tightening his belt too. If we have slain the kind of myths that we all once attached to the presidency we may have done so at a very dangerous time in our national history. I have some fear about the capacity of this country and this government to handle domestic problems which are likely to be first on our agenda. We certainly learned now the dangers of having that kind of president deal with foreign affairs such as Southeast Asia of the sixties. In dealing with that and perhaps preventing that from happening again we may have rendered ourselves less able to deal with the domestic problems that there will be no skirting in the next few years.

PRESSMAN: I hope that the whole experience will be important in setting limits, albeit very broad ones, as to what a president can do. I don't think that the formal structural changes that come out of it will be as important as the revived notions of political legitimacy that Nelson Polsby was talking about—the informal understandings of what people are supposed to do and not supposed to do in the American political system. Also, Congress may now be able to use its impeachment weapon at least as a very strong bargaining tool. I feel that this experience has taken some of the onus off the idea of impeachment that had grown out of the Andrew Johnson case. Of course, Watergate may also have some negative effects in terms of making people leery, perhaps too leery, of government intervention in a whole range of areas. Since that intervention is often to help people who don't have resources, that could pose serious problems for the disadvantaged.

SHERRY: I agree with everything that has been said by the preceding speakers and this I'm afraid brings me back, since the question was put in a very specific way, to a remark which I've already made: namely, that you have the element of limitation of the presidency and the concept of accountability which has been introduced or reintroduced into the American system in a very pronounced way. After all, we've had two presidents in a row who, in effect, have been forced out of office and while it may be exaggerated to say that this introduces a European element of parliamentary responsibility into the American system, there may even be something to that. Now as far as the field of foreign policy is concerned, I do not believe that the implications are very far reaching; the important implications, as you have said, will remain in the field of domestic policy. I mentioned that Nixon's domestic difficulty spilled over into the foreign-policy field and impaired his ability to deliver on various commitments and promises, diminishing his credibility and forcing him into some dubious tactics because he desperately needed "successes." But the chances are that once this is over and done with, the country's foreign policy, the courses of action which will be open to the American government will be determined by the dynamics of world politics in a manner which will not take Watergate into account. The options that are available in foreign policy are not, after all, directly affected by a development such as Watergate, but by events abroad and by the kind of long-term global problems that now preoccupy the United Nations.

POLSBY: I guess that my view is that norms of continuous political accountability have been strengthened by the Watergate experience. Future presidents have been invited in the most imperative terms to participate in the practice of politics and the politics of governing rather than to see in their elections a mandate which carries them around the necessity of being political leaders. I think, however, that the pardon has made much more difficult the problem of achieving public enlightenment and education on precisely what the norms were that were transgressed and how they were transgressed. Therefore I continue, I must say, in my pessimism about the capacity for large masses of people to see clearly what it is that's going on in their government and thereby to achieve the possibility of popular control.

SCHLESINGER: Well, I think Watergate represents a quite dramatic revival of the system of accountability. Foreign comment on it—the mixture of wonder and envy with which other nations look upon what has happened in the United States—is really extraordinary and touching. The idea that the people of a country can rise against the abuse of power by their rulers is a marvelously attractive idea around the world. Many people will regard it as the exemplification of what ultimately democracy ought to be. Its effect might be even stronger abroad than it is at home. I agree that the pardon complicates the lessons to be derived from it; and on balance, in spite of some useful side effects from the pardon, it would obviously have been much better had it never been made. On the other hand, I do think that, even in spite of the pardon, enough has come out to prevent Nixon from mistaking San Clemente for Elba or his successors from supposing that the pardon repeals the lessons of Watergate. In fact, I think it's possible that Congress may be sufficiently exasperated to devise means of getting more of the story on the record.

How you sustain the lessons of Watergate, I'm not absolutely clear. But I do think that an essential part of it is to continue the process of the secularization of the presidency. I'm still not clear in my own mind as to when we fell into this notion of the president as a superior being requiring reverence and awe. One recalls in Dicken's *American Notes* his description of visiting President Tyler in the White House. People wandered in and out. They were irritated if they didn't get an immediate audience. The president had no staff and no office except a room in his residence. Even in our own time, FDR was supposed to be such an imperial president. But he was readily accessible to his staff. He held cabinet meetings twice a week. He held press conferences twice a week. Members of Congress could get appointments to see him rather quickly. Much of this persisted even during the war. Truman was fairly accessible.

POLSBY: Henry Fairlie [in *The Kennedy Promise* (New York, 1973)] dates this from JFK. Do you agree?

SCHLESINGER: I would disagree on that. Kennedy was perfectly accessible to his staff, his cabinet, members of Congress, even the press.

POLSBY: I'm not talking about accessibility now, but secularization and deification.

WICKER: I think it began with Roosevelt.

SCHLESINGER: President-worship may have begun with Roosevelt, but Roosevelt's practices were not those of a man who regarded himself as properly an object of semireligious veneration.

POLSBY: I think it was accelerated seriously by the Kennedy presidency.

SCHLESINGER: It was stimulated in the Eisenhower years. Eisenhower was widely perceived as a man above the battle and therefore exempt from secular criticism. I think that in all these cases sacrosanctity was more imposed on presidents than contrived by them.

WICKER: I think it was seriously accelerated by nuclear weapons . . . the image of the man who could press the button.

POLSBY: There was a lot of contrivance and it can be set at James Hagerty's door and that was continued and systematically exploited, I think brilliantly, during the Kennedy administration. In essence Henry Fairlie is right about Kennedy, but wrong about Eisenhower, in that he doesn't see that it was going on in the Eisenhower period.

WICKER: I think he's wrong in attributing it to personality. Granted, you have personalities that made important differences. You had four or five extraordinarily impressive personalities, all different: Roosevelt, Truman, Eisenhower, Kennedy, and Johnson. Nevertheless, I think what was happening in that period of time had nothing to do with who they were. Much more important, the average living American never even saw a commander-in-chief before Franklin Roosevelt. Woodrow Wilson didn't play that role or try to. With FDR you had the image of the commander-in-chief in his black cape, at Yalta and all that, and Roosevelt's personality which made the role matter more. Then you had nuclear weapons, you had television, and you have the whole development of the new hat the president wears as the manager of the economy. None of that is merely personality and yet it developed a deification.

POLSBY: I'm not attributing it to personality, but rather to the very skillful exploitation of the resources of the office by a politician more and more fixated on bypassing the ordinary political processes and appealing directly to the masses and the press.

WICKER: No question it was exploited, but you've got to have something to exploit.

POLSBY: Granted, and it was there. Nevertheless, it seems to me that that's the mechanism—the one I described.

SCHLESINGER: But none of these presidents really did that particularly. We used to complain in the White House that Kennedy did not make more of an effort to appeal to the people.

POLSBY: You mean all that charisma was overrated?

SCHLESINGER: He shied away from TV. He was always afraid of becoming a bore. I felt at the time that he was intimidated by the narrowness of the margin in 1960. He didn't go out and make great appeals. The charisma is really something of a memory of him. That isn't something that he himself made.

SHERRY: What charisma? Kennedy kept getting clobbered in Congress on most issues. It was only after his death that much of his legislative program was enacted.

POLSBY: I'd like to ask Arthur, just as a point of information, who tells people when they arrive in the White House to call the president "Mr. President"? Men who have been calling him "Jack." Where does that start? Does it just happen? It's a dreadful habit.

SCHLESINGER: In England, for example, they call him "Prime Minister" in meetings; they call him just "Harold" or "Ted" informally. That's what we ought to do. I agree with that.

WICKER: And you know it's all "Hail to the Chief" and everything is pretty impressive. While I don't think it's necessarily true, there's that great story in one of Eisenhower's books. He said what seemed to impress young Mr. Kennedy most was the time when "I reached under the desk and pressed a button and a helicopter landed on the White House lawn."

SCHLESINGER: To complete my point, that is, how you strengthen the movement toward the secularization of the presidency: I think this imposes a particular burden on those who have any role in forming opinion. And I would say that historians, political scientists, and journalists have been guilty in the past of contributing to the presidential mystique. I'm not sure that our self-restraint will have great effect in the ultimate balance of things. But what all of us can do is to remind the world that any president is only a politician luckier than the rest, and that making it to what Disraeli called the top of the greasy pole does not transform his character or increase his wisdom or make him a being beyond our concern or control. The most noxious of all of Nixon's phrases was that idiot phrase about respect for the presidency. So far as I know, no previous president had ever used it.

SHERRY: Well, you only use a phrase like that if you haven't got it.·

SCHLESINGER: We must reject the notion that a president is entitled to any more respect than his words and actions earn him. He's entitled to courtesy, like every other American citizen, but not to worship. Indeed, because of his power, you can make the opposite argument that he deserves more disrespect than anyone else. I think all presidents should hang over their desks Lord Acton's great statement, "There is no more heresy than that the office sanctifies the holder of it."

CARALEY: I think there is another modest way of helping the secularization of the presidency and the strengthening of mechanisms of accountability. That is to demand of all federal judges and especially of all members of Congress when they get appointed or elected and before they draw their first paycheck that they reread or read for the first time *Federalist No. 51*. That essay has all the advice they need:

> ... the great security against a gradual concentration of the several powers in the same department, consists in giving to those who administer each department the necessary constitutional means and personal motives to resist encroachments of the others. ... Ambition must be made to counteract ambition.

Because for a long time they weren't ambitious enough in Congress, were they? It seems to me that members of Congress were simply not ambitious enough to protect their own constitutionally given prerogatives. In my judgment they tolerated presidential encroachments for decades, and by so tolerating them, implicitly invited further ones. Whether members of Congress should be disrespectful to the president or just watch him like a hawk and be completely and immediately intolerant of any attempts on his part to overstep constitutional bounds, I don't know ...

SCHLESINGER: Presidents regard that as disrespect. . . .

9 Separation of Powers
and Executive Privilege:
The Watergate Briefs

CHARLES ALAN WRIGHT, ET AL.
ARCHIBALD COX, ET AL.

INTRODUCTORY NOTE: On July 23, 1973, President Richard M. Nixon was served with a subpoena *duces tecum* "command[ing]" him to turn over to a Washington, D.C., federal grand jury the tape recordings of eight specifically identified meetings and one specifically identified telephone conversation that had taken place in his office between June 20, 1972, and April 15, 1973. The grand jury seeking the tapes was the one that had originally investigated the June 17, 1972, break-in of the Democratic National Committee's headquarters at the Watergate. That investigation had led to the indictment of seven low- and middle-level employees of the Republican "Committee for the Re-Election of the President" and their subsequent conviction after trial in early 1973. At the time of the issuance of the subpoena to the President, the grand jury was investigating whether White House aides, other high government officials, or senior officers of the "Committee to Re-elect" had committed perjury during the earlier investigation and prosecution of the Watergate burglary and whether any of them had otherwise conspired to obstruct justice by "covering up" evidence linking them to the illegal activities of the convicted defendants.

Testimony during the summer of 1973 before the Senate Select Committee on Presidential Campaign Activities (also known as the "Watergate" or "Ervin" Committee) had shown that on each of the nine occasions for which the tapes were being demanded, there had been discussions between the President and others about the Watergate break-in, its investigation, possible cover-ups, or all three. The testimony received by the Select Committee was public and thus available to the grand jury. But much of that testimony was in sharp conflict on a number of crucial points, such as: Had the President indicated awareness of the plans for the burglary or of any cover-up? Had there been discussions of any offers of executive clemency or money pay-offs for the convicted burglars to insure their continued silence about higher-level involvement? To what extent had any of the White House aides, other government officials, and officers of the "Committee to Re-elect" who participated in the discussions with the President revealed that they themselves had authorized or engaged in illegal acts?

The confrontation over the "executive privilege" issue was precipitated by the revelation that tape recordings of the discussions in the President's office existed. In surprise testimony on July 16, a former deputy assistant to the President told the Select Committee that during the period in which the nine conversations took place, the Secret Service had been automatically recording all conversations in which the President participated, in person or by telephone, while in his offices at the White House or Old Executive Office Building. The tapes, which were purportedly in the custody of the Secret Service, were immediately seen as a means of resolving the conflicts in testimony and furnishing almost indisputable proof of what was actually said by the different participants on the nine occasions the Senate Committee testimony indicated had been critical.

A request for the tapes promptly went to the White House from both the Senate Committee and Special [Watergate] Prosecutor Archibald Cox, who was acting as attorney for the government in the grand-jury proceedings. Cox had been appointed Special Prosecutor by Attorney General Elliot L. Richardson in May of 1973. In a departmental order Richardson had delegated to Cox "full authority for investigating and prosecuting offenses . . . arising out of the unauthorized entry into . . . the Watergate, and . . . allegations involving the President, members of the White House staff, or presidential appointees. . . ." Richardson had also specifically authorized Cox to contest any assertion by the President of "executive privilege."

The President's response to the Senate Committee and Cox requests was to announce that he was assuming personal control of the tapes and would not release them. It was after this announcement that Cox, on behalf of the grand jury, issued the subpoena requiring the President or "any subordinate officer, official, or employee with custody or control" to produce the tapes. Two days later on July 25, the President wrote to District Court Judge John J. Sirica that he would "decline to obey the command of [the] subpoena" because he was "not subject to compulsory process from the courts." Sirica was the presiding judge of the United States District Court for the District of Columbia, under whose seal the subpoena had issued. He was also the judge who empaneled the "Watergate" grand jury, and he had presided over the original Watergate burglary trial. After the President's letter refusing to comply with the subpoena, the grand jury unanimously instructed Cox to apply for a court order directing compliance. Judge Sirica on July 26 signed an order for the President to "show cause" why "full and prompt compliance" should not be forthcoming and "the tapes . . . be produced as evidence before the grand jury."

The President, through his attorneys, thereupon entered a "special appearance" on August 7 in which he asserted that the court "lack[ed] jurisdiction to enter an enforceable order compelling compliance with the subpoena." The President argued that it was his "executive privilege . . . in his official capacity as President of the United States to withhold information the disclosure of which would be contrary to the public interest" and that consequently any attempt to enter such an order "would be an unwarranted and unsupportable violation of the Constitutional doctrine of separation of powers."

A constitutional issue of the highest possible import was thus joined:

Does the President enjoy an unreviewable "executive privilege" to withhold evidence of conversations in which he participated from a grand jury investigating serious allegations of obstructions of justice by his White House aides and party leaders solely on the basis of his own assertion that he deems production of the evidence to be "contrary to the public interest" and notwithstanding the relevance of those conversations to the question of whether crimes had been committed?

The Constitution does not contain the term "executive privilege" and therefore does not define it. Since George Washington, however, presidents have asserted the right to withhold information demanded at various times by the courts and by Congress. In all past instances either the President eventually provided some or all of the information voluntarily or the courts or the Congress acquiesced in his continued refusal and did not press for a legal order compelling the production of the desired information. The Supreme Court has not, accordingly, ever had occasion to rule directly on whether such an order could be issued to a President, though enough decisions exist on closely related points to enable legal scholars to fashion strong arguments on both sides of the question.

The *Political Science Quarterly* has chosen to publish both the brief submitted to the District Court by the President's attorneys in opposition to the petition for an order directing the production of the tapes and the Special Prosecutor's brief filed in support of such an order. The two briefs give the competing legal arguments and policy considerations that bear on the grand jury's right of access to the presidential tapes. They demonstrate the great complexity of the "executive privilege" issue and of the many different sub-issues that are intertwined with it. Because these are the briefs that laid the original legal foundation for the unprecedented lawsuit compelling disclosure by the President of his own conversations, we believe that they are historic documents of lasting value.

Unlike court decisions, texts of original briefs are not widely available, nor have these particular briefs been quoted at any length in the public press. We present the "Watergate" briefs here with the thought that readers of the *Quarterly* will be interested in having the full background for understanding the court decisions that have been made and may yet be made in this momentous constitutional confrontation over the extent of presidential powers.

DEMETRIOS CARALEY AND FRANCES PENN

UNITED STATES DISTRICT COURT
FOR THE DISTRICT OF COLUMBIA

IN RE GRAND JURY SUBPOENA)	
DUCES TECUM ISSUED TO)	
RICHARD M. NIXON, OR ANY)	
SUBORDINATE OFFICER, OF-)	MISC. NO. 47-73
FICIAL, OR EMPLOYEE WITH)	
CUSTODY OR CONTROL OF)	
CERTAIN DOCUMENTS OR)	
OBJECTS)	

BRIEF IN OPPOSITION
[TO AN ORDER TO PRODUCE DOCUMENTS OR
OBJECTS IN RESPONSE TO THE SUBPOENA]*

. . .

SUMMARY OF ARGUMENT

The present proceeding, though a well-intentioned effort to obtain evidence for criminal prosecutions, represents a serious threat to the nature of the Presidency as it was created by the Constitution, as it has been sustained for 184 years, and as it exists today.

---

* This brief is printed in its entirety except for an introductory factual statement of the case.

If the Special Prosecutor should be successful in the attempt to compel disclosure of recordings of Presidential conversations, the damage to the institution of the Presidency will be severe and irreparable. The character of that office will be fundamentally altered and the total structure of government—dependent as it is upon a separation of powers—will be impaired.

The consequence of an order to disclose recordings or notes would be that no longer could a President speak in confidence with his close advisers on any subject. The threat of potential disclosure of any and all conversations would make it virtually impossible for President Nixon or his successors in that great office to function. Beyond that, a holding that the President is personally subject to the orders of a court would effectively destroy the status of the Executive Branch as an equal and coordinate element of government.

There is no precedent that can be said to justify or permit such a result. On the contrary, it is clear that while courts and their grand juries have the power to seek evidence of all persons, including the President, the President has the power and thus the privilege to withhold information if he concludes that disclosure would be contrary to the public interest.

The breadth of this privilege is frequently debated. Whatever its boundaries it must obtain with respect to a President's private conversations with his advisers (as well as to private conversations by judges and legislators with their advisers). These conversations reflect advisory opinions, recommendations, and deliberations that are an essential part of the process by which Presidential decisions and policies are formulated. Presidential privacy must be protected, not for its own sake, but because of the paramount need for frank expression and discussion among the President and those consulted by him in the making of Presidential decisions.

The privilege with regard to recordings was not waived by the decision of the President, in the interest of having the truth about Watergate come out, to permit testimony about portions of those conversations by persons who participated in them. Testimony can be limited, as recordings cannot, to the particular area in which privilege is not being claimed. Nor does the privilege vanish because there are claims that some of the statements made to the President by others in these conversations may have been pursuant to a criminal conspiracy by those other persons. That others may have acted in accordance with a criminal design does not alter the fact that the President's participation in these conversations was pursuant to his Constitutional duty to see that the laws are faithfully executed and that he is entitled to claim executive privilege to preserve the confidentiality of private conversations he held in carrying out that duty.

In the exercise of his discretion to claim executive privilege the President is answerable to the Nation but not to the courts. The courts, a co-equal but not a superior branch of government, are not free to probe the mental processes and the private confidences of the President and his advisers. To do so would be a clear violation of the Constitutional separation of powers. Under that doctrine the Judicial Branch lacks power to compel the President to produce information that he has determined it is not in the public interest to disclose.

The issue here is starkly simple: will the Presidency be allowed to continue to function?

ARGUMENT

I. *Introductory Statement*

The extent to which the Executive Branch has a power or privilege to withhold documents or testimony from the other two branches of government has been correctly described as "one of the most difficult, delicate and significant problems arising under our system." Rogers, *Constitutional Law: The Papers of the Executive Branch*, 44 A.B.A.J. 941, 1012 (1958). There are few authoritative judicial decisions on the matter but this is because the other branches of government have respected claims of privilege by the Executive Branch and have recognized that inappropriateness of seeking resolution in the courts of controversies between branches of government.

Although there have been repeated clashes between Presidents and Congress over the issue from 1796 on, there is no judicial decision whatever on controversies of that kind. See *Soucie* v. *David*, 448 F.2d 1067, 1071 n. 9 (D.C. Cir. 1971). There are decisions on the privilege as it exists against the courts, but these decisions tend to be cautious, Hardin, *Executive Privilege in the Federal Courts*, 71 Yale L.J. 879 (1962), and to be resolved on the narrowest possible grounds. E.g., *United States* ex rel. *Touhy* v. *Ragen*, 340 U.S. 462,

467 (1951); *United States* v. *Reynolds*, 345 U.S. 1, 6 (1953). Though there is a fairly substantial literature on the question, it is more argumentative than authoritative.

The question is still further clouded by the tendency of all those who have spoken on this question to lump together questions that may require separate answers. Thus courts and writers have not always been careful to distinguish between the President himself, the heads of departments, and subordinates within the executive departments. Nor is it always recognized that the scope of the privilege may be one question, who is to judge of its existence a second question, and whether a decision adverse to the executive could be enforced a third question.

This case, however, does not require a sweeping analysis of the privilege and all of its ramifications. Rather the court is faced with the narrow question of its application to the President of the United States in his most confidential conversations with his intimate advisers. On this question judicial precedents are almost nonexistent. One fact does stand out. No court has ever attempted to enforce a subpoena directed at the President of the United States. No President —and, for that matter, no department head—has ever been held in contempt for refusal to produce information, either to the courts or to Congress, that the President has determined must be withheld in the public interest. Quite commonly Presidents have voluntarily made available information for which a claim of privilege could have been made. That happens very often—and has happened and is happening in this case. But practice throughout our history shows no exception to the rule that the President cannot be forced to disclose information that he thinks it would damage the public interest to disclose.

We do not question the power of the court to issue a subpoena to the President. In *United States* v. *Burr*, 25 F.Cas. 30, 34, No. 14,692d (C.C.D.Va. 1807), Chief Justice Marshall, sitting at circuit, ruled that a subpoena might issue, though he immediately recognized that "difference may exist with respect to the power to compel the same obedience to the process, as if it had been directed to a private citizen * * *." A subsequent Attorney General has ruled that a subpoena may be directed against the President to produce a paper, though the courts would be without power to enforce their process should the President refuse. 25 Op. Atty. Gen. 326, 330-331 (1905). The cautious reference to the *Burr* ruling in *Branzburg* v. *Hayes*, 408 U.S. 665, 688 n. 26 (1972), goes no further than to note that Chief Justice Marshall had "opined" that a subpoena might issue. For present purposes, we accept that proposition.

But the power to seek information from the Executive Branch does not impose on the Executive any concurrent obligation to disclose that information. Rather the responsibility of a President to disclose information to a grand jury and to the courts is limited by the Constitutional doctrine of separation of powers. The classic statement of that doctrine is contained in the opinion of the Supreme Court in *Kilbourn* v. *Thompson*, 103 U.S. 168 (1880), where the Court said:

> It is believed to be one of the chief points of the American system of written constitutional law, that all powers intrusted to government, whether State or national, are divided into the three grand departments, the executive, the legislative, and the judicial. That the functions appropriate to each of these branches of government shall be vested in a separate body of public servants, and that the perfection of the system requires that the lines which separate and divide these departments shall be broadly and clearly defined.

103 U.S. at 190-191. The Court continued:

> In the main, however, that instrument, the model on which are constructed the fundamental laws of the States, has blocked out with singular precision, and in bold lines, in its three primary articles, the allotment of power to the executive, the legislative, and the judicial departments of the government. It also remains true, as a general rule, that the powers confided by the Constitution to one of the departments cannot be exercised by another.

> It may be said that these are truisms which need no repetition here to give them force. But while the experience of almost a century has in general shown a wise and commendable forebearance in each of these branches from encroachments upon the others, it is not to be denied that such attempts have been made * * *

103 U.S. at 191.

This concept of separation of powers, which was recognized by the Supreme Court as early as 1803 in *Marbury* v. *Madison*, 1 Cranch (5 U.S.) 137 (1803), caused Chief Justice Marshall, in the *Burr* case, to qualify his remarks about subpoenaing the President. He said:

In no case of this kind would a court be required to proceed against the President as against an ordinary individual. The objections to such a course are so strong and so obvious that all must acknowledge them.

United States v. *Burr*, 25 F. Cas. 187, 191-192, No. 14,694 (C.C.D. Va. 1807).

To insist on the doctrine of separation of powers is by no means to suggest that the President is above the law. This is not the case. The President is accountable under the law, but only in the manner prescribed in the Constitution. The distinction was drawn vividly by Attorney General Stanbery in his argument in *Mississippi* v. *Johnson*, 4 Wall. (71 U.S.) 475, 484-485 (1867):

> It is not upon any peculiar immunity that the individual has who happens to be President; upon any idea that he cannot do wrong; upon any idea that there is any particular sanctity belonging to him as an individual, as is the case with one who has royal blood in his veins; but it is on account of the office that he holds that I say the President of the United States is above the process of any court or the jurisdiction of any court to bring him to account as President. There is only one court or quasi court that he can be called upon to answer to for any dereliction of duty, for doing anything that is contrary to law or failing to do anything which is according to law, and that is not this tribunal but one that sits in another chamber of this Capitol. There he can be called and tried and punished, but not here while he is President; and after he has been dealt with in that chamber and stripped of the robes of office, and he no longer stands as the representative of the government, then for any wrong he has done to any individual, for any murder or any crime of any sort which he has committed as President, then and not till then can he be subjected to the jurisdiction of the courts. Then it is the individual they deal with, not the representative of the people.

See the similar statement of position by Alexander Hamilton in *Federalist* No. 69.

Nor is the privilege derived from the doctrine of separation of powers one that is available only to protect the President, or the Executive Branch generally, from the other two branches of government. Each branch of government has claimed, and rightly so, a privilege to do its own business in its own way, without coercion from other branches of government. No other branch of government can compel disclosure of what judges of a court say to each other when the court is in conference. No other branch can require disclosure of discussions about legislative business between a Congressman and his aide. Cf. *Gravel* v. *United States*, 408 U.S. 606 (1972). As Judge Wilkey recently wrote, "the privilege against disclosure of the decision-making process is a tripartite privilege, because precisely the same privilege on conducting certain aspects of public business exists for the legislative and judicial branches as well as for the executive." *Soucie* v. *David*, 448 F.2d 1067, 1080 (D.C. Cir. 1971) (concurring opinion). The Congress has always claimed a privilege for its own private papers. No court subpoena is complied with by the Congress or its committees without a vote of the house concerned to turn over the documents. 448 F.2d at 1081-1082.[1] The Judiciary claims a similar privilege against giving testimony about the official conduct of judges, *Statement of the Judges*, 14 F.R.D. 335 (N.D.Cal 1953); cf. *Fayerweather* v. *Ritch*, 195 U.S. 276, 306-307 (1904). See also the letter of Justice Tom C. Clark, dated November 14, 1953, refusing to respond to a subpoena to appear before the House Un-American Activities Committee, on the ground that the "complete independence of the judiciary is necessary to the proper administration of justice."

All branches of government benefit from the independence secured to them by the Constitutional separation of powers. All

[1] See, e.g., 108 Cong. Rec. 3626 (1962), showing Senate adoption of a resolution permitting staff members and former staff members of a Senate Committee to appear and to testify in a criminal proceeding against James Hoffa but forbidding them from taking any documents or records in the custody of the Senate and from testifying about information that they gained while employed by the Senate. In explaining the resolution to the Senate, Senator McClellan said in part: "The Senate recognizes it has certain privileges as a separate and distinct branch of Government, which it wishes to protect." *Id.* at 3627.

On July 16, 1970, counsel for 1st Lt. William L. Calley, Jr., moved in his court-martial proceeding for production of testimony concerning the My Lai incident presented to a subcommittee of the House Committee on Armed Services in executive session. The subcommittee Chairman, Rep. F. Edward Hebert, refused to make the testimony available, advising defense counsel on July 17, 1970, that Congress is "an independent branch of the Government, separate from and equal to the Executive and Judicial branches," and that accordingly only Congress can direct the disclosure of legislative records. He concluded from this that the material requested by the defense was not within the rule of *Brady* v. *Maryland*, 373 U.S. 83 (1963), nor subject to the requirements of 18 U.S.C. § 3500. Subsequently the military court issued a subpoena to the Clerk of the House of Representatives. The Speaker laid this before the House on November 17, 1970, 116 Cong. Rec. 37652 (1970), but to date the House has taken no action and given no indication that it will supply the information sought.

America has benefited from the sturdy insistence of all three of the branches, over the years, on preserving that independence.

II. *The President Has The Power To Withhold Information If He Deems Disclosure To Be Contrary To The Public Interest*

Executive privilege has been aptly described as "a phase of release from requirements common to private citizens or organizations. It is granted by custom or statute for the benefit of the public, not of executives who may happen to then hold office." *Kaiser Aluminum & Chemical Corp.* v. *United States,* 157 F.Supp. 939, 944 (Ct.Cl. 1958) (per Reed, J.) It is a concept essential to the discharge of highly important executive responsibilities. *Carl Zeiss Stiftung* v. *V. E. B. Carl Zeiss, Jena,* 40 F.R.D. 318, 324 (D.D.C. 1966). Whatever uncertainty there may be about the outer boundaries of executive privilege, discussions by the President in his official capacity are at the very heart of the concept.

This follows logically from the President's broad inherent powers under the Constitution. These broad powers were recognized very early in the decision in *Marbury* v. *Madison,* 1 Cranch (5 U.S.) 137 (1803). There Chief Justice Marshall, speaking for the Court, stated:

> By the Constitution of the United States, the President is invested with certain important political powers, in the exercise of which he is to use his own discretion, and is accountable only to his country in his political character, and to his own conscience. To aid him in the performance of these duties, he is authorized to appoint certain officers, who act by his authority and in conformity with his orders.

> In such cases, their acts are his acts; and whatever opinion may be entertained of the manner in which Executive discretion may be used, still there exists and can exist no power to control that discretion. The subjects are political. They respect the nation, not individual rights, and being entrusted to the executive, the application of this remark will be perceived by adverting to the act of Congress for establishing the department of foreign affairs. This officer, as his duties were prescribed by that act, is to conform precisely to the will of the President. He is the mere organ by whom that will is communicated. The acts of such an officer, as an officer, can never be examinable by the courts.

1 Cranch at 165-166.

This principle was restated 35 years later in *Kendall* v. *United States* ex. rel. *Stokes,* 12 Pet. (37 U.S.) 524, 610 (1838), where the Court said:

> The executive power is vested in a President; and as far as his powers are derived from the Constitution, he is beyond the reach of any other department, except in the mode prescribed by the Constitution through the impeaching power.

A. *Privilege against Demands by Congress.* The privilege asserted here derives from the same Constitutional source as, and closely parallels, the executive privilege that has consistently and successfully been asserted in response to Congressional attempts to require production by the Executive Branch.

This long-standing privilege of the executive to refuse Congressional demands does not require extended discussion. From the administration of Washington to the present, Presidents have repeatedly asserted the privilege, and when forced to a showdown, Congress has consistently yielded. Corwin, *The President: Office and Powers, 1787-1957* 113 (4th rev.ed. 1957). A recent instance was the refusal of President Kennedy to disclose the names of Defense Department speech reviewers. Committee on Armed Services, U.S. Senate, *Military Cold War Escalation and Speech Review Policies,* 87th Congress, 2nd Sess., 338, 369-370, 508-509, 725, 730-731 and 1826 (1962). The Senate Subcommittee, speaking through Senator Stennis, conceded:

> We now come face to face and are in direct conflict with the established doctrine of separation of powers * * *

> I know of no case where the Court has ever made the Senate or the House surrender records from its files, or where the Executive has made the Legislative Branch surrender records from its files—and I do not think either one of them could. So the rule works three ways. Each is supreme within its field, and each is responsible within its field.

Id. at 512.

Reference to the unbroken record of successful assertions of privilege in practice is particularly significant to the doctrine of separation of powers. Uninterrupted usage continued from the early days of the Constitution is weighty evidence of the proper construction of any clause of the Constitution.

Both officers, lawmakers and citizens naturally adjust themselves to any long continued action of the Executive Department—on the presumption that unauthorized acts would not have been allowed to be so often repeated as to crystallize into regular practices. That presumption is not reasoning in a circle but the basis of a wise and quieting rule that in determining the meaning of the statute or the exercise of a power, weight should be given to the usage itself—even when the validity of the practice is the subject of investigation.

United States v. *Midwest Oil Co.,* 236 U.S. 459, 472-473 (1915).

This is especially important because the doctrine of separation of powers is not stated in express words in the Constitution and because the functioning of our government depends largely upon limits on the power of each branch derived from practical adjustments based on a fair regard by each for the rights of the others. "Even Constitutional power, when the text is doubtful, may be established by usage." *Inland Waterway Corp.* v. *Young,* 309 U.S. 517, 525 (1940).

B. *Scope of the Privilege.* It is well settled that the privilege applies to information relating to national security. *United States* v. *Reynolds,* 345 U.S. 1, 10 (1953). Similarly, it has been applied to information relating to diplomatic affairs. *New York Times* v. *United States,* 403 U.S. 713, 728 (1971) (Stewart, J. concurring).

But the privilege is not confined to specific kinds of subject matters nor, as discussed in the next part of this brief, to particular kinds of communications. Reason dictates a much broader concept, that the privilege extends to all of the executive power vested in the President by Article II and that it reaches any information that the President determines cannot be disclosed consistent with the public interest and the proper performance of his Constitutional duties. The touchstone for a broad concept is provided by President Washington and his cabinet, who concluded that "the Executive ought to communicate such papers as the public good would permit and ought to refuse those the disclosure of which would injure the public. Consequently were to exercise a discretion." 1 Ford, *Writings of Thomas Jefferson* 189-190 (1892).

This broad concept of executive privilege has been acted upon by many subsequent Presidents and has been stated by many Attorneys General. Thus, Attorney General Speed gave the following opinion in 1865:

Upon principles of public policy there are some kind of evidence which the law excludes or dispenses with. Secrets of state, for instance, cannot be given in evidence, and those who are possessed of such secrets are not required to make disclosure of them. The official transactions between the heads of departments of the Government and their subordinate officers are, in general, treated as "privileged communications." The President of the United States, the heads of the great departments of the Government, and the Governors of the several States, it has been decided, are not bound to produce papers or disclose information communicated to them where, in their own judgment, the disclosure would, on public considerations, be inexpedient. These are familiar rules laid down by every author on the law of evidence.

11 Op. Atty. Gen. 137, 142-143 (1865). In 1877 Attorney General Devens took the view that production cannot be required of correspondence between the Commissioner of Internal Revenue and a United States attorney if production would be prejudicial to the public interests. 15 Op. Atty. Gen. 378 (1877). In 1893 Attorney General Olney gave the opinion that it is for the President or head of the department having the legal custody of a paper, and "not for the judge presiding at the trial," to determine whether "such general public interest forbids the production of an official record or paper in the courts* * *." 20 Op. Atty. Gen. 557, 558 (1893). In 1905 Attorney General Moody ruled that the head of an Executive Department may properly decline to furnish official records of the department, or to give testimony in a court case, "whenever in your judgment the production of such papers or the giving of such testimony might prove prejudicial for any reason to the Government or to the public interest." 25 Op. Atty. Gen. 326, 331 (1905).

An opinion in 1941 by Attorney General (later Justice) Jackson was directed to investigative reports but rested on a broader principle:

> The courts have repeatedly held that they will not and cannot require the executive to produce such papers when in the opinion of the executive their production is contrary to the public interests. The courts have also held that the question whether the production of the papers would be against the public interest is one for the executive and not for the courts to determine.

40 Op. Atty. Gen. 45, 49 (1941).

President Eisenhower's famous letter of May 17, 1954, directing that persons employed in the executive branch were not to testify before a Congressional committee on matters occurring within the executive branch, was supported by a memorandum of Attorney General Brownell, which said in part:

> Courts have uniformly held that the President and the heads of departments have an uncontrolled discretion to withhold the information and papers in the public interests; they will not interfere with the exercise of that discretion, and that Congress has not the power, as one of the three great branches of the Government, to subject the executive branch to its will any more than the executive branch may impose its unrestrained will upon the Congress.

100 Cong. Rec. 6621 (1954).

More recently Assistant Attorney General (now Justice) Rehnquist made a statement in 1971 to the Foreign Operations and Government Information Subcommittee of the House Government Operations Committee in which he asserted that the privilege of the President to withhold information "the disclosure of which he feels would impair the proper exercise of his constitutional obligations" is "firmly rooted in history and precedent." Hearings before the Subcommittee on Separation of Powers of the Committee on the Judiciary, *Executive Privilege: The Withholding of Information by the Executive*, U.S. Senate, 92nd Cong. 1st Sess., at 429 (1971). He continued:

> The President's authority to withhold information is not an unbridled one, but it necessarily requires the exercise of his judgment as to whether or not the disclosure of particular matters sought would be harmful to the national interest.

Id. at 431.

C. *Confidential Intra-Governmental Communications.* The "public interest" standard is admittedly broad and defies precise definition. Nevertheless, it is clear that it applies to confidential intra-governmental communications. Thus, the court in *Carl Zeiss Stiftung* v. *V. E. B. Carl Zeiss, Jena*, 40 F.R.D. 318 (D.D.C. 1966), *aff'd on the opinion below* 384 F.2d 979 (D.C. Cir.), *cert. denied* 389 U.S. 952 (1967) stated:

> While it is agreed that the [executive] privilege extends to all military and diplomatic secrets, its recognition is not confined to data qualifying

as such. Whatever its boundaries as to other types of claims not involving state secrets, it is well established that the privilege obtains with respect to intra-governmental documents reflecting advisory opinions, recommendations and deliberations comprising part of a process by which governmental decisions and policies are formulated.

40 F.R.D. at 324. The court continued:

This privilege, as do all evidentiary privileges, effects an adjustment between important but competing interests. There is, on the one hand, the public concern in revelations facilitating the just resolution of legal disputes, and, on the other, occasional but compelling public needs for confidentiality. In striking the balance in favor of nondisclosure of intragovernmental advisory and deliberative communications, the privilege subserves a preponderating policy of frank expression and discussion among those upon whom rests the responsibility for making the determinations that enable government to operate, and thus achieves an objective akin to those attained by other privileges more ancient and commonplace in character. Nowhere is the public interest more vitally involved than in the fidelity of the sovereign's decision-and policy-making resources.

40 F.R.D. at 324-325.

These policy considerations are particularly compelling when applied to Presidential communications with his advisers. As stated by the President on July 6, 1973, in his letter to Senator Sam J. Ervin:

No President could function if the private papers of his office, prepared by his personal staff, were open to public scrutiny. Formulation of sound public policy requires that the President and his personal staff be able to communicate among themselves in complete candor, and that their tentative judgments, their exploration of alternatives, and their frank comments on issues and personalities at home and abroad remain confidential.

Earlier Presidents throughout our history have taken a similar position. The principle was well stated by President Eisenhower on July 6, 1956, in connection with the Dixon-Yates controversy:

But when it comes to the conversations that take place between any responsible official and his advisers or exchange of little, mere little slips, of this or that, expressing personal opinions on the most confidential basis, those are not subject to investigation by anybody, and if they are, will wreck the Government.

There is no business that could be run if it—if there would be exposed every single thought that an adviser might have, because in the process of reaching an agreed position there are many, many conflicting opinions to be brought together. And if any commander is going to get the free, unprejudiced opinions of his subordinates, he had better protect what they have to say to him on a confidential basis.

See also. . . .

A distinguished constitutional lawyer has recently observed that refusal to disclose communications of this kind is not only the President's lawful privilege

but his duty as well, for it is a measure necessary to the protection of the proper conduct of his office, not only by him but, much more importantly, by his successors for all time to come.

* * * It is hard for me to see how any person of common sense could think that those consultative and decisional processes that are the essence of the Presidency could be carried on to any good effect, if every participant spoke or wrote in continual awareness that at any moment any Congressional committee, or any prosecutor working with a grand jury, could at will command the production of the verbatim record of every word written or spoken.

Black, *Mr. Nixon, the Tapes, and Common Sense*, The New York Times, Aug. 3, 1973, p. 31. See also . . .

The wise men who wrote the Constitution of the United States surely would have agreed. On May 29, 1787, as one of their first acts at the Constitutional Convention, they adopted a resolution that their deliberations were to be kept secret. 1 Farrand, *The Records of the Federal Convention of 1787* 15 (1966 ed.). They knew that wise decision-making requires the kind of frank discussion for which confidentiality is essential.

The unique status of Presidential papers, that they are the property of the President and that they often require the highest degree of confidentiality for many years, was recognized by Congress in the Presidential Libraries Act of 1955, Pub. L. 84-373, 69 Stat. 695 (1955), now codified in 44 U.S.C. §§ 2107, 2108. That statute encourages Presidents to give their papers to a Presidential library, and provides that papers, documents, and other historical materials so given "are subject to restrictions as to their availability and use stated in writing by the donors or depositors* * *. The restrictions shall be respected for the period stated, or until revoked or terminated by the donors or depositors or by persons legally qualified to act on their behalf." 44 U.S.C. § 2108(c); *Nichols* v. *United States,* 460 F.2d 671 (10th Cir. 1972). The gifts of the papers of Presidents Kennedy and Johnson, for example, both provide that "materials containing statements made by or to" the President "in confidence" are to be held under seal and not revealed to anyone except the donors or archival personnel until "the passage of time or other circumstances no longer require such materials being kept under restriction." Agreement of Feb. 25, 1965 between Mrs. Jacqueline B. Kennedy and the United States; Letter of Aug. 13, 1965, from President Lyndon B. Johnson to the Administrator of General Services.[2]

These reasons apply with special force when recordings of Presidential conversations are sought. Recordings are the raw material of life. By their very nature they contain spontaneous, informal, tentative, and frequently pungent comments on a variety of subjects inextricably intertwined into one conversation. Disclosure of information allegedly relevant to this inquiry would mean disclosure as well as other information of a highly confidential nature relating to a wide range of matters not relevant to this inquiry. Some of these matters deal with sensitive issues of national security. Others go to the exercise by the President of his Constitutional duties on matters other than Watergate. The nature of informal, private conversations is such that it is not practicable to separate what is arguably relevant from what is clearly irrelevant. Once the totality of the confidential nature of the recordings is destroyed, no person could ever be assured that his own frank and candid comments to the President would not eventually be made public. Nor should this Court be misled by the seemingly modest request to hear recordings of a few conversations. These conversations could not be properly understood without listening also to many other conversations, and once the principle was

---

[2] The letter from President Johnson specifically prohibits disclosure to "public officials." It states, as the reason for these restrictions, that "the President of the United States is the recipient of many confidences from others, and * * * the inviolability of such confidence is essential to the functioning of the constitutional office of the Presidency * * *." In both respects this is identical with what President Eisenhower said in giving his papers to the United States. Letter of April 13, 1960, from President Dwight D. Eisenhower to the Administrator of General Services.

established that the most confidential records of the Presidency can be ordered produced for a grand jury, the present subpoena would be only the first installment of requests for many more of the President's most confidential conversations. No government can function if its internal operations are to be subject to that kind of open scrutiny.

This point is recognized by even those who take a hostile view of executive privilege. Fifteen years ago Representative Meader made a slashing attack on what he called "a non-existent, imaginary so-called Executive privilege." 104 Cong. Rec. 3853 (1958). After stating his argument against executive privilege generally, however, he said: "The foregoing reasoning, of course, does not apply to the important constitutional powers of the President, his power to execute the laws, his powers as Commander-in-Chief of the Armed Forces, and his power to conduct diplomatic relations." *Id.* at 3851. A leading contemporary critic of executive privilege is Professor Raoul Berger, who has written a 156-page article setting out his controversial views on the limited scope of the privilege. He recognizes very clearly, however, that discussions between the President and his close advisers stand on a very different footing from the more usual kinds of claim of executive privilege to which he is so strongly opposed.

> President Jackson's refusal to reveal a statement he made *to his Cabinet* is a remote analogy, because such confidential communications—what Marshall labelled "secrets of the cabinet"—are poles apart from an unlimited discretion to withhold any document or communications between the several million subordinate employees in the interest of "administrative efficiency."

Berger, *Executive Privilege* v. *Congressional Inquiry,* 12 UCLA L. Rev. 1043, 1289-1290 (1965) (emphasis in original). Again at 1331 he says:

> "Judicial deliberations" are better compared to conferences between the President and a Cabinet member, for which a privilege was recognized in *Marbury* v. *Madison* or Presidential communications with other high military or civil officers, which at least one congressional committee recognized. But it is farfetched to compare the conferences of two lowly subordinates, or of subordinate with a lower echelon chief; with consultation between a judge and his immediate aide or the President with a department head.

D. *Privilege Not Waived.* It seems to be suggested in paragraph 9 of the Petition for an Order to Show Cause that any claim of executive privilege has been waived with regard to this investigation by the grand jury. This suggestion will not withstand analysis. In his statement of May 22nd, appended to and referred to in the Petition, the President said that "executive privilege will not be invoked as to any testimony concerning possible criminal conduct or discussions of possible criminal conduct, in the matters presently under investigation, including the Watergate affair and the alleged cover-up." It is one thing to permit testimony on a specific subject, for testimony can be confined to information that relates to that particular subject and can avoid reaching extraneous material, the disclosure of which is contrary to the public interest. With these recordings, as has been indicated, that is not possible.

Indeed, the short answer to any claim of waiver with regard to the materials now sought may be found in *United States* v. *Reynolds*, 345 U.S. 1 (1953). In that case the United States refused to produce an Air Force investigation report of an airplane crash as well as written statements by the survivors of the crash. It offered to allow the survivors to give depositions and to testify as to all matters except those of a "classified nature." The Supreme Court sustained the claim of privilege with regard to the documents sought. The offer to allow the witnesses to testify, far from being a waiver of privilege as to the documents, was expressly relied on by the Supreme Court as a reason for upholding the claim of privilege. 345 U.S. at 11.

To apply a waiver notion to executive privilege would be self-defeating, for a President then could not disclose any information without risk that this might be construed as a waiver with regard to other information that, in the public interest, he feels cannot be disclosed. The practice under which Presidents volunteer a great deal of information, because it is in the public interest to do so, would come to an end if the President thus jeopardized the confidentiality of things that cannot be disclosed.

Nor is there any waiver because the President has permitted a few of these tapes to be heard by a very few people. Whenever the President has confidential information, he is free to disclose it to those persons, in and out of government, in whom he has confidence and from whom he seeks advice.

E. *Charges of Criminal Conduct.* Executive privilege does not vanish because the grand jury is looking into charges of criminal conduct. No case so holds. There is no body of practice to this effect. Many of the celebrated instances in the past in which Presidents have refused to produce information in their custody have involved charges of criminal misconduct. It is true that the instances in the past have been refusals to give the material to Congress, but the Presidential privilege to withhold confidential information where the public interest so requires stems from the Constitutional separation of powers. There is nothing in Constitutional theory to suggest that the Chief Executive is separate from the Legislative Branch but inferior to the Judicial Branch. Only last year in *Branzburg* v. *Hayes*, 408 U.S. 665 (1972), the Supreme Court, in recognizing that ordinarily a grand jury has the right to every man's evidence, immediately qualified that by adding "except for those persons protected by a constitutional, common-law, or statutory privilege." 408 U.S. at 688.

In this connection it is worth quoting in part what the Special Prosecutor said in his letter of July 18, 1973, to J. Fred Buzhardt, Esq., in support of his request for the tapes that are now the object of a subpoena.

First, the request is part of an investigation into serious criminal misconduct—the obstruction of justice. The tapes are material and important evidence—quite apart from anything they show about the involvement or non-involvement of the President—because the conversations recorded in all probability deal with the activities of other persons under investigation. Indeed, it is not implausible to suppose that the reports to the President on these occasions may themselves have been made pursuant to a conspiracy and as part of a cover-up.

In that passage the Special Prosecutor quite properly bases his request on his claimed need for the tapes "quite apart from anything they show about the involvement or non-involvement of the President." If there were any question of Presidential involvement in the crimes the Special Prosecutor is investigating—and the President's statements have categorically denied any such involvement—this would not be within the jurisdiction of this Court, the Special Prosecutor, or the grand jury. The President of the United States is, as we have pointed out in the Introductory Statement, not above the law. He is liable to prosecution and punishment in the ordinary course of law for crimes he has committed but only after he has been impeached, convicted, and removed from office. U.S. Const., art. I, § 3; *Federalist* No. 69 (Hamilton); *Kendall v. United States* ex rel. *Stokes*, 12 Pet. (37 U.S.) 524, 610 (1838).

It may well be, as the Special Prosecutor suggests, that statements made by other persons to the President at the meetings for which the recordings have been subpoenaed were made by them pursuant to a conspiracy to obstruct justice. Executive privilege cannot be claimed to shield executive officers from prosecution for crime, *Gravel v. United States*, 408 U.S. 606, 627 (1972). Similarly, it can "never be justified as a means of covering mistakes, avoiding embarrassment, or for political, personal or pecuniary reasons." Rogers, *Constitutional Law: The Papers of the Executive Branch*, 44 A.B.A.J. 941 (1958). It is precisely with these considerations in mind that the President has not asserted executive privilege with regard to testimony about possible criminal conduct or discussions of possible criminal conduct.

But although remarks made by others in conversations with the President may arguably be part of a criminal plan on their part, the President's participation in these conversations was in accordance with his Constitutional duty to see that the laws are faithfully executed. It is the President, not those who may be subject to indictment by this grand jury, who is claiming executive privilege. He is doing so, not to protect those others, but to protect the right of himself and his successors to preserve the confidentiality of discussions in which they participate in the course of their Constitutional duties, and thus ultimately to protect the right of the American people to informed and vigorous leadership from their President of a sort for which confidentiality is an essential prerequisite.

Executive privilege would be meaningless if it were to give way whenever there is reason to suspect that disclosure might reveal criminal acts. It is possible to conceive of circumstances in which discussions of sensitive foreign affairs matters or of the most highly classified military secrets might include remarks that would arguably show criminal conduct by a Presidential adviser. It is unthinkable that discussions of that kind could be produced to a grand jury, a petit jury, or to the public, even though the alternative may be to make a successful prosecution impossible. But it is not only in the realm of national security that it must be for the President to decide what the public interest permits to be disclosed. It is just as important that the President be able to talk frankly with his advisers about domestic issues as about military or foreign affairs. Any other view would fragment the executive power vested in him and would assume that some of his Constitutional responsibilities are more important than others. He—and he alone—must weigh the interest in prosecuting a wrongdoer against the interest in keeping all Presidential conversations confidential.

That choices of this kind must be made is so well accepted that it is surprising that there should be an argument to the contrary. In many contexts in the criminal law the United States will be told that it should make available information in its possession. In these situations, however, the United States is given a choice. Either it must produce the needed information—whether it be a Jencks Act statement, the name of an informer, or information on electronic surveillance—or suffer the consequences to the prosecution, which may well include its dismissal.

> The burden is the Government's, not to be shifted to the trial judge, to decide whether the public prejudice of allowing the crime to go unpunished is greater than that attendant upon the possible disclosure of state secrets and other confidential information in the Government's possession.

Jencks v. United States, 353 U.S. 657, 672 (1957). Accord: . . .

It is not the President's view that refusal to produce these tapes will defeat prosecution of any who have betrayed his confidence by committing crimes. It is his expectation that the other evidence available to the Special Prosecutor, together with testimony from witnesses with regard to whom the President has not claimed executive privilege and documentary evidence that the President has been and will be making available to the Special Prosecutor, will suffice to convict any lawbreakers. But the President has concluded that even if he should be mistaken about this in some particular case, the public interest in a conviction, important though it is, must yield to the public interest in preserving the confidentiality of the President's office.

That is a decision that only the President can make. It is not for the trial judge. Indeed, in the passage just quoted from the Jencks case the Supreme Court stated explicitly that the burden of that choice is "not to be shifted to the trial judge." It is not a choice for the prosecutor. In the ordinary case it is a choice that would have to be made by senior government officials. When Presidential papers are involved, it is a choice that must be made by the President himself.

The President has concluded that it would be detrimental to the public interest to make available to the Special Prosecutor and the grand jury the recordings sought as item 1 of the subpoena. That decision by the President is in itself sufficient cause for this Court to proceed no further to seek to compel production of those records.

III. *This Court Lacks the Power To Compel Production of the Recordings*

There is no case in which the courts have actually compelled the executive to disclose information when the executive thinks it would be detrimental to the public interest to do so, nor is there any case in which the courts have undertaken to hold the President or a department head in contempt for failure to make a disclosure. Admittedly, some courts have claimed the power to decide for themselves whether executive privilege has been appropriately claimed and to weigh for themselves whether the harm to the national interest from disclosure is outweighed by the need of litigants for the information, but no court has compelled production of the information itself if the Executive Branch disagrees with the court's ruling on that issue. Other sanctions may be imposed. Production of executive documents cannot be required.

Although it was a civil case, *United States* v. *Reynolds*, 345 U.S. 1 (1953), is instructive. That was a suit under the Tort Claims Act for the death of three civilians in the crash of a B-29 while it was testing secret electronic equipment. The United States, through the Secretary of the Air Force, made a formal claim of privilege against being required to produce during discovery the Air Force's official accident investigation report and the statements of surviving crew members. The United States asserted that the aircraft in question was engaged in a highly secret mission of the Air Force, and thus invoked the executive privilege for military secrets, which, as the Supreme Court said, is recognized "by the most outspoken critics of governmental claims to privilege." 345 U.S. at 7.

Although the Court in *Reynolds* was unwilling to hold that a claim that military secrets would otherwise be revealed is conclusive on the courts, 345 U.S. at 9-10, it outlined the balancing process that must be followed before a court should call for production or even call for *in camera* inspection. If, from all the circumstances of the case, the claim of privilege is sufficiently strong, "the court should not jeopardize the security which the privilege is meant to protect by insisting upon an examination of the evidence, even by the judge alone, in chambers." 345 U.S. at 10. In considering the claim of privilege, there must be a balancing of the litigant's need for the information against the public interest in keeping it confidential. "Where there is a strong showing of necessity, the claim of privilege should not be lightly accepted, but even the most compelling necessity cannot overcome the claim of privilege if the court is ultimately satisfied that military secrets are at stake." 345 U.S. at 11. In the particular case before it, the Court held that it was obvious from the circumstances that there was a reasonable danger that the accident investigation report would contain references to the secret electronic devices while the plaintiffs' need for the information was slight, since the United States had agreed to allow the surviving crew members to give testimony and plaintiffs might be able to prove negligence through that testimony. Under these circumstances the Court ruled that the claim of privilege should have been upheld . . . and that the district court erred in imposing a sanction against the United States for its refusal to produce the documents for *in camera* inspection.

The principles announced in *Reynolds* have been applied by the lower courts to all claims of executive privilege, whether dealing with military secrets or with other kinds of information. See *Carl Zeiss Stiftung* v. *V. E. B. Carl Zeiss, Jena,* 40 F.R.D. 318, 324 (D.D.C. 1966), *aff'd on the opinion below* 384 F. 2d 979 (D.C. Cir.), *cert. denied* 389 U.S. 952 (1967); 8 Wright & Miller, *Federal Practice and Procedure: Civil* 170-172 (1970). The courts have been circumspect in substituting their judgment for that of the executive officer, or in calling for *in camera* inspection. There are cases in which they have ruled in favor of production, *id.* at 169 n. 23, but none of those cases involve a Presidential claim of the privilege with its obvious special considerations. And, at the risk of repetition, it is worth repeating that in no case has a court used compulsory process or the contempt power to require production of information that the court thinks ought to be produced, either for the parties or for the court *in camera*. Refusal to comply with a court's decision that information ought to be produced has other adverse consequences to the government's position in the litigation but the information itself remains confidential if the executive determines that the public interest requires this resolution.

Although there may be instances where court scrutiny is appropriate, a different question is presented in cases involving intragovernmental confidential communications. Here the privilege takes on a virtual immunity from inquiry. The judiciary, the courts declare, is not authorized "to probe the mental processes" of an executive or an administrative office. *Morgan v. United States*, 304 U.S. 1, 18 (1938). This rule forecloses investigation into the methods by which a decision was reached, *United States v. Morgan*, 313 U.S. 409, 422 (1941), the matters considered, *Fayerweather v. Ritch*, 195 U.S. 276, 306-307 (1904), the contributing influences, *Chicago, B & O Ry. Co. v. Babcock*, 204 U.S. 585, 593 (1907), or the role played by the work of others, *Kaiser Aluminum & Chem. Corp. v. United States*, 157 F. Supp. 939, 946-947 (1958) (per Reed, J.)—results demanded by exigencies of the most imperative character. No judge could tolerate inquisition into the elements making up his decision—indeed "public examination of a judge would be destructive of the judicial responsibility"—and by the same doctrine "the integrity of the administrative process must be equally respected." *United States v. Morgan*, 313 U.S. 409, 422 (1941). Equally sound reasons dictate that a protection no less extensive be afforded the processes by which a President's responsibility for decision-making and policy formulation, legal or otherwise, are discharged.

In the present case, there is no showing whatever of necessity for production of the recordings except for the conclusory statement in the Petition for an Order to Show Cause that the recordings "are relevant and important evidence in the Grand Jury's investigation." Here, as in the *Reynolds* case, testimony of those who participated in these meetings has been made available, because of the President's disclaimer of executive privilege with regard to testimony by his aides concerning possible criminal conduct or discussions of possible criminal conduct in the matters presently under investigation. Much other evidence, both documentary and testimonial, is available to the Special Prosecutor, including a significant amount of material furnished him by the President. Doubtless the Special Prosecutor would like to have the recordings to test their consistency with testimony now being given by participants in the conversations that were recorded. Doubtless the plaintiffs in *Reynolds* would have liked to have had the contemporaneous statements of the survivors of the crash, as well as the report of the Air Force investigation, to test their consistency with the testimony later made available from the survivors. That was not enough to justify even *in camera* inspection in *Reynolds*. It is not enough here, particularly when the circumstances here show that the recordings involved are of confidential conversations with the President of the United States, material raising the strongest possible claim of privilege.

Whatever may be the case with a department head, as in the *Reynolds* case, it is not appropriate for the courts to purport to weigh a claim of privilege by the President himself. Since the courts are without power to compel compliance with a decision overruling a claim of privilege by the President, any consideration by the courts would be a meaningless issue.

> By the constitution of the United States, the President is invested with certain important powers, in the exercise of which he is to use his own discretion, and is accountable only to his country in his political character and to his own conscience.

Marbury v. *Madison*, 1 Cranch (5 U.S.) 137, 165 (1803). Again in *Kendall* v. *United States* ex rel. *Stokes*, 12 Pet. (37 U.S.) 524 (1838), the Court distinguished between requiring a department head to do a purely ministerial act and requiring the President to act in a matter within his discretion. It said of the President, at 610, that "as far as his powers are derived from the constitution, he is beyond the reach of any other department, except in the mode prescribed by the constitution through the impeaching power."

The issue was squarely presented in *Mississippi* v. *Johnson*, 4 Wall. (71 U.S.) 475 (1867). The Court there refused to entertain a bill seeking to enjoin President Andrew Johnson from enforcing the Reconstruction Acts. In his argument in that case Attorney General Stanbery discussed the *Marbury* and *Kendall* cases and noted that the writs sought in those cases ran only against cabinet officers rather than against the President himself. He pointed out that if a cabinet officer could be imprisoned for contempt for disobedience of a court order, his duties could be performed by a deputy or a new member of the cabinet could be appointed. If, however, the President were to be imprisoned for contempt, he would be disabled from performing his constitutional duties, though he would still, in the absence of impeachment, retain the office. 4 Wall. at 489-490.

The Supreme Court ruled that it had "no jurisdiction of a bill to enjoin the President in the performance of his official duties." 4 Wall. at 501. As one of the reasons for this conclusion, it had noted: "Suppose the bill filed and the injunction prayed for allowed. If the President refuse obedience, it is needless to observe that the court is without power to enforce its process." 4 Wall. at 500-501. At another point it said:

> An attempt on the part of the judicial department of the government to enforce the performance of such duties by the President might be justly characterized, in the language of Chief Justice Marshall, as "an absurd and excessive extravagance."

4 Wall. at 499.

In the light of these precedents Attorney General Moody was clearly right when he ruled that "it seems clear that while a subpoena may be directed against the President to produce a paper, or for some other purpose, in case of his refusal to obey the subpoena, the courts would be without power to enforce process." 25 Op. Atty. Gen. 326, 330-331 (1905).

The commentators have agreed. The then-Executive Editor of the Washington Post, an outspoken critic of executive privilege, says: "That the President himself enjoys practical immunity from the enforcement of legal process in wide areas must be acknowledged." Wiggins, *Government Operations and the Public's Right to Know*, 19 Fed. B.J. 62, 74 (1959). See also 8 Wigmore, *Evidence* § 2370 (McNaughton rev. 1961), suggesting that the executive may be under a testimonial duty to be a witness. He regards this as a different question from whether compulsory process can issue to enforce that duty and says: "That the enforcement of the duty is constitutionally impossible is still consistent with its existence."

This is not to suggest that the courts are powerless in the face of executive refusals. In civil litigation to which the United States is a party, sanctions other than contempt are available for failure to produce material that the court thinks not privileged. Thus in *O'Neill* v. *United States*, 79 F. Supp. 827, 830 (E.D. Pa. 1948), the court recognized that because of "the separateness and mutual independence of the three coordinate branches of the government," compulsory process or contempt against the Attorney General would be barred, but held that under Civil Rule 37 other sanctions could be imposed that might cause procedural disadvantages to the United States or even cause it to lose its case. Indeed, this was the sanction applied by the lower courts in the *Reynolds* case itself, and it would have been the appropriate sanction had not the Supreme Court determined that the claim of privilege was so compelling that it was error to order *in camera* inspection. Both the District Court and the Court of Appeals had held that the appropriate sanction, after the government refused to comply with a court order to produce documents for *in camera* inspection, was to rule that the facts on negligence would be taken as established in plaintiffs' favor. See *United States* v. *Reynolds*, 345 U.S. 1, 5 (1953). Even with regard to department heads the courts can neither compel production of documents nor punish the department head for contempt. 8 Wigmore, *Evidence* § 2379, at 815 (McNaughton rev. 1961); 4 Moore, *Federal Practice* par. 26-61 [5. -1], at 26-287 (2d ed. 1970). The immunity of the President from compulsory process is even clearer than that attaching to department heads.

As has been pointed out earlier in this brief, the practice in criminal litigation is similar. The court may require the government to choose between producing documents or damaging its chances for a successful prosecution, but the court cannot require that the documents be produced nor can it even require that they be submitted for *in camera* inspection.

The motion of the Special Prosecutor asks the Court to compel the President of the United States to produce material that he has determined that the public interest requires be kept confidential. It thus asks the Court to substitute its judgment for that of the President on a matter entrusted to the President by the Constitution, and calls for the Court to issue an order of a sort that the Judicial Branch lacks power to enter against the President of the United States.

Conclusion

The result for which we have argued is supported by such precedent as exists. It is supported by premises that are, and have always been, at the heart of our Constitutional system. It is supported by the unvarying practice of 184 years. It is supported finally, and most importantly, by the consequences that would follow if any other result were to be reached.

Were it to be held, on whatever ground, that there is any circumstance under which the President can be compelled to produce recordings or notes of his private conversations, from that moment on it would be simply impossible for any President of the United States to function. The creative interplay of open and spontaneous discussion is essential in making wise choices on grave and important issues. A President would be helpless if he and his advisers could not talk freely, if they were required always to guard their words against the possibility that next month or next year those words might be made public. The issue in this case is nothing less than the continued existence of the Presidency as a functioning institution.

For all of the foregoing reasons, the motion of the Special Prosecutor should be denied.

Respectfully submitted,

LEONARD GARMENT
J. FRED BUZHARDT
CHARLES ALAN WRIGHT
DOUGLAS M. PARKER
ROBERT T. ANDREWS
THOMAS P. MARINIS, JR.
The White House
Washington, D.C. 20050
Attorneys for the President

August 7, 1973

UNITED STATES DISTRICT COURT
FOR THE DISTRICT OF COLUMBIA

IN RE GRAND JURY SUBPOENA)	
DUCES TECUM ISSUED TO)	
RICHARD M. NIXON, OR ANY)	
SUBORDINATE OFFICER, OF-)	MISC. NO. 47-73
FICIAL, OR EMPLOYEE WITH)	
CUSTODY OR CONTROL OF)	
CERTAIN DOCUMENTS OR)	
OBJECTS)	

MEMORANDUM IN SUPPORT OF AN ORDER
TO PRODUCE DOCUMENTS OR OBJECTS
IN RESPONSE TO THE SUBPOENA*

. . .

SUMMARY OF ARGUMENT

I

The President has an enforceable legal duty not to withhold material evidence from a grand jury. The grand jury occupies a fundamental position in the administration of public justice. There is no exception for the President from the guiding principle that the public, in the pursuit of justice, has a right to every man's evidence. These propositions were recognized as early as 1807 in *United States* v. *Burr*, 25 Fed. Cas. 30 (No. 14,692d) (C.C.D. Va. 1807). They have critical importance in a grand jury inquiry into gross misconduct by high officials in the Executive Offices of the President.

The decision in *United States* v. *Burr* is but a specific application of two historic constitutional principles: (1) even the highest executive officials are subject to the rule of law, which it is emphatically the province and duty of the courts to declare; and (2) the rights and obligations of the President and other high executive officers are defined and judicial orders are entered on the premise that these officials, rather than interpose their naked power, will obey the law's

* This brief is printed in its entirety except for an introductory 'factual statement of the case and a detailed description of the conflict in testimony in each of the nine conversations for which the tapes were being demanded.

explicit and particularized commands. Accordingly, the Court of Appeals for this Circuit, like every other Federal court, has rejected the claim that absolute executive privilege flows from the constitutional separation of powers. It has ruled that it is for the Judiciary—not the Executive—to determine what materials may be held confidential because of a particular exigency and what evidence must be produced. *Committee for Nuclear Responsibility, Inc.* v. *Seaborg,* 463 F.2d 788, 792-94 (D.C. Cir. 1971).

The subpoena was properly directed to the President, and the Court has power to enforce it. Counsel's claim that the President, because of his great powers, has immunity from orders enforcing legal obligations is inconsistent with our entire constitutional tradition. The President cannot be limited by judicial intrusion into the exercise of his constitutional powers under Article II. Here, however, the grand jury is not seeking to control the President in the exercise of his constitutional powers, for, as we show, he has no constitutional power to withhold the evidence sought by the subpoena merely by his own declaration of the public interest. The grand jury is seeking evidence of criminal conduct that the President[1] happens to have in his custody—largely by his personal choice. All the Court is asked to do is hold that the President is bound by legal duties in appropriate cases just as other citizens—in this case, by the duty to supply documentary evidence of crime. In the language of the authoritative precedents, this is a "ministerial duty."

Contrary to counsel's argument, enforcement of the subpoena would not create the threat of "potential disclosure of any and all conversations' (Brief in Opposition 212-213),[2] nor does our submission suggest that every participant in a Presidential conversation would have to speak "in continual awareness that at any moment any Congressional committee, or any prosecutor working with a grand jury, could at will command the production of the verbatim record of every word written or spoken" (Brief in Opposition 224). Not only are the facts of the case much narrower, but a settled

---

[1] For the sake of readability, the word "President" was substituted for the legal term "respondent" wherever the latter appeared in the original brief. The citation "S. Tr." refers to the transcript of hearings of the Senate Select Committee on Presidential Campaign Activities. Ed.

[2] The page numbers in citations of the "Brief in Opposition" have been changed to refer to the brief as reprinted in this volume, *supra*, not to the pagination of the original brief. Ed.

rule of evidence protects a broad range of Presidential papers and conversations against disclosure *when the Court decides*—after *in camera* inspection when necessary—that the public interest in the secrecy of the particular items outweighs the need for the evidence in the administration of justice.

II

The present case does not fall within the traditional rule of executive privilege as administered by the courts. Counsel for the President wisely refrain from pressing such a claim. Under the usual rule, the Court—not the President—determines whether particular documents are privileged by weighing the need for the evidence against any governmental interest in secrecy. Here, the only possible governmental interest in secrecy is encouraging openness and candor in giving advice and promoting the free flow of discussion in deliberations upon executive policy by assuring a measure of confidentiality. Preservation of secrecy is unwarranted in the present case for two independent reasons. First, the interest in confidentiality is never sufficient to support an official privilege where there is reason to believe that the deliberations may have involved criminal misconduct. Second, under the particular circumstances of the present case, the need of the grand jury for the critically important evidence provided by the recordings upon a question of wrongdoing by high officials and party leaders easily outweighs the slight risk to the freedom of executive discussions. There will be few occasions upon which a grand jury will have similar cause to believe there may be material evidence of the criminality of high officials in the papers and documents in the Executive Office of the President. The aides of future Presidents are not likely to be timid because of this remote danger of disclosure. If there be some small risk of greater reticence, it is not too great a price to pay to preserve the integrity of the Office of the President.

III

Even if the tape recordings might once have been covered by a privilege, any such claim to continued secrecy has been waived by the extensive testimony, given with the President's consent, publicizing individual versions of the conversations. In his public statement of May 22, 1973, the President announced that "Executive privilege will not be invoked as to any testimony concerning possible criminal conduct, in the matters presently under investigation, including the Watergate affair and the alleged cover-up." In accordance with that statement, Dean, Mitchell, Ehrlichman and Haldeman already have testified extensively before the Senate Committe and/or in other proceedings concerning the conversations specified in the subpoena. Haldeman even was allowed access to various tapes after he left government office and gave testimony based upon his listening to the tapes denied the grand jury. The President and his counsel themselves have made comments for publication upon the content of the conversations. Under familiar legal principles those disclosures waive any right to further confidentiality. Not even a President can be allowed to select some accounts of a conversation for public disclosure and then to frustrate further grand jury inquiries by withholding the best evidence of what actually took place.

ARGUMENT

INTRODUCTION

Our basic submission is that the President of the United States like the humblest citizen, has an enforceable legal duty not to withhold from the grand jury material evidence the production of which the Court determines to be in the public interest. The grand jury serves "the dual function of determining if there is probable cause to believe that a crime has been committed and of protecting citizens against unfounded criminal prosecutions." *Branzburg* v. *Hayes*, 408 U.S. 665, 686-87 (1972). . . . "Its adoption in our Constitution as the sole method for preferring charges in serious criminal cases shows the high place it held as an instrument of justice." *Costello* v. *United States*, 350 U.S. 359, 362 (1956).[3] Because of the grand jury's fundamental importance to the administration of justice, "the long standing principle that 'the public has a right to every man's evidence,' except for those persons protected by a constitutional, common law or statutory privilege . . . is particularly applicable to grand jury proceedings." *Branzburg* v. *Hayes*, 408 U.S. at 688.[4] See also. . . .

---

[3] The Fifth Amendment provides in relevant part:

"No person shall be held to answer for a capital, or otherwise infamous crime, unless on a presentment or indictment of a Grand Jury * * *."

[4] The Court in *Branzburg* quotes Jeremy Bentham's vivid illustration:

The application of these principles to the President was recognized as early as 1807 in *United States* v. *Burr*, 25 Fed. Cas. 30 (No. 14, 692d) (C.C.D. Va. 1807). The decision was recently cited with apparent approval by the Supreme Court in *Branzburg* v. *Hayes*, 408 U.S. at 688-89 n. 26.

The decision in *United States* v. *Burr* conforms to two constitutional principles which history has put beyond dispute. *First*, even the highest executive officials are subject to the rule of law, which —as Chief Justice Marshall observed in *Marbury* v. *Madison*, 1 Cranch 137, 177 (1803)—"[i]t is, emphatically the province and duty" of the courts to declare. *Second*, the rights and obligations of the President and other high executive officers are defined and judicial orders entered on the premise that these officials will obey the law's explicit and particularized commands.

Against these settled principles counsel for the President claim an absolute Presidential prerogative to withhold material evidence from a grand jury merely upon the assertion that production is against the public interest. The only practical argument adduced for so dangerous a claim is that the effective functioning of the Presidency requires confidentiality for papers, memoranda and conversations. Our response is that the practical needs of the Presidency are fully met by the familiar rule of qualified executive privilege defined and administered by the courts. We show below that the separation of powers does not support the claim of unreviewable privilege, that there is no Presidential immunity from judicial orders requiring the production of evidence, and that the nine tapes lie outside the normal qualified executive privilege. Six limiting conditions frame the context for those legal propositions:

Are men of the first rank and consideration—are men high in office—men whose time is not less valuable to the public than to themselves—are such men to be forced to quit their business, their functions, and what is more than all, their pleasure, at the beck of every idle or malicious adversary, to dance attendance upon every petty cause? Yes, as far as it is necessary, they and everybody . . . Were the Prince of Wales, the Archbishop of Canterbury, and the Lord High Chancellor, to be passing by in the same coach while a chimneysweeper and a barrow-woman were in dispute about a halfpennyworth of apples, and the chimney-sweeper or the barrow-woman were to think proper to call upon them for their evidence, could they refuse it? No, most certainly. See 4 The Works of Jeremy Bentham 320-21 (Bowring ed. 1843). See also 8 Wigmore § 2192.

1. The recordings are sought *by a grand jury* as necessary to its investigation of definable criminal conduct. There is no claim here of a right of the Legislative Branch—or of the Judiciary for that matter —to monitor the Executive's decision-making processes by rummaging through confidential files for debatable policy judgments.[5] Even farther afield are the interests of private litigants asserting private rights.

2. The allegations under investigation involve high Presidential assistants and criminal conduct in the Executive Offices. Such involvement is virtually unique. Because it is unlikely to recur, production of White House documents *in this investigation* will establish no precedent for recurrent grand jury investigations.

3. There is a demonstrated and particularized need for the recordings of the nine specific conversations covered by the subpoena. All are demonstrably material to the planning and scope of the alleged criminal conspiracy—as well as to possible perjury—and thus are essential to the grand jury's full discharge of its constitutional responsibilities. This circumstance constitutes still another guarantee that enforcing the subpoena would not set a precedent for prying or politically motivated inquiries even by a grand jury.

4. There is no particularized showing that the public interest would be injured by disclosing the relevant parts of the recordings to the grand jury. On the contrary, the confidentiality of these conversations already has been eliminated by the extensive public testimony given by principals, with the explicit approval of the President.

5. The public testimony about these conversations indicates that some of them may have been part of a criminal conspiracy to ob-

---

[5] Rejection of the claim of executive privilege in the present case does not require a decision upon any claim of executive privilege *vis-a-vis* the Congress. History provides a great variety of opinions on the relative rights of the Executive and the Congress. See generally Berger, *Executive Privilege v. Congressional Inquiry,* 12 U.C.L.A. L. Rev. 1043, 1078-98 (1956). The issue has never been submitted to the courts; at one time it was generally assumed that a claim of executive privilege *vis-a-vis* the Congress presented a nonjusticiable political question. See *e.g.,* L. Hand, The Bill of Rights 17-18 (1958). But see *Powell* v. *McCormack,* 395 U.S. 486 (1969). No one has ever suggested that an application for an order requiring the Executive Branch to produce evidence in the usual course of judicial or grand jury proceedings presents a nonjusticiable political question.

struct justice. To the extent that the conversations do not concern the legitimate affairs of Government and the performance of the official duties and responsibilities of the President and his staff, they could not be protected by executive privilege.

6. The subpoena is directed to the President—admittedly a rare proceeding—only because the President took the unusual step of assuming sole personal custody of the recordings once the existence of the evidence was admitted. In the absence of this attempt on the part of the President or his attorneys to strengthen his hand in a constitutional confrontation, the Special Prosecutor and the grand jury could have pursued the more traditional course of seeking disclosure from a subordinate official.

The confluence of these six factors shapes the entire case. They put the President's claim outside the normal rule of executive privilege and drive counsel for the President to the extraordinary claim that the President has an absolute right to withhold material evidence from a grand jury merely by his own *ipse dixit* whenever he asserts that non-disclosure would be in the public interest and even though he has a personal and private interest in the question. The six factors also limit the issue the Court must decide so sharply that enforcement of the subpoena will set only a narrow precedent, albeit a precedent of historic importance in reaffirming the American constitutional tradition that no man is above the law.

I

THE PRESIDENT HAS AN ENFORCEABLE LEGAL DUTY TO
PRODUCE MATERIAL EVIDENCE FOR THE GRAND JURY
WHERE HE FAILS TO SHOW TO THE SATISFACTION OF THE
COURT A PARTICULARIZED NEED FOR SECRECY

A. *The Courts Have the Final Authority to Determine When Evidence in the Executive Branch Should be Produced in a Judicial Proceeding.*

In accordance with the uniform course of decisions, the claim of an absolute executive privilege based upon the separation of powers was rejected for the District of Columbia Circuit in *Committee for Nuclear Responsibility, Inc.* v. *Seaborg,* 463 F.2d 788 (1971). There, as here, counsel claimed that the Executive Branch's "inherent constitutional powers" include the right to determine conclusively what documents in the possession of the Executive Branch are subject to executive privilege. There, as here, the claim was premised on the contention that the separation of powers prevents the courts from ordering the production of such documents. The courts, however, rejected the claim that "executive absolutism [can] override the duty of the court to assure that an official had not exceeded his charter or flouted the legislative will." 463 F.2d at 793. The opinion goes on to state the rule binding in this Circuit in words foreshadowing the present case:

> [N]o executive official or agency can be given absolute authority to determine what documents in his possession may be considered by the court in its task. Otherwise the head of any executive department would have the power on his own say-so to cover up all evidence of fraud and corruption when a federal court or grand jury was investigating malfeasance in office, and this is not the law. 463 F.2d at 794.

The President's letter to the Chief Judge of this Court, dated July 25, 1973, declining to comply with the subpoena, argues: "It would be wholly inadmissible for the President to seek to compel some particular action by the courts. It is equally inadmissible for the courts to seek to compel some particular action from the President." These assertions mistake the true nature of our constitutional system. The President focuses on the "separation" of functions in our tripartite system of government, and in so doing misses a crucial point: the respective "powers" of each branch frequently interact. Interaction between branches is an essential element of our constitutional arrangement, and one branch frequently requires action by another when it is exercising its constitutional powers. Thus, the Legislative Branch has the power to make the laws. Its enactments bind the Judiciary—unless unconstitutional—not only in the decision of cases and controversies, but in the very procedure through which the Judiciary transacts its business.[6] Congress, in scores of statutes, regularly imposes legal duties upon the President. The very essence of his function is the legal duty to carry out congressional mandates.[7] Indeed, the President, contrary to his letter, may require

[6] See, e.g., 28 U.S.C. 2, 44(c), 45, 144, 331, 332, 333, 455, 1731-1745, 1826, 2254(b), 2284(4), 2403; 18 U.S.C. 2519, 6003(a), 6005(a).

[7] Article II, Section 3, of the Constitution provides in relevant part:

[H]e [the President] shall take Care that the Laws be faithfully executed. . . .

"some particular action by the courts." The courts have a legal duty to give—and do give—effect to executive orders.[8] Where the President or an appropriate official institutes a legal action in his own name or that of the United States, a judge is compelled to grant the relief requested if in accordance with law; should he fail, the appellate court will mandate the performance of the obligation.

For more than a century and a half, all three branches have acknowledged that it is the constitutional function of the courts to interpret the laws, see *Marbury* v. *Madison, supra,* and to issue orders directing the cessation of legal wrongs or the performance of legal duties. We enjoy a constitutional government of laws and not of men because each branch has acknowledged its duties under the functioning of the others. The judicial power is no less potent when the rights and duties of executive officials are at issue.

"Checks and balances were established in order that this should be a 'government of laws and not of men.' . . . The doctrine of separation of powers was adopted by the Convention of 1787, not to promote efficiency but to preclude the exercise of arbitrary power." *Myers* v. *United States,* 272 U.S. 52, 292-93 (1926) (Brandeis, J., dissenting). As Mr. Justice Jackson explained in *Youngstown Sheet & Tube Co.* v. *Sawyer,* 343 U.S. 579, 635 (1952) (concurring opinion):

> While the Constitution diffuses power the better to secure liberty, it also contemplates that practice will integrate the dispersed powers into a workable government. It enjoins upon its branches separateness but interdependence, autonomy but reciprocity.

The doctrine stated in the *Seaborg* case is but a specific application of two historic constitutional principles:

(1) The highest executive officials, like all citizens, are subject to the rule of law and may be required to comply with their legal obligations.

(2) "It is, emphatically, the province and duty of the judicial department to say, what the law is." *Marbury* v. *Madison, supra.*

From the earliest days of the Republic the courts have issued orders requiring executive officials to comply with the Constitution

---

[8] See, *e.g., Environmental Protection Agency* v. *Mink,* 410 U.S. 73 (1973) (security classification).

and laws as judicially interpreted even when the defendant was acting under explicit orders of the President. *E.g., Youngstown Sheet & Tube Co.* v. *Sawyer* (steel seizure case), *supra; United States* v. *United States District Court,* 407 U.S. 297 (1972) (power of the President, acting through the Attorney General, to order domestic national security wiretaps without judicial warrants); *State Highway Commission* v. *Volpe,* —— F.2d —— (No. 72-1512) (8th Cir. April 2, 1973) (highway fund impoundment); cf. *Marbury* v. *Madison, supra* (court with jurisdiction can issue mandamus).[9]

In applying the fundamental principle of our republican form of government that the Executive is not above the law, the courts, as in *Seaborg,* consistently have determined for themselves what evidence is appropriately subject to a claim of privilege. In *United States* v. *Reynolds,* 345 U.S. 1 (1953), the Executive Branch argued that "department heads have power to withhold any documents in their custody from judicial view if they deem it to be in the public interest," 345 U.S. at 6 (footnote omitted),—a position strikingly similar to the one now advanced by the President. The case involved a Tort Claims Act suit arising out of the crash of a B-29 bomber testing secret electronic equipment. The plaintiffs sought discovery of the Air Force's official accident investigation report and the statements

---

[9] *Youngstown Sheet & Tube Co.* v. *Sawyer* is perhaps the most noted instance where the Supreme Court has reviewed the assertion of Presidential power. President Truman, concluding that a threatened work stoppage at the Nation's steel mills during the Korean War "would immediately jeopardize and imperil our national defense," directed the Secretary of Commerce to take possession of and operate specified steel facilities. Executive Order No. 10340 (April 8, 1952). The President asserted that he "was acting within the aggregate of his constitutional powers as the Nation's Chief Executive and the Commander in Chief of the Armed Forces of the United States." 343 U.S. at 582. District Judge Holtzoff denied a temporary restraining order on the ground that what was involved was the action of the President and that the courts could not enjoin Presidential action. Judge Pine, however, granted a preliminary injunction and the Supreme Court upheld him. In doing so, there was no doubt expressed that the Court could adjudicate the claim that the President had no constitutional power to issue the Executive Order. In his concurring opinion, Justice Jackson expressed the fundamental principle underlying the Court's decision:

> With all its defects, delays and inconveniences, men have discovered no technique for long preserving free government except that the Executive be under the law. 343 U.S. at 655.

See also *Korematsu* v. *United States,* 323 U.S. 214 (1944), in which the Supreme Court reviewed and upheld the President's assertion of wartime powers.

of the surviving crew members. Although the Supreme Court agreed that an evidentiary privilege covers military secrets, 345 U.S. at 6-7, 11, it held "[t]he court itself must determine whether the circumstances are appropriate for the claim of privilege. . . . Judicial control over the evidence in a case cannot be abdicated to the caprice of executive officers." 345 U.S. at 8, 9-10 (footnote omitted). See also. . . .

The governing principle is aptly summarized by Wigmore:

> A court which abdicates its inherent function of determining the facts upon which the admissibility of evidence depends will furnish to bureaucratic officials too ample opportunities for abusing the privilege. The lawful limits of the privilege are extensible beyond any control if its applicability is left to the determination of the very official whose interest it may be to shield a wrongdoing under the privilege. Both principle and policy demand that the determination of the privilege shall be for the court. 8 Wigmore § 2379, at 809-10.

There is nothing to the contrary in the cases giving the Government a "choice" between producing evidence and dropping a criminal prosecution or losing a civil action.[10] Clearly, despite the President's apparent implication (Brief in Opposition 230, 232), those decisions do not mark the limits of judicial power. In those particular instances the requirements of justice could be satisfied without compelling production of evidence over an executive claim of privilege if the Government preferred to lose the suit to which it was a party. See generally Rule 16(g), Federal Rules of Criminal Procedure; Rule 37(b), Federal Rules of Civil Procedure. In the instance at bar the requirements of justice cannot be served in that fashion. Counsel for the President even avoid making the choice by expressing the hope that the investigation can be pushed forward with other evidence,

---

[10] See cases cited in Brief in Opposition 230. To the extent there is such a choice in the Executive Branch, it is committed by law to the Attorney General, not to the President. Under 28 U.S.C. 535, the Attorney General is given the responsibility to "investigate any violation of title 18 involving Government officers. . . ." Under U.S.C. 533, he is to appoint officials to "detect and prosecute crimes against the United States." Pursuant to 28 U.S.C. 510 and 515 the Attorney General has now delegated these powers and responsibilities to the Special Prosecutor for this investigation and prosecution, including the authority "to contest the assertion of 'Executive Privilege'. . . ." See 38 Fed. Reg. 14,688 (June 4, 1973).

thus attempting to wash their hands of the risk that any resulting prosecution might have to be abandoned if exculpatory evidence were being withheld (Brief in Opposition 230-231). Nor can it be argued that termination of this grand jury investigation would be a tolerable or just price to pay to allow the President the "choice" of refusing to produce the evidence. The seriousness of the putative offenses and the high offices held by those possibly implicated preclude that solution.

There is not the slightest basis for doubting the power of a court to order the production of evidence from the Executive Branch when justice so requires. Last Term's Supreme Court decision *Environmental Protection Agency* v. *Mink,* 410 U.S. 73 (1973), clearly establishes the proposition that the constitutional separation of powers does not give the Executive any constitutional immunity from judicial orders for the production of evidence. The plaintiffs had sought access under the Freedom of Information Act to a report prepared f r the President by the Undersecretaries Committee of the National Security Council on the proposed underground nuclear test on Amchitka Island. The Government opposed the request partly upon the ground that the documents were exempt from disclosure as "interagency memorandums or letters,"[11] arguing that the need to avoid disclosure of communications with the President was "particularly important." Brief for the Petitioners 39-40. Nevertheless, the Supreme Court remanded for a judicial determination of the claim of privilege; the opinion states explicitly that in opposing disclosure the Government carried the burden of establishing "to the satisfaction of the District Court" that the documents were exempt from disclosure. 410 U.S. at 93. Significantly, the Freedom of Information Act expressly provides that "[i]n the event of noncompliance with the order of the court" to disclose material found unprivileged, the court may punish the responsible executive officer "for contempt." 5 U.S.C. 552(a)(3). Neither in *Mink* nor in any other decision has any doubt been expressed about the constitutional power of the courts to enter mandatory orders for the production of evidence.

[11] Although the Court dealt within the framework of the Freedom of Information Act, 5 U.S.C. 552(b)(5), it recognized that Congress simply had incorporated the common law executive privilege. 410 U.S. at 85-89. The exemption was defined with specific reference to the court decisions that had developed the privilege.

Other precedents confirm the existence of judicial power to require the production of evidence by executive officials when the Court determines the evidence to be material and unprivileged. *United States v. Burr*, 25 Fed. Cas. 30 (No. 14,692d) (C.C.D. Va. 1807), is an early and clear example involving a grand jury. In *Bowman Dairy Co. v. United States*, 341 U.S. 214, 221 (1951), the Supreme Court treated contempt as a proper sanction against government counsel if he refused to obey a subpoena for the production of documents after the court rejected a claim of privilege. Similarly, while holding that an FBI Agent could not properly be held in contempt for refusing to obey a subpoena to produce information for use in a state prisoner's habeas corpus action without permission from the Attorney General, the Court implicitly assumed, and Justice Frankfurter explicitly stated in his concurring opinion, that the Attorney General himself would be subject to compulsory process. *United States ex. rel. Touhy v. Ragen*, 340 U.S. 462, 465-66, 472 (1951). Thus, Professor Charles A. Wright, after explaining that—

> The determination whether to allow the claim of [executive] privilege is then for the court . . .

goes on to say that—

> In private litigation refusal of a government officer to comply with a court order overruling a claim of executive privilege and ordering disclosure could lead to conviction for contempt. . . .

8 Wright and Miller, Federal Practice and Procedure § 2019, at 171-72 (1970) (footnotes omitted). For cases in this Circuit in which the court has assumed the existence of power in private litigation to enforce a subpoena for documents in the Executive Branch over a claim of privilege, see *Westinghouse Electric Corp. v. City of Burlington*, 351 F.2d 762 (D.C. Cir. 1965); *Machin v. Zuckert, supra; Boeing Airplane Co. v. Coggeshall*, 280 F.2d 654 (D.C. Cir. 1960).[12]

---

[12] Counsel's emphasis upon the absence of judicial authority holding an executive officer in contempt is familiar rhetoric. We could assert with equal accuracy that there is no authority whatever excusing an executive official from complying with a valid subpoena after the claim of executive privilege has been determined adversely by the courts. The explanation seems to be that throughout our history, the Executive Branch, though occasionally disappointed with judicial rulings on the law, has complied with the court's decision and not pressed the matter to contempt. This precedent was set in the *Burr* case by President Jefferson, of

The present case underscores the wisdom of the rule vesting power in the courts to pass upon claims of executive privilege and to compel the production of material evidence. The President cannot be a proper judge of whether the greater public interest lies in giving the evidence to the grand jury or withholding it. His highest and closest aides and associates have been accused in sworn testimony. The President is bound to them not only by the natural emotions of loyalty and gratitude, but also by the risk that his present political power and future place in history will be linked to the effect of disclosure to the grand jury on them. The evidence on the tapes also may be material to public accusations against the President himself—a question to which he can hardly be indifferent. We call attention to these facts without disrespect to the President or his office. Even if the President, by extraordinary act of conscience, could judge impartially the relative public advantages of secrecy and disclosure without regard to the consequences for himself or his associates, confidence in the integrity and impartiality of the legal system as between the high and lowly still would be impaired through violation of the ancient precept that no man shall be the judge of his own cause.[13]

B. *The President is Not Immune from Orders Requiring the Production of Material Evidence.*

There is not the slightest basis for counsel's effort to except the President from the usual rule that claims of executive privilege are subject to judicial determination. The President is not above the law. The basic policies are the same as those discussed above.

United States v. *Burr*, 25 Fed. Cas. 30 (14,692d) (C.C.D. Va. 1807), is clear authority for the issuance of a subpoena *duces tecum* in appropriate cases to the person who is President. Although Chief Justice Marshall recognized that the power was one to be exercised with attention both to the convenience of the President in performing his arduous duties and to the possibility that the public interest might preclude coercing particular disclosures, he utterly rejected

___

course, and has been regarded as part of our fine tradition of respect for the authority of the courts.

[13] Compare *Ward* v. *Village of Monroeville*, 409 U.S. 57 (1972); *Mayberry* v. *Pennsylvania*, 400 U.S. 455 (1971); *Offutt* v. *United States*, 348 U.S. 11 (1954).

any suggestion that the President, like the King of England, is absolutely immune from judicial process:

> Although he [the King] may, perhaps, give testimony, it is said to be incompatible with his dignity to appear under the process of the court. Of the many points of difference which exist between the first magistrate in England and the first magistrate of the United States, in respect to the personal dignity conferred on them by the constitutions of their respective nations, the court will only select and mention two. It is a principle of the English constitution that the king can do no wrong, that no blame can be imputed to him, that he cannot be named in debate. By the constitution of the United States, the president, as well as any other officer of the government, may be impeached, and may be removed from office on high crimes and misdemeanors. By the constitution of Great Britain, the crown is hereditary, and the monarch can never be a subject. By that of the United States, the president is elected from the mass of the people, and, on the expiration of the time for which he is elected, returns to the mass of the people again. How essentially this difference of circumstances must vary the policy of the laws of the two countries, in reference to the personal dignity of the executive chief, will be perceived by every person. In this respect the first magistrate of the Union may more properly be likened to the first magistrate of a state; at any rate, under the former Confederation; and it is not known ever to have been doubted, but that the chief magistrate of a state might be served with a subpoena ad testificandum. 25 Fed. Cas. at 34.

The decision was recently noted with apparent approval in *Branzburg* v. *Hayes*, 408 U.S. at 688 n. 26. Furthermore, only two weeks ago, Judge Jones of this Court ordered the custodian of the records of the White House, who had claimed executive privilege at the direction of the President, to produce files for *in camera* inspection. *Nader* v. *Butz*, D.D.C. Civil No. 148-72 (August 1, 1973). See also....[14]

---

[14] The President refers to the Presidential Libraries Act of 1955, 44 U.S.C. 2107, 2108. That statute, of course, is inapplicable, since there has been no effort to donate the tapes sought by the grand jury to a Presidential library under a condition of confidentiality and there is no occasion to consider whether that Act creates a statutory privilege as against a grand jury subpoena.

Furthermore, the assumption that the materials being sought by the grand jury "are the property of the President" (Brief in Opposition 224-225) is unfounded. Public testimony has established that the tape recordings were made by agents

The rule in *United States* v. *Burr* is consistent with contemporary evidence of the intent of the Framers. Contrasted with the explicit privileges in Article I, no comparable privileges or immunities were specified for the President or Executive Branch in Article II, even though they had been commonplace for the King. The Founding Fathers were keenly aware of the dangers of Executive power. Even James Wilson, who favored a strong executive, rejected "the Prerogatives of the British Monarch as a proper guide in defining the Executive powers. . . ."[15]·He stated at the Pennsylvania Ratification Convention:

> The executive power is better to be trusted when it has no screen. Sir, we have a responsibility in the person of our President; he cannot act improperly, and hide either his negligence or inattention; he cannot roll upon any other person the weight of his criminality. . . . Add to all this, that officer is placed high, and is possessed of power far from being contemptible; yet not a *single privilege* is annexed to his character. . . .[16]

One might infer quite plausibly from the specific grant of official privileges to Congress that no other constitutional immunity from normal legal obligations was intended for government officials or papers. Indeed, Charles Pinckney stated in the Senate on March 5, 1800:

> They [the Framers] well knew how oppressively the power of undefined privileges had been exercised in Great Britain, and were determined no such authority should ever be exercised here. . . .
>
> * * * *
>
> No privilege of this kind was intended for your Executive, nor any except that which I have mentioned for your Legislature.[17]

We do not press the argument to this extreme, for the law of evidence has come to recognize a qualified executive privilege defined

---

of the United States Secret Service using government equipment in public buildings. The President can lay no claim to private ownership of materials furnished, produced, and stored by public officials using public money.

[15] 1 Farrand, Records of the Federal Convention of 1787, at 65-66 (1911). See also 4 Elliot's Debates 108-09 (2d ed. 1836) (remarks of Iredell at the North Carolina Ratification Convention).

[16] 2 Elliot's Debates 480 (2d ed. 1836).

[17] 3 Farrand, Records of the Federal Convention of 1787, at 384-385 (1911).

and applied by the courts.[18] The teaching of history is nonetheless persuasive against the claim of an absolute Presidential prerogative.

Interestingly, counsel for the President concede that they do "not question the power of the court to issue a subpoena to the President" (Brief in Opposition 214-215), but then they turn about and assert that the power to issue the command "does not impose on the Executive any concurrent obligation to disclose that information" (Ibid.). The inconsistency is obvious. A subpoena is a judicial command. If it is valid, compliance is a legal duty. Nothing in the separation of powers principle discussed above, or in the President's status as Chief Executive, justifies a contrary conclusion.[19]

It is true that custom dictates that legal process should not be addressed to the President of the United States whenever a Cabinet member or lesser official is available, even though a defendant is acting upon direct order of the President. E.g., Youngstown Sheet & Tube Co. v. Sawyer, supra. We would have followed that course here if the President had been content to leave the tapes under the physical control of his assistant for administration and the Director of the Technical Security Division of the Secret Service (S. Tr. 4145-70). In that event, a subpoena addressed to either of these officials would have been sufficient.[20] In fact, it became necessary to seek this evi-

---

[18] The courts never have decided whether executive privilege derives implicitly from the constitutional separation of powers, or whether it is merely a common law evidentiary privilege. See, e.g., United States v. Reynolds, 345 U.S. at 6; Committee for Nuclear Responsibility, Inc. v. Seaborg, 463 F.2d at 793-94. Professor Charles Alan Wright has observed that "[t]he commentators have not found much substance in the constitutional argument, based, as it is, on separation of powers." 8 Wright and Miller, Federal Practice and Procedure § 2019, at 175 n. 44 (1970 ed.).

[19] Professor Wigmore has stated:

The public . . . has a right to every man's evidence . . . Is there any reason why this right should suffer an exception when the desired knowledge is in the possession of a person occupying at the moment the office of chief executive of a state?

There is no reason at all. 8 Wigmore § 2370, at 748.

[20] Chief Justice Marshall recognized as much in Marbury v. Madison, when he stated: "It is not by the office of the person to whom the writ is directed, but the nature of the thing to be done, that the propriety or impropriety of issuing a mandamus is to be determined." 1 Cranch at 170. Similarly, where the issue is the enforcement of a subpoena, what matters is whether the evidence is lawfully producible, and the office occupied by its possessor is of no decisive consequence.

dence from the President only because he elected to assume personal control. To allow this device to render the tapes immune from ordinary legal process would exalt form over substance and set a President above the law, contrary to our firm constitutional tradition. This tradition was summed up by the Supreme Court in *United States* v. *Lee*, 106 U.S. 196, 220 (1882):

> No man in this country is so high that he is above the law. No officer of the law may set that law at defiance, with impunity. All the officers of the Government, from the highest to the lowest, are creatures of the law and are bound to obey it. It is the only supreme power in our system of government, and every man who by accepting office, participates in its functions, is only the more strongly bound to submit to that supremacy, and to observe the limitations which it imposes upon the exercise of the authority which it gives.

The argument that the President is immune from process rests upon a misreading of *Mississippi* v. *Johnson*, 4 Wall. 475 (1866).[21] In that case the State of Mississippi sought leave to file an original bill to enjoin President Johnson from enforcing the Reconstruction Acts, which provided for reconstitution of the governments of the erstwhile Confederacy. Because the President was named as a defendant in the bill, the Supreme Court heard argument upon the question of jurisdiction before the bill was filed, instead of reserving the question to a later stage.[22] As the President states (Brief in Opposition 216), Attorney General Stanbery did indeed argue that the President is "above the process of any court." 4 Wall. at 484. In order to make the claim, Attorney General Stanbery was forced to challenge Chief Justice Marshall's differentiation between the President and a royal monarch by asserting:

> . . . I deny that there is a particle less dignity belonging to the office of President than to the office of King of Great Britain or of any other potentate on the face of the earth. He represents the majesty of the law

---

[21] Scattered district court opinions seem to have accepted that argument, at least where discretionary executive powers were at issue. See, *e.g.*, *National Association of Internal Revenue Employees* v. *Nixon*, 349 F. Supp. 18, 21 (D.D.C. 1972) (appeal pending D.C. Cir.); *Reese* v. *Nixon*, 347 F. Supp. 314, 316-17 (C.D. Cal. 1972).

[22] Fairman, *Reconstruction and Reunion 1864-88*, 6 History of the Supreme Court of the United States 379-80, 436-37 (1971).

and of the people as fully and as essentially, and with the same dignity, as does any absolute monarch or the head of any independent government in the world. 4 Wall. at 484.

Faithful to the tradition that in the United States no man and no office is above the law, the Supreme Court emphatically refused to accept the Attorney General's claim of royal immunity for the President of the United States:

> We shall limit our inquiry to the question presented by the objection [that the bill seeks to enjoin the President in the performance of his duties as President], *without expressing any opinion on the broader issues discussed in argument, whether, in any case, the President of the United States may be required, by the process of this court, to perform a purely ministerial act under a positive law, or may be held amenable, in any case, otherwise than by impeachment for crime.* 4 Wall. at 498 (emphasis added).

Rather, the Court held that it had "no jurisdiction of a bill to enjoin the President in the performance of his official duties. . . ." 4 Wall. at 501. The Court distinguished the power of the courts to require the President to perform a single ministerial act from an attempt to control the exercise of his broad constitutional discretion:

> In each of these cases [involving ministerial duties] nothing was left to discretion. There was no room for the exercise of judgment. The law required the performance of a single specific act; and that performance, it was held, might be required by mandamus.

> Very different is the duty of the President in the exercise of the power to see that the laws are faithfully executed, and among these laws the acts named in the bill. . . . The duty thus imposed on the President is in no just sense ministerial. It is purely executive and political. 4 Wall. at 499.

That case arose shortly after the Civil War, when there was a bitter political conflict over the proper national policy to be followed in dealing with the secessionist states. In declining to exercise its original jurisdiction over an equitable suit brought by a state seeking to enjoin the President from enforcing congressional policy, the Court had no occasion to decide that *no* federal court could ever issue *any* order to the President, and it did not do so.

Subsequently, the Court declined jurisdiction of similar bills naming the Secretary of War or a military commander as respondent.

Georgia v. *Stanton*, 6 Wall. 50 (1867). Their disposition is further proof that it was the character of the question presented and not the identity of the respondent that determined the issue in *Mississippi* v. *Johnson*. In still later cases, the Supreme Court has recognized explicitly that that decision did not turn on the fact that the respondent was the President, but was an early expression of the nonjusticiability of "political questions." Mr. Justice Harlan has cited the decision as an example of instances where the Supreme Court has refused "to entertain . . . original actions . . . that seek to embroil this tribunal in 'political questions'." *Ohio* v. *Wyandotte Chemical Corp.*, 401 U.S. 493, 496 (1971). See also. . . . In this light, more recent cases[23] have indicated that the President can be named a defendant in an action when that course would be necessary to the granting of effective relief. See Rule 19(a), Federal Rules of Civil Procedure.

A central theme of the argument for the President is that the President has "the power and thus the privilege to withhold information" (Brief in Opposition 212). To link physical power with legal privilege runs contrary to our entire constitutional tradition. It might as well be said that a Secretary of State, acting upon orders of the President, has "the power and thus the privilege" to withhold a signed commission, contrary to the ruling in *Marbury* v. *Madison, supra;* or that a Postmaster General, acting upon instructions of the President, has "the power and thus the privilege" to refuse to pay money owed pursuant to a contract, contrary to the decision in *Kendall* v. *Stokes*, 12 Pet. 524 (1838); or that the President has "the power and thus the privilege" to seize industrial property in a wartime labor dispute, contrary to *Youngstown Sheet & Tube Co.* v. *Sawyer, supra;* or to conduct warrantless electronic surveillance, contrary to the Fourth Amendment as interpreted in *United States* v. *United States District Court, supra*.

The Court never has allowed doubt about its physical power to enforce its commands against the Executive Branch to deter the issuance of appropriate orders.[24] Happily, the possession of the naked

---

[23] See p. 251, *supra*.

[24] Counsel for the President place great emphasis (Brief in Opposition 234-235) upon the portion of the opinion in *Mississippi* v. *Johnson* suggesting that the bill was beyond the Court's jurisdiction because the Court could not, in the final analysis, enforce its will against the President. 4 Wall, at 500-01. We think those passages must be read as part of the explanation of the impossibility of dictating to the President how he was to perform a wide range of discretionary

physical power to frustrate the Court has never led the Executive Branch to disregard a judicial determination of legal rights and obligations.

The irrelevance of physical power to the entry of orders enforcing legal obligations is reflected in many contexts. For example, in *Glidden* v. *Zdanok,* 370 U.S. 530 (1962), the Supreme Court rejected the argument that a money claim against the United States did not present a justiciable issue because the courts were without power to force execution of a judgment against the United States: "If this Court may rely on the good faith of state governments or other public bodies to respond to its judgments, there seems to be no sound reason why the Court of Claims may not rely on the good faith of the United States." 370 U.S. at 571. See also. . . .

The crucial jurisdictional issue is not the physical power to secure compliance with judicial orders, but the ability to resolve authoritatively the conflicting claims of legal rights and obligations. See *Baker* v. *Carr,* 369 U.S. 186, 208-37 (1962). The effect of a President's physical power to disobey a court order is wholly speculative at this juncture, moreover, and undoubtedly will remain so. There is no reason to believe that the President would disregard a final binding order fixing legal responsibilities. Certainly, the contention that the Court could not force him into prison does not strip the Court, as opposing counsel mistakenly argue, of the jurisdiction to order compliance with a valid subpoena.[25]

Of course, the judiciary must be circumspect in issuing process against the President to avoid interference with the proper discharge of his executive functions. For example, it might not be proper in the absence of strong necessity, to require the President to appear personally before a grand jury if personal appearance would interfere with his schedule or the performance of his duties. Similarly, the

---

functions; otherwise, they run contrary to the entire tradition of our constitutional law.

[25] It should be noted, of course, that a contempt citation does not lead automatically to incarceration. Apart from the sanction of imprisonment to enforce a court order or to punish its violation, the courts may be content merely to cite the contemnor for his recalcitrance or to impose a daily coercive fine pending compliance or to assess a penal fine or to strike the name of the contemnor from the roll of attorneys. None of these sanctions involves exercise of physical power over the contemnor's person or any interference with his other activities.

courts should not saddle the Executive with requests that are administratively burdensome. Compare *United States* v. *Burr*, 25 Fed. Cas. 30, 34 (No. 14,692d) (C.C.D. Va. 1807). Nor may the courts review, oversee or direct the performance of the President's constitutional duties which implicate "political questions." See *Mississippi* v. *Johnson*, 4 Wall. at 499-501; *Marbury* v. *Madison*, 1 Cranch at 165-66, 170.

But the question here is very different. We are concerned with the obligation of the President, as a citizen of the United States, to co-operate with a criminal investigation of the grand jury by performing the solely ministerial task of producing specified recordings and documentary evidence. It should be emphasized that compliance with the subpoena will not interfere with or burden in any direct or material way the proper performance of the duties and responsibilities of the President or the Executive Office. The President is not summoned in person.[26] Nor is the Court asked either to command or forbid the performance of any discretionary functions.

Assertion of a personal prerogative to frustrate the practical performance of an important governmental function is particularly empty here, where the Chief Executive is refusing to cooperate in a grand jury investigation. Although its proceedings are conducted by officers of the Executive Branch and are subject to the supervision of the courts, the grand jury's "authority is derived from none of the three basic divisions of our government, but rather directly from the people themselves." *In re April 1956 Term Grand Jury*, 239 F.2d 263, 269 (7th Cir. 1956). As the Supreme Court has noted, grand jurors "are not appointed for the prosecutor or for the court; they are appointed for the government and for the people. . . ." *Hale* v. *Henkel*, 201 U.S. 43, 61 (1906).

Thus, it is a false conflict to see the present controversy as a struggle between the powers of the Judiciary and the prerogatives of the President. Rather, what is involved is the President's refusal to respond to a demand from the people, speaking through their organ, the grand jury. Unlike a monarch, the President is not the Sovereign. As Chief Justice John Jay noted, "Sovereignty is the right to govern.

[26] The Order to Show Cause as well as the subpoena are directed to "Richard M. Nixon *or* any subordinate officer" whom Mr. Nixon may designate as having custody of the tape recordings and other documents.

... [H]ere it rests with the people; ... our governors are the agents of the people." *Chisholm* v. *Georgia*, 2 Dall. 419, 471 (1793). This Court is merely called upon to vindicate the rule of law and to direct compliance with the duty owed by every citizen, including the President—the duty to supply evidence to the grand jury when in accordance with law.

II
THE TAPE RECORDINGS LIE OUTSIDE THE NORMAL EXECUTIVE PRIVILEGE FOR CONFIDENTIAL COMMUNICATIONS

In showing that the President has no absolute right to withhold evidence merely on his own say-so, we noted the familiar rule evidence that there are circumstances in which a claim of executive privilege, based upon a particularized showing of a public interest in secrecy greater than the need for the evidence, should be sustained by the courts.[27] Counsel for the President, although they assert that conversations in the Executive Office must be kept confidential to preserve the vigor and candor of the deliberative processes of government in the future, pitch their entire case upon the claim of absolute right. Having answered that claim, we might appropriately end our brief without elaborating the reasons for concluding that the tapes listed in the subpoena are not protected by a generalized claim of executive privilege, as normally understood, in this grand jury investigation.[28] Because of the public importance of the case,

---

[27] See pp. 239-240, *supra*.

[28] We use the term "generalized claim of executive privilege" to cover claims to privilege based on an asserted interest in the confidentiality of communications within the Executive Branch as distinguished from more specific privileges sometimes linked under the same term.

Thus, the courts also have recognized a specific privilege for "state secrets," covering information bearing on international relations, military affairs and the national security. See, *e.g.*, *United States* v. *Reynolds*, 345 U.S. at 6-7; *United States* v. *Curtiss-Wright Export Corp.*, 299 U.S. 304, 320-21 (1936); 8 Wigmore § 2378. There is also a privilege for "investigative files," including information relating to confidential informants. See, *e.g.*, *Alderman* v. *United States*, 394 U.S. 165, 184-85 (1969); *Roviaro* v. *United States*, 353 U.S. 53 (1957); *Machin* v. *Zuckert*, 316 F.2d at 339; 8 Wigmore §§ 2874-77; cf. *United States ex rel. Touhy* v. *Ragen*, 340 U.S. 462.

however, we go on to show that the recognized privilege would be inapplicable even if it were claimed.

A. *A Claim of Executive Privilege Must Be Resolved by the Court by Weighing the Need for the Evidence Against Any Government Interest in Secrecy.*

Three basic principles furnish important guidance in considering how a claim of executive privilege for confidential communications, if asserted, would apply to the present case.

1. The privilege must be strictly construed. Any evidentiary privilege is "an obstacle to the administration of justice." 8 Wigmore § 2192, at 73. Professor Wigmore has termed all privileges "so many derogations from [the] positive general rule" that the public has a right to every man's evidence. *Id.*, at 70. Accordingly, a privilege must be confined to the narrowest limits justified by its underlying policies.[29] "To hold otherwise would be to invite gratuitous injury to citizens for little if any public purpose." *Doe v. McMillan,* —— U.S. ——, ——, 93 S. Ct. 2018, 2027 (1973). Such strictness in application of executive privilege conforms to the ideas of the Founding Fathers, who were keenly aware of the dangers of Executive secrecy.[30]

2. Whether particular documents or other materials are privileged is *for judicial determination*—upon the extrinsic evidence if sufficient, but otherwise upon *in camera* inspection. "[A] complete abandonment of judicial control would lead to intolerable abuses." *United States v. Reynolds,* 345 U.S. at 8. See also. . . .

3. It is a "settled rule" that "the court must balance the moving party's need for the documents in the litigation against the reasons which are asserted in defending confidentiality." *Committee for*

The President has not identified any of the conversations described in the subpoena as containing state secrets, and, clearly, the privilege for investigatory files compiled for law enforcement purposes is inapplicable.

The courts never have decided whether executive privilege stems implicitly from the separation of powers or whether it is merely a common law evidentiary privilege. See note 18, *supra.*

[29] See 8 Wigmore § 2192, at 73; Morgan, Foreword to ALI Model Code of Evidence 7 (1942).

[30] For a discussion of the intent of the Framers, see pp. 253-254 *supra.*

Nuclear Responsibility, Inc. v. *Seaborg,* 463 F.2d at 791. See also
. . . .[31]

B. *The Executive Privilege Based Upon a Need for Candor in
Governmental Deliberations Does Not Apply Where There is
Reason to Believe That the Discussions May Have Involved
Criminal Wrongdoing.*

The President makes no showing that production of the tapes
would disclose to the grand jury "military secrets" or other state
secrets damaging to the national security.[32] The only privilege remotely pertinent to the present case is the qualified privilege which
attaches to "intra-governmental documents reflecting advisory
opinions, recommendations and deliberations comprising part of a
process by which governmental decisions and policies are formulated." *Carl Zeiss Stiftung* v. *V.E.B. Carl Zeiss, Jena,* 40 F.R.D. at
324; see also. . . . It is based on "two important policy considerations . . .: encouraging full and candid intra-agency discussion, and
shielding from disclosure the mental processes of executive and
administrative officers." *International Paper Co.* v. *Federal Power
Commission,* 438 F.2d 1349, 1358-59 (2d Cir.), cert. denied, 404
U.S. 827 (1971); *Carl Zeiss Stiftung* v. *V.E.B. Carl Zeiss, Jena,* 40
F.R.D. at 324-26.

These reasons for according a measure of confidentiality pale to
insignificance when, as in the present case, there is reason to believe
that the deliberations in the Executive Offices were tainted by criminal wrongdoing. The interest in free discussion by government
officials cannot outweigh the interest in the integrity of government
itself. The veil of confidentiality should not be lifted upon sheer
speculation, but it cannot be used as a cloak when there is substantial

---

[31] Professor Wright has himself observed:

Applying a process of this kind, though not always so clearly articulated,
courts in many cases have sustained claims of executive privilege. But in other
cases, in which the litigant's need for the information has seemed to outweigh the government's interest in secrecy, the claim of privilege has been
overruled and disclosure has been ordered.

8 Wright and Miller, Federal Practice and Procedure, §§ 2019, at 168-69 (1970).

[32] In a case in which it appeared that specific portion of a document contained
such material, those portions could be excised from the copy put into evidence.

reason to believe that serious criminal wrongdoing may have occurred.

According to the testimony of John W. Dean, many of the conversations in which he participated were part and parcel of a criminal conspiracy to obstruct justice by preventing the truth from coming out about the additional participants in the original conspiracy to break into and wiretap the offices of the Democratic National Committee. He has testified that in the presence of H.R. Haldeman he told the President on September 15, 1972, that "all [Dean] had been able to do was to contain the case and assist in keeping it out of the White House." Dean also told the President that he "could make no assurances that the day would not come when this matter would start to unravel." The President allegedly congratulated him on the "good job" he was doing on that task. (S. Tr. 2229-30). Dean also has testified that on March 13, 1973, the President told him that the President had approved executive clemency for Hunt and that there would be no problem in raising $1 million to buy the Watergate defendants' silence (S. Tr. 2324). In addition, there is uncontradicted testimony that the President was briefed on Watergate on June 20, 1972, three days after the arrests, by Haldeman, Ehrlichman and Mitchell, his closest political advisors (S. Tr. 5924, 3407-08). If these three told the President all they allegedly knew, the President would have been aware of details of the nascent cover-up.

It is true, of course, that other testimony indicates that the conversations did not include direct evidence of criminal misconduct. While this is not the time or place to judge credibility, Dean's testimony cannot be dismissed out of hand. In fact, Haldeman has confirmed many of the details of the meetings at which both he and Dean were present. The opposite conclusions he draws are based upon a different interpretation and different recollection of some of the details. It is precisely in this type of situation that recordings of the conversations are important either to confirm or dispel the inferences of criminal misconduct.

In earlier cases it has been squarely held that the protection afforded by executive privilege does not extend beyond the transaction of legitimate official activities so as to protect conversations that constitute evidence of official misconduct. See, e.g., Rosee v. Chicago Board of Trade, 36 F.R.D. 684, 690 (N.D. Ill. 1965); United

States v. *Proctor & Gamble Co.*, 25 F.R.D. 485, 490 (D. N.J. 1960). When the processes which are fostered and protected by a veil of secrecy are abused or subverted, the reasons for secrecy no longer exist and the privilege is lifted. See *United States* v. *Procter & Gamble Co.*, 356 U.S. 677, 684 (1958) (grand jury minutes).[33]

In contending for an absolute and impenetrable executive privilege here, the President's counsel point to the confidentiality normally attaching to certain deliberations in the Legislative and Judicial Branches (Brief in Opposition 216-217). Neither analogy, however, will bear the weight placed on it by counsel. To the contrary, the interpretation of the Speech or Debate Clause, which confers an explicit constitutional privilege on members of Congress, underscores the flaws in that claim.[34] "The immunities [of that Clause] were not written into the Constitution simply for the personal or private benefit of Members of Congress, but to protect the integrity of the legislative process." *United States* v. *Brewster*, 408 U.S. 501, 507 (1972). The purpose of the Clause was to "assure a co-equal branch of the government wide freedom of speech, debate and deliberation without intimidation or threats from the Executive Branch." *Gravel* v. *United States*, 408 U.S. 606, 616 (1972). The policies and interests underlying the Clause are thus similar to those underlying executive privilege.[35] But even though the Clause protects a legislator in the performance of legislative acts, "it does not privilege either

---

[33] Executive privilege compares in many respects to executive immunity. A government official may not be held liable for damages in a civil action for the consequences of acts within the scope of his official duties. See *Barr* v. *Matteo*, 360 U.S. 564 (1959). Immunity, as executive privilege, has been considered necessary to foster "the fearless, vigorous, and effective administration of policies of government." 360 U.S. at 571. But the immunity does not shield him for acts "manifestly or palpably beyond his authority." *Spalding* v. *Vilas*, 161 U.S. 483, 498 (1896); *Bivens* v. *Six Unknown Narcotics Agents*, 456 F.2d 1339 (2nd Cir. 1972).

[34] The Speech or Debate Clause, Art. I, S 6, cl. I, provides that no Senator or Representative may be "questioned in any other Place" for "any Speech or Debate in either House." It prohibits inquiry "into those things generally said or done in the House or in the Senate in the performance of official duties and the motivation for those acts." *United States* v. *Brewster*, 408 U.S. at 512.

[35] Executive privilege, it has been said, is granted "for the benefit of the public, not of executives who may happen to then hold office." *Kaiser Aluminum & Chemical Corp.* v. *United States*, 157 F. Supp. at 944. The re-election of an incumbent President can not automatically be equated with the transaction of the people's business.

Senator or aide to violate an otherwise valid criminal law in preparing for or implementing legislative acts." *Gravel* v. *United States,* 408 U.S. at 626. Nor can even this explicit constitutional privilege be invoked to frustrate a grand jury inquiry into the activities of a Senator or his aide to determine whether criminal acts have been committed. *Ibid.* Thus, *a fortiori,* any shield of official confidentiality under an implicit executive privilege must yield in the face of public testimony indicating that the conversations covered by the subpoena dealt with illegitimate activities.

Similarly, counsel's analogy to confidentiality in the Judicial Branch, when analyzed, shows why the President can invoke no privilege here. Counsel cite *Fayerweather* v. *Ritch,* 195 U.S. 276, 306-307 (1904), for the proposition that judicial deliberations are confidential, as shown by the rule that evidence of jury deliberations ordinarily is not admissible to impeach a verdict. In so doing, however, they overlook the later, qualifying decision in *Clark* v. *United States,* 289 U.S. 1 (1933), holding that this privilege of confidentiality must yield in a criminal case probing alleged misconduct by a juror. Mr. Justice Cardozo's opinion for the Court recognized that the privilege, based upon a need for confidentiality, was generally valid: "Freedom of debate might be stifled and independence of thought checked if jurors were made to feel that their arguments and ballots were to be freely published to the world." 289 U.S. at 13. But Justice Cardozo continued [that] the privilege is subject to "conditions and exceptions" when there are other policies "competing for supremacy. It is then the function of a court to mediate between them." *Ibid.* In explaining that the interest in confidentiality must yield where there is evidence of criminal misconduct, the Court reasoned:

> The privilege takes as its postulate a genuine relation, honestly created and honestly maintained. If that condition is not satisfied, if the relation is merely a sham and a pretense, the jury may not invoke a relation dishonestly assumed as a cover and cloak for the concealment of the truth. 289 U.S. at 14.

The Court then drew an analogy to the attorney-client privilege, one of the most venerable privileges in the law, and emphasized: "The privilege takes flight if the relation is abused. A client who consults an attorney for advice that will serve him in the commission of a fraud will have no help from the law. He must let the truth be told. The attorney may be innocent, and still the guilty client must let the truth come out." 289 U.S. at 15.

That, of course, is exactly what is involved in the present case. The evidence already available tends to show, in counsel's own words, that the "statements made by other persons to the President at the meetings for which the recordings have been subpoenaed were made by them pursuant to a conspiracy to obstruct justice" and that some of the participants in the conversations may "have betrayed his confidence by committing crimes" (Brief in Opposition 228-230). Counsel argue that, despite this, the general principle of confidentiality must be maintained in order to assure the effective functioning of the Presidential staff system! An analogous argument was made in *Clark*, and the rationale was decisively rejected.

> With the aid of this analogy [to the attorney-client privilege] we recur to the social policies competing for supremacy. A privilege surviving until the relation is abused and vanishing when abuse is shown to the satisfaction of the judge has been found to be a workable technique for the protection of the confidences of client and attorney. Is there sufficient reason to believe that it will be found to be inadequate for the protection of a juror? No doubt the need is weighty that conduct in the jury room shall be untrammeled by the fear of embarrassing publicity. The need is no less weighty that it shall be pure and undefiled. A juror of integrity and reasonable firmness will not fear to speak his mind if the confidences of debate are barred to the ears of mere impertinence or malice. He will not expect to be shielded against the disclosure of his conduct in the event that there is evidence reflecting upon his honor. The chance that now and then there may be found some timid soul who will take counsel of his fears and give way to their repressive power is too remote and shadowy to shape the course of justice. It must yield to the overmastering need, so vital in our polity, of preserving trial by jury in its purity against the inroads of corruption. 289 U.S. at 16.

It is hard to imagine a stronger need for piercing the cloak of confidentiality than in the present case. Requiring production of the evidence under these circumstances presents only a minimal threat to a President's ability to obtain advice from his aides with complete freedom and candor; for surely there will be few occasions upon which a grand jury will have similar cause to believe there is material evidence of criminality of high officials in the papers and documents in the Executive Offices of the President.

Counsel cannot seriously claim that the aides of any future President will be so "timid" in the face of such a remote danger of disclosure of their advice, or that some small risk of reticence is too great a price to pay to preserve the President's Office "against the inroads of corruption." In light of the substantial showing that there is reason to believe the conversations described in the subpoena were part of a corrupt criminal plan, they cannot be shielded by a privilege designed to protect the objective, candid, and honest formulation of policy in government affairs.

C. *The Need of the Grand Jury for the Evidence in the Impartial Administration of Justice is Greater Than the Public Interest Served by Secrecy.*

We submit, for the reasons stated, that the need to inquire into the allegations that the nine conversations were linked to criminal conspiracy is alone sufficient to take the present case out of any privilege based upon a generalized interest in preserving the confidentiality of executive deliberations. It is unnecessary, however, to make so broad a ruling. When the interests in secrecy are balanced against the need for the evidence under the circumstances of the present case in accordance with the settled judicial procedure[36], it becomes apparent that the need of the grand jury for the evidence greatly out-weighs any risk of harm from so limited a disclosure.

1. Each of the nine recordings listed in the subpoena is material evidence and may have critical importance in an on-going grand jury investigation into crimes on the part of high government officials. This is no "fishing expedition" where the grand jury is searching blindly for evidence which may or may not be relevant. The subpoena requires the tape recordings of nine specific conversations. Testimony before the Select Committee of the Senate, depositions in civil actions and White House press releases indicate that each of the conversations very probably deals in whole or in part with the activities under investigation. The public testimony given by principals in the conversations has been largely conflicting, hazy or

[36] See authorities cited in Part II(A)(3), p. 262, *supra.*

incomplete. The electronic recordings perhaps may prove garbled in some instances, but it is much more likely that they are the best direct evidence of what was said on those occasions. Cf. *United States* v. *White*, 401 U.S. 745, 753 (1971). Production of the tapes, therefore, will minimize the risk that innocent persons may be indicted or that a guilty person may escape prosecution.[37]

The importance of each of the nine recordings is apparent from the discussion in the Statement, above, and is illustrated by public accounts of the conversation in the President's office on September 15, 1972. John Dean testified that in the presence of Haldeman he told the President that "all [Dean] had been able to do was to contain the case and assist in keeping it out of the White House." Dean also told the President that he "could make no assurances that the day would not come when this matter would start to unravel." The President congratulated him on his "good job" (S. Tr. 2229-30). Haldeman testified, on the other hand, that there were only innocent and casual references to the return of indictments and to a supposedly *bona fide* investigation conducted by Dean on the President's behalf (S. Tr. 6090-93). It is manifestly important for the grand jury to learn, if it can, which accounts of the conversation is correct. If Dean's testimony is true, the tape recording of the conversation will tend to prove that at least he and Haldeman were involved in conspiracy to obstruct justice. If Haldeman's testimony is true, the tape will probably tend to show that Dean is guilty of perjury. Both crimes are within the purview of the present grand jury. Production of the tapes is the best method of resolving the issue.

2. The fact that production is sought only for use by a grand jury under the normal rules of secrecy applicable to such proceedings minimizes any dangers from invasion of confidentiality. This is not a civil proceeding between private parties or even between the United

---

[37] Indeed, perhaps the "most valuable function of the grand jury" is to "stand between the prosecutor and the accused, or to determine whether the charge [is] founded upon credible testimony or [is] dictated by malice or personal ill will." *Hale* v. *Henkel*, 201 U.S. at 59. Speaking of the proper scope of a grand jury's discharge of its responsibilities, the Supreme Court has said: "society's interest is best served by a thorough and extensive investigation. . ." *Wood* v. *Georgia*, 370 U.S. 375, 392 (1962).

States and a private party, where masses of confidential communications might be arguably relevant. Nor is this one of a long history of congressional investigations seeking to expose to the glare of publicity the policies and activities of the Executive Branch. In such instances the evidence is often sought in order to probe the mental processes of the Executive Office in a review of the wisdom or rationale of official Executive action. Compare *Morgan* v. *United States*, 304 U.S. 1, 18 (1938); *United States* v. *Morgan*, 313 U.S. 409, 422, (1941). The threat to freedom and candor in giving advice is probably at the maximum in such proceedings; they invite bringing to bear upon aides and advisors the pressures of publicity and political criticism, the fear of which may discourage candid advice and robust debate. The present grand jury investigation is not an inquisition into official governmental policy or actions, but an attempt to root out possible criminal activity.[38]

3. The allegations under investigation involve high Presidential assistants and criminal conduct in the Executive Offices. Such involvement is virtually unique. Because it is unlikely to recur, production of White House documents in this investigation will establish no precedent for recurrent grand jury investigations. Nor is there substantial likelihood that, because of disclosure under these unhappy circumstances, Presidents and their aides will be deterred from full, frank and vigorous discussion of legitimate governmental concerns.

4. Withholding the recordings may frustrate prosecution of wrongdoers in high places. It is easy for counsel claiming the privilege to express the expectation that prosecution will be possible without the tapes, but under the law (see note 10, *supra*, p. 248), it is now the responsibility of the Special Prosecutor, exercising the powers and duties delegated by the Attorney General, to see to it

[38] Indeed, despite the President's extravagant claim that the separation of powers gives the Executive's deliberative process "a virtual immunity from [judicial] inquiry" (Brief in Opposition 233), it is clear that in certain circumstances it is appropriate for the courts to probe Executive deliberations. See, e.g., *Citizens to Preserve Overton Park* v. *Volpe*, 401 U.S. 402, 420 (1971), holding that, despite the *Morgan* line of cases, "the court may require the administrative officers who participated in the decision to give testimony explaining their actions."

that all relevant evidence is produced for the grand jury in accordance with the frequent admonitions of the Supreme Court. See *United States* v. *Dionisio,* 410 U.S. at 12-13; *Branzburg* v. *Hayes,* 408 U.S. at 688, 701-12; *Wood* v. *Georgia,* 370 U.S. at 392. Nor is it premature to note that if indictments are returned, there may be further demands for access to the tapes under the Jencks Act, 18 U.S.C. 3500, or cases like *Brady* v. *Maryland,* 373 U.S. 83 (1963). Of course, at this stage it is impossible to determine precisely what evidence might be material to the defense in future prosecutions and might be ordered produced. No great amount of imagination is required, however, to foresee the danger that prosecution of some possible indictments—assuming that the available evidence warranted indictments—would have to be abandoned if the recordings were withheld. All this is plainly contingent but it is not amiss to point out that there could hardly be a greater cause for loss of public confidence in our governmental institutions than frustration of the prosecution of a Chief Executive's aides and political associates by his withholding of material evidence.

6. Finally, it is worth noting that the confidentiality of deliberative processes is always subject to unanticipated disclosures. As the President's counsel concede, "Presidents volunteer a great deal of information because it is in the public interest to do so," despite the arguable applicability of executive privilege (Brief in Opposition 227). Thus, at the time of any particular discussion, neither a President nor his advisers can assume that their statements will remain confidential. Indeed, in this very case, even before the grand jury issued its subpoena, the President saw fit to disclose some aspects of these conversations with his closest advisers. Furthermore, he has also acknowledged publicly that he ordered all his conversations to be tape-recorded so that they could be made available to history. This is consistent with the common practice by Presidents and presidential advisers of publishing memoirs disclosing the consultations of the Executive Office. Thus, an order compelling disclosure of contemporaneous evidence in this unique case, which carries no inference of continuing or repeated disclosure of future conversations, can hardly present a substantially increased threat to the freedom and candor of advice available to the President.

The balance of interests, therefore, overwhelmingly mandates production of the evidence.[39]

III
ANY PRIVILEGE ATTACHING TO THE RECORDINGS OF THE CONVERSATIONS HAS BEEN WAIVED BY OTHER DISCLOSURES OF THEIR CONTENT GIVEN WITH THE PRESIDENT'S CONSENT

Even if the conversations recorded on the nine tapes listed in the subpoena could otherwise be regarded as covered by a privilege of executive confidentiality, the privilege cannot be claimed in the face of the voluminous testimony and other public statements concerning the conversations given with the President's consent. "A person who would otherwise have a privilege to refuse to disclose or to

---

[39] The President asserts in his Brief in Opposition (p. 225), without further explanation, that parts of the conversations deal with constitutional duties clearly irrelevant to the Watergate investigation. Obviously, we make no claim that conversations that are subject to a valid privilege and irrelevant to grand jury investigation should be disclosed either to the grand jury or the public. And the Special Prosecutor does not intend to present any irrelevant evidence to the grand jury.

We have made a prima facie, and we suggest, conclusive showing that the recordings that are material to the grand jury's investigation cannot be withheld. Although the President has not suggested any means of accommodating the respective interests, we feel certain that counsel for the President and the Special Prosecutor will be able to agree on a method for excising those portions of the recordings that should not be disclosed.

The President, in his reply, may suggest that *in camera* inspection would be appropriate as has often been done to separate producible material from unproducible. See *Environmental Protection Agency* v. *Mink*, 410 U.S. at 91-93; *United States* v. *Reynolds*, 345 U.S. at 8-10; *Carl Zeiss Stiftung* v. *V.E.B. Carl Zeiss, Jena*, 40 F.R.D. at 331-32. See also 18 U.S.C. 3500(c). We suggest that in the circumstances of this case, where the Special Prosecution is an appointee of the Attorney General and an officer of the Executive Branch, there is no necessity for the Court to burden itself with this procedure.

It is essential at this stage of the proceedings to preserve the authenticity of the recordings. If there is an *in camera* inspection and if it reveals that part of the conversations should be excised, the Court should have transcribed those portions that are to be disclosed. The original recordings should then be maintained by the Court under seal until all proceedings are concluded.

prevent another from disclosing a specified matter has no such privilege with respect to that matter if the judge finds that he . . . without coercion and with knowledge of his privilege, made disclosure *of any part of the matter* or consented to such a disclosure made by any one." Uniform Rules of Evidence, Rule 37 (emphasis added). The rule stated was approved as "sound" by the Court of Appeals for this Circuit in *Ellis* v. *United States*, 416 F.2d 791, 801 m. 26 (D.C. Cir. 1969).[40]

The present case is governed by this familiar rule. Much about the subject matter of the nine conversations has been disclosed by the President or with the President's consent. In his statement of May 22, 1973, the President announced that, in light of the importance of the "effort to arrive at the truth," "executive privilege will not be invoked as to any testimony concerning possible criminal conduct or discussions of possible criminal conduct, in matters presently under investigation, including the Watergate affair and the alleged cover-up."[41] In the weeks following that expression of consent, extensive testimony has been given as to the substance of the communications which are recorded on the tapes subpoenaed by the grand jury.[42] Messrs. Dean, Mitchell, Ehrlichman, and Haldeman have presented testimony on the particular conversations in which they participated. Some parts give a general summary of the discussion. Other parts are an attempt to reconstruct the entirety of the conversations in as detailed a manner as possible. The extent of

[40] The court there also approved what became Rule 511 of the Proposed Federal Rules of Evidence (as transmitted to Congress by the Supreme Court on November 20, 1972):

A person upon whom these rules confer a privilege against disclosure of the confidential matter or communication [including executive privilege] waives the privilege if he or his predecessor while holder of the privilege voluntarily discloses or consents to disclosure of any significant part of the matter or communication. This rule does not apply if the disclosure is itself a privileged communication.

[41] Verified Petition for Order to Show Cause, Exhibit C, 7-8.

[42] This testimony has been given in hearings held before the Senate Select Committee on Presidential Campaign Activities, and in depositions taken in connection with the pending civil action of *Democratic National Committee* v. *McCord, et al.* (D.D.C. Civil No. 1233-72). We are filing an Appendix quoting the testimony already given in various forums about the substance of each conversation covered by the subpoena.

these disclosures is indicated in our statement and earlier portions of this brief. The President neither objected to such testimony nor claimed that it exceeded the scope authorized by his May 22 statement.[43]

The President himself has engaged in public discussion of matters covered in the conversations. On May 22 he outlined a version of the Watergate affair without mentioning the conversations but it now must be read, after Dean's testimony, as direct contradiction of Dean's account. Indeed, in his letter to Senator Ervin on July 23, 1973, after Dean's testimony concerning the conversations, the President reaffirmed his earlier statement. The President also described the conclusions concerning the conversations which he would have drawn from the tapes:

> Before their existence became publicly known, I personally listened to a number of them. The tapes are entirely consistent with what I know to be the truth and what I have stated to be the truth.

J. Fred Buzhardt, Special Counsel to the President, also has discussed the conversations with a view to publication, presumably with the President's consent. On June 21, 1973, *The New York Times* published a "White House analysis of conversations between President Nixon and John W. Dean" which is generally understood to be a memorandum made by an attorney for the Senate Select Committee based upon Mr. Buzhardt's presentation. Some conversations are barely noted. The suggestions as to the others go into considerable detail.[44] Surely, it is fair to presume that Mr. Buzhardt

---

[43] It is true that the President, through his Counsel, J. Fred Buzhardt, did instruct Haldeman not to testify before the Senate Select Committee concerning facts which Mr. Haldeman learned only by listening to the tapes that were made available to him. Insofar as Haldeman testified as to those portions of the March 21, 1973, meeting between Dean and the President which he did not attend, his testimony therefore does exceed Mr. Buzhardt's instruction. It should be noted, however, that the President made no other protest, and that Dean's previous testimony as to those portions of the March 21 meeting falls within the scope authorized by the President.

[44] For example, the suggestions concerning the March 13 conversation read:

March 13—President inquired as to Ken Rietz. Dean said no illegality involved. President asked if Colson or Haldeman knew Segretti. President asked if Mitchell and Colson knew of Watergate. Dean said there was nothing specific on Colson; that he didn't know about Mitchell, but that Strachan could

was acting with authority and that this version of the conversation was not the product of his imagination.

The President has even allowed some of the tapes to be used in preparing public testimony. Haldeman, not a disinterested witness, was allowed to take home the tapes of the conversations of September 15, 1972, March 21, 1973, and other unspecified dates after he had resigned (S. Tr. 6091, 6357-58), and to use them in preparing his testimony.

The short of the matter is that the President waived the confidentiality of the conversations, thus producing a flood of incomplete and contradictory testimony about some of the most important events in this investigation. As to a number of conversations the President has supplied his own version. Now the President asserts a privilege to withhold the most complete record available to supplement faulty recollections, resolve contradictions, and fill in important details.

The law is not so capricious. "[T]he moment confidence ceases, privilege ceases." *Parkhurst v. Lowten*, 36 Eng. Rep. 589, 596 (Ch. 1819). "This much," observes Wigmore, "is universally conceded." 8 Wigmore § 2311, at 599. The rule that disclosure eliminates any privilege that would otherwise attach to confidential information has been applied in cases dealing with claims of governmental privilege, *Roviaro v. United States*, 353 U.S. 53 (1967); *Westinghouse Electric Corp. v. City of Burlington, Vt.*, 351 F.2d 762 (D.C. Cir. 1965); *Fireman's Fund Indemnity Co. v. United States*, 103 F. Supp. 915 (N.D. Fla. 1952), as well as in cases dealing with attorney-client privilege, *Underwater Storage Inc. v. U.S. Rubber Co.*, 314 F. Supp. 546 (D.D.C. 1970), *United States v. Kelsey-Hayes Wheel Co.*, 15 F.R.D. 461 (E.D. Mich. 1954); physician-patient privilege, *Munzer v. Swedish American Line*, 35 F. Supp. 493 (S.D.N.Y. 1940); and marital privilege, *Pereira v. United States*, 347 U.S. 1, 6 (1954).

Counsel try to avoid the consequences of the President's approval

---

be involved. President states again that Dean should compile a written report about the matter. Dean said Sirica was a hanging judge, the President said he liked hanging judges. They discussed fund-raising before April 7. Dean said that everything [that] had been done was legal. *New York Times*, June 21, 1973, p. 28, col. 4.

This account differs in critical respects from Dean's version.

of public testimony about the conversations by arguing that he should be allowed to decide precisely how much should be told (Brief in Opposition 227). They also argue that application of the waiver doctrine to require fuller supplementation of the public statements might discourage Presidents from volunteering selected portions of confidential information in the future (Brief in Opposition 227). Similar contentions have been advanced with analogous privileges and have not proven weighty. If a person holds a valid privilege, he has a choice whether to stand on it or not. If he elects to disclose, the boundaries of the disclosure are no longer within his exclusive control. For example, in cases involving the analogous privileges accorded to attorney-client and physician-patient communications, it is clear that once testimony has been received as to a particular communication, either with the consent of the holder of the privilege or without his objection, the privilege is lost as to the entire communication and not only as to those parts already revealed. There can be no assertion of the privilege to block access to another version of the conversation. See, e.g., *Hunt* v. *Blackburn*, 128 U.S. 464, 470-71 (1888); *Rosenfeld* v. *Ungar*, 25 F.R.D. 340, 342 (S.D. Iowa 1960); *Munzer* v. *Swedish American Line, supra; In re Associated Gas & Electric Co.*, 59 F. Supp 743, 744 (S.D.N.Y. 1944); 8 Wigmore §§ 2327, 2389, at 636 & 855-61. The *Rosenfeld* case is particularly relevant, for there it was held that the oral disclosure of communications between an attorney and his client waived any privilege which might otherwise be invoked with regard to the documents that recorded those communications.

The same principles apply to the Fifth Amendment's privilege against self-incrimination. Once the privilege-holder elects to disclose his version of what happened, a due "regard for the function of courts of justice to ascertain the truth" requires further disclosure "on the matters relevantly raised by that testimony." *Brown* v. *United States*, 356 U.S. 148, 156, 157 (1958). Once the privilege-holder has opened the door, "he is not permitted to stop, but must go on and make a full disclosure." *Brown* v. *Walker*, 161 U.S. 591, 597 (1896). These principles are followed, of course, in this Circuit, even when separate proceedings are involved. See *Ellis* v. *United States*, 416 F.2d 791, 800-805, (D.C. Cir. 1969); *Viereck* v. *United States*, 139 F.2d 847, (D.C. Cir.), *cert: denied*, 321 U.S. 794 (1944).

The possibility that the tapes contain as yet undisclosed details of the recorded conversations, far from justifying preservation of their confidentiality, provides a compelling reason for their disclosure. The extensive testimony already received on the taped conversations indicates that those discussions have critical importance in resolving issues before the grand jury. The tapes, original and contemporaneous recordings, are the best evidence that can be obtained of what actually transpired. *Schuyler v. United Air Lines*, 94 F. Supp. 472 (M.D. Pa. 1950), *aff'd*, 188 F.2d 968 (3d Cir. 1951). Since it is well settled that the best evidence that is obtainable in the circumstances . . . must be adduced to prove any disputed fact," *Sylvania Electric Products, Inc. v. Flanagan* 352 F.2d 1005, 1007 (1st Cir. 1965), the tapes are necessary to the proper functioning of the grand jury. Without the tapes, the grand jury would be relegated to dependence upon the sometimes vague, conflicting, and potentially self-serving recollections of the participants.

Forcing the grand jury to rely upon inferior evidence in its deliberations on a case of this magnitude does a disservice to the administration of justice by needlessly increasing the risk that the guilty may go free or the innocent be wrongly indicted. Since the purposes underlying any executive privilege which arguably might have attached to the subpoenaed tapes can no longer be served, and since the tapes are the best evidence of material allegations, any privilege which might otherwise have protected the tapes from disclosure to the grand jury has dissolved.

CONCLUSION

Counsel for the President pose the issue: "Will the Presidency be allowed to continue to function?" (Brief in Opposition 213.) Our response is that the Presidency can indeed function, strongly and effectively, without the need to set above the law the determination by an incumbent that it will be "in the public interest" to withhold material evidence from a grand jury engaged in investigating serious charges of criminal misconduct upon the part of his aides.

The petition for an order directing the President or any subordinate offical with custody or control of the materials specified in the grand jury subpoena *duces tecum* to produce this evidence forthwith should be granted.[45]

Respectfully submitted.

ARCHIBALD COX,
Special Prosecutor,
PHILIP A. LACOVARA,
Counsel to the Special
Prosecutor,
PETER M. KREINDLER,
Executive Assistant to
the Special Prosecutor,
JAMES F. NEAL,
Special Assistant to the
Special Prosecutor,

Of Counsel:

Sidney M. Glazer
Maureen E. Gevlin
Robert L. Palmer
Richard D. Weinberg

August 13, 1973

Watergate Special Prosecution
Force
1425 K Street, N.W.
Washington, D.C. 20005
*Attorneys for the United States,
on behalf of the Grand Jury.*

[45] The early resolution of the question whether the evidence will be produced is a matter of great importance. For the grand jury to vote to return and not to return indictments covering central aspects of a possible "cover-up" of the Watergate break-in, prior to receipt of this evidence, would be of questionable propriety. The term of the grand jury expires at the beginning of December 1973. Time would be required after the evidence was received not only for pursuit of leads it suggested, but also for adequate deliberation.

CONCLUDING NOTE: On August 29, 1973, District Court Judge Sirica, after having received additional supplemental briefs and listened to oral argument, ruled that the determination of whether a claim of "executive privilege" was properly invoked was a "judicial decision." Sirica ordered the President to produce the tapes "forthwith for the court's examination *in camera*," that is, for examination in his chambers, privately. Sirica declared that if after such examination he found that any portion of the tapes were not properly subject to privilege, those portions would be forwarded to the grand jury.

The President's lawyers filed an appeal on September 6, asking the U.S. Court of Appeals for the District of Columbia for a Writ of Mandamus to direct the reversal of Sirica's decision. They argued that Sirica's order to the President for the production of the tapes even for *in camera* inspection only was "clearly erroneous and beyond the power of the judicial branch." On September 7, Special Prosecutor Cox also appealed. Cox contended that the Court of Appeals should direct Sirica to order the President to deliver the tapes to the grand jury without prior *in camera* inspection or, if the right of *in camera* inspection were upheld, that Sirica be directed to allow the Special Prosecutor to be present during any such inspection in order to "advise and aid the court in determining what parts were relevant to the grand jury's investigations."

The Court of Appeals on October 12 upheld District Court Judge Sirica's ruling that the tapes be turned over to him for *in camera* inspection and determination of whether they should be forwarded to the grand jury. Rejecting the validity of any "all-embracing claim of prerogative" and declaring that the President was "not above the law's commands," the Appeals Court held in a 5 to 2 decision that the President should specify the particular segments of the tapes that he believed should not be disclosed and the particular kinds of privilege on which each claim for non-disclosure was based. Sirica was ordered to hold a hearing in chambers at the request of either the President's attorneys or the Special Prosecutor on any claims of privilege presented. Following the *in camera* hearing and inspection, Sirica was to determine whether to allow the claim of privilege on any portion of the tapes to which it purportedly attached or to disallow it and disclose the relevant segment to the grand jury.

On Friday October 19, the last day allowed for appealing to the Supreme Court, President Nixon made the startling announcement that he would neither appeal the District Court and Court of Appeals decisions nor comply with them by delivering the tapes to Judge Sirica. Instead, the President stated that as a "compromise," he would personally prepare a summary statement of "everything in [the] tapes that has any bearing on Watergate" and forward copies of that summary both to Judge Sirica and the Senate Select Committee.

President Nixon asserted that the authenticity of his statement would be assured by giving "unlimited access to the tapes" to Senator John Stennis of Mississippi so that Stennis could verify that the statement was "full and accurate." The President also announced that in order "that the constitutional tension of Watergate would not be continued," he was directing Special Prosecutor Cox, as an "employe of the Executive Branch, to make no further attempts by judicial process to obtain tapes, notes, or memoranda of Presidential conversations."

Cox immediately issued a statement giving his "judgment" that the President was "refusing to comply with the court decrees." The Special Prosecutor indicated that he would have to bring that point "to the attention of the court" and added that he could not be a party to any "arrangement" precluding him from continuing to use the judicial process to obtain relevant presidential tapes, notes, and memoranda. The next day, Saturday, October 20, Cox reiterated this position at an extended news conference.

That same evening it was announced by the White House that Cox had been discharged as Special Prosecutor and that the Watergate Special Prosecution Force had been disbanded and its functions transferred "into the institutional framework of the Department of Justice." It was also announced that Attorney General Richardson had resigned rather than execute a presidential directive to dismiss Cox and that Deputy Attorney General William D. Ruckelshaus was himself discharged when he too refused to carry out the presidential order. Richardson indicated in his letter of resignation that his discharging Cox would have been contrary to repeated commitments he had made to assure the "independence" of the Special Prosecutor; Ruckelshaus wrote that his "conscience would not permit" him to carry out the President's instruction. The actual discharge order to Cox was delivered by Solicitor General Robert H. Bork, who automatically became Acting Attorney General as a result of the vacanies in the offices of Attorney General and Deputy Attorney General.

On Monday, October 22, the President's attorneys filed a statement with Judge Sirica advising him that they would contend the President's furnishing of the projected "summary statement" of the tapes constituted adequate compliance with the District Court and Court of Appeals orders. But on Tuesday, October 23, there was yet another startling development. One of the President's attorneys appeared personally before Judge Sirica and announced that the President had changed his position and was now prepared "to comply in all respects" with the court orders by delivering the tapes to the District Court.*

D. C. and F. P.

---

* This October 23 declaration of the President's intent to deliver the tapes for *in camera* inspection under the procedures detailed by the District Court and Court of Appeals orders abruptly brought to an end the constitutional issue between the President and the courts. The settlement of the constitutional issue did not, however, immediately produce the tapes called for in the subpoena. At the October 23 hearing, the President's attorney had already indicated that it would "require some time . . . to put [the] materials together." Eight days after this hearing at which compliance was promised "in full" and "in all respects"

with the court orders directing delivery of tape recordings for eight meetings and one telephone conversation, the President's Special Counsel appeared before Judge Sirica and informed him that the tapes for one of the eight meetings and for the one telephone conversation would not in fact be forthcoming. The Special Counsel claimed on behalf of the President that the tapes did not exist because the two conversations in question had never been recorded. On November 21, the President's attorneys went before Judge Sirica again and now announced that an eighteen-minute blank portion existed in the tape recording for one of the remaining seven meetings. Sirica then ordered that the original tapes be delivered to his custody, which they were with various particularized claims of executive privilege on November 26. On November 28 the President's attorneys disclosed, again for the first time, that in addition to the tape with the eighteen-minute gap, blank sections existed in other tapes as well.

10   On the Presidential Succession

ARTHUR M. SCHLESINGER, JR.

On the eve of the bicentennial of independence, the American experiment in self-government was confronted by a startling development: the President and Vice President who would lead the celebrations on July 4, 1976, would be persons who had come to office and power, not through election, like all their predecessors, but through appointment. Even more disturbing was the thought that the source of this President's appointment was a former President whose first Vice President had resigned in disgrace as a confessed felon and who himself had resigned in the face of virtual certainty that he would otherwise have been impeached and removed because of high crimes and misdemeanors against the United States.

Nothing like this had ever happened, or could ever have happened, in the earlier history of the republic. The right of the people to choose their own leaders had been assumed by definition as a fundamental point of self-government. A major premise of American politics had always been —at least up to 1967—that the President was an elected, not an appointed, official. The Constitution (Article II, Section 1) expressly provided that the President and Vice President were to "be elected." The Founding Fathers believed that no one who had not been elected to the Presidency should serve as President any longer than necessary to organize a new

ARTHUR M. SCHLESINGER, JR., Schweitzer Professor of the Humanities at the City University of New York, served as Special Assistant to President Kennedy from 1961 to 1963. His major books include *The Age of Jackson; The Crisis of the Old Order, The Coming of the New Deal, The Politics of Upheaval* (volumes in the Age of Roosevelt); *A Thousand Days: John F. Kennedy in the White House;* and, most recently, *The Imperial Presidency.*

presidential election. The Framers would unquestionably have been astounded and appalled to find as President and Vice President 200 years after the Declaration of Independence two men, neither of whom had ever faced a national election and each of whom owed his office to his direct predecessor.

It was the Twenty-fifth Amendment—ratified in 1967 without, it must be said, any clear view of the consequences[1]—that discarded the wisdom of the Founding Fathers and threatened to introduce so extraordinary an innovation into the American system. Under that amendment President Nixon, after the resignation of Vice President Agnew in 1973, named Gerald Ford as his Vice President. When Nixon himself went under, Ford, now President, was obliged by the same amendment to name a Vice President of his personal choice. "For the first time in the history of this great Nation," John Pastore of Rhode Island cried with pardonable senatorial grandiloquence, "the President and Vice President will both be appointed—not elected by the people and not responsive to any mandate from the citizens. The Nation will no longer be democratically governed."[2]

I

Nixon's Secretary of State, a former professor of political science, had observed in March 1974, "There have been, very rarely, fully legitimate governments in any European country since World War I."[3] This was perhaps an imprudent remark from the representative of a government whose legitimacy lay at that very moment (and for many moments thereafter) under the most serious question. But what would Dr. Kissinger make of the legitimacy of an allegedly democratic government headed by two men receiving their office and power through appointment rather than through election?

No doubt such a government, though on the face incompatible with Article II of the Constitution, had become technically constitutional through the Twenty-fifth Amendment. But it could not be said that those who drafted that ill-considered amendment desired this particular result. The constitutionality of the appointive Presidency was thus inadvertent, not premeditated. And for anyone concerned with democracy in a philosophical sense the prospect raised the sternest difficulties. Not only was the conception of the Presidency as an elected office breached; but the assignment to a President of the personal power to appoint a

---

[1] Certainly not on the part of this writer.
[2] *Congressional Record*, November 15, 1973, S 20429.
[3] *New York Times*, March 12, 1974.

Vice President in case of a vacancy added a quasi-dynastic aspect to the process of presidential succession.[4]

In 1945 President Truman, noting that it lay within his authority to appoint the person (then the Secretary of State) who would be his successor in the event of his own disability or death, said with customary directness, "I do not believe that in a democracy this power should rest with the Chief Executive."[5] The Twenty-fifth Amendment cavalierly tossed away Truman's old-fashioned scruple and thereby contributed its mite to the aggrandizement of the Presidency. And, if Truman had supposed that the principle applied to himself, an elected Vice President, how much more powerfully must it apply to a Chief Executive who was an appointed Vice President and whose name had never been submitted to a national electorate. A system that permitted an appointed President to appoint his own successor was a system that removed the most vital political choices farther and farther from the people. One doubted whether such a regime could be called, in the phrase with which Professor Kissinger flunked a half-century of government in Europe, "fully legitimate."

The fix into which the Twenty-fifth Amendment placed American democracy was emphasized by a striking contrast with events in France soon after the Secretary of State delivered his excommunication of Europe. General de Gaulle had designed a very powerful Presidency for himself; but even that towering leader had not claimed for Presidents of France the authority the Twenty-fifth Amendment bestowed, in special cases, on Presidents of the United States: that is, the power to nominate his own successor. Instead Article 7 of the Constitution of the Fifth Republic said that in case of a vacancy in the Presidency a new presidential election must be held within thirty-five days. In the meantime, the functions of the President (save for the powers of calling a national referendum and of dissolving the National Assembly) are to be exercised by the president of the senate. On April 2, 1974, President Pompidou died. On May 5 the French had their election, followed by a runoff on May 19 and the inauguration of the new President on May 27. In less than two months, in short, France had a new President, freely chosen by the people and equipped by them with a fresh mandate. Which government is the more legitimate—the elected government of France after the death of Pompidou, or the appointed government of the United States after the resigna-

---

[4] The objection that Presidents name their Vice Presidents anyway at the nominating convention is dealt with in the discussion of the Twenty-fifth Amendment below, section X.

[5] H. S. Truman, *Public Papers . . . 1945* (Washington, 1961), p. 129.

tion of Nixon? Which political system is, in this respect at least, the more democratic?

The signal difference between the French and American systems in dealing with a vacancy in the Presidency is obvious: *the French have no Vice President.* The results surely favor the French on essential tests of legitimacy and democracy. The contrast therefore calls on Americans to reconsider the utility of the Vice Presidency in their own .system.

II

History had shown the American Vice Presidency to be a job of spectacular and, I believe, incurable frustration. Gerald Ford, like his predecessors, entered into the office with soothing presidential assurances that he, unlike his predecessors, would be given tasks of substance and responsibility. One could be absolutely certain that these shining prospects would disappear whenever he reached out to grasp them. Nixon, even in his feeble condition of 1974, was no more disposed to share power with Ford than he had shared power with Agnew. When James J. Kilpatrick asked Nixon whether he had told his Vice President of 1971 about the plan for the diplomatic opening to China, Nixon, replying in what Kilpatrick described as an "incredulous" tone, said, "Agnew? Agnew? Oh, of course not."[6] Yet a year later he kept on as his running mate and successor the Vice President he excluded from his councils. Still President Nixon's tone could hardly have been more incredulous than Eisenhower's when interrogated in 1960 about Vice President Nixon's role in the eight years of the Eisenhower Presidency. To the question "What major decisions of your Administration has the Vice President participated in?" Eisenhower responded, "If you give me a week, I might think of one."[7]

Nor was Nixon merely doing unto others what others had done unto him. He was behaving the way all Presidents have behaved—as they appear to have no inclination and perhaps little choice but to behave—toward their Vice Presidents. It is a doomed office. No President and Vice President have fully trusted each other since Jackson and Van Buren.[8]

---

[6] *Washington Star-News,* May 16, 1974. Jeb Stuart Magruder of the Nixon White House writes of Agnew in 1970: "He'd been frozen out by Nixon, for almost two years." J. S. Magruder, *An American Life* (New York, 1974), p. 128.

[7] *New York Times,* August 25, 1960.

[8] It should perhaps be added that Polk had amiable personal relations with George M. Dallas, McKinley with Garret Hobart, and Truman with Alben Barkley, but none of

Antagonism is inherent in the relationship. "The only business of the vice-president," wrote the sardonic Thomas R. Marshall, who served for eight years under Wilson, "is to ring the White House bell every morning and ask what is the state of health of the president."[9] The only serious thing the Vice President has to do is to wait around for the president to die. This is hardly the basis for cordial and enduring friendships. "The Vice President," said Lyndon Johnson, who experienced both ends of the relationship, "is like a raven, hovering around the head of the President, reminding him of his mortality."[10] Presidents inevitably resent the death's head at the feast; Vice Presidents equally resent the monarch who stuffs himself at the banquet table while they scramble for leavings. Elbridge Gerry worried in the Constitutional Convention about the "close intimacy" that he thought "must subsist between the President & vice-president." Gouverneur Morris responded acidly, "The vice president then will be the first heir apparent that ever loved his father."[11]

The single contemporary point of the Vice Presidency is to provide for the succession in case of the death, disability, resignation, or removal of the President. Of course there have been repeated attempts to give it other points. They have all failed. They are all bound to fail. The Constitution does say that the Vice President "shall be President of the Senate, but shall have no Vote, unless they be equally divided." When there was objection to this in the Constitutional Convention, Roger Sherman observed that, if the Vice President did not preside over the Senate, "he would be without employment."[12] Sherman's observation was prophetic, except that the Vice President's constitutional employment soon became a farce. Agnew as Vice President, for example, never went near the Senate if he could help it. Early Vice Presidents of a philosophical bent filled their days by meditating attacks on the power of the national government. Jefferson wrote the Kentucky Resolution as Vice President, Calhoun the South Carolina Exposition. Their successors have lacked a taste for political philosophy. Richard M. Johnson ran a tavern as Vice President. Thomas R. Marshall and Alben Barkley made jokes. But most Vice Presidents, especially in modern times, have lacked a taste for humor too.

---

these Vice Presidents played any significant role in the policy decisions of their respective administrations.

[9] T. R. Marshall, *Recollections* (Indianapolis, 1925), p. 368.

[10] As told by President Johnson in retirement to Professor Doris Kearns, with whose kind permission I am repeating this exceedingly apt aphorism.

[11] C. C. Tansill, ed., *Documents Illustrative of the Formation of the Union of the American States* (Washington, 1927), p. 682.

[12] Ibid.

III

Why have Presidents not given the Vice President serious work? For a long time they supposed themselves constitutionally forbidden to do so. Washington did on occasion ask his Vice President to attend cabinet meetings; but Jefferson as Vice President was quick to erect a wall of separation. "I consider my office," he wrote, "as constitutionally confined to legislative functions, and that I could not take any part whatever in executive consultations, even were it proposed."[13] Most Presidents and Vice Presidents have accepted the Jeffersonian doctrine. Thus Truman wrote in 1955 that the Vice President "is not an officer of the executive branch" and Eisenhower as late as 1963 that the Vice President "is not legally a part of the Executive branch and is not subject to direction by the President."[14]

The practice of vice presidential participation in cabinet meetings is a recent development. In 1896 Theodore Roosevelt thought it would be desirable "to increase the power of the Vice-President. . . . It would be very well if he were given a seat in the Cabinet."[15] But when he became President himself after an exasperating interlude as Vice President, he did not give his own Vice President, Charles W. Fairbanks, a seat in the cabinet or anywhere else. Vice President Marshall presided at cabinet meetings when Wilson was at Versailles. But, since he regarded himself as a "member of the legislative branch," he questioned the propriety of doing so and carefully explained to the cabinet that he was acting "in obedience to a request" and "in an unofficial and informal way."[16] Harding was the first President to make his Vice President, Calvin Coolidge, a regular at cabinet meetings. Coolidge expected his own Vice President to follow this example; but Charles G. Dawes rejected any such entanglement with the executive as a "wrong principle" and in due course supported farm legislation from his office on Capitol Hill that his President opposed and eventually vetoed.[17] Franklin D. Roosevelt, who from the time of his own vice presidential candidacy in 1920 had cherished the hope of making something of the office,[18] reinstituted vice-

[13] J. D. Feerick, *From Failing Hands: The Story of Presidential Succession* (New York, 1965), p. 70.

[14] H. S. Truman, *Year of Decisions* (New York, 1955), p. 197; D. D. Eisenhower, *Waging Peace* (New York, 1963), p. 6.

[15] Theodore Roosevelt, "The Three Vice-Presidential Candidates and What They Represent," *Review of Reviews*, September 1896. TR also thought that the Vice President should be given a vote on ordinary occasions in the Senate and "perchance on occasions a voice in the debates."

[16] I. G. Williams, *The Rise of the Vice Presidency* (Washington, 1956), pp. 109–110.

[17] Ibid., pp. 134, 138.

[18] Franklin D. Roosevelt, "Can the Vice President Be Useful?" *Saturday Evening*

presidential attendance at cabinet meetings, and it became routine thereafter. Truman got Congress in 1949 to make the Vice President a member of the National Security Council by statute. But Vice Presidents continued to operate out of an office at the Hill. It was not till Kennedy that a Vice President was given space in the Executive Office Building.

Nor, despite ritualistic pledges at the start of each new term, have Presidents ever delegated real power to Vice Presidents. FDR did make Henry Wallace head of the Board of Economic Warfare—the only big job handed a Vice President in the history of the American Presidency—but this merely proved the embarrassment bound to arise when an agency chief who happened to be Vice President got into fights with powerful members of the President's cabinet. Nixon as Vice President appointed himself the political hit man of the Eisenhower administration and subsequently as President assigned the same delicate responsibility to Agnew, thereby making him, as Eugene McCarthy wittily said, "Nixon's Nixon." When Ford succeeded Agnew, Nixon began by trying to insert him into the same slot. This is hardly a promising development. If there is anything certain to cast the Vice Presidency into permanent disrepute, it is the theory that the Vice President is the appointed outlet for an administration's partisan rancor.

For the rest the Vice Presidency is make-work. Presidents spend time that could be put to far better use trying to figure out ways of keeping their Vice Presidents busy. "They seek to put him," as Tom Marshall said, "where he can do no harm."[19] So Vice Presidents serve meaninglessly as chairmen of interdepartmental committees like the Aeronautics and Space Council or the Committee on Equal Employment Opportunity. The suggestion is sometimes made that the Vice President could take over the ceremonial side of the President's job. But Presidents perform few ceremonial functions they do not want to perform; and Vice Presidents would be acceptable substitutes only on the most footling occasions. Nor would a purely ceremonial role satisfy any but the most vacuous Vice President. Getting Vice Presidents out of sight through foreign travel is a solution much favored by recent Presidents. This is all make-believe too. Despite the pieties, the Vice Presidency remains "the fifth

---

Post, October 16, 1920. FDR claimed to regard the Vice Presidency as a major example of "industrial waste" in Washington. He did not think that attendance at cabinet meetings would make much difference but argued that the Vice President should be used to overcome the gap between Congress and the executive branch and to help bring about government reorganization. He acknowledged that a constitutional amendment would be required to give the Vice President serious executive authority but thought that even without an amendment there were things a Vice President could do.
[19] Marshall, *Recollections*, p. 16.

wheel in our government" (Albert J. Beveridge), "the spare tire on the automobile of government" (John Garner).[20] As Gertrude Stein said of Oakland, California, there is no there there.

But what of the suggestion, advocated by Roosevelts when they aspired to be Vice Presidents (and forgotten once they became Presidents), that the power of the Vice Presidency might be increased? Carl Kaysen, director of the Institute for Advanced Studies, has made the ingenious proposal, for example, that the Constitution be amended to make the Vice President an officer of the executive branch. Then let the presidential candidate promise the nominating convention that he will appoint his Vice President to one of the four great cabinet offices, State, Treasury, Defense or Justice, and specify which. This would provide a there there. But it would also create problems if the Vice President turned out to fail at the job or to disagree with the policy and could not, like other incompetents or dissidents, be easily dismissed.

Moreover this would have to be an informal, and hence unstable, arrangement; for any formal allocation of power to the Vice President would run up against the clause in the Constitution vesting the undivided "executive power" in the President. And the resistance to any sharing of authority is visceral as well as constitutional. When William O. Douglas, who had been chairman of the Securities and Exchange Commission, suggested to Franklin Roosevelt that he have the heads of the independent agencies report to his Vice President, Henry Wallace, FDR replied, "Would you like to see Henry instead of me? What would Henry know about all those matters?"[21] No President in the nature of things, is going to yield power to a Vice President.

For this reason, Benjamin V. Cohen, that wise veteran of the New Deal, recommends a different approach. He would frankly recognize that there is, and can be, no there there and have presidential and vice-presidential candidates separately voted upon in the general election. This would have meant in 1968, for example, that Nixon would have been elected President and Muskie Vice President. The fact that Muskie could not have taken part in a Nixon administration would have made no difference, since the Vice President has nothing to do anyway; and Muskie would have been an infinitely more attractive heir apparent. But this proposal raises the possibility of a shift in party control of the White House without the intervention of a new election.[22]

[20] A. J. Beveridge, "The Fifth Wheel in Our Government," *Century*, December 1909; Garner quoted in J. MacG. Burns, "A New Look at the Vice Presidency," *New York Times Magazine*, October 9, 1955.

[21] W. O. Douglas, *Go East, Young Man* (New York, 1974), pp. 310–311.

[22] So too would Endicott Peabody's otherwise attractive proposal that the Twenty-fifth Amendment be revised to require the choice of a new Vice President, in case of a

Neither of these ideas goes to the heart of the matter. Nor certainly do the reform proposals generated by the Agnew and Eagleton fiascoes. In 1973 the Democrats appointed a Vice Presidential Selection Committee under the chairmanship of Hubert Humphrey, whose own vice presidential wounds had hardly healed. Its recommendation was that the parties slow up the process of nominating the second man by making the convention longer and even, if necessary, holding the choice over to a later meeting of the party's National Committee.[23] This procedure, it need hardly be said, would not have saved the Republicans from twice anointing Agnew, which did not prevent a corresponding committee of the Republican National Committee from contemplating the same change. Senator Robert Griffin of Michigan, the Republican whip, in what he called, presumably as a recommendation, "a small step in the direction of the parliamentary system," would do away altogether with party participation in the nomination and have the new President submit his choice to Congress in the manner in which Mr. Nixon chose Mr. Ford under the Twenty-fifth Amendment.[24] This would be another formula for Agnews.

Fiddling with the way vice presidential nominees are chosen is beside the point. The real question is why have a Vice President at all? "His importance," as Woodrow Wilson said, "consists in the fact that he may cease to be Vice-President."[25] The only conceivable argument for keeping the office is that it provides an automatic solution to the problem of succession. No doubt it does. But does it provide the *best* solution?

IV

There is first the mystical argument that the Vice President is the proper successor when a President vanishes in mid-course because, as Truman said and many have repeated, "There is no officer in our system of government, besides the President and Vice President, who has been elected by all the voters of the country."[26] Truman's proposition, advanced nine weeks after Roosevelt's death, was natural enough to a man concerned with legitimating his own recent succession to the Presidency. But insofar as it implied that the voters in some sense intended him or any other Vice President (since 1796) for the Presidency, it was a myth. No one

---

vacancy, through special election rather than through appointment. See "On the Threshold of the White House," *Atlantic Monthly*, July 1974.

[23] *Congressional Record*, December 21, 1973, S23756–S23758.

[24] Ibid., October 23, 1973, S19448–S19450.

[25] Woodrow Wilson, *Congressional Government* (Boston, 1901), p. 240.

[26] Truman, *Public Papers . . . 1945*, p. 129.

votes for a Vice President *per se*. He is a part of a package deal, "a sort of appendage to the Presidency" (Truman's own phrase); not an independent choice.[27]

To this hazy theory of an electorally sanctified connection between the Vice Presidency and the succession there is added the conventional wisdom of political science departments (and of Vice Presidents) that the Vice Presidency is the best school for the Presidency. It is above all, we are told, a "learning office" where men educate themselves for the great responsibility that may one day be theirs. Even if the Vice President has nothing to do, he can—we are assured—watch what others are doing and prepare himself to take over if calamity strikes. Thus Richard M. Nixon: "The Vice Presidency . . . is the only office which provides complete on-the-job training for the duties of the Presidency."[28]

This implies, one fears, an unduly romantic view of Presidents. Nixon himself made this perfectly clear as soon as he had a Vice President or two at his mercy. Presidents, whatever they may say, do not pick their running mates because they want to raise them up to be their successors. All Presidents see themselves, if not as immortal, at least as good for a couple of terms. They pick a running mate not because he is the second citizen of the republic and splendidly qualified to replace them in the White House but because of occult and very often mistaken calculations about the contribution he will make to their own victory at the polls. "Whether they should or not," Congressman James G. O'Hara of Michigan has realistically observed, "they will not, in the final analysis, choose their Vice-Presidential candidate to succeed them. They will choose them to help them succeed."[29]

These calculations, I say, are very often mistaken. It is an exceedingly rare case when the vice presidential candidate makes a difference. Very likely Johnson made a difference in 1960. But much more typical was the outcome in 1948. Earl Warren was the most popular governor California had had in a generation, but Truman carried California against the Dewey-Warren ticket. As for the idea, much discussed by the sages of the press, of a "balanced ticket," this is a fraud on the public. It pretends that the Vice President's views will somehow "balance" the views of the President when all our history testifies that they have no impact at all on the President. Should the President die, however, then the difference in views could have a cataclysmic effect. Theodore Roosevelt, recalling what

[27] Truman, *Year of Decisions*, p. 53.

[28] In his testimony in 1964 before the Senate Judiciary Committee, reprinted in Senate Judiciary Committee, *Selected Materials on the Twenty-fifth Amendment*, Senate Document 93–42, 93 Cong., 1 Sess. (1973), 95.

[29] James G. O'Hara, testimony before the Vice Presidential Selection Commission of the Democratic National Committee, November 7, 1973 (mimeo.), p. 10.

had happened when Tyler succeeded Harrison and what might have happened had Grover Cleveland died and Vice President Adlai Stevenson taken over, observed, "It is an unhealthy thing to have the Vice-President and the President represented by principles so far apart that the succession of one to the place of the other means a change as radical as any possible party overturn."[30]

Presidents not only do not choose Vice Presidents to become successors, but, after they make the White House themselves, they do as little as possible to prepare them to become successors. A Vice President can learn only as much as a President is willing to have him learn—which, given presidential resentment of vice presidential existence, is not ordinarily very much. Truman, recalling how little he had been told as Vice President, tried harder than most Presidents to clue in his second man. His conclusion about on-the-job training is not encouraging. "No Vice-President," he wrote three years after he left the White House, "is ever properly prepared to take over the presidency because of the nature of our presidential, or executive, office." In the nature of things, "it is very difficult for a President to take the Vice-President completely into his confidence." The President "by necessity" builds his own staff and makes his own decisions, "and the Vice-President remains an outsider."[31]

Moreover, seeing things as an ill-informed, impotent, and often sullen outsider, the Vice President will very likely "learn" the wrong things. Lyndon Johnson thought Kennedy too cautious at the time of the Cuban missile crisis and in Vietnam. What Johnson "learned" as Vice President led him on to policies of overkill in the Dominican Republic and Indochina. In any case, where does a successor's responsibility lie? "A Vice-President might make a poor President," said Tom Marshall, who had to reflect on this question in Wilson's season of disability, "but he would make a much poorer one if he attempted to subordinate his own mind and views to carry out the ideas of a dead man."[32]

A learning office? With Presidents less generous than Truman—and that in this context is most Presidents, however generous they may be in other relationships—the Vice Presidency is much less a making than a maiming experience. The way most Presidents treat their Vice Presidents, far from preparing them for the succession, is more likely to erode their capacity to succeed. McKinley, wrote Theodore Roosevelt as Vice President, "does not intend that I shall have any influence of any kind, sort or description in the administration from the top to the bottom. This he has made evident again and again. . . . I have really much less influ-

---

[30] Roosevelt, "The Three Vice-Presidential Candidates," p. 292.
[31] Truman, *Year of Decisions*, p. 54.
[32] Williams, *Rise*, p. 110.

ence with the President now that I am Vice-President than I had even when I was governor."[33] Fortunately, for T. R., he only had to endure six months of frustration. When he acquired a Vice President of his own, he could not have been more destructive of poor Charley Fairbanks. He used to regale Washington with Finley Peter Dunne's crack after the President remarked he was going down in a submarine: "You really shouldn't do it—unless you take Fairbanks with you."[34] Tom Marshall, who at least extracted a good deal of shrewd humor out of his predicament, concluded that the Vice President "is like a man in a cataleptic state: he cannot speak; he cannot move; he suffers no pain; and yet he is perfectly conscious of everything that is going on about him."[35] Lyndon Johnson, when Vice President, once remarked to Franklin D. Roosevelt, Jr., "Your daddy never let his Vice Presidents put their heads above water."[36]

In recent years, as men of larger aspirations and capacities have responded to the actuarial attractions of the office, the damage to Vice Presidents has increased. The more gifted and ambitious the Vice President, the more acute his frustration—and the less his President is inclined to do to alleviate it. Everyone knows the humiliation that Eisenhower repeatedly visited on Nixon. Malcolm Moos, the political scientist, after watching that relationship as an Eisenhower special assistant, concluded that the office was "a kind of coffin."[37] Only a man who has the overpowering ego of a Lyndon Johnson and is treated by his President, as Johnson was, with relative consideration can survive the Vice Presidency; and even Johnson was a subdued and shrunken man by 1963. "It's like being naked in the middle of a blizzard with no one to even offer you a match to keep you warm—that's the vice presidency," said Hubert Humphrey in 1969, eight months after he had been released from confinement. "You are trapped, vulnerable and alone, and it does not matter who happens to be President."[38] Few Vice Presidents can survive the systematic demoralization inflicted by the office without serious injury to themselves. Bill Moyers, who was with Lyndon Johnson both as Vice President and President, later remarked that the Vice Presidency "is a man eater. It destroys individuals. This country was very lucky that Harry Truman was the vice president for only a year [actually for less than three months]. When he became President, he still had so much left.

[33] Theodore Roosevelt, *Letters*, ed. E. E. Morison, vol. III (Cambridge, 1951), p. 57.
[34] Williams, *Rise*, p. 89.
[35] Alben Barkley, *That Reminds Me* (New York, 1954), p. 221.
[36] As told by FDR, Jr., to me; Arthur Schlesinger, Jr., *A Thousand Days* (Boston, 1965), p. 704.
[37] *Minneapolis Tribune*, June 2, 1974.
[38] *Time*, November 14, 1969.

If we had gotten Truman three years later, he would have been much different."[39]

V

The Vice Presidency does a poor job of preparing politicians to become Presidents. But it has recently begun to do an excellent job of preparing politicians to become presidential candidates. For the Vice Presidency is the only place except the Presidency itself that insures its occupant automatic and comprehensive national exposure. Moreover, a new sense of the frailty of Presidents—FDR's death in office, the attempted assassination of Truman, Eisenhower's sicknesses, the successful assassination of Kennedy, the movement to impeach Nixon—has focused unprecedented public attention on the Vice Presidency. As a result, the Vice Presidency has returned to somewhat the status it enjoyed in the early republic as the stepping-stone to the Presidency. In the 160 years before 1948 only five Vice Presidents had ever won election to the Presidency on their own. Of the five Presidents elected since, three were former Vice Presidents. Every man who has served as Vice President since 1953 has become a candidate for President, except for Agnew, who was well on his way to becoming a candidate until the law caught up with him, and for Ford, whom the office transformed from a little-known congressman into a national favorite in a few weeks and who, even before he became President, seemed destined to be a presidential candidate in 1976.

The irony is that this process has nothing to do with the presidential qualifications a Vice President might have and everything to do with the publicity in which the office bathes him. Whether or not a Vice President is any good, the office instantly makes him a front-runner in the polls. At the same time the office makes it impossible to find out whether or not he is any good. "The Vice President," Donald Graham has written, "is the one American politician who is not held responsible for what he says."[40] If he makes a hawk or a zealot or a fool of himself, it is always supposed that he is doing so at the behest of his President. No doubt he is, which is one reason why, at the very time the office enhances his political availability, it depletes and despoils his substantive value. So while the Vice Presidency is coming to be the main avenue to the Presidency, it is, alas, an avenue that typically specializes in the delivery of damaged goods.

There is no escape, it seems to me, from the conclusion that the Vice

[39] Jimmy Breslin, "Police Riot," *New York Magazine*, September 16, 1968.

[40] Donald Graham, "The Vice Presidency: From Cigar Store Indian to Crown Prince," *Washington Monthly*, April 1974.

Presidency is not only a pointless but even a dangerous office. A politician is nominated for Vice President for reasons unconnected with his presidential qualities and elected to the Vice Presidency as part of a tie-in sale. Once carried to the Vice Presidency not on his own but as second rider on the presidential horse, where is he? If he is a first-rate man, his nerve and confidence will be shaken, his talents wasted and soured, even as his publicity urges him on toward the ultimate office for which, the longer he serves in the second place, the less ready he may be. If he is not a first-rate man, he should not be in a position to inherit or claim the Presidency. Why not therefore abolish this mischievous office and work out a more sensible mode of succession?

VI

Such a revision of the Constitution would not be an affront to the Founding Fathers. They had no great commitment to the Vice Presidency. Though they had had considerable experience with lieutenant or deputy governors in the colonies and though most of the thirteen states had provided for such officers in their own constitutions, the Constitutional Convention did not resort to the Vice Presidency in order to solve the problem of succession. Instead the August 6 draft from the all-important Committee of Detail proposed that, in case of a vacancy in the Presidency, "the President of the Senate shall exercise those powers and duties, *until another President of the United States be chosen.*"[41] This, it might be noted, was the formula adopted a century and three-quarters later by General de Gaulle for the French Constitution and employed so expeditiously in France in the spring of 1974.

There was some objection to the President of the Senate as acting President of the nation. Gouverneur Morris thought that the Chief Justice should be "provisional successor." Madison suggested that "the Executive powers during a vacancy" be administered by a Council of State.[42] Wherever the line of devolution went, however, all agreed that it was to prevail only until the voters could choose, *de novo*, a new President by special election.

Then a fortnight before the Convention adjourned, a new drafting committee went off for a weekend and came back with the Vice Presidency. The committee did *not* devise the Vice Presidency primarily as a means of dealing with the succession. The delegates already had a solution to that problem. Indeed, as Charles Warren later wrote, they paid surprisingly little attention in considering the Vice Presidency "to the chief

[41] Tansill, ed., *Documents*, p. 479. Emphasis added.
[42] Ibid., p. 621.

part which the Vice-President has, in fact, played in history, that is, to his succession in case of the death of the President."[43] The Vice Presidency came to the fore for entirely distinct reasons. Hugh Williamson of North Carolina, a member of the new drafting committee, frankly told the Convention that "such an office as vice-President was not wanted. He was introduced *only* for the sake of a valuable mode of election which required two to be chosen at the same time."[44]

The Vice Presidency entered the Constitution, in short, not to provide a successor to the President—this could easily have been arranged otherwise—but to ensure the election of a *national* President. For the United States had as yet little conviction of national identity. Loyalty ran to the states rather than to the country as a whole. If presidential electors voted for one man, local feeling would lead them to vote for the candidate from their own state. The new draft now recommended that they be required to vote for two persons, "of whom one at least shall not be an inhabitant of the same State with themselves."[45] By means of the double vote, localism could be overcome, and a President with broad appeal beyond his own state would emerge. "The second best man in this case," as Madison observed, "would probably be first, in fact"[46]— i.e., the favorite second choice would be the person commanding national confidence.

In addition, the double vote was also intended to defeat cabal and corruption in the selection process. Because each elector must vote for two persons without indicating a preference, "the precise operation of his vote," James Wilson observed, "is not known to himself at the time when he gives it." Conspiracy would therefore be "under the necessity of acting blindfold at the election" and would be "defeated by the joint and unforeseen effect of the whole."[47] Hamilton concluded in *Federalist* #68 that through the double vote the Constitution had made it a "moral certainty" that the Presidency would be filled "by characters preeminent for ability and virtue." Popularity and intrigue might enable a man to carry his own state; "but it will require other talents, and a different kind of merit, to establish him in the esteem and confidence of the whole Union."

Under the double vote, the person winning most votes became President, the runner-up Vice President. It was not logically essential to the

[43] Charles Warren, *The Making of the Constitution* (Boston, 1928), p. 635.
[44] Tansill, ed., *Documents*, p. 682. Emphasis added.
[45] Ibid., p. 679.
[46] Ibid., p. 454.
[47] James Wilson, *Works*, ed. R. G. McCloskey, vol. I (Cambridge, Mass., 1957), p. 439.

operations of the system that the runner-up be anything at all; and no doubt considerations of the succession played a larger part here than were reflected in the discussions at the Convention and in subsequent debates at the state ratifying conventions. For both President and Vice President would have been voted on for the Presidency, and both presumably would be well qualified for the office. The primary point of the Vice Presidency, however, was not as a mode of succession but as an organic part, in Williamson's phrase, of the "valuable mode of election."

VII

Even then the new office was not received with great enthusiasm. Elbridge Gerry told the Convention that he was "ag.st having any vice President."[48] Gerry was the only member of the Convention ever to become Vice President. George Clinton, not a delegate, denounced the office from outside as dangerous and unnecessary. Clinton later served as Vice President under two Presidents. James Monroe told the Virginia ratifying convention that he saw no need for the office.[49] The *Federalist* tried to ignore the issue, devoting two quick paragraphs to it in the entire series of eighty-five papers. Noting that the Vice Presidency had been "objected to as superfluous, if not mischievous," Hamilton defended it in perfunctory fashion because the Vice President's casting vote could prevent deadlocks in the Senate and because the Vice President himself could be on occasion a "constitutional substitute" for the President. Privately he complained to James Wilson, "Every body is aware of that defect in the constitution which renders it possible that the man intended for Vice President may in fact turn up President."[50] The First Congress even wrangled over the question of whether the Vice President should be paid a salary. Some members thought he should only receive *per diem* for those days when he actually presided over the Senate. Finally they voted him $5000 a year.

The double vote did produce two remarkable figures, Adams and Jefferson, as the first two Vice Presidents. But as an occupation for a grown man the Vice Presidency proved a disaster. "I am Vice-President," Adams told the Senate. "In this I am nothing, but I may be everything"—a concise statement of the paradox of the office. To his wife Adams complained that the Vice Presidency was "the most insignificant office that ever the invention of man contrived or his imagination conceived. . . . I

---

[48] Tansill, ed., *Documents*, p. 682.
[49] Feerick, *From Failing Hands*, pp. 52, 54.
[50] Alexander Hamilton, *Papers*, ed. H. C. Syrett, vol. V (New York, 1962), p. 248.

can do neither good nor evil." Jefferson called it "the only office in the world about which I am unable to decide whether I had rather have it or not have it."[51] In the meantime, the rise of the party system, a development unanticipated in 1787, was placing the "valuable mode of election" under severe strain. In 1796, the Federalists gave their second ballots to Thomas Pinckney, who was manifestly not the second citizen of the country. Adams himself, the top Federalist candidate, would have preferred, if he had been defeated, to lose to Jefferson rather than to his fellow-Federalist.[52] In 1800 the Republicans gave the same number of electoral votes to Jefferson, their presidential choice, as they gave to Aaron Burr, a man of undoubted talents, who, however, was trusted by no one in the long course of American history, except for his daughter Theodosia and Gore Vidal. Burr was nearly chosen President, though the voters never intended him for the Presidency. The fear of comparable slipups in 1804 led to the adoption of the Twelfth Amendment requiring the electoral college to vote separately for President and Vice President.

With the abolition of the "valuable mode of election," the Vice Presidency lost the function for which it had originally been designed. Separate voting ended any prospect that the Vice President would be the second man in the country. The office would no longer attract men of the highest quality. It would become, as was immediately noted, a bargaining counter in the presidential contest—"a bait to catch state gudgeons," in Gouverneur Morris' scornful phrase.[53] Samuel White, a senator from Delaware, summed up with admirable prescience the consequences of the Twelfth Amendment: "Character, talents, virtue, and merit will not be sought after, in the candidate. The question will not be asked, is he capable? is he honest? But can he by his name, by his connexions, by his wealth, by his local situation, by his influence, or his intrigues, best promote the election of a President?" Roger Griswold of Connecticut said that the Vice Presidency would thereafter be "worse than useless." A number of political leaders, Republicans and Federalists—John Randolph of Roanoke; former Speaker of the House, now Senator Jonathan Dayton; Griswold; Samuel W. Dana—drew the logical conclusion. The Vice Presidency was an organic part of a particular mode of election. That mode of election was now about to be terminated. Should not the Vice Presidency therefore be terminated too? "The reasons of erecting the office," Dayton correctly said, "are frustrated by the amendment. . . . It will be preferable, therefore, to abolish the office." Unfortunately for

[51] Feerick, *From Failing Hands*, pp. 66–67, 63.
[52] Lucius Wilmerding, Jr., *The Electoral College* (Beacon paperback, 1964), pp. 33–34.
[53] Michael Harwood, *In the Shadow of Presidents* (Philadelphia, 1966), p. 27.

the republic the effort failed by 19–12 in the Senate and 85–27 in the House.[54]

But the dismal predictions were correct. The Twelfth Amendment sent the Vice Presidency into prompt decline. The first two Vice Presidents had moved on directly to the Presidency. After the amendment the Vice Presidency became a resting-place for mediocrities. Who can remember Burr's successors—George Clinton, Elbridge Gerry, Daniel D. Tompkins? For a generation the Secretary of State became the stepping-stone to the Presidency; thereafter, until very modern times, Presidents were elected from anywhere except the Vice Presidency. In the 170 years since the Twelfth Amendment only one Vice President—Martin Van Buren—has advanced directly to the Presidency by election. More than half our Vice Presidents in the nineteenth century were actually *older* than their Presidents. William R. King, when nominated as Vice President with Franklin Pierce, was known to have an incurable disease and died six weeks after inauguration. Clinton, Gerry, Henry Wilson, Thomas A. Hendricks, and Garret A. Hobart also died in office. Apart from their families, few cared or even noticed. The Vice Presidency was nothing. "It is not a stepping stone to anything except oblivion," said Theodore Roosevelt when Boss Platt conned him into accepting the vice presidential nomination in 1900. "I fear my bolt is shot." Asked if he planned to attend McKinley's second inaugural, Platt replied with relish, "I am going to Washington to see Theodore take the veil."[55] Four years later the Democrats nominated Henry G. Davis, then 81 years old, for the Vice Presidency (the ticket lost). For thirty-eight years—almost a quarter of the time that has passed since the ratification of the Twelfth Amendment—the republic was without any Vice President at all. No catastrophe resulted.

VIII

Theodore Roosevelt concluded that the Vice Presidency was "an utterly anomalous office (one which I think ought to be abolished)."[56] He was indisputably right. But what would take its place? How else to deal with the succession? Here it would not seem unreasonable to go back for a moment to the Constitutional Convention. The Founding Fathers were not a pack of fools. While they did not suppose that their descendants would be governed forever by what made sense for an agricultural

---

[54] Feerick, *From Failing Hands*, p. 73.
[55] Williams, *Rise*, p. 81.
[56] Roosevelt, *Letters*, vol. III, p. 60.

society of four million souls, they had insights into the principles of self-government that later generations did not conspicuously improve.

Their first thought, as we have seen, had been to give the President a provisional successor—most probably the President *pro tem* of the Senate—and then, as soon as possible, elect a new President. When the Convention, for other reasons, moved on to the idea of a Vice Presidency, the delegates resolved to empower Congress to designate the next in succession in case of a double vacancy. The early proposal was that the officer thus designated by Congress should "act" as President "until the time of electing a President shall arrive." Madison at once pointed out that "this, as worded, would prevent a supply of the vacancy by an intermediate election of the President" and offered language, immediately accepted by his colleagues, stipulating that the designated officer "shall then act as President . . . until the Disability be removed, or a President shall be elected."[57] The constitutional scholar Lucius Wilmerding, Jr., accurately stated the principle of the Founding Fathers in a letter to Walter Lippmann in 1946: "A man who had not been voted on for the Presidency ought not to hold the office for longer than it takes to choose a new President."[58]

Before the adoption of the Twelfth Amendment, Vice Presidents had been voted on for the Presidency. Indeed, as the young republic began to develop and assume a national consciousness, people quickly forgot that the original reason for the double vote was to overcome localism and increasingly supposed that its point was, in the words of Elias Boudinot of New Jersey, "to obtain the second best character to fill the place of the first, in case it should be vacated by any unforeseen accident."[59] If the Vice President were thus so well qualified to act as President, the instant problem of succession seemed under control.

So, when the Second Congress passed the Presidential Succession Act of 1792, the act assumed without specification that, if anything happened to the President, the Vice President would take over. If both the Presidency and the Vice Presidency were vacated, Madison's idea of an "intermediate election" was to prevail. The President *pro tempore* of the Senate (or, if there were none, the Speaker of the House) would "act as President . . . until a President be elected," and a special election would be called for the next November to choose a new President unless the double vacancy occurred in the last months of the presidential term.[60]

[57] Tansill, ed., *Documents*, p. 680. Emphasis added.
[58] Walter Lippmann, "A Letter about Vice Presidents," *Washington Post*, December 7, 1946.
[59] Wilmerding, *Electoral College*, p. 30.
[60] The text of the 1792 Act can be conveniently found in Edward Stanwood, *A History of the Presidency* (Boston, 1901), pp. 36–38.

"It is unlikely," E. S. Corwin, that mordant annotator of the Constitution, has written, "that Congress ever passed a more ill-considered law."[61] This is harsh language. Corwin did not live long enough to see the Twenty-fifth Amendment. Still, the Act of 1792 unquestionably had its defects. Corwin was particularly upset because he regarded the intrusion of the legislative branch into the line of succession as a violation of the separation of powers. (Madison had made this point against the bill in Congress, but Madison was aggrieved because, had Hamilton not intrigued to shift the succession to Congress, Jefferson as Secretary of State would have been next in line. If Jefferson had been President *pro tem* of the Senate and Hamilton Secretary of State, would Madison have cared so much about the separation of powers?) In any case, the Madison-Corwin doubt had not impressed the Committee of Detail in the Constitutional Convention; and it may be considered to have been laid to rest by the long life of the Act of 1792 and by the reenactment of the principle of congressional succession in 1947.

There still remained, though, the more substantial objection that the qualifications for President *pro tem* and for Speaker are less stringent than for the White House. The congressional officers, for example, need not be natural-born citizens; the Speaker may be under 35 (as Henry Clay demonstrated in 1811); and, peculiarly, neither is required to be a member of the body over which he presides, which makes them less than perfect exemplifications of the elective principle. Still, in practice, the congressional officers have met the presidential qualifications most of the time. A graver objection was that they might be on occasion members of the opposite party; in 1792, however, Congress was not thinking in terms of the party system. A still graver objection was that there might be times when there would be neither a Vice President nor a President *pro tem* nor a Speaker.

The Twelfth Amendment came a dozen years after the Act of 1792. It was intended to make it impossible for persons who had not been voted on for the Presidency to become President. It had precisely the opposite effect.[62] After 1804 Vice Presidents were not voted on for the Presidency except in a highly metaphysical sense. But the retention of the office and the ambiguity of the Constitution enabled Vice Presidents to make themselves President.

IX

The Founding Fathers, so far as we can tell, assumed that, if a President died, the Vice President would inherit the powers and duties of the

[61] E. S. Corwin, ed. *The Constitution of the United States of America: Analysis and Interpretation* (Washington, 1953), p. 387.

[62] As Lucius Wilmerding, Jr., pointed out in two penetrating essays on the Vice

President but not the office itself; he would only be acting president. Corwin judged it the clear expectation of the Framers that, if there were a vacancy in the Presidency, "the Vice-President should remain Vice-President, a stopgap, a locum tenens, whatever the occasion of his succession, and should become President only if and when he was elected as such."[63] A careful modern scholar, John D. Feerick, agrees that the men who signed the Constitution accepted the words limiting tenure ("until . . . a President shall be elected") "as applicable to all successors, including the Vice-President."[64]

The final language was a hurried and cryptic condensation by the drafting committee of two resolutions previously adopted by the Convention. This language—that in case of the President's death, resignation, removal "or Inability to discharge the Powers and Duties of the said Office, the same shall devolve on the Vice President"—contained a capital ambiguity. By "same" did the Framers mean merely the powers and duties of the Presidency or did they mean the office as well? Since earlier language consistently had the Vice President acting as President and exercising presidential powers and duties, the Framers plainly thought that the Vice President was *not* to inherit the office. The Twelfth Amendment substantiates this surmise; for it provides that, if a presidential choice went to the House and could not be made before inauguration day, "the Vice-President shall *act* as President, as in the case of the death or other constitutional disability of the President" (emphasis added). But the debate over the Twelfth Amendment showed incipient congressional confusion as to whether the Vice President, in the event of a vacancy in the Presidency, was only to exercise the powers and duties of the office or was to acquire the office as well, thereby becoming President in every sense of the term.[65]

Then in 1841 William Henry Harrison died a month after his inauguration. At last there was brought to test, as John Quincy Adams said, "that provision of the Constitution which places in the Executive chair a man never thought of for it by anybody." Vice President John Tyler in effect staged a constitutional coup by successfully insisting—"in direct violation," Adams testily noted, "both of the grammar and context of the Constitution"[66]—that, when a Vice President inherited the powers and

---

Presidency, "The Presidential Succession," *Atlantic Monthly*, May 1947, and "The Vice Presidency," *Political Science Quarterly*, vol. 68 (March 1953).

[63] E. S. Corwin, *The President: Office and Powers* (New York, 1957), p. 54.

[64] Feerick adds: "The debates at the Convention clearly show that the Vice-President was merely intended to discharge the powers and duties of the President temporarily. All of the drafts before the Committees of Detail and Style were explicit in this regard." Feerick, *From Failing Hands*, pp. 50–51.

[65] Ibid., pp. 74–75.

[66] J. Q. Adams, *Memoirs*, ed. C. F. Adams, vol. X (Philadelphia, 1877), pp. 457,

duties of the presidential office, he inherited the office too and became, not acting President but President in his own right. There were unavailing protests from senators who thought that a man could gain the Presidency only by election.[67] But Tyler won his point, though the point did not gain explicit constitutional sanction until 125 years later in the Twenty-fifth Amendment.

The United States lived under the Succession Act of 1792 for ninety-four years. Since a double vacancy never occurred, the intermediate-election feature, evidently intended by the Founding Fathers as a routine part of the process, never came into play. In 1881 James A. Garfield, shot by an assassin, died at a time when there was neither a President *pro tem* of the Senate nor a Speaker of the House. If anything happened to his vice presidential successor, Chester A. Arthur, the Presidency would have been in limbo. This was strangely also the case when Grover Cleveland's Vice President died four years later. Moreover, the Republicans were in control of the Senate in 1885, which meant that the President *pro tem* of the Senate, when chosen, would be of the opposite party from Cleveland as well as his statutory successor.

The cry for reform produced the Presidential Succession Act of 1886. The new law put the line of descent through the cabinet, thereby making succession automatic and preventing the mechanics of succession from transferring the Presidency from one party to another without an election. Some members of Congress opposed this idea—among them Congressman William McKinley of Ohio—especially on the ground that it would contravene· the elective principle by empowering a President to name his successor.[68] The 1886 law did not, however, eliminate the idea of intermediate elections. It provided that the cabinet successor should "act as President until the disability of the President or Vice-President is removed, or *a President shall be elected.*" It was "the powers and duties of the office of President," and apparently not the office itself, that devolved upon the cabinet successor, and "it shall be the duty of the person upon whom said powers and duties shall devolve" to convene Congress within twenty days, presumably in order to provide for a special election.[69]

463–464. J. Q. Adams' great-great-grandson, Thomas B. Adams, now president of the Massachusetts Historical Society, has speculated that, if a special election had been held following Harrison's death, Henry Clay would probably have been the choice of the nation, in which case there might have been no President Polk, no Mexican War, and a different course of national development. See "On the Threshold of the White House," *Atlantic Monthly*, July 1974.

[67] Feerick, *From Failing Hands*, p. 95.
[68] Ibid., p. 146.
[69] For text, Stanwood, *History of the Presidency*, pp. 451–452. Emphasis added.

The republic operated under this law for another sixty years. Again no occasion arose to call the provision for intermediate elections into play. Then in 1945 Harry S. Truman, abruptly translated to the Presidency, faced the prospect of serving the balance of Roosevelt's term—nearly four years—without a Vice President. The law of 1886 put the Secretary of State next in line. But Truman, as we have noted, thought it undemocratic for a President to have the power to appoint his successor, contending that the Vice President should always be an "elective officer" —i.e., someone who held public office through election. So he proposed a reversion to the principle of the Succession Act of 1792, though with the Speaker of the House first and the President *pro tem* of the Senate second. There were manifest defects in the scheme. Neither the Speaker nor the President *pro tem*, as we have seen, need be elective officers. Both posts were in part the reward of seniority, which often meant long tenure in a safe and therefore unrepresentative district. James F. Byrnes and George C. Marshall, Truman's second and third Secretaries of State in 1947–1948 were far better equipped for the Presidency than Joseph Martin of Massachusetts, who, as Speaker of the House, was heir apparent for the same period under the Truman reform. In general, Secretaries of State have been more impressive figures than Speakers. Polk is the only Speaker to have made it to the White House.

Truman, however, saw this part of the scheme as provisional. Reaffirming the conviction of the Founding Fathers, he said, "No matter who succeeds to the Presidency after the death of the elected President and Vice President, it is my opinion that he should not serve longer than until the next Congressional election or until a special election called . . . to fill the unexpired term of the deceased President and Vice President."[70] As Walter Lippmann put it in 1946, the Founding Fathers "thought the country should never for more than a few months have a President who had not been elected. They did not believe, as we now assume, that there could never be a Presidential election except once every four years."[71] If the country was without an elected President, it should proceed as expeditiously as possible to elect a new one. There was nothing sacrosanct about the four-year election system.

X

Truman's proposal that the intermediate election fill the unexpired term has given some trouble to constitutional scholars who read the language

[70] Truman, *Public Papers . . . 1945*, p. 130.
[71] Walter Lippmann, "Wrong Answer, Right Question," *New York Herald Tribune*, November 12, 1946.

on the Presidency in Article II, Section 1, of the Constitution—"He shall hold his Office during the term of four Years"—as guaranteeing every new President four years in the White House. The Succession Act of 1792 did provide that the term following the special election should be for four years. The Act of 1886 was mute on the point, though the debate assumed a four-year term. It is far from self-evident, however, that the Constitution forbids elections to fill unexpired terms. We have such elections every day for senators and representatives, though they, no less than Presidents, serve for terms specified in the Constitution. The House Judiciary Committee, under the chairmanship of that rugged old Texas strict constructionist Hatton W. Sumners, went into this question at length in 1945 and found no consitutional problem in the case of the Presidency

The Constitution, the House Judiciary Committee said, "does not provide that the term of each incumbent shall be 4 years, but that the President shall hold his office 'during the term of 4 years.' This language appears to have reference to a fixed quadrennial term, permitting the filling of an unexpired portion thereof by elections. The tradition of special elections for unexpired terms of other officers also supports the provision."[72] "During" often means "in the time of"; it does not necessarily mean "throughout the entire course of." Had the Constitution said "*for a Term of four Years*," this would clearly assure a four-year term to every new President. But the Constitution does not say this.

And if John Tyler was correct in saying that a Vice President became President, not just acting president, and if it is correct to construe the Constitution as assuring every President a four-year term, then this reading must surely apply to Presidents who gain the office by inheritance quite as much as to those who gain it by election. This would mean that, when a President dies, the Vice President who succeeds him is entitled to a four-year term of his own. Ben Butler made this point during the impeachment trial of Andrew Johnson. "Whose presidential term is the respondent now serving out?" he asked. "His own or Mr. Lincoln's? If his own, he is entitled to four years up to the anniversary of the murder, because each presidential term is four years by the Constitution."[73] But no one has ever argued, not even John Tyler, that a Vice President has any right to do more than serve out his President's unexpired term. On what principle, when there is no Vice President, should a specially elected "constitutional substitute" be in a more favored position?

The House unwisely deleted Truman's provision for special presiden-

---

[72] The report is reprinted in the *Congressional Record*, June 26, 1947, 7854–7855.
[73] D. M. DeWitt, *Impeachment and Trial of Andrew Johnson* (New York, 1903), p. 411.

tial elections before passing the Sumners bill in 1945, and the Senate took no action on the proposed change in the line of succession. The 1946 mid-term election gave the Republicans control of Congress. The Republican leadership, determined to make Joe Martin Truman's absolute and not provisional successor, now favored Truman's bill while opposing the idea of intermediate elections. As finally enacted, the law thus departed critically from Truman's original intention. He signed it, however, in order to shift the succession back to elective officers.

The elimination of intermediate elections was a bad mistake. The mistake was compounded twenty years later by the ratification of the Twenty-fifth Amendment. Section 2 of that amendment, by authorizing a President, whenever there was a vacancy in the Vice Presidency, to nominate a new Vice President, sanctified the appointive principle at the highest level of government and created the monstrous possibility—within a decade a probability—that an appointed Vice President would himself become President and appoint his own Vice President.

There was some opposition to this procedure. The Presidency, as Charles Mathias of Maryland observed in a brilliant dissent from the House report, would no longer be a purely elective office if the amendment were adopted. The Constitutional Convention "would surely have rejected an appointed Vice President on grounds of principle alone." The amendment, Mathias continued, was based not only on a false view of democracy but on a false view of human nature. It assumed

> that a President will always be enlightened and disinterested in naming a Vice President. While this optimism reflects well on the 20th Century's opinion of itself in contrast to the pragmatic 18th century estimate of human frailty, it may not be a prudent basis for constitutional law.

Mathias dismissed the argument that Presidents picked their Vice Presidents anyway at the nominating convention. A candidate for the Presidency, bent on winning the approval of the electorate, was a different man from an incumbent President safe and secure in the White House. "The electability of the vice-presidential candidate is a form of accountability for the head of the ticket." Once elected, a President could employ any criteria he personally preferred. Since the rest of the proposed amendment gave the Vice President new authority with regard to the declaration of presidential inability, a President might well "hesitate in seeking a vigorous and aggressive Vice President" and prefer instead a "respectable, but pallid" appointment. Congressional confirmation would be "a mere formality in a period of national emotional stress." In addition, the choice by the presidential candidate of his running mate was merely the contemporary political custom. It had not always been the custom in the past and might not be the custom in the future. Putting it into a constitutional amendment would transform a passing practice into a permanent principle.[74]

Nonetheless, Congress, with the support of the establishment press, the American Bar Association, and, alas, an assortment of scholars, voted overwhelmingly for the Twenty-fifth Amendment. The error was deepened in 1973 when Congress, cheering through the nomination of Gerald Ford, acquiesced in Nixon's interpretation of the amendment as making a Vice President thus nominated not a choice genuinely shared with Congress (as some in Congress had ingenuously supposed when voting for the amendment) but a unilateral presidential appointment subject to congressional confirmation.

XI

This removal of the Presidency from the elective principle is unnecessary, absurd, and incompatible with the constitutional traditions of American democracy. It is also not beyond recall. If the American people want to restore authentic legitimacy to their government, it is plain what must be done. We must adopt a constitutional amendment abolishing the Vice Presidency, an office that has become both more superfluous and more mischievous than Hamilton could have imagined when he wrote *Federalist #68*; and then provide for the succession in the spirit of Founding Fathers through a congressional statute reestablishing the principle of special presidential elections. This principle, announced by Madison in the Constitutional Convention, authorized by the Constitution, applied by the Second Congress in 1792 to the prospect of a double vacancy, reaffirmed in this context by the Forty-eighth Congress in 1886, reaffirmed again by Truman in 1945 (and actually again by Eisenhower

---

[74] Senate Judiciary Committee, *Selected Materials on the Twenty-fifth Amendment*, 67–68. Oddly Richard M. Nixon at the time took what superficially appeared to be a similar position, arguing that the selection of the Vice President "should reflect the elective, rather than the appointive process" so that "whoever held the office of President or Vice President would always be a man selected by the people directly or by their elected representatives, rather than a man who gained the office by appointment." On closer examination, however, the Nixon proposal was designed to strengthen the presidential domination of the process. His objection to placing the power of confirmation in Congress was that Congress might be controlled by the opposition party. Instead he proposed that the President make his recommendation to the reconvened electoral college, which "will always be made up of a membership a majority of which is the President's own party," and which would presumably serve as a rubber stamp, as in the quadrennial elections. This seems an emaciated view of an elective process. *Selected Materials*, 94, 97.

in 1965),[75] would, if the Vice Presidency were abolished, work fully as well for a single vacancy. More than this: it would repair the fatal errors of the Twelfth and Twenty-fifth Amendments and make it certain that the republic would never have to suffer, except as a *locum tenens*, a Chief Executive who, in the words of John Quincy Adams, was never thought of for that office by anybody.

The notion is occasionally advanced that intermediate elections would be unconstitutional. This can be ignored. Madison himself introduced language into the Constitution specifically to make such elections possible. The Second Congress, which contained men who had served five years before in the Constitutional Convention, authorized them by statute. Anything with such patriarchal blessing may be taken as safely consitutional.

Most of the objections to intermediate elections seem to spring primarily from a reverence for routine. The quadrennial rhythm, though not regarded as untouchable by the Founding Fathers, has evidently become sacrosanct for their descendants. Thus Lewis Powell (before, it must be said, his ascension to the Court, though he was still holding forth from a respectable eminence as president-elect of the American Bar Association) rejected the idea of intermediate elections as a "drastic departure from our historic system of quadrennial presidential elections."[76] One must regard such an objection, especially in view of the clear expectation of the Founding Fathers, as frivolous. If the specially elected President fills out his predecessor's term, the sacred cadence will not be disturbed. If not, then Congress could consider E. S. Corwin's proposal: if the vacancy occurs in the first half of the time, the special presidential election should take place at the time of the mid-term congressional election, thereby preserving the assumption that the terms of the new President, a new House and one-third of the Senate would start together.[77]

[75] Eisenhower proposed that in case of a double vacancy there should be a return to the 1886 law, but the cabinet successor would be an "acting President" and "unless the next regularly scheduled presidential election should occur in less than 18 months, the Congress should provide for a special election of a President and Vice President to serve out the presidential term." He seemed to believe this would require a constitutional amendment. See Eisenhower, *Waging Peace*, p. 648. It is also of interest that, when the Louis Harris survey put the question in 1973 whether it would be a good idea to have a special election for President in 1974, its respondents favored such an election by 50 to 36 percent. *Washington Post*, January 7, 1974.

[76] Senate Judiciary Committee, *Selected Materials on the Twenty-fifth Amendment*, 124.

[77] Corwin, *The President*, p. 57. Corwin's proposal was directed to the possibility of a double vacancy, but it would serve as well for a single vacancy. If the President vanished after the mid-term election, however, it would risk leaving the country in the hands of a nonelected President for as long as twenty-six months.

There is also the objection, formulated by (among others) that thoughtful and lamented student of the Presidency, the late Clinton Rossiter, that "it would be simply too much turmoil and chaos and expense to have a special nationwide election."[78] But one wonders how carefully Professor Rossiter considered the proposition. This plainly was not the French experience with regard to the Presidency in 1974, nor indeed has it been the experience in parliamentary states where elections are held at unpredictable intervals. Are we to suppose that the French and Italians, for example, are so much more cool and imperturbable, so much more Anglo-Saxon, than the Americans?

It could of course be said that special elections in a time of national disarray might only deepen popular confusions. Would it have been a good idea to hold such elections after the wartime death of Franklin Roosevelt, after the murder of John Kennedy, after a successful presidential impeachment? Hubert Humphrey has made the point that special elections in wartime, for example, might cause dangerous delay and irrelevant bickering at a time when the nation could afford neither.[79] No doubt such elections would test the poise and stamina of American democracy. Yet what is the gain in undue protectiveness? The same argument can be made against holding presidential elections in wartime at all. The elections of 1864 and 1944 were held in the midst of the two greatest crises of our history. They caused much irrelevant bickering. Had Lincoln and Roosevelt lost, there would have been an embarrassing interlude of lame-duckery and interregnum. But the nation survived these elections without undue trauma. Democracy is a system for foul weather as well as for fair. Though a special election in a time of stress might conceivably demoralize the country, it might equally help it to resolve its confusions and restore its nerve. At the very least it would reaffirm the principle of self-government and place in the White House a man chosen by the people to be their President rather than, as the present system has done, a man chosen by a President who himself was forced to resign to avoid the virtual certainty of being then impeached and convicted for high crimes and misdemeanors.

XII

If the principle be accepted—the principle that, if a President vanishes, it is better for the people to elect a new President than to endure a Vice

---

[78] Professor Rossiter's reference, however, was to the proposal of a special election to choose a new Vice President. He might have thought differently if the purpose was to choose a new President. See Senate Judiciary Committee, *Selected Materials*, 136.

[79] "On the Threshold of the White House," *Atlantic Monthly*, July 1974.

President who was never voted on for that office, who became Vice President for reasons other than his presidential qualifications, and who may very well have been badly damaged by his vice presidential experience —the problem is one of working out the mechanics of the intermediate election. This is not easy but far from impossible. The great problem is that there can be no gap, no chink, in the continuity of the Presidency. "The President under our system, like the king in a monarchy," said Martin Van Buren, "never dies."[80] It would require up to three months to set up a special election. In the meantime the show must go on. If the Vice Presidency were abolished, who would act as President until the people have a chance to speak?

The historical preference, except for 1886–1947, has been for the President *pro tem* of the Senate (Committee of Detail in the Constitutional Convention, Succession Act of 1792) or the Speaker of the House (Succession Act of 1947). But given the regularity with which in recent years one party has controlled Congress and the other the executive branch, this formula risks an unvoted change in party control of the White House and in the whole direction of government. Such a change would be a graver infringement of the democratic principle than the provisional service of an appointed officer as acting President. The confusion would be even greater in the event of temporary presidential disability, in which case the Presidency might shuttle back and forth between the two parties in a period of a few months.

Fidelity to the results of the last election and to the requirements of continuity in policy creates, it seems to me, an irresistible argument for returning the line of provisional descent to the executive branch. A convenient way would be simply to make the Secretary of State acting President for ninety days. If the Secretary of State is foreign-born or under thirty-five or has some other disqualifying eccentricity, then the Secretary of the Treasury could be the automatic successor, and so on down the 1886 list of succession.[81]

Then, as soon as possible, let the people make their choice (unless the

[80] Martin Van Buren, *Inquiry into the Origin and Course of Political Parties in the United States* (New York, 1867), p. 290.

[81] In an earlier version of this argument, in the *Atlantic Monthly* (May 1974), I proposed devolution to the Secretary of State only long enough to permit the choice of an acting President from the cabinet. The reason for this was that the Secretary of State might not be the member of the cabinet best qualified to serve as acting President. It then seemed to me that the cabinet itself might well select the acting President, using the corporate authority already bestowed on it by the Twenty-fifth Amendment, which gives a majority of the cabinet, plus the Vice President, power to declare the President *non compos mentis*. An alternative would have been to permit Congress to select an acting President from the cabinet—a device that would preserve continuity, spread re-

President vanishes in his last year in office, in which case it might be simpler to let the acting President serve out the term). Some have argued that a national election is too hard to organize; therefore Congress should choose the person to serve the remainder of the term. But this would give Congress the right, limited as it might be, to elect a President —a right the Founding Fathers carefully denied Congress and reserved for the voters. If it be said that ninety days is not time enough to organize an election, let us recall that the French allow themselves only thirty-five days, and who will say that the French are better organizers than the Americans? This would only be an election to fill out a term and thus would not require the elaborate foreplay of the quadrennial orgy. Candidates can be established with astonishing speed in the electronic age. Let the national committees, which have become increasingly representative bodies under the new party rules, canvass opinion and make the nominations. Short campaigns, federally financed, would be a blessing, infinitely appreciated by the electorate. Perhaps their brevity and their economy might have a salutary impact on the quadrennial elections, which in recent years have stretched out to intolerable length and swelled to intolerable expense.

In doing this, we would not be departing from the spirit and intent of the Founding Fathers. Quite the contrary: we would be reaffirming their view—and what view could be more sensible for a self-governing democracy?—that the Chief Magistrate of the United States must, except for the briefest periods, be a person elected to that office by the people. "We have only to operate the Constitution as the men who wrote it thought it should operate," Walter Lippmann wrote in arguing for inter-

---

sponsibility, afford a choice of sorts, and perhaps stimulate Presidents to choose better cabinets. I agree, however, with Richard Neustadt (in the *Atlantic Monthly*, July 1974) that the temporary succession should be automatic within the cabinet.

I still think there is merit in this more complex approach; but on balance I have come to believe that two acting Presidents in a period of three months before a new President is chosen would be too cumbersome and confusing. I therefore now favor the simpler system outlined in the text. I have also dropped the proposal that the acting President be declared ineligible as a candidate in the special election, this in order to avoid the advantage created by the inevitable rush of sympathy to the new person in the White House. Demetrius Sakellarios has reminded me that democracy implies as few restrictions as possible on a people's right to choose its rulers.

I have not discussed the issue of presidential inability—an issue that may have received attention out of all proportion to its importance. In any case, the Vice President is not indispensable to a solution of the inability issue. The majority of the cabinet, when making its determination of presidential inability as authorized in the Twenty-fifth Amendment, could simply designate one of their own number to serve as acting President until the inability is removed.

mediate elections in 1946. "If we are the prisoners of a rigid system today, the fault lies not in the Constitution but in our own habits which
have only rather recently become so hard and so fixed."[82]

[82] Lippmann, "Wrong Answer, Right Question."

11   Congressional Politics
and Urban Aid

DEMETRIOS CARALEY

If the 1960s were the time of the "violent" or "explosive" urban crisis, 1975 could be called the year of the "quiet" or budgetary crisis. For in 1975 there were no major riots, and the cities were not burning. What was happening in large cities was a drastic further tightening of their perennial "fiscal crunch," as the economic recession produced "short-falls" in anticipated revenues at the same time that inflation caused a rapid increase in costs. The result was that city after city ran a deficit in its adopted (1974–1975 fiscal year) budget and projected a large gap in its new (fiscal 1975–1976) budget. This was a gap between the anticipated increased cost of continuing its existing level of services and benefits and the revenues it could expect from its existing package of taxes plus state and federal aids. Although New York City's near default and bankruptcy was the most dramatic budgetary crisis and received the greatest media coverage, cities like Detroit, Chicago, Boston, Cleveland, Baltimore, Buffalo, and St. Louis, among others, also experienced budgetary problems of varying degrees of severity.[1]

City governments responded to the threatened deficits in their 1974–1975 budgets by combining some decrease in their level of operations (including laying off personnel) with short-term borrowing to meet their payrolls and other bills

[1] See "Painful Cutbacks Forced on Cities by U.S. Economy," *The New York Times,* November 29, 1974; "Many Cities in Crisis Cut Payrolls and Raise Taxes," *The New York Times,* May 27, 1975.

DEMETRIOS CARALEY, the editor of *Political Science Quarterly,* is professor of political science in Barnard College and the Graduate School of Arts and Sciences, Columbia University. He has published books and articles on congressional, party, and urban politics, and his new book, *City Governments and Urban Problems,* will appear in late 1976.

until the end of the fiscal year. To cope with the projected revenue gap in their new budgets, city governments scheduled further curtailments in services and personnel, attempted to freeze salaries, proposed new taxes, sought larger amounts of state aid, and, finally, turned to the federal government for expanded financial assistance.

There were obvious disincentives to city governments cutting services and raising taxes: The inadequate performance level of many large cities in supplying housekeeping services and amenities, reducing slum conditions and poverty, controlling crime, etc., coupled with their high level of taxation was already producing a strong stimulus for middle- and upper-income families as well as for businesses to relocate to the suburbs. If city governments raised taxes while curtailing services, they would simply strengthen that stimulus and speed the long-term erosion of their economic bases. Furthermore, city governments could increase taxes only with authorizing legislation from their state legislatures, something a number of legislatures were unwilling to provide in whole or in part. With respect to increased state aid, most state governments in 1975 were finding that their revenues too were dropping while their costs were increasing, thus limiting their ability to produce a new budget that was balanced and provided significantly more generous state aid to local governments.

The federal government in fiscal 1974–1975 was also running a deficit—one of the largest in its history[2]—as a result of the recession *cum* inflation in the economy and was projecting a record-breaking deficit for the 1975–1976 fiscal year. But unlike city and state budgets, the federal budget is not required to be balanced each year. Mayors of various large cities individually and through their interest group—the U.S. Conference of Mayors—turned therefore to the federal government with the hope that it would provide significant new aid, as it had done during the depression of the 1930s and the "violent" crisis of the 1960s.[3]

The major proposal of the mayors was one that originated in the Senate, primarily by Senator Edmund Muskie, for a new program of "countercyclical" aid to cities, to be put into effect whenever—as in 1975—the unemployment rate exceeded 6 percent. Such countercyclical aid would at least partially compensate city governments for falling tax revenues and increased welfare and other poverty-related costs caused by recession. It would also enable cities to avoid cutting back on spending and on the size of work forces and thus to avoid further depressing the economy and the employment level. In the spring of 1975, the mayors spoke of countercyclical aid at an annual level of $5 billion, but by the time of their yearly meeting in early July, they had dropped their level of aspiration to

---

[2] In terms of the "unified budget" and current dollars, the $43.6 billion deficit for fiscal 1974–1975 had been exceeded only by those for three World War II years—$53.8 billion for 1942–1943, $46.1 billion for 1943–1944, and $45 billion for 1944–1945. Although only marginally larger than the 1974–1975 deficit in dollar terms, the World War II deficits were much larger as a percentage both of overall governmental expenditures and of the gross national product.

[3] "Mayors Step Up Appeals for Federal Aid to Cities," *The New York Times*, March 24, 1975.

$2 billion annually.[4] Later in July the Senate passed an "Intergovernmental Anti-Recession Act of 1975" as a floor amendment to a pending public works bill; the amendment authorized countercyclical aid at the $2 billion annual level.[5] In December a House-Senate conference committee accepted the Senate's counter-cyclical aid amendment. The Senate then adopted the conference report, but the House took no action by the time the first session of the Ninety-fourth Congress expired in late December.

The House and the Senate together did enact in 1975 a $5.3 billion emergency public service jobs appropriation bill in May and a $1.7 billion emergency housing bill in June; the first would have helped city governments directly by funding certain jobs on their work forces while the second would have helped indirectly, by stimulating the economy. President Ford complained that both bills were overly expensive and vetoed them, and his vetoes were sustained in the House of Representatives.[6] (Later, scaled-down compromise versions of these bills were passed by Congress and Ford signed them into law.)

Finally, after President Ford ceased threatening to veto such a measure and just in time to prevent certain default, the House and Senate in early December passed a "New York City Seasonal Financing Act," authorizing federal loans of up to $2.3 billion a year through mid-1978. The city was required to repay the loans made in any fiscal year by the last day of that fiscal year and also to pay interest at a rate 1 percent above the Treasury borrowing rate. The act was widely considered as giving the minimal aid required to stave off default, since it only provided a source of short-term borrowing for New York City to help ease its cash flow shortages but did not provide any expanded federal financing to reduce the city's overall revenue needs.

On the crucial floor votes for each of these measures—the Senate amendment adding countercyclical aid to the public works bill; the House and Senate votes to clear the conference reports on emergency public service jobs and emergency housing and then the House attempts to override the presidential vetoes on both bills; and the House and Senate votes to authorize borrowing for New York City —on all of these votes a majority of the Democrats voted in favor of enacting the prourban measure, while on none of them did a majority of Republicans also vote favorably.

These 1975 votes confirmed the pattern of the past three decades—namely, that for good or ill,[7] the Democrats have been the prourban party in Congress and the

[4] "Mayors Seek $5-Billion in Emergency Aid," *Congressional Quarterly Weekly Report*, April 5, 1975; "Big-City Mayors Ask U. S. for Emergency $2-Billion," *The New York Times*, July 6, 1975. The first version of the bill would have triggered at 6 percent unemployment, a $1 billion spending level and added another $1 billion for each additional percent unemployed. The later version halved these levels—a 6 percent unemployment rate triggering $500 million and each additional percent of unemployment increasing the funding by another $500 million.

[5] See 94 Cong., 1st Sess, S. 1359, Report of the Committee on Government Operations, Report to Accompany S. 1359; *Congressional Record*, July 29, 1975, pp. S14176ff.

[6] *Congressional Quarterly Weekly Report*, June 7, 1975, p. 1159; ibid., June 28, 1975, p. 1353.

[7] And views will differ, depending on one's attitudes toward the desirability of federal finan-

Republicans have been the antiurban party. This has meant that legislation authorizing major new kinds of federal financial aid to cities has been almost impossible to enact unless a Congress with heavy Democratic majorities and a Democratic president were serving in office simultaneously. The *heavy* Democratic majorities have been necessary because the "southern Democratic" members of Congress have typically voted on urban programs more like Republicans than like the remainder of their Democratic colleagues. In order to pass legislation for urban aid, therefore, the number of Democrats had to be large enough to constitute floor majorities even in the face of large-scale southern Democratic defections. Having a Democratic *president* in office has been necessary because typically it has been the Democratic presidents rather than the Republican ones who have served as important sources of legislative proposals for urban aid and have provided approval rather than vetoes for those urban aid measures passed by Congress. The remainder of this article seeks to document these propositions by analyzing the past trends and bases of support for federal aid to cities. In its conclusions, the article also speculates on future prospects for urban aid and specifically on whether Democrats in Congress and in the White House can continue to be as prourban as they have been in the past, despite the continual decrease in the proportion of the nation's population that lives in large cities.

The Basis and Magnitude of Federal-Urban Aid

Federal financial aid programs to cities are based primarily on Congress' so-called "spending power." The "spending power" derives from Congress' constitutional authority "to lay and collect taxes . . . to pay the debts and provide for the common defense and general welfare of the United States."[8] As Congress has exercised it since the founding of the country and as the Supreme Court eventually ruled in 1936,[9] this clause permits the spending of federal monies not only in the substantive areas which Congress can regulate under its various enumerated powers. It also permits federal appropriations for any purpose that comes within the meaning of the broad terms "common defense" or "general welfare" of the United States.

Although some limited and sporadic forms of federal assistance to local governments actually go back to the very beginning of the Republic, it was the year 1932 that constituted, as Roscoe C. Martin has put it, "a sort of geological fault line" in the development of relationships between the federal government and large cities.[10] For with one exception, all the major urban-oriented grant programs that are currently in existence were enacted since 1932. (The exception is highway aid, which was begun in 1916.)

---

cial assistance to large cities.

[8] Article I, Section 8.

[9] *U. S. v. Butler*, 297 U.S. 1 (1936).

[10] *The Cities and the Federal System* (New York, 1965), p. 111.

FIGURE 1

*Direct Federal Aid to Cities as Percentage of City General Expenditures
for Cities Above 300,000 in Population (excluding Washington, D. C.)*

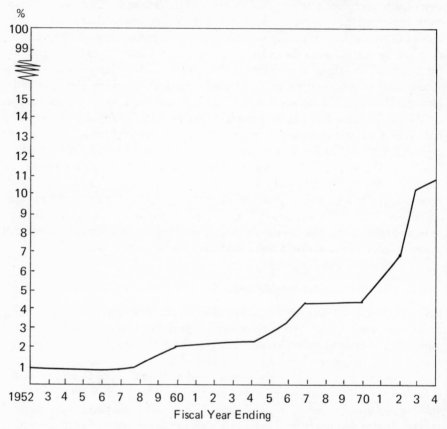

SOURCE: U. S. Bureau of the Census, *City Government Finances,* 1951–1952 to 1973–1974.

The main urban problem areas for which there were federal grant programs in fiscal 1974–1975 were poverty and unemployment (public assistance or "welfare" grants, medical assistance grants, food stamps, antipoverty grants, comprehensive manpower assistance grants); housing and physical decay (urban renewal, low rent public housing, model cities, rent supplements, and neighborhood facilities grants); education (elementary and secondary education grants); crime (law enforcement assistance grants); water pollution (waste treatment works construction and water and sewer facilities grants); health (hospital and medical facilities construction grants); and transportation (federal aid to highways and urban mass transportation grants). The grants in these specific problem areas since 1972 have been supplemented by general revenue-sharing payments.[11]

[11] None of these grant programs is "urban" in the sense of benefiting large cities exclusively.

It should be understood that not all these "urban" grant programs provide for the payment to be made directly to the city governments. Under some programs, the grant is made to the state government, either for eventual redistribution of all or part of the monies to city governments or for the state itself to operate a program that deals with a problem in large cities. A few grant programs benefit city governments more indirectly, by providing subsidies or other payments to individuals (e.g., food stamps) or private groups (e.g., grants to community corporations under the Office of Economic Opportunity) to help them cope with conditions that constitute problems for city governments.

Because only some "urban" grants are paid directly to city governments, while others are paid to the states and still other grants go to private individuals and groups, it is impossible to state with precision the total amount of federal money that is actually spent to help large cities. The Bureau of the Census publication, *City Government Finances* reports only federal grants made directly to local governments. In 1973–1974, federal aid to the nation's largest cities of over 300,000 in population (excluding Washington, D.C.) comprised $2,293,944,000 or some 10.6 percent of their aggregate general expenditures, up from .7 percent in 1951–1952.[12] (See Figure 1.) This represents a dramatic 99-fold increase in the aggregate amount of such grants—one that has been 15 times as fast as the rise in those cities' general expenditures. Even with that increase, however, the federal government's absolute level of "effort" in 1973–1974 for direct aid to large cities remained minimal, at under 1 percent of its total outlays.[13]

Because grants under some of the very largest programs that benefit cities, including public assistance, elementary and secondary education, medical assistance, highways, and food stamps are not paid to city governments, these census figures obviously understate the amount of federal money spent seeking to ameliorate undesirable urban conditions with which city governments must cope. In order to make an exact calculation, it would be necessary to add to the direct federal grants the portion of federal grants to states that are "passed through" to city governments and the payments that go directly to private individuals and groups in large cities. These figures are not, however, available in published census reports on governmental finances.

PARTY DIFFERENCES AND URBAN SUPPORT

In order to identify party differences on urban voting in Congress, an examination was made of all those roll-call votes on urban aid issues that were among the

---

Large cities are, however, direct or indirect beneficiaries of each of the programs and normally have received larger-sized grants under particular programs than other local governments. But local governments other than those of the largest cities are also eligible for grants and are recipients of benefits. Figures showing the allocation of money for particular programs as between large cities and other local governments are not available.

[12] Calculated from U. S. Bureau of the Census, *City Government Finances*, 1951–1952 to 1973–1974.

[13] Calculated from ibid., 1973–1974, and U. S. Bureau of the Census, *Statistical Abstract of the United States: 1975*, table 370.

FIGURE 2

Majorities in Support and in Opposition on Selected Key Urban Votes, 1945–1974, by Party, and for the Democratic Party, by Region

HOUSE OF REPRESENTATIVES

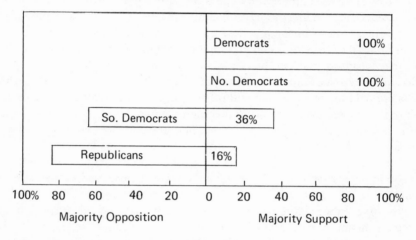

SENATE

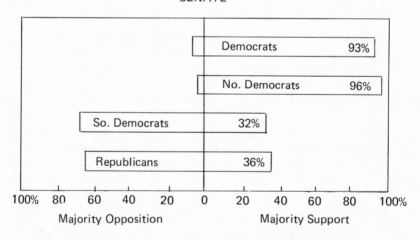

"key votes" selected annually between 1945 and 1974 by the Congressional Quarterly, Inc., a nonpartisan organization that publishes the *Congressional Quarterly Weekly Report* and other reports and books analyzing Congress.[14] These "key votes" were not necessarily the votes on bills on final passage; they are intended to represent the most significant decisions made in the consideration of bills, which are sometimes motions to amend or recommit in order to expand or contract the coverage of a program or to decrease or increase its appropriations.

[14] An identification of the votes and description of the legislative purpose of the bills involved can be found in the Appendix to this article.

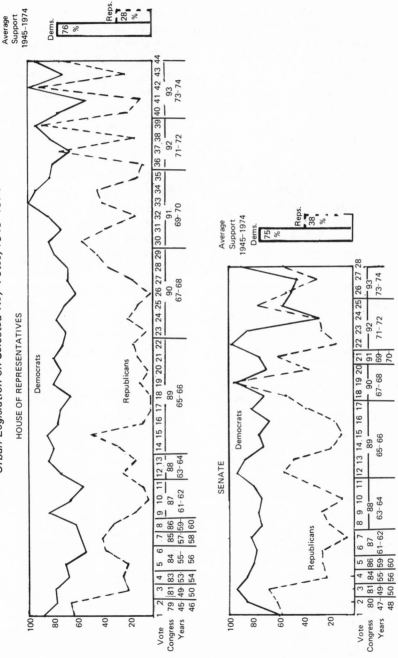

FIGURE 3

Percentage of Democratic and Republican Members of Congress Supporting Urban Legislation on Selected Key Votes, 1945–1974

As Figures 2 and 3 show, on forty-four "key" urban votes taken in the House between 1945 (when the Congressional Quarterly began keeping score) and 1974, a majority of all the Democratic members who voted cast their votes in favor of the prourban position in every one of the forty-four instances. On the other hand, in thirty-seven out of the forty-four cases, a majority of the Republicans who were voting took the antiurban position. Similarly in twenty-eight "key" urban votes taken in the Senate during the same time period, a majority of the voting Democrats was in favor of the prourban position on all but two of the twenty-eight votes while a majority of voting Republicans voted against on all but ten. Inspection of Figure 3 will also show that the majorities from the two parties for and against urban programs typically were not marginal ones but represented sharp differences between the dominant Democratic and Republican point of view: The difference in the average level of support for urban programs in the period 1945 to 1974 was between 76 percent for the Democrats and 28 percent for the Republicans in the House, and between 75 percent for the Democrats and 38 percent for the Republicans in the Senate.

It should be noted that the difference between the dominant Democratic and dominant Republican positions on urban issues becomes even more striking if the votes of those Democrats defined as "southern"[15] by the Congressional Quarterly Service are not included in the overall Democratic totals but are treated separately. Since the late 1930s majorities of this bloc of "southern" Democrats have voted more consistently with the Republicans than with the remaining "northern" Democrats[16] on urban issues. On the key votes already referred to, a majority of "southern" Democrats voted with a majority of their northern Democratic brethren in support of the urban position only sixteen out of forty-four times in the House, giving an average level of support of 45 percent, and nine out of twenty-eight times in the Senate, giving an average level of support of 47 percent (see Figures 2 and 4). Thus, the plotting of urban voting scores of the northern Democrats alone raises the average support level from 76 to 94 percent in the House and from 75 to 90 percent in the Senate and therefore shows even more accurately the very dramatic difference on urban issues that has existed between the "nonsouthern" or "national" Democratic party and the Republican party (see Figure 5).

Given these very strong characteristic positions on urban issues of "northern" Democratic, "southern" Democratic, and Republican members of Congress, a necessary condition for a particular Congress to enact major prourban legisla-

[15] The *Congressional Quarterly* defines as "southern" all those Democrats coming from the states of the old Confederacy—Alabama, Arkansas, Florida, Georgia, Louisiana, Mississippi, North Carolina, South Carolina, Tennessee, Texas, and Virginia—and the two border states of Kentucky and Oklahoma.

[16] The *Congressional Quarterly* defines as "northern" all other Democrats, whether they are in fact from the "North," strictly speaking, or from the Midwest, West, Pacific Coast, etc. It is with these meanings that the terms "southern" Democrats and "northern" Democrats are used in this article.

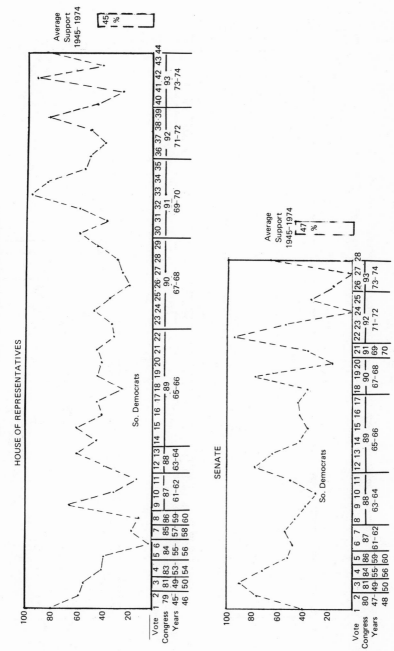

FIGURE 4

Percentage of Southern Democratic Members of Congress Supporting
Urban Legislation on Selected Key Votes, 1945–1974

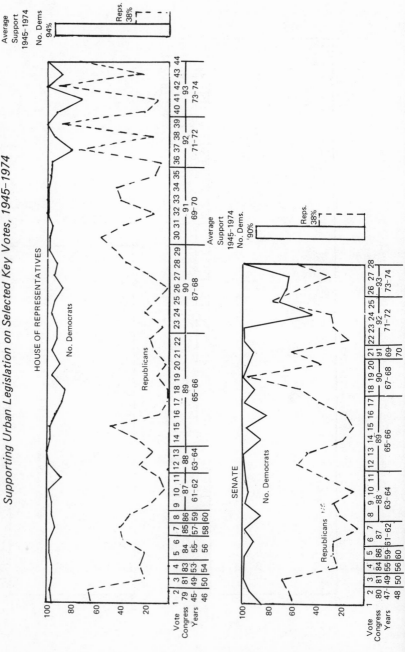

FIGURE 5

Percentage of Northern Democrats and Republican Members of Congress Supporting Urban Legislation on Selected Key Votes, 1945–1974

tion has been the existence and large size of a Democratic majority. Accordingly, in the four years since 1945 with Republican majorities in Congress (1947–1948, 1953–1954), no new urban aid programs were passed and only one old program was expanded. The converse is not true, however, and prourban positions did not fare equally well in all the years that the majorities were Democratic. Persistent success for prourban positions in Congress depended on the Democratic majority being sizable enough so that even with large-scale southern Democratic defections, enough Democratic votes were left from the preponderant majorities of northern members who consistently supported the prourban stand and from the varying-sized minorities of southern Democrats who voted with them to constitute majorities on the floor. On a few occasions, the majorities also required the votes of the handful of Republicans who deserted the dominant antiurban point of view of their party and voted for the prourban position.

Party Differences in Action:
The Eighty-seventh and Eighty-ninth Congresses

An analysis of two specific sessions of the House of Representatives may make clearer the impact of differences in the distribution of seats between parties from Congress to Congress. During most of[17] the Eighty-seventh Congress—the Congress that was elected with President Kennedy in 1960 and was in session in 1961–1962—there were 263 Democrats and 174 Republicans in the House of Representatives. This lineup gave the appearance of the House being safely in the control of the prourban Democratic party. And the Democrats did in fact have "nominal" control, being able to elect members of their party as speaker of the House and as chairmen of the various standing committees. The appearance was, however, deceptive as only 159 of the Democrats were "northern" and 104 came from the South. The result was that the total number of 174 Republicans plus 104 southern Democrats greatly exceeded the number of 159 northern Democrats so that "working control" of the House—as President Kennedy used to refer to it—with respect to enacting urban legislation was largely in the hands of the Republican-southern Democratic, antiurban, "conservative coalition." Thus on two issues that led to an urban "key" vote—passage of the Emergency Educational Act of 1961 and the attempt to establish a cabinet-level Department of Urban Affairs and Housing—the prourban position lost, even though northern Democrats voted in favor by 97 percent on the first and 87 percent on the second. On both these votes, heavy southern Democratic majorities joined the near unanimous Republicans to defeat the nominal Democratic House majority party.[18]

---

[17] "Most of" because through deaths and resignations, the number of northern Democrats, southern Democrats, and Republicans changes slightly over the course of a Congress.

[18] H.R. 8890, Emergency Educational Aid Act of 1961, authorizing grants for school construction, etc. Question, under "Calendar Wednesday" procedures, on whether bill should be considered. Consideration rejected 170–242: Democrats (D) 164–82 (northern Democrats [ND] 132–4, southern Democrats [SD] 32–78); Republicans (R) 6–160. H. Res. 530, Resolution disap-

FIGURE 6

Distribution of Seats by Party and for Democratic Party, by Region, House of Representatives, Eighty-seventh and Eighty-ninth Congress

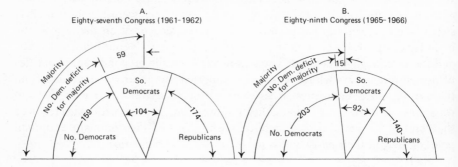

A.
Eighty-seventh Congress (1961–1962)

B.
Eighty-ninth Congress (1965–1966)

Only on the third urban key vote—that on passage of the Emergency Housing Act of 1961—where 66 percent of the southern Democrats voted with a 98 percent northern Democratic majority, did the nominal majority win out.[19] In short, for the northern Democratic supported, prourban position to prevail, some two-thirds of the southern Democrats had to shift away from their characteristic, long-term stance and vote with their nonsouthern colleagues (see Figure 6A). Since this rarely happened on "key" or other votes, almost no urban programs were voted upon favorably by the House in the Eighty-seventh Congress.

A sharp contrast to the Eighty-seventh Congress is the Eighty-ninth, which was elected in 1964, during President Johnson's landslide victory, and served in 1965–1966. When it began, the Eighty-ninth Congress had 140 Republicans and 295 Democrats, of which only 92 were southerners and 203 were from outside the South. This meant that the total number of Republicans and southern Democrats combined barely exceeded that number of northern Democrats alone. It also meant that when only a small minority of 20 percent of the southern Democrats voted with the rest of their party, the northern Democratic, prourban position prevailed in roll-call votes in the House (see Figure 6B).

The Eighty-ninth Congress consequently saw the passage of the Elementary and Secondary Education Act, "Medicaid" for recipients of public assistance, the Department of Housing and Urban Development Act, rent supplements and expansion of other housing programs, model cities, and the expansion of anti-poverty programs. On the "key" vote on each of these issues a majority of the voting Republicans and (with one exception on Medicaid) a majority of southern Democrats took the antiurban position. But each time the number of northern

---

proving President Kennedy's Reorganization Plan No. 1 of 1962 to create cabinet-level Urban Affairs and Housing Department. Resolution of disapproval agreed to 264–150: D 111–137 (ND 18–124, SD 93–13); R 153–13.

[19] H.R. 6028. Passed 235–178: D 210–38 (ND 141–3, SD 69–35); R 25–140.

Democrats available to vote favorably was so large that with only minority support from southern Democrats (plus sometimes a small handful of Republicans), the prourban position won.[20] On only one "urban key vote" during the Eighty-ninth Congress—that to delete funds for rent supplements from a supplemental appropriation act—did the "conservative coalition" come out the winners. This happened when an unusually small number of northern Democrats turned out on the floor to vote and in addition an unusually large percentage of those northern Democrats—some 15 percent—voted with the conservative coalition, a combination of factors that caused the postponement of rent supplements funding for a few months.[21]

The lineup of forces in the House for the two years of the Eighty-ninth Congress was exceptional; the Democratic party had not enjoyed such large majorities since the early Roosevelt Congresses of 1933–1938. The typical House situation since 1939 has been something like the lineup of the Eighty-seventh (or first Kennedy) Congress or worse. Prourban majorities have therefore been difficult to put together in the House most years, even though it has almost always been under nominal Democratic control.

The Ninety-fourth Congress and the Role of the President

In the 1974 congressional elections the Republicans suffered sharp defeats, creating a potentially very prourban House of 204 northern Democrats, 87 southern Democrats, and 144 Republicans. But unlike the 1930s and the Eighty-ninth Congress of the Johnson administration, the current Ninety-fourth Congress is not serving with a prourban Democratic president. A major aspect of the president's importance in determining the federal government's responsiveness to the financial needs of large cities comes from the fact that it is he who provides in his messages to Congress and his annual budget most of the major proposals that

[20] H.R. 2362, Elementary and Secondary Education Act of 1965, providing grants to school districts with large numbers of children from low-income families. Passed 263–153: D 228–57 (ND 187–3, SD 41–54); R 35–96. H.R. 6675, Social Security Amendments of 1965, establishing "Medicare" for the aged and medical assistance or "Medicaid" for public assistance recipients and other medically needy. Passed 313–115: D 248–42 (ND 189–2, SD 59–40); R 65–73. H.R. 6927, Department of Housing and Urban Development Act, establishing cabinet-level department. Passed 217–184: D 208–66 (ND 170–10, SD 38–56); R 9–118. H.R. 7984, Housing and Urban Development Act of 1965, extending public housing, urban renewal, etc., and providing for "rent supplements" to low-income families. Motion to recommit to delete rent supplements provisions rejected 201–208: D 72–204 (ND 21–163, SD 51–41); R 130–4. S. 3708, Demonstration Cities and Metropolitan Development Act of 1965, authorizing "model cities" grants. Passed 178–141: D 162–60 (ND 141–11, SD 21–49); R 16–81. H.R. 15111, Economic Opportunity Act amendments of 1966, continuing program and authorizing appropriations for 1967. Motion to strike enacting clause (thereby killing the bill) rejected 156–208: D 49–193 (ND 5–159, SD 44–34); R 107–15.

[21] H.R. 11588, General Supplemental Appropriations Bill. Amendment to delete funding of rent supplements in fiscal 1966 accepted 185–162: D 86–160 (ND 24–141, SD 62–19); R 99–2.

Congress seriously considers for new or for expansion of existing grant programs and for increased spending levels. And among presidents as among members of Congress, party differences have been clear: Presidents Roosevelt, Truman, Kennedy, and Johnson—all Democrats—were inclined to propose and support new and expanded "urban" programs and to ask for sizable appropriations increases to fund those that were already in effèct. Presidents Eisenhower, Nixon, and Ford—all Republicans—were more inclined to consolidate rather than expand, and sometimes even to cut back or scrap some existing programs; they also attempted to keep spending levels from arising abruptly from what they had been in previous years.

Congress itself does on rare occasions consider proposals for major additions to or expansions of urban grant programs that are originated by its own members and do not constitute a part of the president's "legislative program." This happens most often when as in 1975 the president and majorities in Congress belong to different parties. Even then, however, the president's support or at least acquiescence is almost a prerequisite for any major increases in federal financial assistance to cities. The president can normally defeat congressionally enacted proposals with a veto, since vetoes can be overridden only by a very difficult to attain two-thirds vote in both the House and the Senate. Two dramatic examples of the huge weight of a presidential veto were President Ford's disapproving in 1975 the "emergency [public service] jobs appropriations bill" and the "emergency housing bill." Although on the first bill 99 percent of the northern Democrats and 79 percent of the southern Democrats (as well as 13 percent of the Republicans) voted to override, the veto was sustained by five votes; on the second bill, 95 percent of the northern Democrats and 71 percent of the southern Democrats (as well as 13 percent of the Republicans) voted to override; that attempt failed also, by sixteen votes.[22]

Various presidents have also claimed the right to "impound," i.e., not spend, funds even after they were appropriated by Congress with the president's signature or over his veto. The Congressional Budget and Impoundment Control Act of 1974 may, however, have all but eliminated presidential impoundments that Congress opposes.[23]

---

[22] H.R. 4481, Emergency Jobs Appropriations, Fiscal 1975. Passage over the president's veto. Rejected 277–145 (282 required for two-thirds): R 19–123; D 258–22 (ND 192–4; SD 66–18). H.R. 4485, Emergency Housing Assistance. Passage over the president's veto. Rejected 268–157 (282 required for two-thirds): R19–122; D 249–35 (ND 186–9; SD 63–26). Many Democratic freshman members of Congress expressed great dismay at the failure of the Democrats to override these two vetoes when the total Democratic majority in the House exceeded the two-thirds necessary. In light of long-term trends, however, the northern Democratic-inclining members should have been pleased that the southern Democrats gave the votes to override 71 percent support in each case, whereas their long-term support of urban legislation has, as already reported, been only 45 percent.

[23] See Public Law 93-344, Title X.

A More Prourban Senate

The Senate in recent decades, incidentally, has not been as antiurban in voting behavior as much of the time as has been the House. Although since World War II the combined total of Republican and southern Democratic senators has always exceeded the number of northern Democrats, during this period aid to education, mass transit, expanded housing, and other kinds of prourban bills that could not be enacted in the House did pass in the Senate. This relatively more prourban complexion has existed despite the fact that all states have equal voting power in the Senate regardless of the size of their population, thus giving tremendous overrepresentation to sparsely populated rural states. There appear to be two reasons for the basically more prourban Senate complexion: First, the northern Democratic strength has normally been larger in proportion to total membership in the Senate than in the House—especially since 1959—meaning that smaller defections from the southern Democratic or Republican ranks were sufficient to enable the northern Democratic position to prevail on floor votes.[24] Second, the relatively small defections needed were frequently forthcoming in the Senate. This held true not only for the southern Democrats but even for the Republicans who in significant minority—and occasionally even in majority—strength supported a number of housing and education bills that were overwhelmingly opposed by Republican members in the House.

Party Lineups and Committee Action

The distribution of seats in Congress among the northern Democrats, southern Democrats, and Republicans affects the outcome of controverted legislation, incidentally, not only through votes taken on the floor of the two houses. It also has great effect through its impact on the makeup and policy complexion of the standing committees. It is these committees that shape and report the legislation to be voted upon on the floor. These committees also can choose to preclude, for all practical purposes, favorable floor action by failing to report particular legislation out of committee. On most committees including the ones that handle the bulk of urban legislation—Education and Labor; Banking, Currency, and Housing; and Appropriations in the House; and Labor and Public Welfare; Banking, Housing, and Urban Affairs; and Appropriations in the Senate—the "ratio" of seats between Democratic and Republican members has been set by each Congress to reflect the "ratio" of seats between the parties in the entire parent body. Thus, to the extent that the House or Senate was Republican-controlled or Democratic-

---

[24] Thus, in the five Congresses beginning with the Eighty-sixth (1959–1968), northern Democrats have held an average of 43 (or 44 percent) of the seats by themselves. As a result whenever the northern Democratic ranks stayed solid, they needed to pick up the votes of very few southern Democrats and Republicans to have a absolute majority of the Senate. On the other hand in the House, northern Democrats held an average of 170 (or only 39 percent) of the seats by themselves, thus requiring larger defections from the southern Democratic or Republican ranks in order to prevail.

controlled by only a very small margin, the committees were controlled by majorities of Republicans or by coalitions of Republicans and southern Democrats and thus typically took committee action consistent with the antiurban point of view. To the extent, on the other hand, that the House or Senate was controlled by heavy Democratic majorities, the Democratic majorities on committees were large. Under these circumstances, even with the bulk of the southern Democratic members of the committee voting with the Republicans, the northern Democrats had a majority and thus were able to exercise working control over the committee and report urban legislation favorably.

BASES OF PARTY DIFFERENCES IN URBAN SUPPORT: IDEOLOGY AND CONSTITUENCY

Why the Democratic party in Congress has been prourban and the Republican party, most especially in the House, has been antiurban is a question that cannot be answered definitively in the space available here. One part of the explanation is that since Woodrow Wilson's time, the leading Democratic national officeholders, in the presidency and in Congress, have been persons ideologically committed to using the power and funds of the federal government to alleviate widely felt problems. This was so whether the problems were experienced by farmers, businessmen, union laborers, or more currently, urban dwellers and city governments. The dominant Republican ideological position has been that for the most part, social and economic problems should be dealt with not by the federal government, but by the states or by private efforts. The Republicans have, however, been willing to flex their ideological principles to support the federal government's coming to the aid of some big businesses (e.g., Lockheed, Penn Central) and of farm operators facing economic problems. In addition to ideology, almost all Republicans have also been committed to holding down spending by the federal government, and federally aided urban programs are usually costly. Persons who self-select themselves to try to gain the congressional or senatorial nominations of a particular party—Republican or Democratic—are likely to be those who for the most part find that party's broad ideological image or policy orientation appealing. If elected they therefore carry to Congress ideological or policy outlooks that provide motivation to support their party's traditional position.

Another part of the explanation for the difference in prourban and antiurban stance between the Democrats and Republicans in Congress is that they have tended to come from different kinds of constituencies: since the 1930s, the main bulk of northern Democratic strength in the House and Senate has been from urban districts and urban states that are directly experiencing the problems of urbanization. The main bulk of Republican strength on the other hand, has been from more rural districts and states where the urban problems are not felt at first hand and where big cities antipathies have traditionally existed. For the great bulk of northern Democratic and of Republican members of Congress, therefore, ideological inclinations and the perceived needs of their constituencies neatly coincided to provide mutually reinforcing motivation for prourban and anti-urban positions respectively.

The case of the southern Democratic members of Congress is a unique one. Certainly since the 1930s, the bulk of southern Democratic representatives and senators have been much closer, with respect both to personal ideological outlook and characteristics of their constituency, to the Republican party rather than to the Democratic. And accordingly, most of them have supported the Republican rather than the northern Democratic positions on urban and other welfare and "expansion of federal role" issues. The explanation for this anomaly of Republican-oriented members of Congress being even nominally Democratic is, of course, historical: from the Reconstruction era after the Civil War to the early 1960s, it was impossible for Republican candidates to be elected to the House or to the Senate from the states of the old Confederacy. This was the result not of policy agreement or disagreement with Republican party positions or of constituency characteristics, but of a strong tradition, passed on from generation to generation, of automatic allegiance to the Democratic party among all but a tiny fraction of white southerners. Broadly speaking, that tradition was based on the fact that President Lincoln, General (and later President) Grant, and General Sherman had been Republicans and that the Republican party was perceived as being responsible for freeing the slaves and imposing the indignities of northern military occupation on the South in the decades after Appomattox.[25]

Given this overwhelming opposition to anyone running for Congress under the Republican label, any policy differences among aspirants to Congress were fought out not in the general election as party opponents, but in the primary election for the Democratic senatorial or congressional nomination, whose victor was virtually guaranteed subsequent election. Accordingly, senators and representatives were elected to Congress as Democrats and gave the minimal required support to be counted as nominal members of their party by voting with their northern Democratic colleagues on the organization of the Congress, including the election of presiding officers, floor leaders, and committee chairmen. But the bulk of those southern Democratic members of Congress voted on urban legislation the way that persons with their "conservative," "antiexpansion-of-federal-role," "antifederal-spending" ideological outlook and from their basically rural and small town constituencies could be expected to do—that is, in support of the dominant Republican position.

It should be clearly understood that not all northern Democrats have represented urban districts or states and not all Republicans and southern Democrats have represented rural ones. Their dramatic difference in support for urban programs has therefore not been merely a reflection of their representing different kinds of constituencies. There is no comprehensive analysis of relative influence of party and constituency on urban voting, but whatever scattered evidence exists all points in the same direction, namely that party is much more important than

[25] See V. O. Key, Jr., *Southern Politics* (New York, 1949).

TABLE 1

Percentage of Time House Members Supported Larger Federal
Role on Selected Roll Calls, 1961

	Urban		Suburban		Rural	
	Republican	Democrat	Republican	Democrat	Republican	Democrat
East	23.3	96.4	23.6	92.7	19.8	88.0
South	0.0	64.5	10.0	75.0	14.0	55.0
Midwest	4.0	98.8	5.1	97.5	5.2	91.0
West	8.3	98.9	0.0	98.3	20.2	97.2

SOURCE: Congressional Quarterly Weekly Report, February 2, 1962, p. 155.

constituency in accounting for roll-call voting. That is, regardless of type of constituency—city, suburban, or rural—northern Democratic members of the House
have been much more prourban than Republicans or southern Democrats. Studies
that do exist, for example, of voting on a 1959 aid to airports bill, a series of votes
between 1959 and 1962 on water pollution control, a 1958 and a 1964 vote on
the food stamp program, and of voting on the 1964 mass transit bill show that
*in every single case Democratic members from rural districts voted more heavily
in favor of the urban program—from three to fifteen times—than Republican
members from urban districts, even when the votes of southern Democrats were
included within the overall Democrat scores.*[26] Obviously, if support of the northern Democratic members from rural districts had been calculated separately and
compared to the votes of urban Republicans, the differences in support would
have been even more striking.

A 1962 study by the Congressional Quarterly Service which measured support
for a "larger federal role" (defined as including but not restricted to urban programs) and did differentiate according to party, type of constituency, and region,
came up with similar findings. What this study indicated was that the percentage
of rural Democrats from outside the South supporting such an expansion was
three to four times as large as among urban and suburban Republicans from the
East and ten times as large as among urban and suburban Republicans from other
parts of the country. Indeed, on the bills on which this study was based, even
rural Democrats from the South on the average supported this kind of federal
expansion more than twice as heavily as Republicans from any region or type of
constituency including the urban and suburban East (see Table 1).

Still another study of House voting in 1973 on four key urban votes—per-

[26] Calculated from tables in Frederick N. Cleaveland et al., *Congress and Urban Problems*
(Washington, D. C., 1969), pp. 65, 103, 285, 305, 345. Further supportive evidence for the
proposition that party has been more important than constituency in roll-call voting on issues
defined in this article as "urban" can be found in Julius Turner, *Party and Constituency: Pressures on Congress*, rev. ed. by Edward V. Schneir, Jr. (Baltimore, 1970), esp. pp. 88–95; and in
David R. Mayhew, *Party Loyalty Among Congressmen: The Difference Between Democrats and
Republicans 1947–1962* (Cambridge, Mass., 1966), esp. chap. 3.

TABLE 2

Support for Four Selected Urban Votes from Northern
Democrats and Republicans, by Constituency, House of Representatives, 1973

	Urban	Suburban	Rural	All
No. Democrats	98% (52)	84% (28)	50% (17)	85% (97)
Republicans	29% (14)	30% (57)	4% (45)	20% (116)

SOURCE: Recalculated from *Congressional Quarterly Weekly Report,* April 6, 1974, p. 880.

mitting use of highway trust funds for mass transit, authorizing funds for mass transit operating subsidies, increasing funds for community comprehensive planning grants, and increasing funds for urban renewal—showed that northern Democratic or Republican party affiliation was far more determinative of a pro-urban or antiurban position than type of constituency (see Table 2).

There are no specific studies of the relative influence of party and constituency on "urban voting" in the Senate. But analysis of roll-call votes shows that an extremely high degree of support has been given to urban measures by Democratic senators from outside the South, whether they represented highly urbanized states with large cities, like Massachusetts, Connecticut, California, or New York, or western farm or other types of nonurban states like Montana, Alaska, Idaho, New Hampshire, or Maine. This suggests that in the Senate, too, party has been more determinative of prourban or antiurban position than the urban or nonurban characteristics of the state being represented. Additional evidence for this interpretation is provided by the voting of senators from the same state who belong to different parties. Almost invariably the Democratic senator votes prourban on many more issues than the Republican senator. In the Ninetieth Congress (1969–1970), for example, such states as Arizona, Idaho, Maine, Michigan, New Hampshire, North Dakota, South Dakota, Utah, and Wyoming each had one Democratic and one Republican senator. A Congressional Quarterly study of "Senate Support for Larger or Smaller Federal Role" shows that during this Congress, the Democratic senator provided significantly greater support for an expanded federal role in urban and other programs than his Republican colleague in *every* case.[27] Similarly, a Congressional Quarterly study of "conservative coalition" voting in the Ninety-third Congress (1973–1974) shows that of twenty-one states that had one Democratic and one Republican senator, in all but one case the Republican senator gave greater support to the "conservative coalition," one of whose positions is typically against increased spending for urban programs.[28]

Of course, all these studies show also that the kind of constituency represented does exert some influence. As could be expected, within each party, support for

[27] See "Fact Sheet on Federal Role," *Congressional Quarterly Weekly Report,* November 15, 1968.
[28] See ibid., January 25, 1975, pp. 189–194.

urban programs and other similar expansion of the "federal role" normally is greatest from representatives and senators with the most urban districts or states, is slightly less from those whose districts or states are more suburban, and least from members with the most rural constituencies. (See Tables 1 and 2.) The difference in urban support within each party according to types of constituency, however, has been sharply less than the differences between the parties, even when southern Democrats are not factored out of the Democratic scores, let alone when they are.

Prospects for Increased Federal Aid to Cities

Looking to the future, what are the prospects for any greatly increased federal financial help to cities? There will probably be proposals in the years ahead to establish additional kinds of programs purported to provide new or more effective remedies or solutions for urban problems and to increase the overall level of urban funding, either through expansion of categorical grants or of revenue-sharing, or both. There will most likely also be proposals to redesign ongoing programs that are widely felt not to be working well or to be producing undesirable side effects. At least over the short-run future, there is little reason to doubt that under Democratic presidents and "northern" Democratic controlled Congresses, there will be a greater probability of new programs, greater additional spending, and proportionately more federal aid channeled to cities rather than under Republican presidents or Republican-southern Democrat, "conservative coalition" controlled congresses.

What the longer-term prospects are for drastic increases in federal spending to help solve the problems of large cities is more uncertain. The basic factor here is the decreasing proportion of the nation's population that every year lives in large cities, particularly in the older large cities of the East and Midwest which are experiencing the greatest difficulties and financial needs, and the increasing proportion living in the suburbs.

It is important to recognize that despite much talk of the United States being an "urban" nation, the reality of the matter is that it is "urban" only in the sense of being "metropolitan area-living," but not in the sense of being "large city-living." That is, while according to the 1970 census 69 percent of all Americans lived in metropolitan areas (defined essentially as a central city of at least 50,000 in population and those contiguous counties that are economically and socially integrated with the central city), only 31 percent lived in the central city portions, with 38 percent living in the "outside central city" or suburban portions. The 31 percent included all those living in cities of 50,000 and larger, and represents a decline from 33 percent in 1960 and 35 percent in 1950 (see Figure 7). Moreover when one looks at what percentage of Americans in 1970 remained in the really large cities which are most seriously experiencing various kinds of urban problems, one finds that only 21 percent were in cities of 250,000 or more, 16 percent in those of half-million and larger, and a mere 9 percent in the cities with popula-

FIGURE 7

Distribution of Population by Place of Residence: Central City,
Outside Central City, Nonmetropolitan, 1950–1970

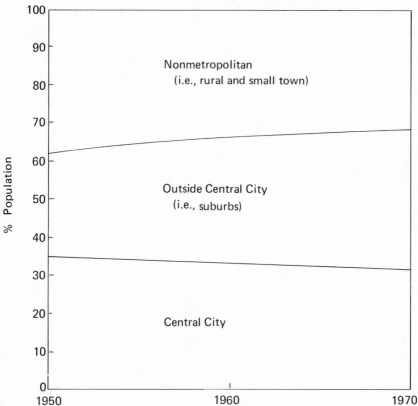

SOURCE: U. S. Bureau of the Census, *Statistical Abstract of the United States:1974*, p. 17, table
16; p. 23, table 23.

ions of a million or over.[29] Actually of the fifty-six largest cities with a 1970
population of 250,000 or more, twenty-three lost population between 1960 and
1970 in absolute terms and twenty-two lost population between 1950 and 1960.

The decline in the proportion of the American population living in large cities
will result in a steadily decreasing number of members in the House of Representatives who will be representing large city districts. The impact of the 1960–
1970 population shifts on the distribution of House seats through reapportionment caused a decrease of 7 percent—from 110 to 102—in those seats primarily
representing central cities of 50,000 or larger in population, and an increase of
26 percent—from 104 to 131—with basically suburban constituencies. The non-

[29] U. S. Bureau of the Census, *Statistical Abstract of the United States: 1974*, tables 16, 23.

FIGURE 8

Distribution of Seats in House of Representatives by Type of Constitutency, 1968 and 1973

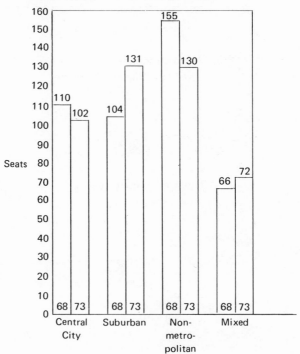

SOURCE: *Congressional Quarterly Weekly Report, April 6, 1974, p. 878.*

metropolitan constituencies dropped 16 percent—from 155 to 130—while the number of seats from "mixed" constituencies rose from 66 to 72. (See Figure 8.) The strength of House representation from city constituencies not only remained smaller than the total nonmetropolitan strength, as before, but it also became smaller than total suburban strength.

What this long-term shift in types of districts is likely to do to the policy complexion of the House of Representatives is extremely difficult to predict. Thus far Democrats from suburban districts have been voting almost as strongly prourban as members from central city districts. If the Democratic party can maintain its present relative strength among suburban constituencies and if any additional suburban Democrats who are elected continue to share the policy outlooks of the central city representatives who will still be the dominant contingent in the northern Democratic membership, sources of support for urban programs will not be fundamentally weakened. Indeed, to the extent that rural Republicans and rural southern Democrats are replaced by suburban Republicans and suburban southern Democrats, the resistance to urban programs from the "conservative coalition" may actually weaken to some extent. If, on the other hand, the bulk of the new suburban seats can be captured by the Republican party, the low-spending, anti-big-city, conservative coalition forces in the House will be strengthened.

The impact of present population trends on the Senate is more difficult to nail down: senators in general, and even Democratic senators from urban states, will inevitably be recognizing the increasingly suburban nature of their overall constituencies. Therefore, even those who may be so inclined personally, may be less able to afford politically, the developing of reputations as out-and-out champions of big cities.

Incidentally, if the historical attachment to the Democratic party continues to weaken in the South and the emergent pattern of more two-party, competitive congressional politics spreads, most of the more conservative and antiurban southern aspirants for House and Senate seats may run as Republicans.[30] Since so many present southern Democrats are conservative and antiurban, the election of individuals with such outlooks as Republicans would have no great impact on the amount of congressional support for urban programs. But it would have the utility of better rationalizing party alignments in Congress by making the nominal distribution of seats between Democrats and Republicans more indicative of the true relative strength available for the different policy positions with which the dominant numbers of those parties have been traditionally associated.

The increasing suburbanization of the population, finally, may affect the intensity of presidential leadership that will be forthcoming for increased federal assistance to cities. For in a nation whose suburban population will be increasingly in a position to outvote its big city citizens, even Democratic presidents, let alone Republican ones, may not find it electorally profitable to assign their highest policy and budgetary priorities to programs that are perceived as basically benefiting large cities.

In short, the most probable long-term impact of the decline in the proportion of the nation's people living in large cities is that most of any additions to, expansions of, and increased spending on "urban" programs probably will be on those that interest and benefit suburbs as much or more than large cities. Examples are increased spending for education, mass transit, intercity rail transportation, environmental pollution, and general or special revenue-sharing programs based on

30 A new factor promoting such a change is the action of the House Democratic caucus at the beginning of the Ninety-fourth Congress in January 1975, when it denied the chairmanships of three standing committees to the most senior members and previous chairmen of those committees. If this break with the seniority principle continues, southern aspirants to seats in the House of Representatives can no longer take for granted, if they run as Democrats, their eventual elevation to committee chairmanships through seniority and regardless of whether their policy stances deviate sharply with the dominant majority of their party colleagues. The Senate Democratic caucus' adoption of a rule requiring a secret ballot on the choice of committee chairman if 20 percent of the caucus members so desired, appeared to lay the groundwork for future challenges to Senate Democratic committee chairmen on similar grounds.

formulas that are also favorable to suburbs. On the other hand, those "urban" programs whose thrust is primarily to improve the social and physical conditions of the poor, and especially of black, urban slum dwellers, will most likely receive treatment varying from only marginal improvement to "benign neglect."[31]*

APPENDIX

House of Representatives

Urban Key Vote	CQ Key Vote, Year and Number	Bill Number	Legislative Purpose
1	1945,6	H.R. 3615	Federal aid to airports
2	1946,2	H.R. 3370	School lunch grants
3	1949,2	H.R. 4009	Public housing and urban development
4	1954,1	H.R. 7839	Housing development
5	1955,6	S. 2126	Public housing
6	1956,4	H.R. 7535	School construction
7	1957,6	H.R. 1	School construction
8	1960,2	H.R. 10128	School construction
9	1961,4	H.R. 6028	Housing
10	1961,6	H.R. 8890	Emergency educational aid
11	1962,1	H. Res. 530	Creation of Department of Urban Affairs and Housing
12	1964,3	H.R. 3881	Urban mass transportation
13	1964,5	S. 2642	Economic opportunity (antipoverty) act
14	1965,3	H.R. 2362	Aid to elementary and secondary education
15	1965,5	H.R. 6675	Medicaid for welfare recipients
16	1965,8	H.R. 6927	Creation of Department of Housing and Urban Development
17	1965,9	H.R. 7984	Public housing and urban renewal
18	1965,10	H.R. 11588	Rent supplements appropriations
19	1965,12	H.R. 8283	Economic opportunity
20	1966,2	H.R. 14012	Rent supplements appropriations
21	1966,9	H.R. 15111	Economic opportunity
22	1966,11	S. 3708	Model cities
23	1967,3	H.R. 9960	Rent supplements appropriations
24	1967,4	H.R. 9960	Model cities appropriations

[31] Space did not permit taking into account in the analysis the factor of suburban diversities. It should be noted, however, that not all suburbs are problem-free white, upper middle class residential havens. Some suburbs—especially those that are older and closest to central cities—are already experiencing increases in crime, poverty, physical deterioration, and ghettoization. Members of Congress from constituencies that include such suburban areas may, therefore, turn out to be a source of long-term support even for programs aimed at alleviating the pathologies associated with slum poverty.

* I thank Bruce Feld, Gerald Finch, Jeffrey Pressman, Douglas Price, and Robert Reischauer for constructive comments on an earlier draft of this article.

Urban Key Vote	CQ Key Vote, Year and Number	Bill Number	Legislative Purpose
25	1967,7	H.R. 11000	Rat control and extermination
26	1967,8	H.R. 5037	Law enforcement assistance
27	1967,12	H.R. 2388	Economic opportunity
28	1968,7	H.R. 18027	OEO appropriations
29	1968,11	S. 3497	Low-income housing
30	1969,3	H.R. 13111	Elementary and secondary education appropriations
31	1969,10	H.R. 12321	Economic opportunity
32	1970,1	H.R. 13111	Labor, HEW, and OEO appropriations
33	1970,5	H.R. 11102	Hospital construction
34	1970,9	H.R. 16916	Education appropriations
35	1970,10	H.R. 17548	HUD appropriations
36	1971,3	H.R. 7016	Education appropriations
37	1972,4	H.R. 14370	General revenue-sharing
38	1972,7	H.R. 15417	Labor-HEW appropriations
39	1972,12	S. 2770	Water pollution control
40	1973,8	H.R. 6452	Urban mass transit
41	1973,10	H.R. 8870	Labor-HEW appropriations
42	1974,10	S. 3066	Housing and community development
43	1974,11	H.R. 12859	Urban mass transit
44	1974,15	H.R. 16596	Public service jobs

Senate

Urban Key Vote	CQ Key Vote, Year and Number	Bill Number	Legislative Purpose
1	1948,2	S. 866	Low rent housing
2	1948,4	S. 472	Educational financing
3	1949,2	S. 1070	Public housing and urban development
4	1955,4	S. 2126	Public housing
5	1960,1	S. 8	School construction and salaries
6	1961,3	S. 1021	Schools and teachers' salaries
7	1961,4	S. 1922	Expanded housing programs
8	1963,2	S. 6	Urban mass transit
9	1963,3	S. 1	Youth employment
10	1963,5	S. 1321	National service corps
11	1964,4	S. 2642	Economic opportunity
12	1965,3	H.R. 2362	Elementary and secondary education
13	1965,10	H.R. 6675	Medicaid for welfare recipients
14	1965,11	S. 2212	Rent supplements
15	1965,13	H.R. 8283	Economic opportunity appropriations
16	1966,3	H.R. 14012	Rent supplements appropriations
17	1966,8	S. 3708	Model cities
18	1967,9	H.R. 9960	Rent supplements
19	1968,8	S. 3497	Housing and urban development
20	1968,11	H.R. 18037	Economic opportunity appropriations

Urban Key Vote	CQ Key Vote, Year and Number	Bill Number	Legislative Purpose
21	1970,7	H.R. 17912	Food stamps appropriations
22	1971,5	S. 575	Public works jobs
23	1971,14	S. 2007	Day-care program
24	1972,11	H.R. 14370	General revenue-sharing formula
25	1972,14	S. 3939	Rail transportation
26	1973,2	S. 502	Bus and subway construction
27	1974,4	S. 1539	Aid to schools formula
28	1974,14	H.R. 14449	Economic opportunity funding

SOURCE: Full details on each of these votes can be found in *Congress and the Nation,* Vol. I (1945–1964) (Washington, D. C., 1965), "Key Votes," pp. 38a–97a; ibid., Vol. II (1965–1968) (Washington, D. C., 1969), "Key Votes," pp. 5a–41a; ibid., Vol. III (1969–1972) (Washington, D. C., 1973), "Key Votes," pp. 5a–47a; *Congressional Quarterly Almanac,* 1973 (Washington, D. C., 1974), pp. 929–941; ibid., 1974 (Washington, D. C., 1975), pp. 973–985.

12 Official Secrecy and Informal Communication in Congressional-Bureaucratic Relations

LEON V. SIGAL

Item: When Daniel Ellsberg decided to disclose the Pentagon papers, he first delivered a set to Senator J. William Fulbright, chairman of the Senate Foreign Relations Committee and perhaps the most prominent dove in Congress. Fulbright took the material and placed it in his office safe, where it remained unexamined. Subsequently, Ellsberg decided to leak the documents to *The New York Times.*

Item: While serving as national security adviser to the president, Henry Kissinger met periodically with senior members of the Senate Foreign Relations Committee over breakfast at Senator Fulbright's home. The existence of these meetings was not publicly acknowledged by any of the participants until Kissinger's nomination as secretary of state.

These incidents are somewhat puzzling. Why Senator Fulbright would choose not to make a political issue out of the information contained in the Pentagon papers until after Ellsberg had leaked them to the press, and why Henry Kissinger would meet with Foreign Relations Committee members while keeping secret the fact that he had done so, have a common strand of explanation. They are both instances of *informal communication* between the executive branch and Congress about matters which are officially secret. How such exchanges of information take place often affects how those who receive the information can exploit

LEON V. SIGAL teaches government at Wesleyan University. He is the author of *Reporters and Officials: The Organization and Politics of Newsmaking.*

what they know, as well as what outcomes emerge from the policy process.

THREE CHANNELS OF INFORMAL COMMUNICATION

Informal communication is a commonplace around Washington. In its most mundane form, it is gossip—"inside dope" on what really transpired, the likes and dislikes of the key players in the current political game in town, the fleshing out of the organizational charts. It rises above the mundane, though, when a significant area of governmental activity is veiled from public view by executive attempts to keep it secret. Then, informal communication may provide the only information that most congressmen have to act upon.

Individual congressmen have access to a number of regular channels of information. There are committee hearings and formal reports, their fellow congressmen, their own staffs and those of their committees, and various supporting staffs—the Government Accounting Office, the Congressional Research Service, and the new Office of Technological Assessment. They can also call upon the services of various experts, private organizations, and lobbyists in and out of Washington to provide them with information. Yet these channels are not always helpful in supplying the information that congressmen need in order to make a political issue out of some governmental activity. To the extent that they can garner attention or votes from an issue, these channels may dry up at the source—inside the federal bureaucracy. Especially when administrative secrecy is invoked, routine channels alone become insufficient for supplying congressmen with the politically exploitable information they need most.

Even under these circumstances, though, secrecy seldom prevails; *official secrecy* does. Word about supposedly secret matters still tends to get around town informally. Elected officials in Congress, and even specialists in the press and the general public, can usually gain at least a general awareness of what the government is doing even when information is closely held. Sometimes as the result of a decision by senior officials in the government, but more often as a political maneuver by subordinates in the bureaucracy to circumvent the directives of their putative superiors, informal communication takes place between the executive branch and the Congress.

Informal communication flows through three principal channels:

1. Bootlegging. "Bootlegging" is Washington's name for covert dissemination of information, usually copies of internal documents given to a government official not authorized to receive them, either because he lacks a security clearance or because, though cleared, he does not have a

"need to know" and therefore is excluded from the routing list. Congressmen and their aides fall into the latter category. Insofar as this channel supplies copies of actual documents, congressmen may regard it as the most authoritative of the three informal channels and tend to rely more on the information provided through it. While bootlegging sometimes is practiced by senior officials, it is a maneuver more common to lower-level bureaucrats who thereby may attain a measure of political support from the congressmen they supply, without themselves risking exposure and administrative sanction.

2. Informal briefings. Government officials occasionally brief selected groups of congressmen about activities not formally reported to the Congress as a whole. Because more than one, and often large numbers of congressmen or their aides are invited to these briefings, the channel is less secure than bootlegging, and lower-echelon officials concerned with preserving their anonymity tend not to use it. Usually administration officials communicate through this channel in order to mobilize political support *in advance of* a forthcoming act or announcement. Sometimes, however, informal briefings serve *as a substitute for* formal consultation or testimony before committees of Congress, whether in open or executive session. By restricting invitations to supporters of administration policy, officials can avoid leaving themselves open to the charge of failing to "inform" the Congress, while helping to ensure that those in attendance will use discretion in their handling of the information. Even administration antagonists, when invited to attend these briefings, may feel constrained by considerations of national security and their desire for continued access not to reveal the substance discussed, or the fact that the meeting took place. The congressmen who attend, for their part, receive information which the administration wants them to have, helping them to anticipate and encourage future developments, while permitting them to deny any "knowledge" of, and hence responsibility for, what is happening. The Kissinger briefing was one example; another was the ongoing relationship secretaries of state in the Truman administration fostered with Senators Tom Connally and Arthur Vandenberg.[1] Informal briefings are rooted in the organization of Congress—and the allocation of bargaining advantages to members that results from this organization. Knowledge of what is going on in the executive branch is perhaps the most important resource the leadership and committee chairmen have for controlling backbenchers.

3. "Leaks" to the press. The press is the best informal channel for disseminating information to the entire Congress in a hurry. Of the three channels, congressmen may consider it the least reliable because

---

[1] Harry S. Truman, *Memoirs*, I: *Year of Decisions* (New York, 1955), p. 272.

they often find it difficult to identify the source, and hence to establish the authenticity of the information provided to reporters. At the same time, however, it is the most public of the informal channels and thus the hardest to ignore: others in and around Washington are reading the same information as the congressmen, and they may wonder why their representatives are not doing anything about the situation.

"Secrets" and "Official Secrets"

The existence of informal communication makes it necessary to distinguish between secrets and official secrets. Although a piece of information may not remain a secret forever, so long as it is an official secret, those who know it may feel politically constrained from using it or even discussing it. Herein lies the essence of the distinction Washingtonians draw between having information and "knowing." For example, the following colloquy took place between Senator Harold Hughes and Army Chief of Staff Creighton W. Abrams in the course of hearings on the Cambodia bombing:

> Senator Hughes. Did you at any time get information from Prince Sihanouk that he would tolerate bombing in Cambodia willingly?
> General Abrams. No, sir. I have read all those things. Where I was I did not know those things.[2]

Gleaning information from the newspaper is one thing; knowing things officially by virtue of his position—"where he was"—is quite another.

Official secrecy nevertheless may severely curtail congressmen's ability to exploit politically the information that comes into their possession. Moreover, administrative efforts to enforce official secrecy by preventing unwanted informal communication often have as their unintended consequence, loss of control over other actions of subordinates.

The way in which informal communication takes place and some of its political and administrative ramifications may be inferred from two examples: the building of the atomic bomb from 1939 to 1945 and the bombing of Cambodia from March 1969 through April 1970.

---

[2] U. S. Congress, Senate, Committee on Armed Services, Hearings: Bombing in Cambodia, 93rd Cong., 1st Sess., 1973, p. 349. A variation of the same theme came earlier in the hearings in an exchange between Senator Hughes and General Abrams' predecessor as army chief of staff, Earle G. Wheeler:
"Senator Hughes. General, if I ask you some questions that are still classified that you don't want to respond to, just tell me. I may ask without knowing about the classification.
General Wheeler. I will beg your indulgence, because I have been out of office so long that I am not too sure of what I do know and what I don't know" (p. 188).

APPROPRIATIONS FOR THE ATOMIC BOMB

The building of the atomic bomb followed an ideal-type bureaucratic strategy—not in the sense that every step proceeded according to a preconceived plan, but rather in the sense that it was a typical path for decisions and actions to take within the government—partly as a result of some tactical planning by bureaucrats trying to attain their objectives and partly through happenstance. Among the characteristics of this strategic path are (1) compartmentalization of information, disclosing significant details to other bureaucrats as well as to congressmen only on a "need to know" basis—to those whose governmental responsibilities necessitated their having the information in order to do their jobs; (2) avoidance of outside evaluation; (3) circumvention of regular budgetary procedures; and (4) involvement of experts in and out of government in the program, committing them to its success and exploiting their presumed expertise and prestige to deflect criticism of it. Although building the bomb in the course of World War II cost $2.2 billion, the rationale of national security was used in circumventing the regular appropriations process. Instead, officials devised a makeshift process.

Still, the bomb did not remain a secret. Most senior officials in the national security process—including many who did not qualify as having a "need to know"—had at least a general awareness of the bomb's existence, usually gained through private conversations with their colleagues. Secretary of State Cordell Hull, War Mobilization Director James F. Byrnes, and Treasury Secretary Henry Morgenthau all learned of the project this way.[3] At least a dozen congressmen found out, as did William L. Laurence, Turner Catledge, and Arthur Sulzberger of *The New York Times*, and even Supreme Court Justice Felix Frankfurter. Many in scientific circles were aware of it, both in the United States and abroad.[4]

While it might strike the Washingtonian of today as extraordinary how few officials learned of so substantial and long-lived a project as the building of the bomb, word of mouth nevertheless did get around. It is

[3] Cordell Hull, *Memoirs*, II (New York, 1948), p. 1110; James F. Byrnes, *All in One Lifetime* (New York, 1958), p. 247; Henry L. Stimson, *Stimson Diary*, October 17, 1944, Stimson Papers, Yale University Library.

[4] Richard G. Hewlett and Oscar E. Anderson, Jr., *A History of the United States Atomic Energy Commission*, I: *The New World, 1939–1946* (University Park, Pa., 1962), p. 327; Turner Catledge, *My Life and The Times* (New York, 1971), pp. 174–176; William L. Laurence, *Dawn Over Zero* (New York, 1946), p. xi. Within the Manhattan Project itself, some scientists chafed at the restrictions and eventually rebelled against the rigid compartmentalization enforced by army security personnel. Testimony of Leo Szilard, December 10, 1945, U. S. Congress, Senate, Special Committee on Atomic Energy, *Hearings Pursuant to S. Res. 179*, 79th Cong., 1st Sess., part III, pp. 293, 295.

virtually impossible to keep a secret in a town whose denizens pride themselves on being "in the know." But being aware of the project and having detailed official knowledge of it are not equivalent. Because most officials who did know of its existence did not know officially, they could not put their knowledge to political use in any official forum. Not secrecy, but official secrecy, involving the lack of formal, regular provision of information to Congress, characterized the appropriations process with respect to the bomb.

How did congressmen learn of the bomb's existence prior to August 6, 1945? None seems to have learned through the press, although a staff man who had even a rudimentary understanding of atomic energy might have made correct inferences from stray news reports which appeared in the press from time to time.[5] William Laurence of the *Times* had attended several lectures prior to the outbreak of World War II at which scientists described the revolutionary developments in nuclear physics. On Sunday, May 5, 1940, a seven-column article by Laurence appeared on page 1 of the *Times* telling of the first chemical separation of U_{235} in a laboratory. While he made no specific mention of a bomb, he did point out that 1 pound of U_{235} would yield the energy equivalent to 5 million pounds of coal or 15,000 tons of TNT and told of German research efforts. "I had hoped that the facts would galvanize Washington into action," he later wrote.[6] One member of Congress was sufficiently galvanized to insert the article into the *Congressional Record*—a California senator who appended it to a long statement about the threat that atomic energy posed to his state's petroleum industry. Laurence followed up this effort with a long article for the *Saturday Evening Post*, which appeared in the September 7 issue. The Federal Bureau of Investigation subsequently requested that the *Post* take that issue out of circulation and asked libraries to remove it from their shelves and report the name of anyone who asked for that issue to agents of the FBI.[7] Despite security precautions, news stories did appear in the regional press alluding to massive plants producing an unspecified weapon. To anyone with the least awareness of atomic energy, furthermore, the very absence of speculation might have

[5] Lansing Lamont, *Day of Trinity* (New York, 1965), p. 163. Elsewhere in the public domain, the 1943 edition of *Minerals Yearbook* contained these two nuggets: "Uranium production in 1943 was greatly stimulated by a government program having materials priority over all other mineral procurements, but most of the facts were buried in War Department secrecy." And later: "Most of the 1943 uranium supply was used by physics laboratories for research on uranium isotopes as a source of energy." Testimony of Alexander Sachs, November 26, 1945, *Hearings Pursuant to S. 179*, part I, p. 16.

[6] Laurence, *Dawn Over Zero*, p. ix.

[7] Ibid., pp. ix–x.

provided a clue, too. There is little evidence, however, that any congressman made the connection between press reports and the manufacture of the bomb.

Some congressmen seem to have learned by a variant of "bootlegging." One was the junior senator from Missouri and chairman of the Senate Committee to Investigate the National Defense Program, Harry S. Truman. Previous queries from inquisitive congressmen had been satisfied by replies from the commanding officer of the Manhattan Engineering District, General Leslie R. Groves.[8] But Truman was not so easily dissuaded. Having learned of the Oak Ridge facility, he sent a long-time associate to investigate the project. The aide managed to gain access to Oak Ridge, apparently surreptitiously, but security personnel quickly detected his presence. It took a telephone call from Secretary of War Henry Stimson on June 17, 1943, to convince Truman to call off the inquiry. As transcribed by Stimson, their exchange on the bomb went as follows:

> *Stimson.* Now that's a matter which I know all about personally, and I am one of the group of two or three men in the whole world who know about it.
>
> *Truman.* I see.
>
> *Stimson.* It's part of a very important secret development.
>
> *Truman.* Well, all right then—
>
> *Stimson.* And I—
>
> *Truman.* I herewith see the situation, Mr. Secretary and you won't have to say another word to me. Whenever you say that to me, that's all I want to hear.[9]

Later, when Truman contemplated sending two staff members to Hanford, Washington, to investigate construction costs connected with the project facility there, though not the bomb itself, Stimson again took responsibility and refused access. This example is too easily dismissed as typical of an era of trust between politicians in the legislative and executive branches of government, especially when one party controlled both. Tactical considerations played a part, too. Conducting an investigation of the defense effort in order to improve efficiency and cut down waste could be made to seem patriotic in wartime, but breaching security regulations to conduct a preliminary investigation without a formal

---

[8] Leslie R. Groves, *Now It Can Be Told* (New York, 1962), p. 361.

[9] Transcript of telephone conversation between Secretary of War Stimson and Senator Truman, June 17, 1943, Stimson Papers, Yale University Library, quoted in Elting E. Morison, *Turmoil and Tradition* (Boston, 1960), p. 616. See also, Truman, *Year of Decisions*, pp. 10–11; Groves, *Now It Can Be Told*, p. 365; Michael Amrine, *The Great Decision* (New York, 1959), pp. 29–30, for slightly different versions.

congressional mandate to do so was politically far riskier—better to take the secretary's word for it now and pin the blame on him later if the project did not succeed.

Informal briefings eventually became necessary as congressional protests mounted along with project costs. Money for the bomb—$16 million in calendar year 1942, $344 million in 1943, and about $100 million a month in early 1944—had mostly been concealed in two lines of the War Department budget: "Engineer Service, Army" and "Expediting Production."[10] Senior officials concluded in early 1944 that the time had come to let a few selected congressmen in on part of the secret. General Groves writes:

> We realized from the start that this could not go on forever, for our expenditures were too vast and the project was too big to remain concealed indefinitely. And, as always happens in the case of any large construction job, rumors and distortions of the facts abounded, and could understandably become a source of concern to any congressman who heard them.[11]

On February 18, 1944, Stimson, Groves, and Vannevar Bush met with House Speaker Sam Rayburn, Majority Leader John W. McCormack, and Minority Leader Joseph W. Martin, Jr. Stimson outlined the "general state of the project" and current and projected expenditures, Marshall related the bomb to war plans, and Bush sketched the scientific background and military potential of the weapon. With only that general briefing, the congressmen gave their approval to circumventing the appropriations process. Speaker Rayburn would be notified in advance of requests for appropriations for the project, whereupon he would inform his two colleagues and then tell a few Appropriations Committee members that the two items in the budget had been reviewed with Stimson and Marshall and should not be questioned. "The other members of Congress," says Groves, "would be given only the most general reasons for the need to accord special handling to our requests for funds."[12] On June 10, a similar briefing was given to four Senate leaders: Majority Leader Alben Barkley, Minority Leader Wallace H. White, and Senators Elmer Thomas and Styles Bridges, the chairman and ranking minority member of the Military Subcommittee of the Senate Appropriations Committee, who would vouch for the item on the Senate side of the Capitol. Carefully omitted from these briefings and whatever questioning that followed was one

[10] Groves, *Now It Can Be Told*, p. 361; Hewlett and Anderson, *The New World*, p. 290, Appendix 2.

[11] Groves, *Now It Can Be Told*, p. 362.

[12] Ibid., p. 363. See also, Vannevar Bush, *Pieces of the Action* (New York, 1970), p. 133, for a slight variant.

salient detail—that the bomb might not be ready for use before the end of the war.[13]

The Appropriations Committees never challenged Stimson and Bush on the bomb. After the war had ended, Bush recalls, he appeared before the House Appropriations Committee for the last time in his capacity as director of the Office of Scientific Research and Development. Chairman Clarence Cannon chided him for not telling the committee about the bomb:

> So I told them, "You remember, every time I appeared before you, I put a red-covered book on the table and told you that it contained an account of everything my agency was doing." "I remember all right," said Cannon, "and I remember stating that it was a very dangerous book, and telling the clerk to guard it carefully. But the atomic energy matter was not in it." "Oh, yes, it was, Mr. Chairman." "But," said Cannon, "we would not have understood it if we had read it." "No, you would not have understood it," said I, "but it was there."[14]

Bush draws a lesson from the charade: although no member of the committee ever opened the book, "it was a symbol, and an important one." He writes:

> By its use I had said, in effect, to the Committee, "You are entitled to know anything you wish to know about the program of the OSRD," and they had replied, "We wish to know nothing."

Not all members of Congress went along, however. When an attempt was made in February 1945 to transfer other War Department funds to the line, "Expediting Production," as a first step in turning them over to the Manhattan Engineering District, Representative Albert J. Engel, having earlier raised questions about the project, demanded a detailed justification. Stimson and Groves met with the congressman at the Pentagon, and without giving him any details about the project itself, assured him that the costs of purchasing land and constructing plants, roads, and housing were not incommensurate with similar costs in the private sector, thereby allaying his suspicions of waste.[15]

As congressional restrictiveness grew, Groves proposed extending informal consultation to include a visit to Oak Ridge by a carefully chosen contingent from the Hill. Five congressmen, among them, Cannon and Engel, were allowed to inspect the Clinton Works at Oak Ridge—but

---

[13] Hewlett and Anderson, *The New World*, pp. 289–290. It is also unclear whether or not the words "atomic bomb" were ever used. Alben Barkley, *That Reminds Me* (New York, 1954), p. 266.

[14] Bush, *Pieces of the Action*, p. 134.

[15] Groves, *Now It Can Be Told*, p. 363.

only from the outside. None was permitted to enter any of the plants. According to Groves,

> They appeared to be entirely satisfied with what they saw, and like everyone else were impressed with the hugeness and complexity of the installation. They did not raise a single question about possible waste. . . . [16]

The issue on the Hill was whether or not the project was a boondoggle, even a fraud; there seems to have been little controversy over the question of whether nor not to build the bomb at all.

BOMBING IN CAMBODIA, 1969–1970

On February 11, 1969, less than a month after President Nixon had taken office, the joint chiefs of staff renewed a request, first made in 1968, for authority to bomb enemy sanctuaries in Cambodia, in particular, to attack a suspected enemy headquarters commonly identified as "COSVN." After a round of meetings with advisers, the president approved the request in early March despite some opposition from Defense Secretary Melvin Laird. At the same time, Secretary Laird recommended withdrawal of 50,000 to 70,000 troops from Vietnam over the course of the year. The coincidence of somewhat contradictory acts suggests a quid pro quo, granting authority to bomb in return for military acceptance of the start of withdrawals.[17]

Between March 18, 1969, the date of the first raid, and April 30, 1970, when new bombing authority took effect in conjunction with the United States invasion of Cambodia, the Air Force flew 3,875 sorties against targets inside that neutral country, dropping 108,823 tons of ordnance at a cost of roughly $150 million.[18] None of the bombing was reported to the Congress. Moreover, since Congress had given no authorization, expending money for the bombing may have constituted a violation of law.

Unlike the case of the atomic bomb, secrecy was designed to keep the fact of the bombing from the Congress as much as from any foreign power. In order to do so, the Joint Staff, at the express request of the president, devised an elaborate system of double reporting on the bombing there, as well as in Northern Laos.[19] Requests for authority to hit specific

---

[16] Ibid., pp. 364, 365–366.

[17] U. S. Congress, *Bombing in Cambodia*, pp. 132, 138, 140, 502. For circumstantial evidence of a deal, pp. 347, 349, 445–446.

[18] Sorties and tonnage are from "Department of Defense Report on Selected Air and Ground Operations in Cambodia and Laos," September 10, 1973, ibid., p. 487. The cost estimate is based on comparable figures for bombing in South Vietnam over the same period.

[19] Ibid., pp. 17–18, 132, 144–145, 155, 164.

targets in Cambodia were passed up through the chain of command from the commander of MACV, to CINCPAC and the SAC commander on Guam, to the chairman of the joint chiefs of staff, and finally to the secretary of defense under security procedures which limited distribution to "eyes only" of those with a "need to know." At the same time, a request to hit "cover" targets in South Vietnam was routinely processed through normal channels. Upon receipt of authority, the mission would fly over or near its "cover" target in South Vietnam, but release its bombs only when it had arrived over its actual target in Cambodia. After the planes had returned to base, operations reports on the mission were filed through the "back channel," while routine reports were filed in normal channels without revealing the actual coordinates of the strike. This procedure enabled the Air Force to keep track of logistical requirements—fuel and munitions, spare parts, crewmen—without revealing the nature of its operations to the thousands of people who had access to that data. Reports to the Congress on sorties flown and bomb tonnage dropped were based on data from the logistics reports and failed to show any bombing strikes in Cambodia. In order to operate the dual reporting procedure, ground controllers who guided the B-52's to their destination and signaled the time for releasing their bomb load had to be briefed on the actual nature of their missions. So did the pilots and navigators who, alone among the crewmen on board, had access to navigational equipment that revealed the plane's exact position. Others did not.[20]

Administration officials insisted that secrecy was necessary in order to avoid diplomatic embarrassment for Cambodia's chief of state, Prince Sihanouk, who was said to have "acquiesced" to the bombing so long as it was not officially acknowledged—although his acquiescence seems to have taken the form of an inability to stop the bombers from going about their business, rather than discreet silence and lack of protest.[21] Notwithstanding administration assertions, it is difficult to understand why it became necessary to devise so elaborate a reporting system if the purpose was simply not to acknowledge the raids officially. The regular classification system seems to have sufficed to keep comparable information out of foreign hands.

The system enabled the administration to avoid officially informing the Congress of the Cambodia strikes. In public statements, officials who were aware of the bombings, from the president down, either lied or avoided responding directly to questions about the bombing. For instance,

---

[20] The details of procedures are in "Department of Defense Report on Selected Air and Ground Operations in Cambodia and Laos," September 10, 1973, ibid., pp. 482–487.

[21] Ibid., pp. 169, 366, 389, 392–400, 460–461.

President Nixon, in a speech of April 30, 1970, announcing the invasion of Cambodia, said, "For five years, neither the United States nor South Vietnam has moved against these enemy sanctuaries because we did not want to violate the territory of a neutral nation."[22] In testimony before Congress administration officials who knew provided evasive answers to questions bearing on the bombing. Secretary of Defense Laird told a House appropriations subcommittee soon after Nixon's speech: "We moved across the border from time to time when we were under attack and when such movement was necessary to protect our forces—with tactical air at times, and at times with artillery. But we did not have the opportunity, primarily because of political reasons, to move into the sanctuary areas and destroy these facilities."[23] That same day, committee chairman George Mahon and Army Chief of Staff Earle G. Wheeler discussed air operations over Cambodia:

> *Mr. Mahon.* To what extent, General Wheeler, during past months and years have we bombed the fringes of Cambodia? I don't mean that we made any public statements about it, but have we over a period of months and years bombed the fringes of Cambodia?
>
> *General Wheeler.* We have responded to attacks from Cambodia with artillery fire and air strikes.[24]

On at least three occasions those who did not know were allowed to provide—unwittingly—false reports on sorties flown and tonnage dropped, based on data from logistical reports which failed to show any bombings of Cambodia.[25]

Despite elaborate precautions, the Cambodia bombing, like the atomic bomb, was no secret; it was an official secret. Word of mouth spread through Air Force ranks in Vietnam concerning the bombings in Cambodia and the accompanying border crossings by Special Forces units engaged in ground reconnaissance. Unofficially, word slowly got around

[22] U. S. Congress, House, Committee on Foreign Affairs, *Hearings: U. S. Policy and Programs in Cambodia*, 93d Cong., 1st Sess., 1973, p. 152.

[23] Testimony of Defense Secretary Laird and General Earle G. Wheeler, U. S. Congress, House, Committee on Appropriations, Subcommittee on the Department of Defense, *Hearings: Department of Defense Appropriations for Fiscal Year 1971*, 91st Cong., 2d Sess., part VI, pp. 796, 800; also, p. 826.

[24] Ibid.

[25] Air Force Secretary Robert C. Seamans, Jr., who was not in the chain of command on the Cambodia bombing, was one victim of this practice. U. S. Congress, Senate, Committee on Armed Services, *Hearings: Fiscal Year 1972 Authorization for Military Procurement*, 92d Cong., 1st Sess., 1971, pp. 1245, 1284. Although the classified numbers were deleted, the figures for Cambodia were zero. U. S. Congress, *Bombing in Cambodia*, p. 85; also pp. 75–77, 90–91.

Washington, too.[26] At least eight members of Congress learned of the bombing informally at its inception.

Seven of them, all supporters of administration policy in Southeast Asia, learned of the bombing through informal briefings by the president, his national security adviser Henry Kissinger, Defense Secretary Laird, or their staffs.[27] They included the chairmen of the Senate Armed Services Committee, Richard Russell and John Stennis; minority leaders of the Senate and House, Everett Dirksen and Gerald Ford; the chairman and ranking minority member of the House Armed Services Committee, L. Mendel Rivers and Leslie Arends, and House Appropriations Committee chairman George Mahon. The choice of whom to tell seems to have been made by the president or his national security adviser.[28] That they all were in favor of the bombing seems to have been one criterion: they could thus be trusted to keep the secret.[29] In singling out some congressmen for private briefings, the Nixon administration was following in the footsteps of previous administrations. To objections from those congressmen who were not among the chosen few, administration officials defended their action on grounds that the Congress had acquiesced to the practice in the past. One colloquy between Senator Stuart Symington and Deputy Defense Secretary William P. Clements, Jr., gave the essence of the legislative and executive stands on the issue:

[26] Air Force Secretary Seamans, for one, seems to have learned of the bombing through the informal grapevine. U. S. Congress, *Bombing in Cambodia,* p. 96.

[27] On June 17, 1973, Secretary Laird stated, "I did, of course, advise key members of the Congress from both political parties regarding those missions." Ibid., p. 73.

[28] "The Department understands that the decisions on whom to advise in the Congress were made by the notifying Executive Branch individuals who apparently took into account the extremely sensitive diplomatic situation and the strict orders for security." "Department of Defense Report on Selected Air and Ground Operations in Cambodia and Laos," ibid., p. 489; also, pp. 401, 420.

[29] Senator Stennis, for one, came close to revealing the secret in a 1970 appropriations subcommittee hearing on the defense budget while trying to encourage continuation of the bombing overtly:

"*Chairman Stennis.* And with no bombing he [the enemy] is free to make that supply line what he wants.

General Wheeler. He is reasonably free, yes, sir.

Secretary Laird. We are hitting that supply line pretty well though, Mr. Chairman. We are making it difficult for him to get supplies in there. I don't want to discount it. I am sure General Wheeler doesn't want to indicate that we are not causing him some difficulty.

Chairman Stennis. I should have said no bombing in certain areas.

General Wheeler. In North Vietnam."

U. S. Congress, Senate, Committee on Appropriations, Subcommittee on Defense Appropriations, *Hearings: Department of Defense Appropriations for Fiscal Year 1971,* 91st Cong., 2d Sess., part I, p. 130.

Senator Symington. If you did not give the information to the whole committee, which is the legislative committee responsible for authorization, then how could you expect the constitutional process of appropriating money to be exercised?

Mr. Clements. Mr. Chairman, I can only abide by the existing procedures within the committee, and what your procedures have been in the historical past. As you might change these procedures, I would certainly abide by them. Now, if these procedures have changed, and it is your considered judgment that we should act accordingly, then you need to so advise us and I am sure that we will be responsive.[30]

Bootlegging was the channel through which at least one influential senator, Barry Goldwater of Arizona, learned of the Cambodia bombing. Goldwater, who had long argued against imposing limits on United States bombing in Southeast Asia, found out not from a briefing in Washington, but from officers in the field while he was on a trip to Southeast Asia.[31] Goldwater's support of the bombing was doubtless a consideration in the minds of those in Vietnam who passed on the information: they could expect him to use his awareness and his influence to encourage overt bombing against Cambodia. If so, their expectations were not at all misplaced. On numerous occasions, Goldwater spoke out in favor of attacking enemy base areas across the borders from South Vietnam. He also encouraged military officers who testified before the Armed Services Committee to air their views on the need for such attacks. An exchange he had with the commander of United States forces in Vietnam, General William Westmoreland, on March 19, 1969, is typical:

Senator Goldwater. Suppose you had been allowed to deny them the great bulk of their supplies that continue to come down from the north by railroad through China, by ships into certain ports, suppose that you would have no restraints to go into Cambodia and Laos to hit the sanctuaries, don't you feel this would very materially shorten the war?

General Westmoreland. I think it would put the enemy in quite a predicament. It would materially weaken his military posture and limit his freedom of action. I think it would have a major impact on the course of the war.[32]

Although informal consultation and bootlegging had informed a

---

[30] U. S. Congress, *Bombing in Cambodia*, p. 379; also, p. 156.

[31] As Goldwater put it, "I did know of this, but I did not learn it from the Pentagon, I learned it from the field, and I will not go further than that. I did not know any of the details, I only knew that it had taken place, and I believe this is the way a few others on this committee learned about it." Ibid., p. 106.

[32] U. S. Congress, Senate, Committee on Armed Services, *Hearings: Authorization for Military Procurement, Research and Development for Fiscal Year 1970*, 91st Cong., 1st Sess., part I, March 19, 1969, pp. 357–358.

few congressmen of the Cambodia bombing at its inception, two months after it had begun a leak made the fact of the bombing public to the rest. *The New York Times* on May 9, 1969, ran a page-one story by its Pentagon correspondent, William Beecher, disclosing that Air Force planes had "raided several Vietcong and North Vietnamese supply dumps and base camps in Cambodia for the first time." Attributed only to "knowledgeable sources," who have yet to be identified, the story could have been partially the product of reportorial enterprise.[33] But those on Beecher's beat with the greatest incentive to talk were advocates of bombing in the Air Force, who, while chafing under the bombing restrictions, may nevertheless have preferred to avoid assuming responsibility for covert bombing. By making the fact of the bombing public, they were, in effect, making the bombing overt. They also might have succeeded in demonstrating congressional support for what the article implied was only occasional limited penetration of Cambodian airspace. A month later, a four-sentence item appeared in the "Periscope" column of *Newsweek* (June 2, 1969), adding details of the use of back-channel reporting procedures pursuant to a presidential directive ordering strict secrecy about the operations.

Doves in the Congress did not make a major issue out of the disclosure of the bombing. Tactical considerations can account for the reticence of the doves, as well as the talkativeness of the hawks who had made the disclosure. Soon thereafter, President Nixon announced the first of a series of troop withdrawals which even some dovish congressmen interpreted as leading to an end to American involvement in Vietnam. Under these circumstances, a nose count on the Hill would have indicated that a vote to halt the Cambodia bombing was an "iffy" proposition. For the doves, putting the issue to a vote and losing would have been tantamount to sanctioning overt bombing there.

A second tactical consideration in the doves' failure to raise an outcry was that in relying on information communicated informally, they ran the risk of political embarrassment; if either their information was less

---

[33] Persistent questioning to follow up a reported sighting of bomb craters in Cambodia may have induced someone familiar with the bombing to talk. U. S. Congress, *Bombing in Cambodia*, pp. 380, 383, 402. Previous *New York Times* articles had mentioned reported bombings in Cambodia as early as 1968, January 13, 1968, p. 10; November 11, 1968, p. 19; November 13, 1968, p. 14; and April 28, 1969, p. 6, which included the "protective reaction" rationale. Just after the covert bombing began, the *Times* ran a story stating that General Abrams had requested permission to conduct B-52 strikes in Svay Rieng province, but that the State Department opposed the request. Defense Secretary Laird's change of line in testimony to Congress the previous week also was cited: "Laotian and Cambodian sanctuaries are of great importance in the enemy's ability to withstand our overwhelming superiority in mobility and firepower." *The New York Times*, March 26, 1969, p. 5.

than the whole story or the circumstances of its disclosure involved an administrative transgression, they would have been vulnerable to the charge of "playing politics with the nation's security," even if none dared call it treason. Apart from the grave constitutional questions raised by the administration's deliberate effort to withhold information from congressmen, though, even when the walls of secrecy had been breached, channels through which members learned of the bombing affected their ability to exploit that information.

Three years passed before the Cambodia bombing became the subject of a major congressional inquiry. In the course of hearings by a subcommittee of the Senate Armed Services Committee, disclosures by career subordinates in the Air Force would greatly enhance the doves' ability to make an issue of the bombing.

Informal Commmunication and Bureaucratic Tactics

Tactical considerations affecting the use to which informal communications can be put are not confined to the Cambodia bombing alone, but apply in general to instances of informal communication. On many occasions in which information is not officially transmitted to the Congress as an institution, individual congressmen do obtain information informally—through informal briefings, bootlegging, and leaks. Having to rely on information acquired through these channels, however, puts congressional opponents of administration policy at a bargaining disadvantage. Seeking to contest the merits of the government's actions, opponents may find the public debate recast in terms of the *information about* those actions rather than the actions themselves; that is, the issues become: Was that information lawfully obtained? How harmful to national security is its disclosure? What are its accuracy and validity? Anticipating this turn of events, an opponent may be reluctant to proceed on the basis of the information in hand, lest he be undercut or embarrassed by it. This seems to have been the case with Senator Fulbright and the Pentagon papers.

Moreover, the bureaucratic strategy of exploiting security procedures to maximize organizational autonomy from political control has its congressional complement in what might be called the "Calhoun strategy." Calhoun refers not to John C. Calhoun, but to the hard-running fullback starring on an otherwise hapless football team whose exploits Lyndon Johnson used to recount when he was Senate majority leader. In the course of a particularly lopsided contest, Calhoun's team was totally unable to move the ball. Unaccountably, however, Calhoun did not even carry the ball once, while runner after runner piled into the opposing line only to be stopped cold at the line of scrimmage. Exasperated, his coach began yelling from the sidelines, "Give the ball to Calhoun!" Instead, the quarterback pitched out to a halfback who lost two yards. Again the coach shouted his instructions and again they went unheeded—resulting in more lost yardage. Finally, the coach called time out and beckoned his quarterback to the bench. "Why don't you give the ball to Calhoun?" he demanded. " 'Cause Calhoun says he don't want the ball, Coach," was the reply.

Letting executive branch officials take full responsibility for a program and going along with their appropriations requests on the basis of only the most perfunctory and informal consultation, however, does not necessarily preclude subsequent investigations if the program proves unsuccessful. Underlying this strategy are three tactical considerations in obtaining information from the executive branch: (1) the information that congressmen care about most is information which may prove politically useful in making issues; (2) timing is often the most critical consideration in deciding to make something an issue; and (3) the means of acquiring information is itself an issue which can favor one side or another in a policy dispute. Disclosing secret activity in its early stages may leave a congressman vulnerable to the charge of endangering the nation's security, but once that project shows signs of failing and an investigation is launched, he can exploit the issue of excessive secrecy as well.

Informal communication not only fails to satisfy the Congress' need for information in order to perform its oversight function, but also lessens the opportunity for senior officials in the executive branch to exercise control and monitor compliance with their own objectives. The necessity of preparing periodic formal reports to Congress is an action-forcing process for those in executive authority, giving them a pretext, indeed a need, to examine what their subordinates are doing. The elimination of congressional checks on bureaucratic behavior goes hand in hand with the elimination of executive checks.

Official secrecy entailed considerable political risk for the handful of senior officials who had personally assumed full responsibility for the $2.2 billion program to develop an atomic bomb. As Army Chief of Staff George C. Marshall would acknowledge after the war, "There was a great deal of difficulty persuading them on the Hill to put up all this money on a gamble, and one that they had to take our word for."[34] In the fall of 1944, Undersecretary of War Robert P. Patterson, who was personally authorizing the expenditure of funds appropriated to the Manhattan Project, became concerned as total spending on it neared the $2 billion mark. Over General Groves' objections, he insisted that his special as-

---

[34] General George C. Marshall, conversation with David Lilienthal, June 12, 1947, quoted in *The Journals of David Lilienthal*, II: *The Atomic Energy Years* (New York, 1964), p. 200.

sistant, a New York consulting engineer Michael J. Madigan, conduct a personal investigation of the construction under way. After several weeks of touring, Madigan returned to Washington to report to Patterson. In a rush to get to the White House for a cabinet meeting, Patterson asked him to come back later. As Patterson related the incident to Groves,

> Madigan replied, "It won't take me five minutes—I can give you my report in thirty seconds." Intrigued by this, Mr. Patterson told him to go ahead, and Madigan reported, "If the project succeeds, there won't be any investigation. If it doesn't, they won't investigate anything else."[35]

Groves, too, appreciated the political predicament that he was in as a result of official secrecy. "If this weapon fizzles," he told his staff on Christmas Eve 1944, "each of you can look forward to a lifetime of testifying before congressional investigating committees."[36] The need to have something to show Congress was not without consequence for future decisions: it predisposed those in charge of the Manhattan Project to press for use of the weapon in combat.

Official secrecy enveloping the Manhattan Project had a second consequence unintended by many of those who had instigated it: it kept not only the Congress but also the secretary of war and the president in the dark about many details critical to the decision on the bomb, among them, the feasibility of dropping it on targets other than large cities. The compartmentalization imposed by security procedures narrowed the circles of advisers within the executive branch. It did not permit those working on various aspects of the Manhattan Project to raise alternatives, or even to compare notes on how the bomb might be used. Paradoxically, then, officially secrecy did not eliminate informal communication about the bomb, but it did limit formal discussion in official forums where knowledgeable participants might raise and evaluate options for its use.

The reporting procedures devised to keep the bombing in Cambodia a secret from the Congress produced unforeseen administrative problems of a related sort. First, the disclosure of the bombing in the *Times* prompted an immediate investigation, which failed to identify the source of Beecher's story. Within three days, it also served as pretext for wiretapping the first of at least thirteen officials engaged in national security affairs, including Defense Secretary Laird's principal military aide, as well as Beecher and three other newsmen. Finally, it contributed to a concern over leaks and the inability of government security agencies to

---

[35] Quoted in Groves, *Now It Can Be Told*, p. 360. See also Laurence, *Dawn Over Zero*, pp. 92–93; William L. Laurence, *Men and Atoms* (New York, 1959), p. 108.

[36] Groves quoted in Fletcher Knebel and Charles W. Bailey, *No High Ground* (New York, 1960), p. 75.

seal them which ultimately prompted the establishment of a highly irregular unit in the White House to conduct its own investigations of leaks—the so-called plumbers.[37] Thus, a preoccupation with keeping secret operations secret led to new operations of dubious legality, which then had to be kept secret too.

The reporting procedures established to maintain secrecy for the bombing of Cambodia and Northern Laos also would have enabled the president, had he wanted to postpone the Paris peace talks, to authorize renewed bombing of North Vietnam in secret under the guise of conducting "protective reaction" strikes. Indeed, he could have done so by going outside the chain of command and circumventing Defense Secretary Laird by hand-carrying orders directly to the Air Force commander in the field.[38] With only minor modifications, however, the same reporting procedures could also permit the Air Force commander in Vietnam to order preplanned "protective reaction" strikes against North Vietnam on his own authority—which is precisely the step General John D. Lavelle took. Lavelle's deputy was struck by the "supreme confidence" of his boss in conducting the raids outside the rules of engagement in force at the time.[39] Lavelle's confidence was not rooted in the certainty that his commander would back him up: when he sought such assurances from

[37] Henry Kissinger, in a sworn affidavit, has since said of the leak to Beecher, "While there were obvious adverse diplomatic repercussions from this disclosure, its greatest effect was to raise a serious question in the mind of the President as to the ability of the Government to maintain the necessary security required for this and other sensitive military and diplomatic operations, and whether in the future he could make critical foreign policy decisions on the basis of full and frank discussions." Affidavit of Secretary of State Kissinger in a civil suit, Ellsberg, et al. v. Mitchell, reprinted in The New York Times, July 19, 1974, p. 15. See also, statement of President Nixon, reprinted in The New York Times, May 23, 1973, p. 28.

[38] This contention was part of John Ehrlichman's defense of his coverup of the plumbers' activities on national security grounds. Both General Wheeler and General Moorer denied ever having transmitted an order to the field without first getting the approval of the secretary of defense. U. S. Congress, Bombing in Cambodia, pp. 133, 381; The New York Times, June 22, 1974, p. 13; The Washington Post, June 22, 1974, p. 1; U. S. Senate, Committee on Armed Services, Hearing: Nomination of Admiral Thomas H. Moorer, USN, for Reappointment as Chairman, Joint Chiefs of Staff, 92d Cong., 2d Sess., pp. 6–7. See also, Hugh Sidey, "Nixon in a Crisis of Leadership," Life, LXVIII (May 15, 1970), 28.

[39] When he asked Lavelle about the raids, General Alton D. Slay testified, "His answer was supreme confidence that—my impression was that General Lavelle knew exactly what he was doing and also my impression was 'That is my worry; you run your end and I will run mine' and it never—as a matter of fact, Charlie Gabriel and I discussed this very point and we both agreed that well, he is a big boy and that is the way he wants to run it; that is his show. . . . "U. S. Senate, Committee on Armed Services, Hearings: Nomination of John D. Lavelle, General Creighton W. Abrams, and Admiral John S. McCain, 92d Cong., 2d Sess., p. 301. Also pp. 289–291.

General Abrams, he did not get them.[40] It stemmed, instead, from his assumption that no one above him would be willing to make an issue over his stretching the rules of engagement at the risk of revealing the extensive secret bombing that had been authorized.

Subsequent events suggest that his confidence was not misplaced. In December 1971, the plumbers' investigation of the India-Pakistan leaks to Jack Anderson uncovered a bootlegging operation in the White House. A liaison office between the joint chiefs of staff and the National Security Council staff was accused of passing the joint chiefs "eyes only" memoranda from Henry Kissinger to the president. The discovery infuriated Kissinger.[41] Yet shortly thereafter, his fury seems to have abated: Admiral Moorer was nominated for another term as chairman of the joint chiefs and the two military aides involved, Rear Admiral Robert O. Welander and a yeoman, were quietly transferred out of the White House. No formal charges were ever brought, on advice of Defense Department counsel, J. Fred Buzhardt, Jr., who argued that the evidence was circumstantial, the law was not very favorable, and because of the line of defense opposing counsel was likely to take, disclosure of additional secrets was probable—presumably, the existence of the plumbers and the Cambodia bombing.[42] There is some evidence that one of Admiral Welander's functions in the liaison office was to serve as a courier to carry secret bombing orders from the White House to a nearby airbase for a flight to the theater of war and to retrieve incoming operational reports from the field for the joint chiefs of staff.[43] By conducting the Cambodia bombing in secret, the administration had made itself vulnerable to political blackmail at the hands of those who knew of the raids.

[40] Although General Lavelle tried to make the most of his conversation with General Abrams, he never asserted that he had received a go-ahead, only that Abrams had not said no. All Lavelle had was the knowledge that Secretary Laird had warned against seeking any expanded bombing authority at such an "inopportune time" and the encouragement from CINCPAC to use whatever authority he had to the utmost. *Nomination of John D. Lavelle*, pp. 38–39, 45–51, 103–105, 443–445, 451, 456.

[41] U. S. Senate, Committee on Armed Services, *Hearings: Transmittal of Documents from the National Security Council to the Chairman of the Joint Chiefs of Staff*, 93rd Cong., 2d Sess., part I (February 6, 1974), pp. 51, 57, 59.

[42] Ibid., part III (March 7, 1974), pp. 5–7, 47. Also, *The Washington Post*, January 13, 1974, p. 1.

[43] Admiral Welander testified that "my staff communications to and from Dr. Kissinger and General Haig which dealt with military operational matters were allowed to be transmitted by hand delivery outside the usual staff correspondence processing channel through the Secretariat." *Transmittal of Documents from the National Security Council to the Chairman of the Joint Chiefs of Staff*, p. 119. In the course of his second interrogation by investigators, Welander balked on grounds of national security: "This time the questioning had an entirely different tone and thrust and began to probe my exact duties and relationship with Dr. Kissinger and Admiral

CONCLUSION

Secrecy thus has a constant companion: *informal communication*. Sometimes as a matter of high-level choice, other times as a political maneuver by bureaucratic subordinates, information is passed along to selected congressmen about governmental activity that was not disclosed formally to the Congress as a body. If informal communication is a constant in the policy process, its importance is magnified in times of deliberate official secrecy.

By adopting a strategy of official secrecy coupled with informal communication with the Congress, an administration can put its opponents on Capitol Hill at a temporary disadvantage. Unable to obtain an authoritative picture of what is going on, reluctant to rely on bits of information informally transmitted, they may choose to remain silent. But policies and programs require coalitions both in and outside of the executive branch for continued political support. At the first whiff of trouble, opposition within the government, often latent, is frequently quite ready to coalesce and locate legislative allies. Then, the flow of informal communication may be sufficient to nourish open opposition in the Congress, as well as arm them with the issue of executive coverup.

Official secrecy and informal communication may conspire to render opposition temporarily ineffective. Deliberately contrived to carry out an action in violation of congressional strictures, official secrecy and informal communication may provide a legislative-executive confrontation tantamount to a constitutional crisis. Even such grave consequences as these, however, may not be as serious as the consequences of official secrecy and informal communication for control of the bureaucracy. Congress may not be able to rely on informal communication to do its job

---

Moorer and various operational matters. I suggested to the investigators that this didn't seem germane to the subject of their inquiry and, furthermore, got into security classification areas for which they were not demonstrably cleared." Ibid., p. 125; also pp. 144, 183, 198–199. The next interrogation session took place in John Ehrlichman's office, in the presence of David Young of the plumbers and another White House aide. Welander testified: "After a few preliminary questions about my background, Ehrlichman presented me a prepared statement on White House stationery for my signature. This statement would have had me admit to the wildest possible, totally false charges of 'political spying' on the White House." Welander reacted "rather strongly" and refused to sign but was puzzled about Ehrlichman's motive afterward. He told the committee, "But, I would say it would be a perfect way to set me up for something of this sort, to implicate me in something where I could not feel free to go ahead and take any action on anything else." Ibid., pp. 125, 151; also, p. 160. Yet, after the closing of the liaison office and his transfer, he received a telephone call from Kissinger, who "said words to the effect, 'Welander, it has been a hell of a mess. You have acted honorably in all of this.' I thanked him and I said, 'Well, Happy New Year.' " Ibid., p. 158.

of oversight, but neither can an administration. The formal provision of information to Congress often enables senior officials to monitor and control the activity of their own bureaucratic subordinates. Even with informal communication, the suppression of information may lead to the loss of political control over the bureaucracy—whether legislative or administrative. Secrecy seems to beget more secrecy, expanding both the security apparatus and its domain. Less information may be circulated within the bureaucracy, lest it seep out to the Congress. The less information in circulation, the easier it is for those who possess it—often subordinates—to manipulate those who do not. As fewer officials are made privy to information, the circle of those who influence decisions narrows, often biasing outcomes in the policy process.

Part IV.

The Courts

13 The Burger Court in Historical Perspective

ALPHEUS THOMAS MASON

Every court is the product of its time and reflects the predilections of fallible men in black robes. Whatever the orientation of conflicting values, judicial activism involves a paradox at the heart of constitutional orthodoxy: the Supreme Court considered as the mouthpiece of self-interpreting, self-enforcing law.[1] While wearing the magical habiliments of the law, Supreme Court justices take sides on controversial issues. In a moment of judicial candor, Justice Robert H. Jackson remarked: "We are not final because we are infallible, but we are infallible only because we are final."[2]

Even those inclined to think of the Supreme Court as "brushed with divinity" do not accept constitutional theology at face value. Few Americans were shocked in 1968 when the GOP presidential candidate made the Court a major political issue, and bluntly announced his determination to restore "law and order" by changing

[1] Alpheus Thomas Mason, "Myth and Reality in Supreme Court Decisions," *Virginia Law Review* 48 (1962), 1385 and "The Supreme Court: Temple and Forum," *Yale Review* 49 (Summer 1959), 524.

[2] *Brown* v. *Allen*, 344 U.S. 443 (1953) at 540 (Jackson concurring).

ALPHEUS THOMAS MASON is McCormick Professor of Jurisprudence Emeritus at Princeton University. His major books include *Harlan Fiske Stone: Pillar of the Law; The Supreme Court from Taft to Warren; The Supreme Court: Palladium of Freedom; William Howard Taft: Chief Justice;* and *Free Government in the Making.*

judicial personnel. Presumably the president, given an opportunity, can mold the Constitution simply by a discriminating choice of Supreme Court nominees.

Richard M. Nixon is not the first president to recognize the judicial function as unavoidably political.[3] When Chief Justice Marshall died in 1835 after thirty-four years on the Supreme Court bench, soothsayers and politicians, mindful that President Jackson would choose Marshall's successor, predicted the deluge. President Taft rated his six Supreme Court appointments during four years in the White House a signal achievement, glorying in the fact that President Wilson made only three appointments in twice that time. In the 1920 presidential campaign, former President Taft spoke out emphatically. Not unlike Nixon in 1968, Taft underscored the major domestic issue—appointment of judges who would maintain the Supreme Court as the "bulwark" of property.[4] Thanks to Warren G. Harding's landslide election, Taft himself as chief justice translated political conviction into Supreme Court decisions.[5]

President Eisenhower's most noteworthy act during eight years in the White House was the appointment of Earl Warren as chief justice of the United States. Under Warren's leadership the Court spearheaded a revolution. Looking back dourly on the unforeseen consequences of his choice, Ike called it "the biggest damn fool mistake I ever made in my life."

It fell to Richard M. Nixon, vice president during Eisenhower's administration, to attempt the undoing of the Warren Court's revolutionary decisions. It was, and is a large order. Can President Nixon fulfill this commitment? The answer is uncertain. Significant clues may be found in the context of history.

[3] More, however, than any president in this century, perhaps more than any in our history, President Nixon's nominations have been made with an eye to politics and ideology rather than to merit or professional distinction. Even the conservative American Bar Association deplored his narrow, political approach to Supreme Court nominations. *American Bar Association Journal* 57 (December 1971), 1209-10.

Nixon was especially critical of the Warren Court's decision expanding the rights of criminal suspects. He supported Title II of the Omnibus Crime Control Act, designed to nullify the Warren Court's decisions in this area. See Louis M. Kohlmeier, *God Save This Honorable Court* (New York, 1972), 250.

[4] William Howard Taft, "Mr. Wilson and the Campaign," *Yale Review* 10 (October 1920), 19-20.

[5] Mason, *William Howard Taft: Chief Justice* (New York, 1964), chap. 10.

The Judicial World of Penumbra

Descriptive labels enter the stream of judicial politics long after the values and techniques they reveal are commonplace in practice. There are numerous examples: "judicial activism," "judicial self-restraint," "preferred freedoms," "separate but equal," "penumbra." All these catch phrases are well known except "penumbra." In 1965, Connecticut's anticontraceptive statute, though violative of no express provisions of the Constitution, foundered on the penumbral right of privacy. "Specific guarantees of the Bill of Rights," Justice Douglas reasoned for a majority of seven (mentioning Amendments 1, 3, 4, 5, 6, 8, 9, and 14), "have penumbras, formed by emanations from those guarantees that give them life and substance."

"We do not sit," the justice observed, "as a super-legislature to determine the wisdom, need, and propriety of laws that touch economic problems, business affairs or social conditions. This law, however, operates directly on an intimate relation of husband and wife and their physician's role in one aspect of that relation."[6]

The reasonable inference is that, in Justice Douglas' mind, the Court *does sit* as a superlegislature in safeguarding the penumbral right of privacy. The distinction thus drawn between the Court's responsibility toward economic and personal rights, if legitimate, could be important, even crucial, as we shall see.

Dissenting justices, Black and Stewart, exploded. Black accused the majority of amending the Constitution under the guise of interpreting it, thus converting the Court into "a day-to-day Constitutional Convention." "I like my privacy as well as the next one," the eighty-year-old justice commented feelingly, "but I am, nevertheless, compelled to admit that government has a right to invade it unless prohibited by some specific constitutional provision."[7]

Nor, according to Black, is the Court's veto power enlarged, as Justice Douglas implied, when confronted with government regulation of personal rather than economic rights. Sounding the note of "strict construction," Justice Black declared war on penumbral embellishments.

Webster defines *penumbra* as a "marginal region or borderland of partial obscurity or some blighting influence as of doubt or cha-

[6] *Griswold v. Connecticut*, 381 U.S. 479 (1964) at 482.
[7] *Ibid.*, at 570 (Black dissenting).

grin." Small wonder Justice Black was outraged. Yet penumbra was not unprecedented. It is, in fact, among the most conspicuous weapons in the arsenal of constitutional interpretation.[8] There are numerous illustrations.

In 1895, Chief Justice Fuller fashioned the "direct and indirect effects" penumbra to undermine the national commerce power, permitting a 95 percent monopoly in the manufacture of sugar to do what the Court denied to Congress—the power to regulate commerce.[9] To dilute the state police power, defined as the authority "to govern men and things," the Court invoked a penumbral right not mentioned in the Constitution—"liberty of contract."[10] Scores of state statutes, including hours-of-labor and minimum-wage laws for women, fell under this nebulous label. The phony "separate but equal" formula kept public schools racially segregated for half a century.[11] A newcomer in the ever-lengthening list of penumbra is "executive privilege."[12] For none does Webster's foggy definition seem more apt.

Less esoteric are the terms "preferred freedoms" and "judicial activism." Both have recently gained widespread currency. Yet both denote values and procedures going back to the beginning of judicial history. "Preferred freedoms" first appeared in a Supreme Court opinion of 1940 to describe constitutional values entitled to special judicial scrutiny.[13] Thereafter it was used to identify the priority

[8] Paul G. Kauper, "Penumbras, Peripheries, Emanations, Things Fundamental and Things Forgotten: The Griswold Case," *Michigan Law Review* 64 (1965), 235; Robert G. Dixon, Jr., "The Griswold Penumbra: Constitutional Charter for an Expanded Law of Privacy?," *Ibid.*, 197; Robert B. McKay, "The Right of Privacy: Emanations and Intimations," *Ibid.*, 259.

[9] *U.S.* v. *E. C. Knight*, 156 U.S. 1 (1895). Dissenting Justice Harlan (the elder) commented: "We have before us the case of a combination which absolutely controls, or may, at its discretion, control the price of all refined sugar in the country." Denial of Congress' power to regulate this monopoly meant that "the Constitution has failed to accomplish one primary object of the Union, which was to place commerce *among the states* under the control of the common government of all the people, and thereby relieve or protect it against burdens or restrictions imposed, by whatever authority, for the benefit of particular localities or interests," at 24, 44.

[10] *Lochner* v. *N.Y.*, 198 U.S. 45 (1905).

[11] *Plessy* v. *Ferguson*, 163 U.S. 537 (1896).

[12] See Louis Henkin, *Foreign Affairs and the Constitution* (Mineola, N. Y., 1972) and Raoul Berger, *Executive Privilege: A Constitutional Myth* (Cambridge, 1974).

[13] The first use of the term, apparently, is in Chief Justice Stone's dissent, *Jones* v. *Opelika*, 316 U.S. 484 at 600, 608.

Justice Rutledge (*Thomas* v. *Collins*, 323 U.S. 516 at 529-30) speaks of "the

accorded speech, press, religion, and sometimes other Bill of Rights freedoms. Previously property rights were "preferred," but that term was not used to identify them.

Since 1938, Supreme Court justices have tended to rank traditional individual freedoms and assign a larger degree of constitutional protection to one rather than another, depending on judicial preference. This tendency has an illuminating historical background.

John Locke listed man's natural rights as life, liberty, and estates, the latter being his "general name for property." In the Declaration of Independence the Lockean trilogy became "life, liberty, and the pursuit of happiness." Did Jefferson intend his euphonious third category to convey something more than property? Commentators are still debating whether this historic sequence implies ranking according to importance. But there can be no doubt that the Revolu-

---

preferred place given in our scheme to the great, the indispensable democratic freedoms secured by the First Amendment. . . . That priority gives these liberties a sanctity and sanction not permitting dubious intrusions. And it is the character of the right, not of the limitation, which determines what standard governs the choice."

In *Lloyd* v. *Tanner*, 407 U.S. 551 (1972), Justice Powell refers to "a special solicitude" which the "courts properly have shown for the guarantees of the First Amendment," at 568.

For an all-out attack on "preferred freedoms," see Justice Frankfurter, concurring, *Kovacs* v. *Cooper*, 336 U.S. 77 (1948) at 90-91. Frankfurter deplored not only the concept itself but also the way in which it entered the stream of constitutional politics. "This is a phrase that has uncritically crept into some recent opinions of this Court. I deem it a mischievous phrase, if it carries the thought, which it may subtly imply, that any law touching communication is infected with presumptive invalidity. . . . I say the phrase is mischievous because it radiates a constitutional doctrine without avowing it. . . . A footnote hardly seems to be an appropriate way of announcing a new constitutional doctrine. . . ."

In 1972 (*Lynch* v. *Household Finance Corp.*, 405 U.S. 538), Justice Stewart, speaking for the Court, declared:

The dichotomy between personal liberties and property rights is a false one. Property does not have rights. People have rights. The right to enjoy property without unlawful deprivation, no less than the right to speak or right to travel, is in truth a "personal right," whether the "property" in question be a welfare check, a home, or a savings account. In fact, a fundamental interdependence exists between the personal right to liberty and the personal right in property. Neither could have meaning without the other. That rights in property are basic civil rights has long been recognized.

Cf. Madison's 1792 *Essay on Property*. Quoted in Mason and Beaney, *American Constitutional Law*, 5th ed. (Englewood Cliffs, N.J., 1972), 292.

The dichotomy Justice Stewart adumbrated is increasingly evident in the Burger Court. See *Lloyd* v. *Tanner*, 405 U.S. 551 and *Pittsburgh Press Co.* v. *Commission on Human Relations*, decided June 21, 1973. *Law Week* 41 (June 21, 1973), 5055.

tionary Fathers had an abiding concern for property. Eighteenth-century Americans warmly endorsed John Adams' deep-seated conviction that "property is as sacred as the laws of God."[14]

The Founding Fathers, recognizing life, liberty, and property as basic, rejected legislative supremacy. Our Constitution embodies a variety of institutional and written restrictions on all organs of government, capping these with the peculiarly American device—judicial review. In England the fate of property depends primarily on the legislature, in America on courts. Judicial review has been described as "an attempt by American democracy to cover its bet."[15]

During a good part of our history, especially between 1890 and 1937, courts, including the Supreme Bench, gave property priority. In 1922 a federal district court judge declared: "Of the three fundamental principles which underlie government—life, liberty, and property—the chief of these is property."[16] Supreme Court decisions in the 1920s reflect this ranking. While resisting legislative encroachments on property, the justices often upheld government restrictions on freedom of thought. Noting an apparent inconsistency, Professor Felix Frankfurter tried to explain it.

> That a majority of the Supreme Court which frequently disallowed restraint on economic power should so consistently have sanctioned restraints of the mind is perhaps only a surface paradox. There is an underlying unity between fear of ample experimentation in economics and fear of the expression of ideas.[17]

Frankfurter's comment was both perceptive and prophetic. At that very moment—1938—the Court was beginning to reassess constitutional priorities.

Another caption of recent vintage is "judicial activism." Some observers would have us believe that this phenomenon, so conspicuous in decisions of the Warren Court, has no antecedents. The fact is that all Courts have been activist in one way or another.[18]

---

[14] Quoted in Mason, *Free Government in the Making* (New York, 1965), 179.

[15] Edward S. Corwin, *Book Review, Harvard Law Review*, 56 (1942), 484, 487.

[16] Justice van Orsdel, *Children's Hospital* v. *Adkins*, 284F. (November 6, 1922). Said the humanist, Paul Elmer More: "To the civilized man *the rights of property are more important than the right to life.*" *Shelburne Essays*, 9th series (Boston, 1915), 136. More's italics.

[17] Felix Frankfurter, *Mr. Justice Holmes and the Supreme Court* (Cambridge, 1938), 62.

[18] See Mason, "Judicial Activism: Old and New," *Virginia Law Review*, 55 (1969), 385-426.

John Marshall was an activist. His Court focused on nation building. Under his leadership, national power was expanded and state power curtailed. Property and contract rights ranked high in Marshall's scale of constitutional preferences.

Roger Brooke Taney was an activist. His Court wrestled with sectionalism, asserting for the states a power-generating doctrine called "police" and fashioning at the national level the power-hampering theory of "dual federalism."[19] The Taney Court's misguided activism in *Dred Scott* helped to precipitate the Civil War.[20]

The Courts headed by Chase, Field, and Fuller, preferring an unregulated economy, read the laissez-faire dogma into the Constitution, carrying judicial activism to unprecedented heights. Judicial *review* was rapidly becoming *supremacy*.

The Taft, Hughes, and Stone Courts tried to reconcile conventional "hands off" attitudes with a popular-legislative mandate for government regulation of the economy. In the 1930s judicial activism in defense of property led to a crucial impasse between President Franklin D. Roosevelt and the Supreme Court. To break that deadlock FDR threatened Court-packing. In an incredibly short time—one year—the justices first vetoed and then legitimatized the New Deal.[21]

Revealed, almost overnight, was the capricious element in the judicial process. In 1936 judicial activism in defense of property had been the Court's posture. One year later, without a single change in judicial personnel, "self-restraint" became the order of the day.

Any inference, however, that the justices abdicated is in error. The Court had merely relinquished its self-acquired guardianship. Under the "self-restraint" banner, the justices would leave protection of property to what Madison called the primary control on government—"dependence on the people," the ballot box.[22] Judicial activism old style was dead; judicial activism new style was just around the corner.

Shortly after the judicial backtrack, Princeton's Professor Edward S. Corwin suggested what lay ahead. The Court, having abandoned

[19] Corwin, "The Passing of Dual Federalism," *Virginia Law Review* 36 (1950).

[20] 19 *Howard* (1857) 393.

[21] See Mason, *The Supreme Court from Taft to Warren* (Baton Rouge, 1968), chaps. 2 and 3.

[22] "A dependence on the people is, no doubt, the primary control on the government; but experience has taught mankind the necessity of auxiliary precautions." Edward G. Bourne, ed. *The Federalist* (New York, 1937), No. 51, 354-55. Judicial review is among the "auxiliary precautions."

its role as defender of property, would thereafter "be free, as it had not been in many years, to support the humane values of free thought, free utterance, and fair play"[23] Corwin predicted that surrender of the Court's protective role for economic privilege would allow the justices "to give voice to the conscience of the country." The Court would have plenty to do if it intervened "on behalf of the helpless and oppressed against local injustice and prejudice, rather than intervening in the assertion of out-of-date economic theories, as it has done too often since 1890."[24]

The same year that Professor Corwin made these prognostications Justice Stone, leader of the drive for judicial self-restraint before 1937, pondered with his law clerk, Louis Lusky, the Court's future course. If the judicial baby was not to be thrown out with the bath, the Court must find other interests to guard. The upshot was the three-paragraphed *Carolene Products* footnote, suggesting special scrutiny—judicial activism—in three areas: legislative encroachments on First Amendment freedoms; government action impeding or corrupting the political process; and official conduct affecting adversely the rights of racial, religious, or national minorities.[25] In other words, the limits of judicial self-restraint are reached when First Amendment freedoms are encroached upon, when rights of minorities are infringed, and when the political process itself is thwarted or corrupted.

The brand of judicial activism Professor Corwin and Justice Stone adumbrated reached a high point under the leadership of Earl Warren. Coming to grips with the hard, often unpleasant facts of contemporary American life, the Warren Court translated our long-time commitment to racial equality into a certain measure of social and constitutional reality. The reapportionment decisions brought us closer to the ideal professed in 1776, just governments rest on the consent of the governed. New rules of criminal procedure were formulated, giving a ring of truth to Equality under Law. Of course, it would have been better if reform could have been accomplished by the political arm of government. But this had not been forthcoming, and the prospects were dim.

Opposing the new activism were powerful and persistent dis-

---

[23] "Statesmanship on the Supreme Court," *American Scholar* (1940), 159, 163.
[24] Corwin, *Constitutional Revolution, Ltd.* (Claremont, Ca., 1941), 110-12.
[25] *United States* v. *Carolene Products Co.* 304 U.S. 144 at 152-53, n.4 (1938). For the story of the footnote's evolution, see Mason, *Harlan Fiske Stone: Pillar of the Law* (New York, 1956), 512-17.

senters, notably Justices Frankfurter, Harlan, and, finally, erstwhile libertarian Black. All deplored it as vehemently as did critics of the old activism prior to 1937. Rejecting any particular ranking of constitutional verities, calling for across-the-board judicial self-restraint, they repeatedly warned that "the Constitution does not confer on courts blanket authority to step into every situation where the political branch may be thought to have fallen short."[26] The Court, they argued, was not only ill-equipped but also unauthorized to do so. The dissenters' primary target was Chief Justice Warren himself, who held with Jefferson that the Bill of Rights is "the heart of any constitution."[27]

Once again the judicial fat was in the fire. Once again the Court became a major political issue, in Congress and in the hustings. Just as judicial activism of the 1930s in defense of property and contract rights (then preferred freedoms) became an explosive political issue in 1937, so the Warren Court's activism in support of civil rights (the new preferred freedoms) heated up the 1968 presidential campaign.

Judicial Activism in the Burger Court

The 1968 GOP candidate committed himself to the appointment of "strict constructionists"—presumably those who would call a halt to the Warren Court's activism. During his first term, President Nixon made four appointments, including a chief justice. Yet, even with a nucleus of support carried over from the Warren Court, his pledge remains unfulfilled.

The three major pillars in the Warren Court's constitutional edifice—Race Relations, Reapportionment, and Rules of Criminal Procedure—though somewhat eroded, are still virtually intact. Within a few weeks after taking the Court's center chair, Chief Justice Burger announced, in the face of Attorney General Mitchell's foot-dragging, that "continued operation of segregated schools under a standard of allowing all deliberate speed for desegregation is no longer permissible."[28] A break in the solid judicial dike erected in 1954 against the "separate but equal" formula occurred in 1972,

[26] Dissenting in *Baker* v. *Carr*, 369 U.S. 186 (1962) and *Reynolds* v. *Sims,* 377 U.S. 533 (1964). Addresses of John M. Harlan at the American Bar Center, August 13, 1963, and at the Dedication of the Bill of Rights Room, New York City, August 9, 1964.
[27] Henry M. Christman, *The Public Papers of Earl Warren* (New York, 1959), 7.
[28] *Alexander* v. *Holmes County Bd. of Ed.,* 396 U.S. 19 (1969).

when four Nixon appointees, voting as a bloc and speaking through the chief justice, declared: "The goal is to dismantle dual school systems rather than to reproduce in each classroom a microscopic reflection of the racial proportions of a given geographical area."[29] Underscored are the complexities and limitations of school desegregation. The historic *Brown* decision remains unaltered.

The reapportionment pillar, constructed by a six to three margin, shows least disintegration. Despite decisions endorsing deviations in congressional and state redistricting that departed from the one man, one vote formula, judicially mandated reapportionment is still the "success story of the Warren Court."[30]

New rules of criminal procedure, the Warren Court's most audacious and controversial innovation, have been whittled down but not eliminated. The record is mixed; the rules have been both qualified and extended. Inroads on the rights of the accused occurred in an area where tradition had become almost sacrosanct—trial by a jury of twelve.[31] Arguing that the unanimous vote of twelve jurors was a historical accident, the Nixon-appointed justices, joined by swing-man Byron White, struck a blow for "law and order," upholding a nine-to-three jury conviction in Louisiana and a ten-to-two vote in Oregon. In a biting dissent, Justice Douglas deplored the Burger Court's activism. The majority had discarded two centuries of American history, "restructuring American law . . . for political, not for judicial action."[32] The activist shoe was now on the other foot.

The rights of defendants apparently suffered another setback on December 1, 1973, when the Court upheld two unrelated convictions, one for a traffic violation, the other possession of narcotics.[33] Rejecting the defendants' contention that their Fourth Amendment guarantees against "unreasonable searches and seizure" had been violated, the majority ruled that after a "custodial arrest," no additional justification was necessary to search for other incriminating evidence. Justices Marshall, Douglas, and Brennan dissented. Denouncing the decision as "a clear departure from our long tradition,"

---

[29] *Wright* v. *Emporia*, 407 U.S. 451 (1972) at 474.

[30] *Connor* v. *Williams*, 404 U.S. 549 (1972); *Mahan* v. *Howell*, 404 U.S. 1201 (1971); *Gaffney* v. *Cummings, Law Week*, 41 (June 18, 1973), 4891; *White* v. *Weiser*, 41 (June 18, 1973), 4900. See Robert B. McKay, "Reapportionment: Success Story of the Warren Court," *Michigan Law Review*, 67 (1968), 223.

[31] *Johnson* v. *La.*, 406 U.S. 356 (1972): *Apodaca* v. *Oregon*, 406 U.S. 404 (1972).

[32] *Johnson* v. *La.*, at 394.

[33] *U.S.* v. *Robinson*, 14, *Criminal Law Reporter*, 3043.

they were concerned lest "a police officer, lacking probable cause to obtain a search warrant, will use a traffic arrest as a pretext to conduct a search." This decision, along with others of a similar nature, indicate a cutting back rather than full retreat from the Warren Court's advances.

On occasion, the Burger Court has extended the rights of defendants. In the 1963 landmark Gideon case, the Warren Court had ruled that an indigent convicted of a felony must be furnished counsel.[34] The Burger Court went further, holding that no person can be jailed for a petty offense unless he has been furnished free counsel or had waived that right. Chief Justice Burger, exponent of efficiency equaled only by William Howard Taft, was relaxed in the face of a more crowded docket certain to result from the ruling. Calmly reassuring his colleagues and the bar, he declared: "The dynamics of the profession have a way of rising to the burdens placed on it."[35]

President Nixon's "law and order" pledge was dealt its most serious blow in the Court's ruling against capital punishment as "cruel and unusual," violative of the Eighth Amendment.[36] The Nixon appointees, voting solidly, could not win the support of Justices Stewart and White. Stewart, stressing the moral and capricious aspects of the death penalty, compared it to being struck by lightning. White's major objection was that capital punishment failed to accomplish its objective—deterrence. For the Nixon-appointed justices the outlawing of capital punishment was judicial activism at its worst. Once again, as before 1937 and in the heyday of Earl Warren, the justices apparently entered an area reserved for legislators.

It is as risky to apply labels—"preferred freedoms," "judicial self-restraint," "judicial activism," or even "strict construction"—to Nixon appointees as to the justices they replaced.[37]

A striking illustration occurred January 22, 1973, when the Court, voting seven to two, upset abortion laws in Texas, and many other states.[38] Ironically, to buttress its ruling the majority, speaking

[34] 372 U.S. 335 (1963).

[35] *Argersinger* v. *Hamlin*, 407 U.S. 25 (1972) at 44.

[36] *Furman* v. *Georgia*, 408 U.S 238 (1972).

[37] Justice Frankfurter, admired by President Nixon as a "strict constructionist," observed: "The words of the Constitution are so unrestricted in their intrinsic meaning, or by their history or by tradition or by prior decisions that they leave the individual justice free, if indeed they do not compel him, to gather meaning not from reading the Constitution but from reading life." Cited by James Simon, *In His Own Image: The Supreme Court in Richard Nixon's America* (New York, 1973), 6.

[38] *Doe* v. *Wade*, *Law Week*, 41 (January 22, 1973), 4233.

through Justice Blackmun, drew on Justice Douglas' penumbral weapon—"right of privacy." In 1973, three Nixon appointees (Burger, Blackmun, and Powell), all presumably "strict constructionists," opposed to judicial activism, sanctioned a constitutional embellishment too extreme even for Justice Black!

Dissenting Justice White called the abortion decision "an exercise of raw judicial power." Refusing to fly in the face of President Nixon's avowed opposition to abortion, Justice Rehnquist charged that the Court's usurpation of the legislative function rivaled Justice Peckham's discredited activism in the Lochner case of 1905, which featured the "liberty of contract" penumbra. Reputedly the most conservative member of the present Court, Rehnquist placed himself in the enviable self-restraint tradition of Mr. Justice Holmes.

The Supreme Court: Bastion of Freedom

The line-up in the abortion and other cases indicates continuing cleavage among the justices concerning the Court's role. Raised are questions of enduring significance:

Is it reasonable to censure judicial activism on behalf of economic interests and applaud more searching judicial scrutiny of encroachments on First Amendment and other Bill of Rights freedoms?

Does our political and constitutional heritage accord weightier sanction to judicial activism on behalf of human rights than to its activism in halting legislative effort to make government an instrument of economic and social reform?

Can the Supreme Court, a politically nonresponsible body, block the will of the majority in the name of minorities and still be considered a democratic institution?

These questions may be narrowed to two: If the Court has any positive or creative role, what is it? What interests, rights, or values should the Court serve?

Supreme Court history provides conflicting answers to these queries. One is that social and economic change should be left to the political process rather than to the judiciary. The contrasting view is that the Court should bring about needed adaptations which, for one reason or another, have failed in their accomplishment by other means.[39]

The most persistent and outspoken exponent of judicial hands-off

[39] For Justice's Harlan's views, see *U.S. News and World Report*, December 18. 1967, 36.

in the Warren Court was Justice Harlan. Often joined by Frankfurter, Harlan made no bones, in judicial opinions and in off-Court pronouncements, concerning his endorsement of judicial self-restraint. Justice Abe Fortas endorsed Harlan's position. During the Senate Judiciary Committee Hearings on Fortas' nomination to the chief justiceship, a committee member asked: "To what extent and under what circumstances do you believe that the Court should attempt to bring about social, economic or political changes?" Justice Fortas, an activist second only to Chief Justice Warren and Justice Douglas, gave an answer as surprising as it was self-serving. "Zero. Absolutely zero."[40]

Other justices, including some of the most eminent, insist that the Court has a positive function. The Court's "chief worth," Justice Cardozo declared, is in making "vocal and audible the ideals that might otherwise be silenced."[41] "Our judges are not monks or scientists," Chief Justice Warren observed, "but participants in the living stream of our national life."[42] At the Conference on World Peace Through Law in 1973, Justice Thurgood Marshall argued that "Courts have a special responsibility to preserve and enforce the moral pillars on which society is built."[43]

Activism, not restraint, has been the judicial practice. In 1896, seven Supreme Court justices put "separate but equal" into the Constitution. In 1954, nine justices took it out. Each of these decisions illustrates judicial activism—one restricting human freedom, the other enlarging it. "Judicial self-restraint" is itself sometimes a disguise for promotion or protection of a deeply cherished interest.

The Warren Court's constitutional jurisprudence, in all its aspects, stands as a testimonial to the conviction that the Supreme Court should reflect and enforce the social conscience of the nation. Change of judicial personnel may have dimmed but not erased this image. With the support of Chief Justice Burger and Justice Blackmun, in 1970 the Court attributed to the Founding Fathers the intention to make courts "palladiums of liberty," "citadels of justice."[44]

The cleavage that one witnesses in the Supreme Court throughout its history and in our own time is rooted not so much in an ideo-

---

[40] *U.S. Congress Senate Committee on the Judiciary Hearings.* Nomination of Abe Fortas, 90th Congress, 2nd session; July 16, 1968, 105-06.

[41] Benjamin N. Cardozo, *The Nature of the Judicial Process* (New Haven, 1921), 94.

[42] Quoted in Christman, p. 226.

[43] *New York Times*, September 21, 1973.

[44] *Illinois* v. *Allen*, 397 U.S. 337 (1970) at 346-47.

logical clash as in fundamental differences concerning what judges, as judges, should do. Justice Holmes waged unrelenting war on the social Darwinism that motivated the judicial activism of his day. Yet, in off-Court comments, Holmes warmly endorsed the laissez-faire dogma. For Holmes the "Constitution is made for people of fundamentally differing views, and the accident of our finding certain opinions natural and familiar or novel, and even shocking, ought not to conclude our judgment upon the question— whether statutes embodying them conflict with the Constitution of the United States."[45] Justice Holmes was the champion even of opinions "we hate." Justice Stone, a New Hampshire Republican, distrusted the New Deal and all its works, but cast his vote to sustain it. The explanation is simple: neither Holmes nor Stone could discover anything in the Constitution forbidding the contested legislation.

Black and Douglas' latter-day quarrels stemmed from divergent conceptions of the Court's role, not from ideology. The division among Nixon-appointed justices in the abortion case reflects basic differences concerning the judicial task. After donning the robes of Chief Justice, Warren Burger commented: "Six months ago if you asked what the Supreme Court should and should not do, I probably could have given you a quick answer. But now I'm not so sure. The hardest question is when the Court should step in."[46]

Logic, history, judicial precedent, eminent Supreme Court justices, and the Constitution itself indicate that the Supreme Court has a special responsibility toward human rights; toward minorities, helpless in the face of majority rule; and toward the unimpeded, uncorrupted functioning of the political process. In 1941, after the Court had reversed its position on preferred freedoms, Robert H. Jackson rationalized the Court's new posture. The justice saw "nothing covert or conflicting" in decisions upholding social legislation, while vetoing legislative repression of religious freedom, free speech, and free assembly.

> Ordinarily, legislation whose basis in economic wisdom is uncertain can be redressed by the processes of the ballot box or the pressures of opinion. But when the channels of opinion and of peaceful persuasion are corrupted or clogged, these political correctives can no longer be relied on, and the democratic system is threatened at its most vital point. In that event the Court, by intervening, restores the processes

---

[45] *Lochner v. N.Y.*, 198 U.S. 45 (1905) at 76.
[46] Quoted in Mason and Beaney, *American Constitutional Law*, XXV-VI.

of democratic government; it does not disrupt them.[47]

Two years later, as a Supreme Court justice, Jackson expressed these views as the Court's spokesman: "The very purpose of a Bill of Rights was to withdraw certain subjects from the vicissitudes of political controversy, to place them beyond the reach of majorities and officials and establish them as legal principles to be applied by Courts."[48]

Jackson echoed Justice Stone's *Carolene Products* footnote, the groundwork for which had been laid, as Stone acknowledged, in the opinions of certain of our most distnguished justices, including Hughes and Holmes. In 1937, Chief Justice Hughes wrote:

> Freedom of speech and of the press are fundamental rights. The rights themselves must not be curtailed. The greater the importance of safeguarding the community from incitements to the overthrow of our institutions by force and violence, the more imperative is the need to preserve inviolate the Constitutional rights of free speech, free press and free assembly in order to maintain the opportunity for free political discussion to the end that government may be responsive to the will of the people and that changes, if desired, may be obtained by peaceful means. Therein lies the security of the Republic the very foundation of constitutional government.[49]

[47] Robert H. Jackson, *The Struggle for Judicial Supremacy* (New York, 1941), 284-85.

In Jackson's final pronouncements, commentators note qualifications of his liberal stance. See Robert H. Jackson, *The American Supreme Court in the American System of Government* (New York, 1955), 57-58. Likewise, libertarian Justice Black felt obliged to respond to "current comments that I have changed my views." *A Constitutional Faith* (New York, 1968), xiv. In 1945, when Chief Justice Stone found himself pitted against judicial activists on the left, he dolefully reminisced. See Mason, *The Supreme Court from Taft to Warren* (Baton Rouge, 1968), 168.

[48] *West Virginia Bd. of Ed. v. Barnette*, 319 U.S. 624, 638 (1942). Cf. letter from Madison to E. Randolph, May 31, 1789. *The Writings of James Madison* 381 (G. Hunt, ed., 1904). Madison said: "The great object in view is to limit and qualify the powers of Government, by excepting out of the grant of power those cases in which the Government ought not to act, or to act only in a particular mode. They point these exceptions sometimes against the abuse of the Executive power, sometimes against the Legislative, and, in some cases, against the community itself; or, in other words, against the majority in favor of the minority."

[49] *D. Jonge v. Oregon*, 299 U.S. 353 at 365 (1937). In an off-court pronouncement, Hughes said: "We protect the fundamental rights of minorities, in order to save democratic government from destroying itself." *Proceedings in Commemoration of the 150th Anniversary of the First Congress*, H.R. Doc. no. 212, 76th Congress, 1st session 32 (1939).

Of Holmes, Professor Frankfurter said: "He attributed very different legal significance to those liberties of the individual which history has attested as indispensable conditions of a free society" and "was far more ready to find legislative invasion in this field than in the area of debatable economic reform."[50]

Justice Jackson penetrated and reconciled the "surface paradox" Frankfurter detected five years earlier in the Court's decisions of the 1920s—a jaundiced eye toward government regulation of property and leniency toward restrictions on First Amendment freedoms. Yet, in 1943, when Jackson took up the judicial cudgels in support of religious freedom, Frankfurter, then a Supreme Court justice, dissented. Deploring the new activism, Frankfurter protested that "judicial review is itself a limitation on popular government."[51] So it is. That is what the Founding Fathers intended it to be. Judicial review is not an alien appendage, not, as Alexander Bickel says, "a deviant institution in American democracy."[52] "Fear of popular majorities," Professor Corwin observes, "lies at the very basis of the whole system of judicial review, and indeed our entire constitutional system."[53] In a free government (and that is what we have), judicial review is an essential auxiliary, safeguarding minorities against the arbitrary will of majorities.

For Jefferson and Madison the argument of "great weight" in support of the Bill of Rights was the "legal check which it puts in the hands of the Judiciary."[54] "Independent tribunals of justice," Madison predicted, "will consider themselves in a peculiar manner the guardian of those rights . . . against every assumption of power in the Legislative or Executive."[55]

Former Justice Goldberg's Northwestern University lectures of 1971 propound this theme, and apply it to contemporary issues. Building on a long and eminent judicial tradition, he observed:

A proper view of judicial restraint applies with far greater force to laws that regulate economic and social matters than to laws that inhibit the

---

[50] Mr. Justice Holmes and the Constitution, p. 51.
[51] Justice Frankfurter in Minersville School District v. Gobitis, 310 U.S. 586 (1940) at 600.
[52] Alexander Bickel, The Least Dangerous Branch (Indianapolis, 1962), 18.
[53] Edward S. Corwin, "The Supreme Court and the Fourteenth Amendment," Michigan Law Review, 7 (1909), 643, 670.
[54] Letter from Jefferson to Madison, March 15, 1789, Julian P. Boyd, ed., The Papers of Thomas Jefferson (Princeton, 1950), 659.
[55] 1 Annals of Congress (1789-90), 1834, 432, 439.

exercise of basic personal liberty. . . .[56] "judicial restraint" has only limited applicability when the treatment of minorities, the fundamental liberties of individuals, or the health of the political process are at issue. . . .[57]

Goldberg believed that inevitable change in personnel would not end judicial activism in this area:

> Our system has now been operating under a Supreme Court for almost two centuries. Yet during all that time the Court has never overruled precedent to any significant degree in order to facilitate a significant contraction of human liberties. . . . Once fundamental rights have been recognized, there has never been a general reversal of direction by the Court, a going back against the trend of history.[58]

"There is an enormous difference," Goldberg concludes, "between not opening new frontiers of human liberty and closing ones formerly open, between declining to move forward and legitimatizing repression."[59]

Justice Goldberg was speaking in 1971. In the Pentagon Papers case, the Court, headed by Warren Burger, had outlawed prior restraint on the right to publish.[60] Though the vote was six to three (Burger, Blackmun, and Harlan dissenting) the chief justice told an interviewer that on the substantive issue the justices were "actually unanimous."[61]

In June 1972, with four Nixon appointees in their seats, the Court adjudicated a hotly contested issue at the heart of the administration's "law and order" commitment. Involved was the government's claim that electronic surveillance approved by Attorney General Mitchell, but without prior judicial endorsement, was lawful as a reasonable exercise of the president's power to protect national security. Two lower federal courts had ruled against Mitchell and the president. The case had been appealed and was then pending in the High Court.

Disinclined to speculate on the outcome, Goldberg argued that the

[56] Arthur Goldberg, *Equal Justice: The Supreme Court in the Warren Era* (Evanston, Ill., 1971), 41.

[57] *Ibid.*, 61.

[58] *Ibid.*, 90.

[59] *Ibid.*, 93. Goldberg's thesis was anticipated in Mason, *The Supreme Court from Taft to Warren* (1958), chaps. 5 and 6. See also Mason, *The Supreme Court: Palladium of Freedom* (1962), chap. 2.

[60] *New York Times* v. *United States*, 403 U.S. 713 (1971).

[61] *New York Times*, July 6, 1971, p. 15, col. 2.

Supreme Court ought to rule in accordance with its function as ultimate guardian of constitutionally protected fundamental rights. The justices, speaking through Powell, a Nixon appointee, did just that —unanimously. Framed in the idiom of basic principles, the Court's words are pointed and unqualified:

> There is, understandably, a deep-seated uneasiness and apprehension that [electronic surveillance] will be used to intrude upon cherished privacy of law-abiding citizens. . . . Those charged with investigative and prosecutorial duty should not be the sole judge of when to utilize constitutionally sensitive means in pursuing their tasks. . . . Official surveillance, whether its purpose be criminal investigation or on-going intelligence gathering, risks infringement of constitutionally protected privacy of speech. . . .
>
> History abundantly documents the tendency of government—however benevolent and benign its motives—to view with suspicion those who most fervently dispute its policies. The danger to political dissent is acute where the government attempts to act under so vague a concept as the power to protect "domestic security". . . . The price of lawful public dissent must not be a dread of subjection to an unchecked surveillance power. Nor must the fear of unauthorized official eavesdropping deter vigorous citizen dissent and discussion of Government action in private conversation. For private dissent, no less than open public discourse, is essential to our free society.[62]

Upheld was the people's right to know. Protected were rights deemed fundamental in both the Declaration of Independence and the Constitution—the right to consent, to criticize and oppose, the right to persuade, and the willingness to be persuaded. As to these values, Justice Powell expressed sentiments worthy of Jefferson, of Oliver Wendell Holmes, Louis D. Brandeis, Harlan Fiske Stone, and Earl Warren.

Without equal opportunity to utilize crucial preliminaries—press, speech, and assembly—the idea of government by consent becomes an empty declamation. In a free society, majorities are in flux. Tomorrow's majority may have a different composition as well as different goals. Judicial defense of the political rights of minorities thus becomes, not the antithesis of majority rule, but its very foundation. The current majority must leave open the political channels

[62] *United States* v. *United States District Court,* 407 U.S. 297 (1972) at 312, 314, 317, 320.

by which it can be replaced when no longer able to command popular support.

Free interchange of ideas and integrity of the political process became all the more urgent after 1937, when the Court, surrendering its self-acquired activism, restored the primary control on government— "dependence on the people." Thereafter, the justices exercised the "auxiliary" function Jefferson and Madison anticipated in urging Bill of Rights amendments. Ironically, the Supreme Court, in structure and organization the most oligarchical branch of our government, bears the responsibility for maintaining the sine qua non of free government—uninhibited discussion and dissent as valid forces in public action.

"Those who begin coercive elimination of dissent," Justice Jackson warned, "soon find themselves exterminating dissenters. Compulsory unification of opinion achieves only the unanimity of the graveyard."[63]

Identification of the Warren Court's constitutional jurisprudence with the Bill of Rights is its hallmark. President Nixon is committed to the selection of Supreme Court justices who will undercut it. Will he succeed? Thanks to a vigilant Senate, he has not yet done so. On the basis of the record to date, it is safe to predict he will not prevail even with the appointment of a Court entirely of his own making.

[63] 319 U.S. 623, at 641.

14 The Supreme Court and School Desegregation: Twenty Years Later

HARRELL R. RODGERS, JR.

Since 1954 school desegregation has been the focus of perhaps more litigation, legislation, administrative action, rhetoric, and controversy than all other areas of civil rights combined. Yet, by all signs, the struggle to desegregate schools has only begun. The struggle will continue because progress in school desegregation has been limited and because difficult questions and problems raised by school segregation in metropolitan areas and in northern school districts are beginning to be dealt with only now.

This article has a single thesis: that school desegregation can be achieved in all American communities and that successful school desegregation will ultimately have positive consequences for American society. In an effort to establish the validity of this thesis, this article will (1) review the progress of school desegregation to identify the areas in which this conflict must expand in the future if full school desegregation is to be achieved; (2) identify the factors that have limited progress to suggest the obstacles which must be overcome if progress is to continue; and (3) assess the current standards of the Supreme Court on school desegregation and speculate on the implications of these standards for achieving further desegregation in both southern and northern districts.

HARRELL R. RODGERS, JR., is professor of political science at the University of Houston. A contributor to social science and law journals, he is the author of the books *Community Conflict*; *Public Opinion and the Law*; and coauthor of *Law and Social Change: Civil Rights Laws and Their Consequences* and of *Racial Equality in America: In Search of an Unfulfilled Goal.*

PROGRESS TOWARD DESEGREGATION

The starting point for school desegregation was the 1954 decision of the Supreme Court in *Brown* v. *Board of Education*.[1] In *Brown*, the Court ruled that dual school systems were inherently unequal and therefore unconstitutional. It ordered southern school boards to dismantle the dual system "with all deliberate speed." Resistance was ubiquitous. Governors denounced the decision, state legislators subverted it, school boards ignored it, United States district courts frequently refused to enforce it, and President Eisenhower pleaded innocence and ignorance in the whole matter.[2] Understandably, therefore, progress was slow, almost unusual. Ten years after *Brown* seven of the eleven southern states had not placed even 1 percent of their black students into integrated schools.[3] As late as fifteen years after the decision, only one of every six black students in the South attended a desegregated school.[4]

The first signs of real progress in school desegregation were not evident until the 1966–1967 school year; in that year 12.5 percent of all black students in the eleven southern states attended schools with whites.[5] A breakthrough in the stalemate over school desegregation was made possible by the 1964 Civil Rights Act. Title VI of this act provided that federal funds could be terminated in school districts that refused to desegregate, and the attorney general was given authority to file suit against recalcitrant districts. The Office for Civil Rights (OCR) in the Department of Health, Education and Welfare (HEW) was given responsibility for enforcing Title VI. The OCR formulated guidelines for desegregation and began to put pressure on those districts that failed to comply. As the guidelines were made sharper and the pressure on districts became more intense, progress began in earnest. In the 1967–1968 school year 18.4 percent of all black students in the eleven southern states

[1] 347 U. S. 483 (1954). Until 1954, seventeen states and the District of Columbia required racial segregation in public schools. Four other states permitted school districts to opt for segregation without requiring it statewide.

[2] See Jack W. Peltason, *Fifty-Eight Lonely Men: Southern Federal Judges and School Desegregation* (New York, 1961); Benjamin Muse, *Ten Years of Prelude: The Story of Integration Since the Supreme Court's 1954 Decision* (New York, 1964), and Harrell R. Rodgers and Charles S. Bullock, III, *Law and Social Change: Civil Rights Laws and Their Consequences* (New York, 1972), pp. 69–111.

[3] See Thomas R. Dye (ed.), *American Public Policy Documents and Essays* (Columbus, Ohio, 1969), pp. 18–19.

[4] *Federal Enforcement of School Desegregation*, Report of the United States Commission on Civil Rights, September 11, 1969, p. 4. The U.S. Commission on Civil Rights, like the Department of Health, Education and Welfare, defines a desegregated school as a majority-white school with racial mixing.

[5] *Revolution in Civil Rights* (Washington, 1968), p. 93. These figures indicate how many black students were attending schools with whites, not how many were attending majority-white schools.

attended majority-white schools—triple the number in the 1965–1966 school year.[6] During the next two years school desegregation doubled in the southern states (see Table 1). In the 1969–1970 school year 39.4 percent of southern blacks attended majority-white schools. During the next two years progress slowed considerably, with only a 5 percent increase over the 1969–1970 school year—44.4 percent. Northern and western states lagged behind the South; in the 1971–1972 school year only 29.1 percent of black students in these areas attended majority-white schools.

Table 1 allows us to assess the progress of school desegregation. It is clear that some very substantial gains have been made since 1963, especially in the South. In 1968, 78.8 percent of southern black students attended schools that were 80 to 100 percent black. By 1972 this figure had dropped to 31.6 percent. Moreover in 1972 only 9.2 percent of southern blacks attended 100 percent minority schools, compared to 68 percent in 1968. These are important and dramatic changes, but progress may be more substantial than HEW's figures (based on the number of black students in majority-white schools) indicate. Since many school districts in the South are majority black, it would be impossible for schools in these districts to become predominantly white once they are integrated. In fact, the more desegregation occurs in these districts, the fewer black students there will be in majority-white schools. If these largely black districts were considered, progress might be shown as having increased by another 8 to 10 percent. Also if the data were divided on an urban-rural basis, we would see much greater compliance in rural areas where the logistics of desegregation are less severe.

Although much remains to be done, considerable progress in school desegregation has been achieved in the South. Nationwide, however, progress has been minimal. In both rural and urban areas of the North and West school segregation is pervasive. A 1972 study revealed the extensiveness of segregation nationwide:

> 5.9 million out of 9.3 million minority-group students, or more than 60 percent, still attend predominantly minority-group schools. At the same time 72 percent of the nation's nonminority-group students attend schools which are at least 90 percent nonminority. Four million minority-group students attend schools which are 80 percent or more minority, and 2 million are in classes which are 99–100 percent minority.[7]

Thus, substantial problems remain in the area of school desegregation, the most serious of which involve the North and West, and metropolitan areas in all regions of the United States.

[6] U. S. Department of Health, Education and Welfare, "Staff Report," January 4, 1970, p. 1 (mimeo.).

[7] *Toward Equal Educational Opportunity*, The Report of the Select Committee on Equal Education Opportunity, United States Senate (Washington, 1972), p. 11.

TABLE 1

Fall 1972 Projections of Public School Black Enrollment Compared with Final Fall 1968 and 1970 Data

Geographic Area	Black Pupils Attending Schools which Are:						Total Pupils	Black Pupils	
	0–49.9% Minority		80–100% Minority		100% Minority				
	Number	%	Number	%	Number	%		Number	%
Continental U.S.									
1968	1,467,291	23.4	4,274,461	68.0	2,493,398	39.7	43,353,568	6,282,173	14.5
1970	2,223,506	33.1	3,311,372	49.4	941,111	14.0	44,877,547	6,707,411	14.9
1972 (est.)	2,446,239	36.8	2,953,991	44.5	721,757	10.9	44,485,568	6,641,343	14.9
(1) 32 North and West									
1968	746,030	27.6	1,550,440	57.4	332,408	12.3	28,579,766	2,703,056	9.5
1970	793,979	27.5	1,665,926	57.6	343,629	11.9	29,451,976	2,899,858	9.8
1972 (est.)	822,480	29.1	1,581,871	55.9	284,273	10.0	28,970,304	2,831,080	9.8
(2) 11 South									
1968	540,692	18.4	2,317,850	78.8	2,000,486	68.0	11,043,485	2,942,960	26.6
1970	1,230,868	39.1	1,241,050	39.4	443,073	14.1	11,570,351	3,150,192	27.2
1972 (est.)	1,405,435	44.4	1,001,211	31.6	289,638	9.2	11,601,027	3,165,229	27.3
(3) 6 Border and D.C.									
1968	180,569	28.4	406,171	63.8	160,504	25.2	3,730,317	636,157	17.1
1970	198,659	29.8	404,396	60.6	154,409	23.1	3,855,221	667,362	17.3
1972 (est.)	218,323	33.8	370,909	57.5	147,844	22.9	3,914,255	645,034	16.5

(1) Alaska, Ariz., Calif., Colo., Conn., Idaho, Ill., Ind., Iowa, Kans., Maine, Mass., Mich., Minn., Mont., Nebr., Nev., N. H., N. J., N. Mex., N. Y., N. Dak., Ohio, Oreg., Pa., R. I., S. Dak., Utah, Vt., Wash., Wis., Wyo.

(2) Ala., Ark., Fla., Ga., La., Miss., N. C., S. C., Tenn., Tex., Va.

(3) Del., D. C., Ky., Md., Mo., Okla., W. Va.

PAST OBSTACLES TO DESEGREGATION

A host of factors are responsible for the slow rate of progress in school desegregation.[8] To start with, from the beginning southern officials had no intention of obeying the *Brown* ruling unless they were forced to do so. The decision played into the hands of southern officials because it was ambiguous to the point of not placing school districts under any real obligation. In arguing the *Brown* case on behalf of the NAACP, Thurgood Marshall asked the Court to establish specific deadlines for the start of school desegregation.[9] Hindsight reveals that the Supreme Court made a serious mistake in ignoring Marshall's plea.

In *Brown* the Supreme Court directed the district courts to ensure that communities in their jurisdiction make a "good faith start" toward school desegregation. However, southern judges were little inclined to take on this obligation. Most federal judges in the South were native southerners and knew only too well that they would be ostracized in their own communities if they enforced the law; and some of the judges disagreed with the decision.[10] Generally, therefore, the Supreme Court was abandoned by the lower courts, which ignored the Court's ruling.

The Supreme Court became completely isolated when the Congress and President Eisenhower refused to endorse or systematically back up the decision. As a result, school boards were under almost no real legal or political pressure to desegregate. Southern blacks were themselves reluctant to pressure local officials for compliance. In many communities if blacks pressured local officials they risked physical violence or economic coercion. When private pressure failed, most southern blacks could not afford to hire an attorney to press their case.

The passage of the 1964 Civil Rights Act signaled a number of important changes. First, the act constituted strong backing by Congress of civil rights goals. Acts had been passed in 1957 and 1960 but they were weak, largely symbolic, and focused primarily on voting rights. Although the 1964 act failed to provide strong enforcement mechanisms for some civil rights, it put Congress firmly behind the principle of school desegregation. The act also allowed a much more systematic attack on school desegregation, since a case-law strategy could be abandoned by civil rights forces for more uniform standards to be applied by HEW. With this new law, and a president, Lyndon B. Johnson, who supported the goal of school desegregation, real progress seemed imminent.

The first guidelines generated by HEW (in the school year 1965–1966) reflected a gradual approach by requiring that all school districts

---

[8] This topic is extensively dealt with in the three works cited in footnote 2.

[9] Peltason, *Fifty-Eight Lonely Men*, p. 15.

[10] Ibid., passim.

make a "good faith start" toward desegregation. This was interpreted by HEW to mean that districts were required to integrate "the first and any other lower grade, the first and last high school grades, and the lowest of junior high where schools were so organized."[11] Despite the fact that the guidelines were timidly enforced and contained obvious loopholes, some progress resulted. HEW allowed school districts to use any of three methods of compliance: (1) Execution of an Assurance of Compliance form, stipulating that race, color, and national origin were not factors in student assignment, reassignment, or transfer; and faculty and staff were not segregated; that the facilities, activities, and services of the school system were not segregated; and that no other vestige of segregation remained. (2) Submission of a final desegregation order by a federal court, together with a statement from the school district of its willingness to comply and a progress report. (3) Submission of a desegregation plan approved by the United States commissioner of education. This plan would have to specify that the school system had designed a workable desegregation program.

Many school districts submitted voluntary plans and then backed away from them at the last moment. Other districts voluntarily submitted to court orders whose requirements were considerably weaker than HEW's standards.[12] If a district was judged dilatory by HEW, the procedure for cutting off federal funds was long and torturous; it included an appeals procedure that allowed a district to continue to receive federal funds for six to twelve months after being judged noncompliant by HEW field officers. Nevertheless, federal funds to several hundred districts were cut off between 1967 and 1969.

Perhaps the greatest weakness of the HEW guidelines was that "freedom of choice" was considered an acceptable approach to school desegregation. Under freeom of choice, any black who dared was "free" to attend a white school. The U. S. Commission on Civil Rights documented many violent acts by whites reminding blacks that they had better not dare.[13] In 1968 the Supreme Court ruled that desegregation plans that relied on freedom of choice could not be used if any other method would more quickly achieve desegregation.[14] Inasmuch as freedom of choice has never been known to produce any real integration, the decision in effect overruled its use. Still, many school districts managed to avoid making progress for another year while it was being "proven" that freedom of choice did not work in their community.

[11] *Revolution in Civil Rights*, p. 92.
[12] This series of events is best covered and documented in *Federal Enforcement of School Desegregation*, passim.
[13] Ibid., pp. 21–22.
[14] 391 U. S. 430.

Just as the momentum of compliance with HEW guidelines was building up, Richard Nixon was elected president.[15] During his 1968 campaign Nixon made it "perfectly clear" that his support for civil rights was weak, and that he favored neighborhood schools and opposed busing to achieve desegregation. During the campaign Senator Strom Thurmond and other prominent segregationists stumped the South spreading the word that Nixon, if elected, would take the heat off school desegregation.

Nonetheless, retreat did not immediately follow the election. Nixon's secretary of HEW, Robert Finch, and the director of the Office for Civil Rights, Leon Panetta (who was appointed by Finch), were liberal Republicans who felt obligated to enforce the law. Although southerners felt betrayed by Nixon's campaign pledges to take the pressure off school desegregation, Finch and Panetta were able to pursue desegregation efforts for some fourteen months. During this period, however, southern politicians and Congressmen put considerable pressure on the White House for relief. This pressure was transmitted constantly from the White House to the OCR; as a result, the earnest but beleaguered Panetta lost a number of battles to enforce the law.[16] During this period the White House persisted in making statements about deemphasizing school desegregation, while Panetta continued to show by actions and words that he had no intention of doing so. The result was considerable confusion over the direction the administration would take; many school districts abandoned desegregation plans in the anticipation that a federal retreat was just around the corner.

After fourteen months, Panetta was fired by Nixon, Finch later resigned, and the retreat on civil rights began.[17] After the departure of Panetta, the administration would probably have brought progress to a halt had the Supreme Court not overruled some compromise maneuvers by HEW (see the section "Current Supreme Court Standards"), thus holding HEW to the obligations of the law. Still, under the newest secretary of HEW (Casper Weinberg) the administration began a "spirit of cooperation rather than coercion" in enforcing civil rights laws. The result was a mere 5 percent increase in desegregation between 1970–1972 in the eleven southern states, a 4 percent increase in the six southern border states and the District of Columbia, and a mere 1.6 percent increase in the thirty-two northern and western states. Obviously in the area of school desegregation, cooperation is a poor substitute for coercion.

What the past tells us about accomplishing school desegregation is

[15] On this section see Rodgers and Bullock, *Law and Social Change*, pp. 88–97.
[16] See Leon Panetta and Peter Gall, *Bring Us Together: The Nixon Team and the Civil Rights Retreat* (New York, 1971), passim.
[17] Ibid., pp. 350–367.

fairly obvious: (1) School officials, especially but not exclusively in the South, will normally obey civil rights laws only under coercion. (2) Legal standards for school desegregation must be unambiguous and forceful. (3) Greater progress is achieved if the three branches of the federal government are reasonably unified and uncompromising in their approach to desegregation. (4) The burden for achieving school desegregation must rest with school officials, not with black citizens and their children. (5) The executive branch may have to be prodded and carefully supervised by the federal courts if significant progress is to be made.

CURRENT SUPREME COURT STANDARDS: IMPLICATIONS FOR COMPLETING DESEGREGATION IN THE SOUTH

As noted, the *Brown* case was the catalyst for little change in school desegregation for some ten years. By 1964 the Supreme Court was beginning to show displeasure with the slow progress of desegregation. In *Griffin* v. *County Board*[18] the Supreme Court noted the long history of dilatory and unlawful behavior of southern officials in avoiding their obligation under *Brown* and concluded that the standard of "all deliberate speed" never contemplated an infinite number of delaying tactics to defeat desegregation.[19]

Progress continued to lag, however, and in 1968 the Supreme Court became specific about the obligations of southern school districts. In *Green* v. *New Kent County School Board* the Supreme Court ruled against the use of nonproductive "freedom of choice" plans; school boards were obligated to "come forward with a plan that promises realistically to work . . . now . . . until it is clear that state imposed segregation has been completely removed."[20] School boards were charged with the responsibility of taking whatever steps were necessary "to convert to a unitary school system in which racial discrimination would be eliminated root and branch."[21]

The *Green* decision was extremely important because it set a much more explicit standard and made it clear that school boards were responsible for undoing the consequences of their past actions. Equally important was the case of *Alexander* v. *Holmes County Board of Education* in 1969 which removed any doubt about the time-frame within which school boards were required to make significant progress. The suit challenged

[18] 377 U. S. 218.
[19] *Watson* v. *City of Memphis*, 373 U. S. 526 (1964).
[20] 391 U. S. 430.
[21] 391 U. S. 438.

an attempt by HEW to grant thirty-three dilatory school districts in Mississippi a one-year delay in implementing desegregation plans. Noting that fifteen years had already passed since *Brown* and the long-standing recalcitrance of the districts, the Court disapproved the delay and declared that school districts were "to terminate dual school systems at once."[22] The *Green* and *Alexander* decisions constituted enough combined force to produce considerable desegregation in many communities throughout the South by a variety of means. The controversy stimulated by many district court orders based on these decisions led to one of the most important of recent Supreme Court cases on school desegregation.

The Swann Decision

In *Swann* v. *Charlotte-Mecklenburg Board of Education et al.* (1971),[23] a North Carolina case, the Supreme Court dealt forcefully with a number of problems left unresolved in earlier decisions. Basically, the case raised questions about the extent of a school board's obligation to achieve desegregation and the extent of a district court's authority to produce desegregation if the school board defaulted on its obligation. The Court's answers were direct. First, school boards were obligated to achieve *immediate* desegregation; plans for gradual progress were no longer adequate. Second, if the local board defaulted on its obligation to achieve desegregation, the district courts had broad discretion to develop desegregation plans. In *Swann* the school board had devised a plan that would have substantially desegregated the junior and senior high schools but would have left the elementary schools segregated. A district judge had ordered the school board either to devise a plan that would desegregate all the schools or to accept a comprehensive desegregation plan already formulated by a court-appointed expert. The court's plan included extensive busing, rezoning, pairing,[24] clustering,[25] closing of schools, and specific ratios for the assignment of students, faculty, and staff.

---

[22] 396 U. S. 19 (1969).

[23] 402 U. S. 1 (1971).

[24] Pairing involves combining the facilities of two schools. For example, if a community has separate elementary schools for black and white students, one school can be converted to handle all students attending grades K–3 and the other can handle all students in grades 4–6. Because desegregation techniques have been discussed so frequently in other works they will not be surveyed here. For an excellent discussion see Gordon Foster, "Desegregating Urban Schools: A Review of Techniques," *Harvard Educational Review*, 43 (February 1973), 5–36.

[25] Clustering is basically the same concept as pairing except that more than two schools are involved.

Racial Ratios

The Supreme Court upheld both the district court's decision to impose the expert's plan on the board and the specific techniques in it. In a 1969 case the Court had upheld the use of fixed ratios for faculty assignment and they merely restated their position on this point.[26] For the first time, however, the Court held that ratios could also be used in student assignment. Although it said that it would not uphold inflexible mathematical formulas, the Court held that ratios were acceptable as "a starting point in the process of shaping a remedy."[27] Whereas some people have argued that the fourteenth amendment requires "color-blindness," the Court took the position that blacks could only be protected by color *consciousness*.[28] "Awareness of the racial composition of the whole school system is likely to be a useful starting point in shaping a remedy to correct past constitutional violations."[29]

Attendance Zones

In the *Swann* case the Court also defined the district courts' authority to alter the attendance zones of school districts. Since it was the obligation of school districts to *achieve* desegregation, assignment policies that were merely "racially neutral" or based on a "neighborhood schools" plan would not be adequate if they did not promote desegregation. To accomplish desegregation, the district courts were given authority to alter attendance zones by pairing, clustering, closing, or grouping schools. Further, the Supreme Court stated that new zones need not be compact or contiguous. The impact of zone restructuring was duly noted by the Court.

> The remedy for such segregation may be administratively awkward, inconvenient, and even bizarre in some situations and may impose burdens on some, but all awkwardness and inconvenience cannot be avoided in the interim period when remedial adjustments are being made to eliminate the dual school systems.[30]

One-Race Schools

The Court was somewhat ambiguous about whether one-race schools could be left in a unitary school system. It noted that under some cir-

---

[26] *United States* v. *Montgomery Board of Education,* 395 U. S. 225 (1969).

[27] 402 U. S. 25.

[28] On this point see Paul R. Diamond, "School Segregation in the North: There Is But One Constitution," *Harvard Civil Rights-Civil Liberties Law Review,* 7 (January 1972), 8–9.

[29] 402 U. S. 25.

[30] 402 U. S. 28.

cumstances one-race schools might remain until housing patterns changed or new schools were constructed; existence of a few one-race schools would not itself indicate that a school system had continued to practice discrimination. However, the Court held that in a system with a history of discrimination, "The Court should scrutinize such schools, and the burden upon the school authorities will be to satisfy the Court that their racial composition is not the result of present or past discriminatory action on their part."[31] Since the *Swann* decision seems generally to consider school segregation in a district that once operated a dual system to be state imposed,[32] it would seem extremely difficult, if not impossible, for such districts to prove that one-race schools were *not* the result of past or present discrimination.

Busing

In perhaps its most important statement in *Swann*, the Court placed its imprimatur on the use of busing to achieve desegregation. This decision was based on three points. First, the Court noted that because busing is such a common practice there could be no legitimate reason for excluding it as a method of achieving desegregation. Backing for this conclusion was provided by an HEW survey in 1970 which found that "42 percent of all American public school students are transported to their schools by buses; an additional 25 percent ride public transportation."[33] This survey also revealed that only 3 percent of all busing is for the purpose of achieving desegregation and that only 1 percent of the annual increase in student transportation was attributable to school desegregation.[34]

Second, the Court noted that the busing ordered by the lower court in Charlotte was comparable to busing practices *before* the desegregation plan: "This system compares favorably with the transportation plan previously operated in Charlotte under which each day 23,600 students on all grade levels were transported an average of 15 miles one way for an average trip requiring over an hour."[35] The one-hour bus ride to school required in Charlotte seems to be common to many communities.

Third, the Court pointed out that busing might be the *only* way to achieve desegregation. "Desegregation plans," the Court said, "cannot be limited to the walk-in school."[36]

[31] 402 U. S. 26.
[32] See Owen M. Fiss, "The Charlotte-Mecklenburg Case—Its Significance for Northern School Desegregation," *The University of Chicago Law Review*, 38 (Summer 1971), 700.
[33] *Toward Equal Educational Opportunity*, p. 188.
[34] Ibid.
[35] 402 U. S. 30.
[36] Ibid.

The Court noted that busing could not be unlimited and that at some point it might even become harmful. It felt, however, that it could not articulate any specific guidelines for busing. It stated only that "An objection to transportation of students may have validity when the time or distance of travel is so great as to either risk the health of the children or significantly impinge on the educational process."[37] The Court also said that "the limits on time of travel will vary with many factors, but probably with none more than the age of the students."[38] Since sixty- and ninety-minute bus rides by school children seem to be rather common, the Court's statements imply that there can be little limitation on the use of busing to achieve desegregation.

In sum, the *Swann* decision came close to being the last nail in the coffin of dual school systems. The presumption of guilt for segregation was weighted toward school boards, the mandate was for immediate change, and the courts were given authority to employ broad remedial powers to dismantle dual schools.

After *Swann* the major obstacle left in the path of the complete dismantling of dual systems was the lack of vigorous enforcement efforts by HEW and OCR. In early 1973 a district court decision took a step toward remedying this problem. In *Adams* v. *Richardson*[39] declaratory and injunctive relief against HEW and OCR for default of their administrative responsibilities under the 1964 Civil Rights Act was sought. The case against HEW and OCR was substantial. For example, the record showed the following:

1. Between January 1969 and February 1970 ten states were judged guilty by HEW of operating segregated systems of higher education in violation of Title VI. Each state was given 120 days to effect a suitable remedy. By early 1973 none of the states had responded adequately but no action had been taken by HEW and all still received Title VI funds.

2. Seventy-four districts judged noncompliant in 1970–1971 were still not in compliance in early 1973 but all continued to receive federal funds.

3. Eighty-seven districts had been allowed an additional year to desegregate after the Supreme Court ruled in *Alexander* v. *Holmes* that districts were to desegregate "at once."[40]

4. After *Swann* established "a presumption against schools that are substantially disproportionate in their racial composition,"[41] HEW continued to take no action against districts with substantial minority schools.

5. Six-hundred-and-forty districts that were subject to court-ordered deseg-

[37] 402 U. S. 31, 32.
[38] 402 U. S. 31.
[39] 351 F. Supp. 636 (1972).
[40] 396 U. S. 19 (1969).
[41] 402 U. S. 26 (1971).

regation plans were presumed in compliance by HEW without the benefit of any monitoring.

6. Between 1964 and 1970 HEW initiated approximately 600 administrative proceedings against noncomplying school districts, with about 100 proceedings a year in 1968 and 1969. With the appointment of Panetta's successor no proceedings were initiated for some twelve months. Since February 1971, only a token number of proceedings have been initiated and no funds have been terminated since the summer of 1970.

The district court made three points: First, HEW and OCR were obligated to achieve compliance with Title VI. Second, HEW and OCR could not exercise unlimited discretion in seeking voluntary compliance. Third, when a substantial period has passed without compliance HEW and OCR must see that Title VI is enforced. Judge Pratt's words were explicit:

> As the undisputed record demonstrates, defendant's efforts toward voluntary compliance have been unsuccessful in the case of many state and local educational agencies which continue to receive substantial federal funds in violation of the statute. Defendants now have no discretion to negate the purpose and intent of the statute by a policy described in another context as one of "benign neglect" but, on the contrary, have the duty, on a case-by-case basis, to employ the means . . . to achieve compliance.[42]

HEW and OCR made three trips to the Courts of Appeal in efforts to reverse the decision, but failed. They then announced that the decision would be obeyed. In April 1973 letters were sent to the ten states in which higher-education systems had been judged segregated and to some 200 school districts telling them to achieve compliance. In addition, OCR announced that it was doing the paperwork necessary to enforce the decision. By May 1974, however, OCR was still shuffling papers and making excuses.

CURRENT SUPREME COURT STANDARDS: IMPLICATIONS FOR ACHIEVING SCHOOL DESEGREGATION IN THE NORTH

The implication of the *Green, Alexander, Swann,* and *Adams* decisions for states that formerly operated dual school systems is quite clear—they must completely dismantle the dual school system and all vestiges thereof. Until lately the implications of the Supreme Court's more recent decisions for school segregation in northern communities has been rather unclear. Traditionally the courts have made a distinction between segregation based on legal or official acts (de jure) and segregation that is supposedly fortuitous (de facto). Until recently most northern districts have escaped the obligation to correct segregation on the ground that the

[42] 351 F. Supp. 642 (1973).

Supreme Court's mandates have been directed toward de jure segregation and that northern segregation is de facto.

The logic of this approach to school segregation is not very persuasive. There would seem to be no justification for forcing southern districts to eliminate segregation while northern districts remain segregated. If school segregation is unconstitutional and harmful in one part of the country, surely it is equally invidious wherever it exists. As noted earlier, school segregation is now more extensive in the North than in the South and it is particularly acute in northern metropolitan areas. Recent figures indicate that "over 80 percent of all black metropolitan residents live in central cities, while more than 60 percent of white metropolitan residents live in suburbs. Of minority group students, 62.4 percent outside the South attend center-city school districts in which a majority of students are from minority groups."[43] Segregation in the North is pervasive, then, but the question is whether northern districts are now obligated to desegregate.

During the 1960s three of the U. S. Courts of Appeal held northern segregation to be constitutional,[44] while one circuit and a number of district courts reached the opposite conclusion.[45] These cases arose, however, at a time when freedom of choice was the only obligation being placed on most southern districts.[46] Since *Green* established an affirmative obligation on districts to remedy segregation many more school districts outside the South have been required by the courts to correct segregated school conditions.

The Discrimination Theory

There are basically two broad theories under which northern districts have been held responsible by federal and state courts for school segregation.[47] Most frequently the courts have held that while school segre-

---

[43] *Toward Equal Educational Opportunity*, p. 32.

[44] *Deal* v. *Cincinnati Board of Education*, 396 F. 2d S5 (6th Cir. 1966), certiorari denied, 387 U. S. 847 (1967); *Bell* v. *School City*, 324 F. 2d 209 (7th Cir. 1963), certiorari denied, 377 U. S. 924 (1964); *Downs* v. *Board of Education*, 336 F. 2d 988 (10th Cir. 1964), certiorari denied, 380 U. S. 914 (1965).

[45] *Taylor* v. *Board of Education*, 294 F. 2d 36 (2d Cir.), certiorari denied, 368 U. S. 940 (1961); *Blacker* v. *Board of Education*, 226 F. Supp. 208 (E.D.N.Y. 1964); *Branche* v. *Board of Education*, 204 F. Supp. 150 (E.D.N.Y. 1962); *Clemons* v. *Board of Education*, 288 F. 2d 853 (6th Cir.), certiorari denied, 350 U. S. 1006 (1956).

[46] See Diamond, "School Segregation in the North," p. 12.

[47] The various theories are best discussed in Diamond, "School Segregation in the North"; Frank I. Goodman, "De Facto School Segregation: A Constitutional and Empirical Analysis," *California Law Review*, 60 (March 1972), 275–437; Robert I. Richter "School Desegregation After Swann: A Theory of Government Responsibility," *The University of Chicago Law Review*, 39 (Winter 1972), 421–447.

gation in the North may not be based on a formal legal mandate, it is still the product of intentionally discriminatory actions. For example, in a recent case the United States Court of Appeals for the Ninth Circuit said: "In context of . . . racial segregation the term 'de jure' does *not* imply criminal or evil intent but means no more or less than that school authorities have exercised powers given them by law in a manner which creates, continues, or increases racial imbalance. . . . "[48] When actionable segregation is based on this broad a theory of de jure segregation the courts can investigate such factors as whether segregated schools have resulted from discriminatory actions on the part of state and local officials in the areas of housing laws and codes, bank-lending policies, school attendance and construction policies, school-site selections, etc. This theory of actionable segregation could probably be sustained in most northern communities with substantial numbers of black students since they often use discriminatory techniques to create and maintain segregation and because it could probably be shown that the actions of most school boards have worked to minimize integration at one time or another.

In recent years this theory has been used to hold school segregation actionable in Detroit,[49] San Francisco,[50] Los Angeles,[51] Denver,[52] Pasadena (Calif.),[53] Oxnard (Calif.),[54] Pontiac (Mich.),[55] Las Vegas,[56] and Indianapolis.[57] In the Detroit case the court ruled that school segregation was de jure rather than de facto because of:

Federal Housing Administration and Veterans Administration loan policies that encourage "racially and economically harmonious neighborhoods"; judicial enforcement of racially restrictive covenants prior to their prohibition by the Supreme Court in 1948; and such school board acts as altered attendance zones, transfer programs that allowed whites to escape from identifiably black neighborhood schools, and busing programs that operated to move only black students out of geographically closer overcrowded white schools into predominantly black schools with available space.[58]

[48] *Johnson* v. *San Francisco Unified School District*, 339 F. Supp. 1316 (1971).
[49] *Bradley* v. *Milliken*, 388 F. Supp. 582 (E.D. Michigan 1971).
[50] *Johnson* v. *San Francisco Unified School District*, 339 F. Supp. 1315 (N.D. Cal. 1971).
[51] *Crawford* v. *Board of Education*, Civil No. 822854 (Sup. Ct. L.A. Cty. 1970).
[52] *Keyes* v. *School District No. 1*, 445 F. 2d 990 (10th Cir. 1971).
[53] *Spangler* v. *Pasadena Board of Education*, 311 F. Supp. 501 (C.D. Cal.).
[54] *Soria* v. *Oxnard School District Board of Trustees*, 328 F. Supp. 155 (C.D. Cal. 1971).
[55] *Davis* v. *School District*, 309 F. Supp. 734 (E.D. Mich. 1970), affirmed, 443 F. 2d 573 (6th Cir.), certiorari denied, 92 S. Ct. 23 (1971).
[56] *Kelley* v. *Brown*, Civil No. LV-1146 (D. Nev. 1970).
[57] *United States* v. *Board of School Commissioners*, 332 F. Supp. 665 (S.D. Ind. 1971).
[58] Richter, "School Desegregation After Swann," p. 427.

In a number of the other communities the courts relied on a less extensive catalog of discriminatory actions but ruled that school segregation was de jure because the school boards had used their powers over attendance zones, school site construction, and faculty assignment to perpetuate racial imbalance that had been caused primarily by residential patterns.[59] For example, in the Indianapolis case the United States Court of Appeals for the Seventh Circuit held that the school board had practiced discrimination because:

> It has built additions at Negro schools and then zoned Negro students into them from predominantly white schools; it has built additions at white schools for white children attending Negro schools; it has generally failed to reduce overcrowding at schools of one race by assigning students to use newly built capacity at schools of the opposite race. The Board has also constructed simultaneous additions at contiguous predominantly white and Negro schools, and has installed portable classrooms at schools of one race with no adjustment of boundaries between it and neighboring schools of the opposite race.[60]

In addition, the court found that there had been "approximately 350 boundary changes in the system since 1954. More than 90% of these promoted segregation."[61] In the Pasadena case the court held that if it could be shown that racial discrimination caused segregated housing patterns, "school officials have the burden to show that there are no educationally sound and administratively feasible alternatives available to overcome the existence of segregated schools."[62]

The Equal Education Theory

The second broad theory involves some showing that minority children are being denied equal educational opportunities. In its most forceful form this theory is unconcerned with past discriminatory actions and centers attention exclusively on segregated educational patterns. The mere existence of segregated patterns would be plenary evidence of a constitutional violation. In this form the theory has been applied only in a few instances but it is perhaps the most sensible approach. Either segregation is evil or it is not. The assumption that school segregation is inherently wrong must basically underlie the Supreme Court's reasoning. Surely it would not be reasonable for the Supreme Court to make the South correct segregated schools *only* because they resulted from

[59] These findings were made in Denver; Pontiac, Mich.; Las Vegas; and Indianapolis.
[60] 332 F. Supp. 667.
[61] 332 F. Supp. 670.
[62] 311 F. Supp. 503.

past discrimination. As the Supreme Court said in *Brown*: "Separate educational facilities are inherently unequal."[63]

In the case of *People* v. *San Diego Unified School District* the theory that an unbalanced school system constitutes a denial of equal protection was adopted. The State Court of Appeals held that when segregation exists within the schools the burden is on the state to prove that all children in the system are receiving a genuinely equal education or that achieving desegregation is impossible.[64] This same reasoning was applied in a case involving Springfield, Illinois.[65] In a somewhat more moderate theory, the Courts of Appeal in the District of Columbia and in San Francisco held that segregated schools deny black children an equal education.[66] In the District of Columbia case the court held that black children had also been denied equal protection of the law because minority schools manifested inferior physical facilities and received fewer economic resources.[67]

The Court's Interpretation

A careful reading of *Swann* provides some support for both theories, but much more for the discrimination than the equal education theory. It may be inherent in the *Swann* opinion that segregated schools are unconstitutional[68] but repeatedly the Court bases the right of relief on the existence of discriminatory state actions. For example, at one point in *Swann* the Court says: "Policy and practices with regard to faculty, staff, transportation, extracurricular activities, and facilities are the most important indicia of a segregated system, and the first remedial responsibility of school authorities is to eliminate invidious racial distinctions in those respects."[69] The reference to facilities indicates that any type of inequality between black and white schools would be considered a constitutional violation. However, the Court seems to be saying that separate facilities that are basically equal would not necessarily be unconstitutional. To be ruled unconstitutional a showing of discrimination in creating or maintaining the separate facilities would be required.

Another section of the opinion supports this reasoning. In perhaps its most revealing words the Court said:

Absent a constitutional violation there would be no basis for judicially

---

[63] *Brown* v. *Board of Education*, 347 U. S. (1954).

[64] *Kelly* v. *Gruinn*, 456 F. 2d 108 (9th Cir. 1972).

[65] *Barksdale* v. *Springfield School Committee*, 237 F. Supp. 543 (1965).

[66] *Hobson* v. *Hansen*, 269 F. Supp. 401 (D.D.G. 1967); *Johnson* v. *San Francisco Unified School District*, 339 F. Supp. 1315 (1971).

[67] *Hobson* v. *Hansen*, 269 F. Supp. 419 (D.D.G. 1967).

[68] This argument is made by Fiss, "The Charlotte-Mecklenburg Case," pp. 697–709.

[69] 401 U. S. 18.

ordering assignment of students on a racial basis. All things being equal, with no history of discrimination, it might well be desirable to assign pupils to schools nearest their homes. But all things are not equal in a system that has been deliberately constructed and maintained to enforce racial segregation.[70]

Thus, a showing of a constitutional violation in the form of discriminatory actions of some type seems critical to relief.

Additionally, when the Court discusses the type of conditions that go to make up a constitutional violation, they are phrased in terms of discriminatory acts, not in the mere existence of segregated attendance patterns. For example, the Court said:

> Independent of student assignment, where it is possible to identify a "white school" or a "Negro school" simply by reference to the racial composition of teachers and staff, the quality of school building and equipment, or the organization of sports activities, a prima facie case of violation of substantial constitutional rights under the Equal Protection Clause is shown.[71]

The Court's phrasing here is very important because it seems to be discussing actions that are independent of laws mandating segregated schools.[72] The acts described seem to define separate constitutional violations that undoubtedly are engaged in by many districts (North and South). In defining the type of activities that make up constitutional violations the Court also said: "In ascertaining the existence of legally imposed school segregation, the existence of a pattern of school construction and abandonment is . . . a factor of great weight."[73] Again it would appear that if it can be shown that school site and construction policies have been manipulated to perpetuate school segregation, a constitutional violation has occurred regardless of where the district is located.

This reasoning was substantiated in June 1973 when the Supreme Court heard *Keyes et al.* v. *School District No. 1, Denver, Colorado,*[74] the first full hearing of a segregation case from a nonsouthern city. The Court ruled that if the district judge found that intentional racial discrimination by school authorities had caused substantial school segregation in any part of Denver, then the whole district could be considered a dual system subject to full constitutional relief. "Common sense," the Court said, "dictates the conclusion that racially inspired school board actions have an impact beyond the particular schools that are the subjects of those actions."[75] In addition, the Court said that the distinction

---

[70] 402 U. S. 28.
[71] 402 U. S. 18.
[72] This point is made by Diamond, "School Segregation in the North," p. 3.
[73] 402 U. S. 21.
[74] 404 U. S. 407 (1973).
[75] Ibid.

between de jure and de facto segregation hinged on whether there had ever been any intent to segregate the races in a community, not on whether segregation had been mandated by law. Thus a community has a "history of segregation" if "a pattern of intentional segregation has been established in the past."[76] Also, the remoteness of past discriminatory actions would not be important if the effects of past discrimination persist. "If the actions of school authorities were to any degree motivated by segregative intent and the segregation resulting from those actions continues to exist, the fact of remoteness in time certainly does not make these actions any less 'intentional.' "[77]

Equally important, the Supreme Court said that if the district judge did not find that the city was operating a dual system, the burden would be on the school board to prove that they had not caused or contributed to the existing segregation. The Court said that the burden would be on the board to show that its policies with respect to construction, site, and location of schools, student transfers, and other factors such as the "so-called 'neighborhood schools' concept," were not adopted to maintain segregation in the core city, or "were not factors in causing the existing condition of segregation in these schools."[78]

The implications of *Swann* and *Keyes* for northern school segregation seem obvious. The message is that northern school segregation is unconstitutional if it can be shown that the segregation is de jure rather than de facto. More important, however, the Court has defined de jure segregation broadly and has put the burden of proof on school boards. For northern boards to prove that their policies have not contributed to, or caused, segregation should be extremely difficult since the specific school board activities that the Supreme Court has identified as evidence of discrimination are activities that are practiced widely both North and South. This is not an ideal approach to school desegregation but it is viable to the extent that segregated conditions can be attacked, North and South.

CONSOLIDATION AND OTHER TRANSDISTRICT REMEDIES

The most important issue presently unanswered by the Supreme Court is exactly how much authority the courts have to devise desegregation plans that cross political boundaries. In many areas of the United States, especially large central cities, it is impossible to eliminate "racially identifiable" schools because the white population of the inner city and es-

[76] Ibid.
[77] Ibid.
[78] Ibid.

pecially the number of white children attending public school is too small. The critical question, therefore, is the conditions under which inner city and suburban students can be assigned across city or county school district boundaries to overcome segregation.

This issue was first raised in the recent case of *Bradley* v. *School Board*.[79] A district judge was faced with the problem of dismantling a dual school system in the city of Richmond, Virginia. Richmond has only a 30 percent white student population. The judge felt that the school system was charged with the affirmative duty under *Green*, *Alexander*, and *Swann* to achieve a unitary school system. The only way to accomplish this goal, however, would have been to combine the schools of Richmond with those of two surrounding counties which were predominantly white. Weighing the merits, the judge ordered the Richmond schools combined with those of the two counties for the purpose of achieving a desegregated system.

The decision was based on three points. First, Judge Merhige concluded that the duty to provide all children with an equal education is an obligation of the state not the local government. Consequently local divisions were irrelevant to this obligation. Second, the court found that all three districts were guilty of having operated dual school systems, of which the district lines were a vestige. Judge Merhige held that maintenance of the district lines had the effect of perpetuating segregation, and that they had been deliberately maintained for that purpose. Third, the boundaries between Richmond and the two counties had been ignored for purposes of achieving and maintaining segregation. Under the dual school system, Judge Merhige found that massive busing over long distances and over the county lines had been employed to segregate the schools. The busing had been so extensive that the judge concluded that in reality the tri-jurisdictional area was one community.

Support for Judge Merhige's decision would seem to be substantial. If district lines could be crossed for purposes of segregation, surely they can be crossed for purposes of overcoming the resulting imbalance. The judge's conclusion that education is a state, not a local, obligation also seems sound. Under the Fourteenth Amendment the states are obligated to see that all their citizens are provided equal protection under the law, and the state is held responsible for the actions and consequences of the acts of its agents.

There also seems to be legal precedent for assuming that intrastate boundaries cannot stand as obstacles to legal rights. In the reapportionment cases the Supreme Court held that political boundaries could not be continued if they denied citizens an equal vote. Furthermore the Court

---

[79] *Bradley* v. *School Board*, 338 F. Supp. 67 (E.D. Va. 1972).

said: "Political subdivisions of states—counties, cities, or whatever—never were and never have been considered sovereign entities. Rather they have been traditionally regarded as subordinate governmental instrumentalities created by the state to assist in the carrying out of state governmental functions."[80]

Surprisingly perhaps, the Court of Appeals for the Fourth Circuit reversed *Bradley* and the decision was upheld when the Supreme Court, Mr. Justice Powell abstaining, divided 4–4. The Circuit Court held that: "Because we are unable to discern a constitutional violation in the establishment and maintenance of these school districts, nor any unconstitutional consequences of such maintenance, we hold that it was not within the district judge's authority to order the consolidation of these separate political subdivisions."[81] The Supreme Court's nondecision did not indicate agreement with the Circuit Court's reasoning but left the lower court decision intact.

There have been a number of other cases which have involved various aspects of this problem. It seems clear that if it can be shown that district lines were purposely drawn or redrawn to achieve segregation, they can be overturned or transgressed. For example, in *Turner* v. *Littleton-Lake Gorton School District* the Fourth Circuit held that the school districts had been reorganized for the purpose of achieving and maintaining segregation.[82] Also, in the case of *U.S.* v. *Scotland Neck City Board of Education*[83] the Supreme Court refused to allow a new school district to be established in a county where the effect was to remove most of the white students from the county. Similarly, in *Lee* v. *Macon County* the Fifth Circuit refused to uphold the secession of a city from a county school system. Judge Wisdom ruled that "the city cannot secede from the county where the effect—to say nothing of the purpose—of the secession has a substantial adverse effect on desegregation of the county school district."[84]

However, if the boundaries are neutrally drawn and later become barriers to integration they are not necessarily unconstitutional. In *Spencer* v. *Kugler*[85] a New Jersey statute establishing school districts coterminous with political boundaries was challenged on the ground that the boundaries created severe racial imbalance in some parts of the state. The district court held that the statute was constitutional since it was

[80] *Reynolds* v. *Sims*, 377 U. S. 533, 575 (1964).
[81] *Bradley* v. *School Board*, Civ. No. 72–1058 (4th Cir., 1972).
[82] 442 F. 2d 584 (4th Cir. 1971).
[83] 442 F. 2d 575 (4th Cir. 1971).
[84] 455 F. 2d. 978 (5th Cir. 1972).
[85] 327 F. Supp. 1235 (D.N.J. 1971).

not based on a racial motive and the Supreme Court affirmed.[86] This decision does not rule out the possibility that the Supreme Court might allow neutral boundaries to be breached for the purpose of executing a specific desegregation plan.

The Supreme Court was directly faced with the issue of consolidation during the 1973–1974 term but their decision still left the issue clouded.[87] The Court heard arguments in a case involving Detroit, Michigan. The Sixth Circuit Court of Appeals had agreed with a district court ruling that the schools in Detroit were segregated by official action and inaction on the part of local and state officials.[88] The court also agreed that a Detroit only desegregation plan would not achieve significant desegregation and that only a metropolitan plan including fifty-two suburban districts in three counties would be effective. The court said:

> The discriminatory practices on the part of the Detroit School Board and the State of Michigan revealed by this record are significant, pervasive and causally related to the substantial amount of segregation found in the Detroit School system by the district judge. . . . The Court feels that some plan of desegregation beyond the boundaries of the Detroit School District is both within the equity powers of the district court and essential to a solution to this problem.[89]

In a 5–4 decision the Supreme Court refused to uphold the lower courts. Chief Justice Berger, speaking for the majority, refused to hold either that local divisions were irrelevant or that school desegregation is a state rather than a local obligation. However, Berger said that "Boundary lines may be bridged where there has been a constitutional violation calling for interdistrict relief." The type of constitutional violation that would warrant an interdistrict remedy seemed to be a showing that all the districts involved in a consolidation plan were guilty of some form of intradistrict or interdistrict school discrimination. Thus Berger stated that relief would be forthcoming for Detroit if it could be shown that "petitioners drew the district lines in a discriminatory fashion, or arranged for white students residing in the Detroit district to attend schools in Oakland and Macomb counties. . . . " Since Berger felt that the record before the Court did not document any significant violations "by the 53 outlying school districts and no evidence of any interdistrict violation or effect," he remanded the case to the Court of Appeals for further investigation.

[86] Affirmed Mem., 92 S. Ct. 707 (1972).
[87] *Milliken* v. *Bradley*, 94 S. Ct. 3112 (1974).
[88] *Bradley* v. *Milliken*, 338 F. Supp. 582 (E. D. Mich. 1971).
[89] Ibid.

Four judges vigorously dissented from Berger's position but the most important opinion in the case may have been written by one of the members of the majority. Justice Stewart concurred in the decision of the Court but he listed a much broader and more liberal set of conditions that would warrant an interdistrict remedy. "Were it to be shown, for example, that state officials had contributed to the separation of the races by drawing or redrawing school district lines, or by purposeful, racially discriminatory use of state housing or zoning laws, then a decree calling for transfer of pupils across district lines or for restructuring of district lines might well be appropriate." This seems to indicate that officials in the outlying districts would not necessarily have to be found personally guilty of any illegal acts. If the actions of state officials produced discrimination in a district, it would be liable to a consolidation plan.

Until the Court deals with some cases that try to document intradistrict violations, the implications of the Detroit case will not be clear. It would seem that the conditions documented in the Richmond case would certainly warrant an interdistrict plan, and this would probably be the case for most southern cities. But the implications for many northern communities must await further litigation.

If the Court will not allow forced consolidation, or if they limit it to only a few instances, it will be difficult or even impossible to desegregate many inner-city schools. With consolidation, however, even the schools of such cities as Washington, D. C., and Detroit could be successfully desegregated. Even though metro plans would lead to more desegregation, some reservations about such systems have been expressed. Most frequently it is argued that metro systems would be large to the point of being unwieldy and that children would have to be bused excessive distances in these systems. The evidence suggests that such arguments may be inaccurate. Many large cities have metro school systems (e.g., Houston, Charlotte, and all cities in Florida) and they have not found such systems to be unmanageably large. In fact, a recent report reveals that metro desegregation plans have proceeded smoothly in Florida districts involving Jacksonville, Orlando, St. Petersburg, Tampa, and Ft. Lauderdale.[90]

The evidence also indicates that metro school districts have some distinct advantages over the typical city or suburban school district. Gordon Foster of the Florida Desegregation Center points out six advantages: (1) A metro plan may require less busing. For example, rather than busing students across a city to achieve desegregation, they may be able to travel only a short distance to a suburban school. (2) Experience indicates

---

[90] Foster, "Desegregating Urban Schools," p. 6.

that in a metro system the physical facilities and resources of all schools quickly are equalized. (3) Metro tends to stabilize communities because there are no segregated communities to which whites can escape. (4) Metro contributes to an equalization of tax burdens and revenues. (5) Metro reduces competition between city and suburban schools for the best teachers. (6) Metro can combine the best of efficient centralization of operation with considerable decentralized control.[91] Metro systems, therefore, seem to offer advantages that go beyond the issue of desegregation.

THE EDUCATIONAL PARK AS A TOOL OF DESEGREGATION

Even if the Supreme Court does rule that central city and suburban schools can be combined for the purpose of desegregation, it may still be difficult to desegregate some schools without burdensome busing. As noted earlier, consolidation does not necessarily lead to more busing; it may in fact substantially reduce the need for busing. Still, the considerable geographical separation of the races in most cities and in some metropolitan areas may necessitate considerable busing. Defining the point at which busing becomes dysfunctional is, of course, very difficult. An hour trip each way seems excessive although this time span is rather common in American communities. If a limitation of an hour trip each way was placed on busing, however, it might be difficult to desegregate some communities.

The educational park is a concept that might be combined with consolidation and busing to produce viable desegregation plans.[92] The educational park is a large and comprehensive public school that can be located advantageously for purposes of desegregation. The educational park would be located on 60 to 100 acres, contain 10 to 20 schools ranging from kindergarten to twelfth grade, and accommodate 10,000 to 20,000 students.

There are good reasons besides achieving desegregation for serious consideration of the educational-park system. First, school consolidation saves money on expensive items that are duplicated massively under the present system—libraries, science labs, swimming pools, gymnasiums, etc. These savings can go into teachers' salaries, innovative teaching methods and aids, individualized instruction, and a broader curriculum.

The construction of an educational park would, of course, be expensive,

[91] Ibid., pp. 33–35.
[92] For a more thorough examination of the educational park see Thomas F. Pettigrew, *Racially Separate or Together?* (New York, 1971), pp. 69–81; and N. Jacobson (ed.), *An Exploration of the Educational Park Concept* (New York, 1964).

but no more so than current school policies. Some have argued that the size of the parks would make them very impersonal. Most city schools are already large and impersonal so the situation would probably not worsen, especially since students would be headquartered in specific units of the park. It is also argued that the idea is extravagant since present schools would be wasted. This is only partially true. Many schools are ready to be razed, some can be sold to private interests, and some can be used for other community purposes (e.g., meeting halls, city offices, etc.).

In sum, the educational park deserves serious consideration, both as a tool of desegregation and as an educational device. Through the use of educational parks, consolidation, and busing, even the largest metropolitan areas could be desegregated.

CONCLUSIONS

This analysis suggests two conclusions. First, school desegregation can be achieved. The legal grounds for attacking school desegregation have been amply established by the Supreme Court. There is probably no community with substantial school segregation that is not obligated to desegregate under the Supreme Court's recent decisions. In the next five years there should be much additional progress in school desegregation because northern segregation will come under full legal scrutiny and because the legal obligations on the South and on the government are so specific that few dilatory ploys are left.

Second, achieving desegregation is easier than many people believe. With honest effort there are probably few school systems in America that cannot be substantially desegregated and most can be desegregated "root and branch." The technology to achieve full desegregation is available—pairing, grouping, clustering, rezoning, site selection, busing, etc. As Foster says "there is nothing mysterious about the techniques of desegregation. Indeed, all of the tools for desegregation can be and have been used to create or maintain a segregated status for school populations."[93]

We also believe that school desegregation will prove worthwhile. Although controversial and frequently hard on those involved, in the long run school desegregation should be beneficial to society. The available empirical evidence only hints at the full potential of school desegregation but the limited insights gleaned are promising.[94] In addition, it seems only reasonable that integrated schools are a necessary prepara-

[93] Foster, "Desegregating Urban Schools," p. 26.
[94] For a review of this literature see Charles S. Bullock, III, and Harrell R. Rodgers, Jr., *Racial Equality in America: In Search of an Unfulfilled Goal* (Pacific Palisades, Calif., in press), chap. 5.

tion for interracial living. As a black parent in Rochester said: "Education . . . is preparing yourself to live and work in the world, and in this respect your education is definitely lacking if you are not being prepared to live and work with all types of people."[95] Jencks et al. make a similar point:

> The most important effect of school desegregation may be on adults, not on students. School desegregation can be seen as part of an effort to make blacks and whites rethink their historic relationship to one another. If blacks and whites attend the same schools, then perhaps they will feel more of a stake in each other's well-being than they have in the past.[96]

In the opinion of the author, the situation can be succinctly summed up as follows:

> [T]he case for or against desegregation should not be argued in terms of academic achievement. If we want a segregated society, we should have segregated schools. If we want a desegregated society, we should have desegregated schools.[97]

[95] *Racial Isolation in the Public Schools*, Report of the U. S. Commission on Civil Rights (Washington, D. C., 1967), p. 159.

[96] Christopher Jencks et al., *Inequality: A Reassessment of the Effect of Family and Schooling in America* (New York, 1972), p. 156.

[97] Ibid., p. 106.